C. Craft
12-4-72

Mr. Lincoln's
Army

BOOKS BY BRUCE CATTON

This Hallowed Ground
Banners at Shenandoah (juvenile)
U. S. Grant and the Military Tradition
A Stillness at Appomattox
Glory Road
Mr. Lincoln's Army
The War Lords of Washington

THE ARMY
OF THE
POTOMAC

DOUBLEDAY & COMPANY, INC.
Garden City, New York

BRUCE CATTON

Mr. Lincoln's Army

Contents

TO CHERRY

Preface

The books which make up this trilogy began, very simply, as an attempt to understand the men who fought in the Army of the Potomac. As a small boy I had known a number of these men in their old age; they were grave, dignified, and thoughtful, with long white beards and a general air of being pillars of the community. They lived in rural Michigan in the pre-automobile age, and for the most part they had never been fifty miles away from the farm or the dusty village streets; yet once, ages ago, they had been everywhere and had seen everything, and nothing that happened to them thereafter meant anything much. All that was real had taken place when they were young; everything after that had simply been a process of waiting for death, which did not frighten them much—they had seen it inflicted in the worst possible way on boys who had not bargained for it, and they had enough of the old-fashioned religion to believe without any question that when they passed over they would simply be rejoining men and ways of living which they had known long ago.

This was too much for an adolescent to understand. Perhaps it is too much for anybody to understand, in a skeptical age. But there it was: these old gentlemen, drowsing out the greater part of their lives in the backwoods, had once been lifted beyond themselves by an experience which perhaps was all the more significant because it was imperfectly understood. They gave a tone and a color to the lives of the people who knew them, and they put a special meaning on such a word as "patriotism"; it was not something you talked about very much, just a living force that you instinctively responded to. I can remember one old man who had lost his left arm in the Wilderness, and he used to go about town in the summer peddling cherries and blackberries in a bucket—there was just enough of his left forearm so that he could hook it over the bail of the bucket and carry it conveniently—and it never once entered my childish head to feel sorry for him because he had been a cripple for half a century. On the contrary, I thought he was rather lucky. He carried with him forever the visible sign that he had fought for his country and had been wounded in its service. Probably only a very backward boy could have thought anything of the kind.

Still, that was what it was like. A generation grew up in the shadow of a war which, because of its distance, somehow had lost all resemblance to everyday reality. To a generation which knew the war only by hearsay, it seemed that these aged veterans had been privileged to know the greatest experience a man could have. We saw the Civil War, in other words, through the distorting haze of endless Decoration Day reminiscences; to us it was a romantic business because all we ever got a look at was the legend built up through fifty years of peace.

We do learn as we grow older, and eventually I realized that this picture was somewhat out of focus. War, obviously, is the least romantic of all of man's activities, and it contains elements which the veterans do not describe to children. This aged berry-peddler, for instance, who lost his arm in the Wilderness: he had never told me about the wounded men who were burned to death in the forest fire which swept that infernal stretch of woodland while the battle was going on; nor had any of his comrades who survived that fight and went on through the whole campaign to the last days at Petersburg ever mentioned the lives that were wasted by official blunders, the dirt and the war-weariness and the soul-numbing disillusionment that came when it seemed that what they were doing was going for nothing. There was a deacon in the church, who used to remind us proudly that he had served in the 2nd Ohio Cavalry. Not until years later did I learn that this regiment had gone with Sheridan in the Shenandoah Valley, burning barns, killing livestock and pillaging with a free hand so that the Southern Confederacy, if it refused to die in any other way, might die of plain starvation. In a sense, the research that went into these books was simply an effort to find out about the things which the veterans never discussed.

Yet, in an odd way, the old veterans did leave one correct impression: the notion that as young men they had been caught up by something ever so much larger than themselves and that the war in which they fought did settle something for us—or, incredibly, started something which we ourselves have got to finish. It was not only the biggest experience in their own lives; it was in a way the biggest experience in our life as a nation, and it deserves all of the study it is getting.

In any case, these books try to examine a small part of that experience in terms of the men who did the fighting. Those men are all gone now and they have left forever unsaid the things they might have told us, and no one now can speak for them. Here is my attempt to speak about them.

1962   B. C.

ONE

Picture-Book War

1. There Was Talk of Treason

The rowboat slid out on the Potomac in the hazy light of a hot August morning, dropped down past the line of black ships near the Alexandria wharves, and bumped to a stop with its nose against the wooden side of a transport. Colonel Herman Haupt, superintendent of military railroads, a sheaf of telegrams crumpled in one hand, went up the Jacob's ladder to the deck—clumsily, as was to be expected of a landsman, but rapidly, for he was an active man—and disappeared into a cabin. A moment later he returned, and as he came down the ladder he was followed by a short, broad-shouldered, sandy-haired man, deeply tanned by the sun of the Virginia peninsula, with thin faint lines of worry between his eyes: Major General George Brinton McClellan, commander of the Army of the Potomac, which had been coming up from the south by water for a week and more and which at the moment was scattered all the way from Alexandria to the upper Rappahannock, most of it well out of the general's reach and all of it, as he suspected, soon to be out from under his authority.

There was an air about this youthful general—an air of far-off bugles, and flags floating high, and troops cheering madly, as if the picture of him which one hundred thousand soldiers had created had somehow become real and was now an inseparable part of his actual appearance. He could look jaunty and dapper after a day in the saddle, on muddy roads, in a driving rainstorm; like a successful politician, he lived his part, keeping himself close to the surface so that every cry and every gesture of the men who adored him called him out to a quick response that was none the less genuine for being completely automatic. It was impossible to see him, in his uniform with the stars on his shoulders, without also seeing the army—"my army," he called it proudly, almost as if it were a personal possession, which was in a way the case: he had made it, he had given it shape and color and spirit, and in his mind and in the minds of the men he commanded the identification was complete.

He sat in the stern of the rowboat, beside the superintendent of military railroads, and he was silent as the boat went back upstream to the landing. The docks and the river front were a confusion of steamboats and barges and white-topped wagons and great stacks of boxed goods and equipment, and the quaint little town itself was lost in a restless, lounging concourse of soldiers: loose fringes of a moving army, convalescents and strays and detailed men, and here and there a regiment moving off with cased flags at route step toward some outlying camp. From this same town the general had set out, nearly five months ago, to take his army down to the swamps and forests below Richmond and win the war; he had known in his heart that he was destined to save the country, and the army had gone forth with unstained uniforms and gleaming rifle barrels, and with proud flags that had never touched the ground.

But nothing had worked quite the way he had expected. The Army of the Potomac, made in his own image, had spent some months on the Virginia peninsula—that long neck of land which runs southeast between the James and the York rivers, and which the army remembered as composed chiefly of mud, mosquitoes, and steaming heat, with a great tangle of gloomy forests infested by lean and hairy men with rifles who uttered shrill, nerve-splitting screams as they came forward endlessly to the attack. The luck of the army and the general had been all bad. Many battles had been fought, and while no great defeat had been suffered there had been a weary retreat from in front of Richmond to a dismal camp far down the river. The general considered that this retreat had been a masterful accomplishment, but the government considered it sheer disaster, and it was trying now—

in August 1862—to strike the southern Confederacy with another instrument.

This new instrument, as McClellan was frank to state, had been
poorly chosen. Scattered fragments of commands had been swept
together and entrusted to a self-confident soldier from the Western
armies, General John Pope, and Pope had been sent down into Virginia overland, following the line of the Orange and Alexandria Railroad to the Rappahannock River. Leaving McClellan and his army
to swelter in their camp on the James, the Rebels had promptly concentrated against Pope's army and had been giving him a bad time
of it—so bad, indeed, that McClellan's army was now being pulled
back to Washington and was being forwarded to Pope by bits and
pieces. McClellan was not being sent forward with it; and this morning, as he passed through the sprawling base of supplies, where white
door fronts of the colonial era looked down on muddy streets churned
by endless wagon trains, it seemed likely that he would presently be a
general without an army.

The general went with the colonel to the colonel's office. They
were both West Pointers, and when the war broke out they had both
been railroad men, and they could talk the same language. As soon
as they were seated Haupt gave McClellan such news as he had.
None of it was good. Seen thus, from behind the lines, the war was
untidy, misdirected, discouraging.

Enemy forces, said Haupt, were across the railroad line at Manassas Junction. It had been thought at first that these were merely a
handful of roving cavalry—cavalry had descended on the railroad a
few days earlier, farther down the line at Catlett's—but it was beginning to be clear now that they were more important than that.
A New Jersey brigade had gone forward to restore the situation and
had run into rifle and artillery fire too heavy to come from any
cavalry; had, as a matter of fact, been most distressingly cut to
pieces. Two Ohio infantry regiments were holding on where the railroad crossed Bull Run, but they were obviously in grave danger and
would probably have to come back. Confederates apparently were
either on or near the railroad this side of them, between Bull Run and
Alexandria; the bridge over Pohick Creek near Burke's Station, only
thirteen miles out, was rumored to have been burned, and the telegraph line had been cut. Nor was it just the two Ohio regiments that

were in peril. The seizure of Manassas Junction meant that General
Pope was out of forage for his horses and rations for his men.

Colonel Haupt did not know where Pope was, and it seemed that
the War Department did not know either. It was bombarding Haupt
with inquiries and had evidently developed the jitters—McClellan saw
a wire complaining that there had been "great neglect and careless-
ness" on the Manassas plain. To McClellan that seemed obvious.
He did not admire General Pope, either as a man or as a soldier, and
his present prospect of forwarding his own troops to Pope at a time
when Pope's position was unknown and the road leading in his direction was blocked by Rebel soldiers was not one that McClellan
could think about with any pleasure.

Clearly, this was no time for an army commander or a superintendent of military railroads to sit holding his thumbs. With the
plight of Pope's army and the dire fix of those two Ohio regiments
Colonel Haupt had no direct concern, except that it was up to him to
get the railroad back in working order so that these and other troops
could be fed, supplied, and, if necessary, transported; and for this he
had a plan of action, which he now asked McClellan to approve. A
wrecking and construction train, ready to go forward and repair
damaged tracks and bridges, was standing on a siding with steam up.
Also ready was a freight train loaded with forage and rations. Haupt
proposed to send out ahead of these a train of flatcars carrying a
battery of field artillery and a few hundred sharpshooters. This could
go as far as the condition of the track permitted, and the guns and
riflemen could then advance by road and clear out such Rebel marauders as might be in the vicinity. The wrecking train could then get
the bridges repaired in short order—Haupt kept a stock of prefabri-
cated bents and stringers on hand, ready for just such emergencies as
this, and if they had to, his construction gangs could build a bridge
with timber from torn-down farmhouses along the right of way—and
when that had been done the supply trains could be leapfrogged
through with subsistence for Pope's army.

The thin lines between McClellan's eyes deepened slightly and he
shook his head slowly. He could not approve the plan. It would be
attended with risk. Haupt was primarily a railroad man; any kind of
expedient was all right, for him, if it just gave him a chance to put
his track gangs on the job and get the line opened up again. Also,

there was not, inherently, any very great difference between a Rebel army and a spring freshet on a Pennsylvania mountain river—both broke up a railroad, and when the damage had been done one went out and fixed it as quickly as possible. But McClellan's mind was full of the mischances that can befall troops which are incautiously thrust out into enemy territory; he repeated that he could not approve. Haupt was irritated. All military operations, he said, were attended with risk, as far as he could see, and the risk here did not seem to be excessive. Surely, if the advance guard were properly handled, nothing very disastrous could happen. The trains could be kept safely in the rear while the skirmishers went forward. If the enemy were found in force, the men could retire to their train and the whole expedition could quickly be brought back out of harm's way.

McClellan shook his head again. The situation was too obscure. Enemy troops, possibly in very substantial numbers, appeared to be between Pope's army and Washington; the first thing to do was to arrange the troops actually present in such a way that the capital itself would be safe. Then preparations could be made for an advance in force. Meanwhile—the general had grown pale beneath his tan and appeared genuinely unwell—did the colonel have any brandy and water? The colonel did. McClellan took it and seemed revived, borrowed a scratch pad, and wrote a telegram to the War Department, reporting that he was ashore in Alexandria and describing the situation as he had found it. Then he departed.

Left to himself, Haupt fumed and pondered, and wished that he had not succeeded in finding McClellan at all. Earlier in the morning he had telegraphed his proposal to General Henry W. Halleck, commander, under the President, of the armies of the United States. Halleck, who never made a decision himself if it could possibly be passed along to someone else, had replied: "If you can see Gen. McClellan, consult him. If not, go ahead as you propose." Haupt had now seen General McClellan and he wished he hadn't; if he had only missed him, the expedition could be under way by now.

Although he had been trained as a soldier—he had been graduated from West Point in 1835, in the same class with George Gordon Meade—Haupt was essentially a civilian. Resigning his commission shortly after graduation, he had gone into railroad work, had built a good part of the Juniata division of the Pennsylvania Railroad, and had become, successively, division superintendent and chief engineer for that line. He had been brought into the army, somewhat against his will, as a railroad and construction expert, and he was admired in high places. President Lincoln liked to tell about the marvelous bridge Haupt had built "out of beanpoles and cornstalks" down on the Aquia Creek line out of Fredericksburg. Haupt actually belonged in the next century; as it was, in the Civil War most generals failed to appreciate him. He was used to direct action, and generals irritated him. His present job gave them many occasions to do this, and they never seemed to miss a chance. Three days ago, for example, Haupt had bestirred himself to assemble trains to send General Joe Hooker's division forward to Pope. He got the trains lined up, Hooker's troops were at hand ready to go aboard, but Hooker himself had vanished—presumably to seek the fleshpots in Washington. Haupt telegraphed to his good friend and brother railroad man, P. H. Watson, Assistant Secretary of War. Back came Watson's reply:

"General Hooker was in Alexandria last night, but I will send to Willard's and see if he is there. I do not know any other place that he frequents. Be as patient as possible with the generals; some of them will trouble you more than they do the enemy."[1]

That was a judgment with which Haupt was ready to agree. He had no sooner got Hooker out of his hair than General Samuel D. Sturgis got into it. Sturgis showed up with a division of troops, demanding immediate transportation to the front. To make sure that his request for transportation got top priority Sturgis had moved his soldiers out and had seized the railroad—or that part of it which lay within his reach, which was enough to tie up the entire line—swearing that no trains would go anywhere until his division had been moved. Haupt tried to reason with him, but it was no go—Haupt was a colonel and Sturgis was a general, and Sturgis would not listen. Sturgis had the rank and he had the soldiers, and for the moment he had the railroad, too, and no temporary colonel was going to tell him what to do.

Haupt had had to go through that sort of thing before. General Pope had had similar ideas when he first took command in northern Virginia, announcing that his own quartermaster would control the movement of railroad cars just as he ran the wagon trains, and informing Haupt that his function was to do as he was told. Within two weeks the line had got into such a snarl that no trains could move in any direction. Pope came to see that it took a railroad man to run a railroad—he could get a point now and then if it was obvious enough, could John Pope, for all his bluster—and he was glad to hand the road back to Colonel Haupt: particularly so since Haupt by this time had got from the Secretary of War an order giving him complete and unqualified control over the railroad and everything on it, regardless of the orders any army commander might issue. Haupt, therefore, was ready to take Sturgis in his stride; but Sturgis had troops and guns and swore he would use them. Furious, Haupt telegraphed Halleck, getting in return a bristling order which specifically authorized him, in the name of the general-in-chief, to put Sturgis under arrest if there was any more funny business. Haupt summoned Sturgis to his office. Sturgis came, rather elevated with liquor, accompanied by his chief of staff.

Haupt showed Halleck's order and explained that he was getting all sorts of troops and supplies forward to General Pope and that Sturgis would simply have to wait his turn. Sturgis was not impressed, and he somehow got the idea that the order Haupt was exhibiting had been issued by General Pope.

"I don't care for John Pope one pinch of owl dung," said Sturgis solemnly—a sentiment which had its points but was hardly germane. Patiently Haupt explained: this order was not from Pope, it was from Halleck, who held the power to bind and to loose. Sturgis shook his head and repeated his judgment of Pope, savoring the sentence as if the thought had been bothering him for a long time. Haupt fluttered the order at him and went over it a third time. Sturgis, his needle stuck in one groove, repeated:

"I don't care for John Pope——"

His chief of staff tugged at his sleeve to stop him, and hastily and earnestly whispered in his ear. Sturgis blinked, finally got the point, and rose to his feet ponderously.

"Well, then," he said—with what, all things considered, might be called owlish dignity, *"take* your damned railroad."[2]

So that had been settled, and Sturgis had awaited his turn. But the episode had tied up the railroad for the better part of a day and had canceled the movement of four troop trains. Haupt was more than ready to agree with Assistant Secretary Watson about the generals.

Anyway, that was over. Now there was the problem of reopening Pope's supply line. Pope's soldiers must be getting hungry; and besides, with the outer end of the line gone, the Alexandria yards were clogged with loaded freight cars that had no place to go. Across the river, in Washington, the Baltimore and Ohio was complaining that boxcars consigned to Pope's army were filling the tracks on Maryland Avenue; the available B. & O. engines were too heavy to go over the Long Bridge; would Colonel Haupt please send an engine over from Alexandria and get them, so that the B. & O. could go on with its regular work? This Haupt could by no means do, having more cars in Alexandria now than he could handle. The B. & O. needled the War Department, which sent plaintive messages; and the day wore on, and the situation did not improve. Haupt reflected that he was, after all, in charge of the railroad, and that somewhere off to the southwest there was an army that greatly needed supplies. He determined to go ahead on his own hook. After dark he sent a message to McClellan—who by now had established his headquarters on shore—notifying him that at four in the morning he would start his construction train forward, followed by the subsistence train. Would McClellan at least let him have two hundred soldiers to go along as train guard? If the men did not report, Haupt added, the trains would go ahead without them.

He got no answer. At midnight he gave up on McClellan, got on his horse, and set out to appeal to the first general he saw—any general, just so long as he had a few troops to spare and was willing to loan a few of them to help open a vital railway line.

By good luck the first general Haupt found was Winfield Scott Hancock, a brigade commander in the Army of the Potomac, recently back from the peninsula, where in spite of the fact that his brigade had not had too much fighting to do he had somehow marked both it and himself as men who would be very useful indeed before the war was over. Late as it was, Hancock had only just gone to bed. He liked to do all his paper work around midnight and had a habit, whenever he encountered a report that was in any way faulty, of having the author hauled out of bed at once and brought to brigade headquarters to receive a dressing-down that was usually loud enough to arouse the nearby regiments. This trait was a trial to Hancock's staff, but it meant that most reports by now were letter-perfect before they ever reached the general.

Hancock was a direct actionist, who both looked and acted like a soldier—a burly, handsome man, who somehow managed always to be wearing a clean white shirt even when the army had been in the field for weeks, and who, in an army where the officers were notably profane, was outstanding for the vigor, range, and effectiveness of his cursing. His men liked to tell how, at the battle of Williamsburg, he had galloped up, outdistancing his staff, to order his troops to the charge—"the air was blue all around him," one of them recalled admiringly. There was a great breezy vigor and bluffness about the man. Earlier in the war, when his brigade was still in training, his men had taken to killing and eating the sheep of farmers near camp, and Hancock had determined to stop it. One afternoon, riding the lines near his camp, he had seen a knot of soldiers in a meadow, bending over the body of a sheep. Putting his horse to the fence, he galloped up, shouting mightily, and the men of course scattered—all except one who tarried too long and whom Hancock, flinging himself from his saddle, seized with strong hands.

"Now, you scoundrel, don't tell me you didn't kill that sheep—I saw you with my own eyes!" roared the general. Just then the sheep, not yet knifed, realized that it was no longer being held and sprang to its feet and scampered nimbly away. Hancock stared at the rocketing sheep, looked blankly at the quaking soldier in his hands—and then threw his head back and made the meadow ring with shouts of laughter.[3]

It was this Hancock whom Haupt found on his midnight quest for troops. Hancock heard his story and immediately detailed the men for him, and early in the morning Haupt's trains went lurching off into Virginia. By ten in the morning Haupt was notified that the bridge near Burke's Station had been rebuilt. He also learned that enemy troops were still somewhere in the vicinity of Manassas in very great strength; the head of the construction gang had been told that Lee himself was with them. A little later trains came steaming back from Fairfax Station loaded with wounded men.

For the moment this was all the news there was. Haupt's line of track went off into the darkness where moved shadowy forces made large by rumor. For all anyone knew, Lee and his whole army might be between Pope and Washington. McClellan picked up a report that 120,000 Confederates were moving toward Arlington and the Chain Bridge, bent on the capture of Washington and Baltimore. Halleck sagely remarked that the thing to be afraid of at that moment was the danger that Rebel cavalry might dash forward by night and enter the city—"Rebel cavalry" in those days being terrifying words, since the plow hands and mechanics whom the Federals were earnestly trying to turn into cavalrymen were no match at all for Jeb Stuart's incomparable troopers.

McClellan sent four infantry regiments out to the works at Upton's and Munson's hills, covering the main highway in from Centreville, and instructed them to hold the lines there at all hazards. The two divisions of Franklin's army corps, just disembarked, loitered about Alexandria waiting for orders; Halleck and McClellan agreed that they ought to go forward to aid Pope, but nobody knew quite where Pope was to be found, and anyway, Franklin had no horses to pull his artillery and no wagon train to carry food and ammunition, and there seemed to be no cavalry at hand to scout the road for him. Haupt darkly remarked to himself that a march of twenty-five miles would put Franklin in the fortified lines at Centreville, which would surely be within reaching distance of Pope, and felt that Franklin's men could carry on their backs enough food and ammunition to take them that far. Besides, Haupt seriously doubted that there was anything hostile this side of Centreville which could hurt a whole army corps. But nobody asked Haupt's opinion, McClellan and Halleck began to bicker fruitlessly about the advance, and Franklin's troops stayed where they were.

The next day was August 29, and outposts reported hearing the rumble of gunfire from beyond Centreville. Somewhere off in the outer darkness the armies apparently had collided. Later in the day Haupt was able to confirm this. Sitting at the end of the railway telegraph line, he got a message from Pope himself—in Centreville, by now—and Pope seemed to be in good spirits, reporting that he was engaged with sixty thousand Confederates, that Joe Hooker was driving them handsomely, and that McDowell and Sigel were cutting off the enemy's retreat. McClellan ordered Franklin to move forward, telling him: "Whatever may happen, don't allow it to be said that the Army of the Potomac failed to do its utmost for the country"—a remark which is a

complete tip-off to the strange jealousies, rivalries, and antagonisms
that were besetting the high command just then. The troops started to
move that morning, Franklin remaining behind in an attempt to get
supply wagons, of which he finally rounded up a scant twenty; then
McClellan began to have second thoughts, wired Halleck that he did
not think Franklin's men were in shape to accomplish much if they
ran into serious resistance along the road, and finally ordered Franklin
to halt at Annandale, seven miles out. Haupt had his railroad open
as far as the Bull Run Bridge and was pushing supplies forward as
fast as the trains could move.

As far as Haupt could see, things were on the mend. Pope was in
touch with Washington and with his supply line again, his wagons
were moving the stores up from Fairfax Station to Centreville, and
the fighting seemed to be going favorably. But on the following day
the luckless railroad man entered into a full-fledged nightmare, which
was visited on him by order of the Secretary of War, Mr. Edwin M.
Stanton.

Stanton, with his pudgy, bustling figure, his scraggly beard, and
his hot little eyes, was prone to disastrous impulses when the going
got tough, and he gave way to one on the thirtieth of August, 1862.
Late the night before, Pope reported having fought a heavy battle in
which he had lost ten thousand men and the enemy twice that many.
The Confederates, he assured the Secretary, were in full retreat and
he was about to pursue with vigor, which was all to the good. But
Stanton, reflecting on those ten thousand casualties—plus the Rebel
wounded, who must be tended for humanity's sake—suddenly concluded that the wounded would never in the world be cared for unless
he departed swiftly from regular channels, and he immediately departed therefrom with restless energy. He publicly issued an invitation
to government clerks, private citizens, and all the sundry to volunteer
as nurses and stretcher-bearers for the wounded out beyond Centreville. Simultaneously he ordered Haupt to stop whatever he was doing
and prepare to transport this volunteer brigade to the field at once.
(He also rounded up all the hacks and carriages he could find in
Washington and sent them off to Centreville by road, but that did not
affect Haupt; it just clogged the highway that Pope's men had to use.)
Shortly thereafter scores and hundreds of civilians began to pour into
Alexandria demanding transportation. Most of them were drunk, and

those who were not were carrying bottles of whisky and obviously would be drunk before very long.

Haupt's head swam at the thought of dumping this howling mob down on a battlefield. Orders were orders, to be sure, but he was enough of an army man to know that there are ways and ways of rendering obedience. He delayed the train as long as he could; then, when he finally sent it off, he wired the officer in command at Fairfax Station to arrest all who were drunk. Also, he bethought himself that while he had been ordered to take this mob out he had not been ordered to bring it back, so as soon as the train had been unloaded he had it hauled back to Alexandria.

"Those who were sober enough straggled off as soon as it was light enough to see, and wandered around until all whisky and provisions became exhausted, when they returned to the station to get transportation back," Haupt wrote later. "In this, most of them were disappointed."

It seemed cruel, he added, to make these people walk all the way back to Washington in the rain, but it was better to do that than to ignore the wounded; besides, his opinion of the volunteer nurses was not high—"generally it was a hard crowd and of no use whatever on the field." He learned later that some of the men bribed army ambulance drivers to leave the wounded and carry the civilians back to Washington.[4]

And as this affair began to be straightened out the news from the front abruptly became worse. Having announced that he had won a great victory, Pope was slow to report bad news, but the news came trickling back anyway. One of the first to get the drift was General Jacob Cox, an Ohioan who had gone to the lines at Upton's Hill in command of the four regiments McClellan had sent out to hold the ground "at any hazard." On the morning of August 30, Cox saw the ambulances coming in from Centreville, accompanied by the walking wounded. These were men who had left the field the night before, and their impression was that they had won the battle and that the enemy was in retreat. Cox noticed that the sound of the firing, which he had been hearing all the previous day, was not nearly so loud. Adding that to the reports from the wounded men, he assumed that Pope was pursuing the foe and that the gunfire came from rear-guard actions—an assumption which Pope himself held until he finally

reached the point at which further delusion was impossible. During
the afternoon, however, Cox could hear that the sound of the firing
was getting louder—much louder and much heavier, with long, sustained, reverberating rolls of gunfire in which the individual shots
could no longer be distinguished. Toward evening the pathetic parade
of wounded was coming in greater numbers. It was accompanied by
stragglers, and by dark the evidence of a disastrous defeat was all
too visible.[5] The spirits of the soldiers in the camps around Alexandria, which had been raised mightily by the early report of a victory,
began to sag, and the provost marshal notified the War Department
that he needed more men if he was to preserve order—"we are being
overrun with straggling officers and men." The colonel of the 55th
New York Infantry, landing at the Alexandria wharves next morning,
noted an air of great depression as soon as he stepped ashore. Nobody knew just what had happened, but all sorts of rumors were
afloat; he found the word "treason" being used freely.

Treason: betrayal, treachery, a will to lose when the means to win
are at hand; a dark, frightening word, coming up out of the shadows,
carrying fear and distrust and panic unreason with it, so that the
visible enemies in gray and butternut off toward the Bull Run Mountains seemed less to be feared than those who might be standing, all
unsuspected, at one's elbow. The word was used everywhere: in the
President's Cabinet, in the War Department, in the tents of the generals, and—most disastrously of all—in the ranks of the tired army
that was plodding back toward Washington. All of the disillusionment which began when the army was repulsed before Richmond, all
of the sudden war-weariness which had come so soon to a land that
had been long at peace, all of the bewilderment felt by men who saw
themselves striking ineffectually at targets that mysteriously shifted
and dissolved as one struck—all of this, welling up in the hearts of
men who had done their best to no avail, began to find expression in
that word. There had been betrayal: of high hopes and noble pur-
poses, of all the army meant to itself and to the country. The country
had suffered more than a defeat. What was happening now was the
beginning of disintegration.

2. We Were Never Again Eager

In the end it would become an army of legend, with a great name
that still clangs when you touch it. The orations, the brass bands and
the faded flags of innumerable Decoration Day observances, waiting
for it in the years ahead, would at last create a haze of romance,
deepening spring by spring until the regiments and brigades became
unreal—colored-lithograph figures out of a picture-book war, with
dignified graybeards bemused by their own fogged memories of a
great day when all the world was young and all the comrades were
valiant.

But the end of August in the year 1862 was not the time for
taking a distant and romantic view of things. The Army of the Potomac was not at that moment conscious of the formation of legends;
it was hungry and tired, muddy and ragged, sullen with the knowledge that it had been shamefully misused, and if it thought of the
future at all it was only to consider the evil chances which might
come forth during the next twenty-four hours. It was in a mood to
judge the future by the past, and the immediate past had been bad.
The drunken generals who had botched up supply lines, the sober
generals who had argued instead of getting reinforcements forward,
the incredible civilians who had gone streaming out to a battlefield
as to a holiday brawl, the incompetents who thought they were winning when they were losing were symbols of a betrayal that was paid
for in suffering and humiliation by the men who were discovering
that they had enlisted to pay just such a price for other men's errors.

The army had developed a high spirit down on the peninsula in
spite of its troubles; a certain cockiness, even, a feeling that it knew
of no other soldiers who were quite as good, plus a deep certainty
that there was no general anywhere who could be trusted as much
as its own commander, General McClellan. But this spirit was dis-
solving and the certainty was being mocked; and as it plodded on
toward the fortified lines at Alexandria it was on the verge of ceasing
to be an army at all. Men drifted off through the fields or formed
little knots about campfires in the woods and farmyards. The winding
columns on the roads stretched as they moved, the head of each
column moving just a little faster than the tail. There was no panic,

as there had been a year earlier after the first fight at Bull Run, when what had been thought to be an army simply melted into a frantic mob. Save for a bad hour or so at the Bull Run Bridge on the night of August 30, there had been no headlong rush to get away. But the miracle of the spirit which takes thousands of young men, ties them together in strange self-forgetfulness, and enables them to walk stead-fastly and without faltering into the certainty of pain and death was wearing very thin. Bickerings and blunderings had sapped its power; where the men went now they went sullenly and only because they must. It would take little more to cause the men to realize that "must" had force only so long as they consented to it.

The army had been gay when it went out. The point that is so easy to overlook nowadays, when all of the illusions about war have been abraded to dust, is that those young men went off to war eagerly and with light hearts, coveting the great adventure which they blithely believed lay just ahead. They went to war because they wanted to go, every man of them, and the obvious fact that in their innocence they did not have the remotest idea what the reality was going to be like does not change the fact. The bounty jumpers and the drafted men had not yet appeared. This was the army of the nation's youth, consciously trying to live up to its own conception of bravery, con-vinced that a soldier marched forward into high romance; an army with banners that postured pathetically and sincerely as it followed its own boyish vision.

That posturing was of the very essence of the army's spirit, and it caused things to happen that could not happen in the armies of today. We read, for instance, of the father and son who enlisted together in a regiment of Massachusetts infantry. In the fighting at Bull Run the son was killed, and a comrade took the news to the father in the midst of the action. "Well," said the father grimly, "I would rather see him shot dead, as he was, than see him run away." And there is a glimpse of a New York regiment holding the line in another battle under heavy fire. The colonel of an adjoining regi-ment came over to report that this New York outfit was an especial target because its colors were being held too high: lower them a bit and the fire wouldn't be so costly. The colonel of the New York regiment—himself the most conspicuous target of all, riding slowly back and forth on horseback in rear of his men, who were lying behind a rail fence—looked at the waving flag and said: "Let it wave

high. It is our glory." Then there was the colonel of another New York
regiment, mortally wounded in a charge, who ordered his men to
lift him and prop him up against a tree facing the firing. This done,
at whatever cost in pain to the dying man, he said faintly: "Tell
Mother I died with my face to the enemy"—and, the message duly
noted, died.[1]

The spirit of the first campaign these soldiers made comes down
to us in a journal written by young Captain George Freeman Noyes,
a pea-green but ardent officer on General Abner Doubleday's staff,
who found himself making a night march up the Rappahannock
when Pope was concentrating his army against Stonewall Jackson
early in August. Wrote Captain Noyes:

"And so over a heavily-wooded, rolling country, through roads
arched with foliage, the moonlight filling them with fantastic shapes
and shadows, we pursued our romantic way. The peculiar quiet of
the hour, and the weird influence of the forest scenery, with patches
of moonlight flung in here and there among the prevailing shadow,
every turn of the road seemingly a narrow pass over which giant and
grotesque trees stood guard to oppose our progress, added mystic
significance to those reflections which our anticipated battle naturally
awakened. No longer Yankee soldiers of the nineteenth century, we
were for the nonce knights of the ancient chivalry."[2]

Those fanciful old ideas about the glory of a waving flag, the shame
of running from danger, the high importance of dying with one's face
to the foe—since that war they have come to seem as out of date as the
muzzle-loaders that were used for weapons in those days. The American soldier of later, more sophisticated eras may indeed die rather
than retreat, and do it as courageously as any, but he never makes a
song about it or strikes an attitude. His heroism is without heroics,
and fine phrases excite his instant contempt, because he knows even
before he starts off to war that fine phrases and noble attitudes and
flags waving in death's own breeze are only so many forms of a come-
on for the innocent; nor does he readily glimpse himself as a knight of
the ancient chivalry. But in the 1860s the gloss had not been worn off.
Young men then went to war believing all of the fine stories they had
grown up with; and if, in the end, their disillusion was quite as deep
and profound as that of the modern soldier, they had to fall farther
to reach it.

The fall was acutely painful, and it was taking place rapidly in the late summer of 1862. The easiest way to see what was going on—in the soldiers' emotions, and in the war itself—is to follow briefly the career of the Black Hat Brigade, which was to become famous.

This outfit was made up of the 2nd, 6th, and 7th Wisconsin regiments and the 19th Indiana—Western troops in an army predominantly of Easterners—and it was assembled in Fredericksburg in the spring and put under the command of young John Gibbon, lately jumped to a brigadier's commission from his position as captain of regular artillery. Gibbon was a West Pointer—a lean, sharp-nosed, bearded man with a habit of blunt speech, who was quietly sorry to have to leave his guns and his tough regulars, where he felt at home, for infantry and volunteers, where he felt strange. He had served on the Western plains under Albert Sidney Johnston before the war; came from North Carolina, had three brothers in the Confederate Army, but for his part had elected to stand by the Union.

Rather to his surprise, he found that he liked his new command, and he wrote that all the men needed was discipline and drill to make first-class soldiers: a judgment that was to be vindicated, for these Westerners turned out to be fighters as good as any the army ever possessed. Gibbon applied the drill and discipline, discovered that volunteers were unlike regulars—praise and the promise of reward were more effective than the fear of punishment which the regulars required—and to tone up their morale he saw to it that they were outfitted, beyond regulations, with black felt hats and white gaiters; hence their nickname, the Black Hat Brigade.

The first combat veterans the boys encountered—Shields's division, down from the Shenandoah Valley after a bloody fight with Stonewall Jackson—jeered at them for bandbox soldiers, but the Westerners retorted that they would rather wear leggings than be lousy like some people, and anyway, they liked their own natty appearance. Like all new troops in that army, when they started cross-country marching in the hot summer they threw their coats and blankets in the nearest ditches, knowing that they could draw new ones, and no questions asked, from the regimental quartermasters. This pained Gibbon's regular-army soul, and he forced the company commanders to receipt for the issue of clothing thereafter, and compelled them to make regular returns on the requisitions, under penalty of drawing no pay.

The brigade carried its coats and blankets henceforward: a thing which caused muttering at first, but morale was high and Gibbon made the men feel like soldiers, and the muttering died away.[3]

So far the war had been a romantic frolic for these boys. They liked to remember the period of training around Washington, when they had been camped along a stream on the far side of which were home-state neighbors, the 5th Wisconsin. The 5th belonged to General Hancock's brigade, and Hancock had a bull voice that could be heard halfway to Richmond, and the 5th was commanded by a Colonel Cobb, very much of a leading citizen back home but strictly an amateur soldier here like all the rest of them. One day when Hancock was drilling his brigade Colonel Cobb got mixed up and took his regiment off the wrong way in some evolution, and the delighted Wisconsin boys across the river could hear Hancock roar: "Colonel Cobb! Where in the damnation are you going with your battalion?" Thereafter, as long as they were neighbors, it struck the Black Hat Brigade as amusing to go down to the riverbank in the still of the evening and chant in unison: "Colonel Cobb! Where in the damnation are you going with your battalion?"

They had worked out a gag for rainy days, when it was too muddy to drill and all hands were snuggled under their pup tents trying to keep dry and were afflicted by boredom. Some private possessed of a great voice would sing out: "When our army marched down to Bull Run, what did the big bullfrog say?" And hundreds of men would croak: "Big thing! Big thing!" ("Big thing" was Civil War slang for any notable event or achievement—a great battle, promotion to a corporal's chevrons, a two-week furlough, the theft of a crock of apple butter, or anything else worth talking about.) Then the leader would call: "And when our army came back from Bull Run, what did the little frogs say?" To which the answer, in unmelodious screeching trebles, was: "Run, Yank! Run, Yank!" And to close it, the question was: "What does the Bully Sixth say?" The answer, in deep pinewoods bass: "Hit 'em again! Hit 'em again!"

The whole brigade took a queer, perverse pride in the regimental band of the 6th Wisconsin—not because it was so good, but because it was so terrible. It was able to play only one selection, something called "The Village Quickstep," and its dreadful inefficiency (the colonel referred to it in his memoirs as "that execrable band") might have been due to the colonel's quaint habit of assigning men to the band not for musical ability but as punishment for misdemeanors—or so, at least, the regiment stoutly believed. The only good thing about the band was its drum major, one William Whaley, who was an expert at high and fancy twirling of his baton. At one review, in camp around Washington, the brigade had paraded before McClellan, who had been so taken with this drum major's "lofty pomposity" (as a comrade described it) that he took off his cap in jovial salute—whereupon the luckless Whaley, overcome by the honor, dropped his baton ignominiously in the mud, so that his big moment became a fizzle.[4]

At the end of July the brigade moved out of its camp at Fredericksburg and tramped up the Rappahannock to join Pope—the same movement which led Captain Noyes to see knights of the ancient chivalry marching along the moonlit roads. The men were impatient. They belonged to General Irvin McDowell's corps, and they had been sorely disappointed because orders to go to Richmond and join McClellan's forces there had been canceled at the last minute. Now they looked ahead to action, for it was believed that Pope would plunge at once into battle. Reaching the point of concentration, they did a great deal of marching and countermarching and heard the rumble of artillery duels from afar, and once or twice long-range shells fell among them, but they got into no fighting. And finally they found themselves, with the three other brigades in the division of General Rufus King, trudging off to the northeast on the Warrenton turnpike, heading in the direction of Centreville. Along the way they captured their first prisoner—a straggler from Stonewall Jackson's corps, who had had his fill of fighting and surrendered willingly enough, but who was an authentic armed Rebel for all that. This lanky soldier looked with interest at the full packs carried by Gibbon's boys and remarked: "You uns is like pack mules—we uns is like race horses. All Old Jackson gave us was a musket, a hundred rounds, and a gum blanket, and he druv us like hell."

The men did not know exactly where they were going, but they understood vaguely that Old Jackson was somewhere up ahead; it looked as if they would get into a sure-enough fight this time, and their spirits rose. To be sure, if they were being hurried into action their course was obstructed by numerous mix-ups. They had got into

Warrenton at dusk, hungry, their rations exhausted, and were met by
General McDowell in person, who regretted that they could not have
any supper but ordered them to move out on the turnpike at once:
this was a forced march, no time to draw rations, they had to keep
moving. So they started on, found the road blocked by stalled wagon
trains, and made a supperless bivouac two miles from Warrenton.
The next day they were led down a country lane and thrown into
line of battle on some deserted farm, and held there for several hours
in complete solitude, before they were recalled and taken back to the
main highway; and there they were halted again, to butcher some of
their beef cattle and make a leisurely meal. But the men had been
soldiers long enough to understand that that sort of thing just went
with army life, and their enthusiasm was undimmed. At last, after an
afternoon in which they had heard occasional sputters of musket fire
far ahead, they went tramping along the pike a mile or two out of
the little hamlet of Gainesville, the brigade well closed up, General
Gibbon riding at the head, a mile of empty road in front and behind separating it from the rest of the division. It was getting on
toward sunset, and the trees on the left of the road were casting long
cool shadows. A regimental band was playing a quickstep—one hopes,
somehow, that it was the band of the 6th Wisconsin—and the boys
were enjoying the war.

The road led straight ahead, like a white dusty arrow, and General
Gibbon trotted on in advance to the top of a little rise, where he
pulled up to see if he could see anything of the leading brigade. It
had vanished, and Gibbon glanced off to the west, to the left of the
road. The ground was more or less open there, and it rose in a long,
gentle slope; and as Gibbon looked he saw several slim columns of
horse—roving cavalry, most likely, he told himself—come trotting out
of a grove on the hillside, half a mile away. He was just beginning to
speculate whether this cavalry was Federal or Confederate when all
the little columns swerved simultaneously, presenting their flanks. At
sight of this familiar maneuver something clicked in the mind of this
young general who had always been a gunner: that wasn't cavalry at
all, it was field artillery going into battery!

Gibbon sent an aide galloping back to the rear of the column to
bring up the brigade artillery—Battery B, 4th U.S., the one Gibbon
himself had commanded before he became a brigadier of infantry.

The aide had hardly started when six shells came screaming over the road, to burst in the woods off to the right. The colonels of the four infantry regiments, without waiting for orders, swung their men into line facing to the west and got them off the road and had them lie down under cover of a low bank. Battery B came clattering madly up the pike in a cloud of dust, while another salvo from the hostile battery crashed into the treetops. As he cantered into a field west of the road to post the guns Gibbon noticed with approval that his soldiers, although they had been taken completely by surprise, did not seem to be nervous. Perhaps half a dozen men, out of more than eighteen hundred present, had scurried hastily off into the woods when the first shells came over, but they were coming back now with shame-faced grins to rejoin their comrades. Battery B came up, the men tore down a rail fence to make a gateway, and the guns went lumbering into the field beside Gibbon, swinging around and unlimbering with the sure precision of the regulars. In a moment counterbattery fire had been opened.

Up to this point nothing had been seen of the enemy but his six guns. The natural supposition was that they were horse artillery attached to Jeb Stuart's cavalry, engaged in cavalry's favorite practice of harassing infantry on the march. The logical thing to do was to shake a line of infantry out to chase the guns away, and this—after a quick study of the ground in front—Gibbon proceeded to do. The 2nd Wisconsin and 19th Indiana moved forward from behind the protecting bank, broke through a little belt of bushes and scrub trees, and started out across the field to make the Rebel battery cease and desist. The whole thing was done with earnest care, just as it had been done on the drill ground so many times: colonel and lieutenant colonel of each regiment full of business, carefully sighting the lines of direction, sending guides forward, fussing mightily about alignment, trying their level best to do it all regular-army style—doing it just a little self-consciously, one gathers, because General Gibbon came riding over from the guns to watch, and the general was a regular, and this was the first time under fire. The lines were formed presently and the men went forward, a fringe of skirmishers in advance, and they came to the top of a low ridge. The Confederate artillery suddenly ceased firing, and a line of gray-clad skirmishers rose from the grass in front of the guns and began a pop-pop of small-arms fire.

Then, from the woods beyond, a great mass of Confederate infantry emerged, coming down the slope to give the Westerners their first trial by combat, red battle flags with the starred blue cross snapping in the evening breeze—Stonewall Jackson's men, whose measured conviction it was that they could whip any number of Yankees at any time and place, and whose record gave them tolerably good reason for the belief.

And a long, tearing crackle of musketry broke over the shadowed field, and the Wisconsin and Indiana boys learned what it was like to fight. Gibbon, who had thought he was quelling impudent horse artillery, went spurring back to bring up his other two regiments, couriers galloped down the road to ask for help from the other brigades, and presently the 6th Wisconsin came up to take position at the right of the line. Many years later its colonel recalled with pride the military precision with which his regiment deployed for action under fire. Gibbon threw the 7th Wisconsin in where the 2nd was fighting, and the battle was on.

It was a strange battle—a straightaway, slam-bang, stand-up fight with no subtleties and no maneuvering, no advancing and no retreating. Some of the Confederates found cover around a little farmhouse, and the 6th Wisconsin got some protection because the ground sagged in an almost imperceptible little hollow right where it was posted, so that most of the bullets that came its way went overhead. But for the most part the men did not seek cover—did not even lie down on the ground, which was the way many fire fights took place in those days, but simply stood facing each other in even, orderly ranks, as if they were on parade awaiting inspection, and volleyed away at the murderous range of less than one hundred yards.

On the right, Battery B fired rapidly and accurately, and some other brigade had brought another battery into action off on the left, and before long General Doubleday sent up the 56th Pennsylvania and the 76th New York—virgin regiments, like those of Gibbon—to join in the fight; and this amazing combat of two dress-parade battle lines at point-blank range sent its echoes resounding across the Manassas plain, while a dense cloud of acrid smoke went rolling up the evening sky. Years later General Gibbon remarked that he heard, that evening, the heaviest musket fire he heard during the entire war.

The fight lasted for an hour and a half. When it ended both sides were exactly where they were when it began, except that a Confederate brigade which tried a flanking movement around the Federal right had got tangled up in a ravine full of underbrush, in the smoky dusk, and couldn't find its way out, while the 19th Indiana had been edged off to the left rear to cope with what looked like a flank attack from that direction. Gibbon was proud of the way his Hoosiers managed this maneuver while under fire. Toward evening, with the Confederate fieldpieces out of action, Stuart's incredible artillerist, John Pelham, brought a section of guns up to within seventy paces of Gibbon's line and opened fire, without any visible effect whatever except to add to the total of killed and maimed.

Night came at last, mercifully, and put an end to it, the rival battle lines slowly drew apart, and, as General Gibbon wrote, "everything except the groans of the wounded quieted down." The Black Hat boys could call themselves veterans now; they had had their baptism of fire—baptism by total immersion, one might say. The 2nd Wisconsin—which, over the length of the war, was to win the terrible distinction of having a higher percentage of its total enrollment killed in action than any other regiment in the United States Army—had taken 500 men into this fight and left 298 of them dead or wounded on the field; it got a leg on the record that evening. The 7th Wisconsin and the 19th Indiana had lost nearly as heavily. The 6th Wisconsin had been lucky by comparison, losing 72 men out of 504 engaged. A regimental historian wrote later that to the end of the war this brigade was always ready for action, "but we were never again eager."

All in all, more than a third of the Federal soldiers who went into action that evening had been shot. Over on the Confederate side, though the Federals didn't know it at the time, the story was about the same. The famous Stonewall brigade had lost 33 per cent of its numbers, the 21st Georgia had lost 173 out of 242 in action, and two division commanders had gone down, one of them the famous General Dick Ewell. Next morning one of Jeb Stuart's staff officers came out to take a casual look at the scene of action. "The lines were well marked by the dark rows of bodies stretched out on the broomsedge field, lying just where they had fallen, with their heels on a well-defined line," he wrote. "The bodies lay in so straight a line that they looked like troops lying down to rest. On each front the edge was sharply defined, while towards the rear it was less so. Showing how men had staggered backward after receiving their death blow."5

The Federals drew a line of battle in the woods next to the turnpike, sent out parties to bring in as many of the wounded as possible, established crude field hospitals under the trees, and in general tried to catch their breath. A staff officer, coming up the pike from the rear, found a campfire blazing in the road, with the generals grouped around it, staff officers seated outside the inner circle, orderlies holding the reins of saddled horses still farther out, the firelight gleaming on tanned faces, a ribbon of wood smoke climbing up out of the glow to disappear in the arching branches above. The brigadiers were assembled and the division commander, General King, who had been taken ill that afternoon and had had to seek shelter back at Gainesville and so had not been present during the fight, came up to join them, weak and pale. His division was part of McDowell's corps, but nobody could find McDowell, who had ridden off in midafternoon to seek General John Pope in the vicinity of Manassas and who, it developed later, had got completely lost in the woods and found neither Pope nor anyone else until the next day. Since neither King nor McDowell had been around while the fighting was going on, the battle had really been fought under nobody's direction—except Gibbon's, and he was responsible only for his own brigade. Now that the generals were in council nobody knew quite what to do, for King's original orders were to march to Centreville, and it was painfully obvious that before he could do that he would have to drive Stonewall Jackson out of the way, which was clearly too much of a task for any single division.

In the end it was agreed that the command had better withdraw in the direction of Manassas Junction, which lay several miles to the east, and it was so ordered. Sometime after midnight the tired troops withdrew and tramped silently off down a country road in the blackness, all the gay banter of their earlier marches quite forgotten; and in a cloudy dawn they dropped down in a field near Manassas to get a little sleep, while the staff hurried off to try to find Pope, McDowell, or somebody who could tell them what the brigade was supposed to do next.

The soldiers didn't get much sleep. Orders came in presently: Fitz-John Porter and his V Corps from the Army of the Potomac were

coming up and would be backtracking along the road toward Gainesville, and King's division—now commanded by General John Hatch,
for King's illness had put him out—would go with them. So the men
drew up in marching order by the roadside, and pretty soon the head
of Porter's corps came along, marching with an indefinable swagger
even in the informal route step of the cross-country hike, and the
young Westerners cheered mightily in boyish hero worship—this was
the Army of the Potomac, these were veterans of the fabulous fighting around Richmond, McClellan's men were joining Pope's, and
everything would be all right now.

Porter's men received the cheers with high disdain. They included a
solid division of regulars, plus some volunteer regiments which had
acquired much esprit de corps, which means that they looked down
on practically all soldiers who did not belong to their own outfit. They
had taken the worst the Confederates had to give at Gaines's Mill,
and at Malvern Hill they had seen the furious Southern assault waves
break up in a swirling foam of bloody repulse on the hard rock of
massed artillery and rifle fire, and their immeasurable contempt for
John Pope was quite broad enough to include all of his troops. They
called out loftily: "Get out of the way, straw-feet—we're going to go
up to show you how to fight." ("Straw-foot" was the Civil War term
for rookie. The idea was that some of the new recruits were of such
fantastic greenness that they did not know the left foot from the
right and hence could not be taught to keep time properly or to step
off on the left foot as all soldiers should. The drill sergeants, in des-
peration, had finally realized that these green country lads did at
least know hay from straw and so had tied wisps of hay to the left
foot and straw to the right foot and marched them off to the chant of
"Hay-foot, straw-foot, hay-foot, straw-foot." Hence: straw-foot—
rookie, especially a dumb rookie.) Gibbon's boys were hurt—after
last evening they felt entitled to join any brotherhood whose entry
fee was courage under fire—and they yelled back: "Wait until you've
been where we've been—that'll take some of the slack out of your
pantaloons"; but they still admired those hard veterans and were
glad to be with them. After a while they swung into column and
followed the V Corps along the road, heading back toward what
they had just marched away from—perfectly ready to fight again,
but not hankering for it any longer.

3. You Must Never Be Frightened

If any of Gibbon's boys had had the speculative bent to sit down and figure out just what their prodigious valor had bought for the Union cause, a most dismaying fact would have come to light. The chief result of that desperate fight in the meadow was that the befuddlement of General John Pope became complete instead of only partial.

General Pope had been having his troubles for some time. He had not been entirely sure where his own army was, and he had not in the least known where the enemy was, and he had been frantically trying to use the one to find the other. For several days he had been holding the line of the Rappahannock, guarding the fords, dueling with his artillery whenever Rebel forces showed themselves on the far side of the river, sending his cavalry dashing about with vast energy, and he had about concluded that a great battle would be fought soon in the vicinity of Warrenton. It would be a desperate encounter, because he was outnumbered, or at least believed that he was. As he understood the top strategy in Washington, he was supposed to hold the line at all costs until McClellan's army could join him, whereupon General Halleck would ride down from Washington and take active command in the field of both Pope and his troops and McClellan and his—Pope and McClellan then becoming, as Pope believed, wing commanders under the general-in-chief.

Pope was deceived in this belief: the last thing Halleck wanted was to command troops in the field against Robert E. Lee; but at the moment no one but Halleck knew this. So on August 26 Pope had been drawing his forces together near Warrenton, spattering the landscape with galloping couriers, as he called outlying divisions to his rendezvous. From McClellan's army, grumpily returning from the peninsula, Fitz-John Porter and the V Corps were coming up the river from Fredericksburg, and General Ambrose Burnside and the IX Corps had landed at Aquia Creek and presumably were making their way to him overland, while the rest of McClellan's men were coming in via Alexandria. A few days more and the reunion would be complete and the responsibility would pass from his shoulders.

But then things started to happen. First Stonewall Jackson disappeared from Pope's front. He was detected marching off to the north-west, and it seemed likely he was heading for his old haunts in the Shenandoah Valley, but on second thought Pope considered a flank attack on his lines at Warrenton probable, and he sent out new orders to hurry the concentration. Then, after dark, the telegraph wire to Washington went dead, and it appeared that Confederate cavalry was up to its old trick of jumping the supply lines. Joe Hooker—who had at last caught his train and got to the front—was ordered to take his division up the railroad and attend to it. Next day it developed that it was Jackson, not cavalry, on the supply line, and the tired couriers galloped off with new orders: concentration at Gaines-ville, now, with the cavalry under Buford swinging west through Thoroughfare Gap to see what had become of the rest of Lee's army. Toward evening Hooker collided with Confederate infantry at Bristoe Station and chased it north across Broad Run after a sharp fight, and orders were changed once more: the army will concentrate at Manassas, Jackson has delivered himself into our hands, and if we move fast we shall "bag the whole crowd."

Pope rode in haste to Bristoe, set out next morning for Manassas, lost Jackson's trail, and changed orders still further: concentrate at Centreville now, Jackson is somewhere near here, if we are alert we can destroy him. And finally, late that night, Pope got news of the fight Gibbon and Doubleday had stumbled into near Gainesville, and the picture became very clear to him—or so he thought. Jackson, having raided the Union supply depot, was trying desperately to get away. King's division had intercepted his retreat and rebuffed him (as Pope conceived), and Jackson was caught squarely between the two wings of the Union Army and could be crushed the very next day. Pope sat down at Centreville, to which place he had by now gyrated, sent jubilant messages to Washington, and made ready for his apotheosis: triumph, confusion to the enemies of the Republic, and a brilliant demonstration that Pope had the secret of victory which Mc-Clellan lacked.

The only trouble with this picture was that it was completely false. Jackson was not trapped and he was not trying to get away. On the contrary, he very much wanted to stay and fight, and while Pope's troops had been countermarching so feverishly he had found a good position near the old Bull Run battlefield, had established himself

there, and had waited to be discovered. Pope being quite unable to
find him, Jackson had moved out to give a prod to the first Union
troops that came within reach—King's division—as a means of calling
attention to his whereabouts. Jackson's primary mission was not
simply to loot and destroy Pope's base of supplies, enjoyable though
that task had been. General Lee had determined that Pope must be
beaten ("suppressed" was his contemptuous word for it) before all
of McClellan's army could join him, and he had reached out with the
long, muscular arm of Stonewall Jackson to pin the Northerner down
on some good fighting ground suitably remote from the Rappahannock. Now, with Pope rushing to fall on Jackson, Lee was coming
up with all speed. Pope, who believed himself to be casting a cunning
net, was walking straight into one.

The soldiers whom General Pope was bringing up to Bull Run
were by no means happy. Knowing nothing of the high strategy involved, they were perfectly aware that they had been marched back
and forth to no good purpose for the better part of a week, and they
had been around long enough to understand that this meant the high
command was confused and jittery. They had outmarched their supplies, in all the confusion, and most of them were hungry, and the
shuttling back and forth, up hill and down dale, had brought many
to the point of exhaustion. The cavalry was deadbeat: some detachments came in from outpost duty on foot, leading horses that were
too worn to carry weight even at a walk. The colonel of one regiment
reported that his men had not had their coats off for three weeks, and
in many squadrons there were not half a dozen men who could get
their horses up to a trot.

To make things worse, what Pope was commanding was not an
army but simply a thrown-together collection of troops. Technically,
Pope's army—named, for its brief life, the Army of Virginia—consisted of three army corps: those of Franz Sigel, Nathaniel P. Banks,
and Irvin McDowell. Sigel's men included a large number of German
regiments—immigrants, for the most part, who had had German army
training and should have been first-rate soldiers, but who somehow
seemed to lose their effectiveness under the loose discipline of the
American volunteer army. They had originally belonged to the famous
but unmilitary General John Charles Frémont, who had ingloriously
led them to failure in the mountain country to the west. Their morale

was low, and Sigel was by no means the man who could pull them together. Banks was a political general—a distinguished Massachusetts businessman and politician, former Republican Speaker of the House of Representatives, a man who, by the strange custom of that war, was "entitled" to a major general's commission because of his importance as a political leader and a public figure. He was a good man and devoted to the cause, but he was no soldier; up in the valley Stonewall Jackson had routed him and run rings around him, and the Confederates had consumed his stores so regularly that they derisively dubbed him "Old Jack's commissary general." He had first-rate soldiers in his command—Easterners, mostly, with a fair number of Ohioans and a sprinkling from Indiana and Wisconsin—and they would do well if they ever got competent leadership.

McDowell was the only real soldier in the group, and he commanded excellent troops. King's division, now led by Hatch and later to go to Doubleday, contained some of the best soldiers in the army, and John Reynolds led a solid division of Pennsylvanians, who were good men under a good general. Ricketts, commanding the third division, had been an artillerist at the first battle of Bull Run. His division included a number of men who had fought well under poor leaders in the valley. All in all, this army corps was basically as good as any in either army, but it suffered from the fact that McDowell, a good man and a capable general, was one of those soldiers born to bad luck. Nothing ever went right for him. The aura of failure, born of that first fight at Bull Run, trailed after him. The men disliked him violently—even a special hat which he had devised for his summer comfort, a cool but rather weird-looking contrivance of bamboo and cloth, they chalked up as a point against him—and for some unaccountable reason they widely believed that he was in cahoots with the enemy. He and McClellan disliked each other, and McClellan blamed him for not coming down from Fredericksburg to help him during the Seven Days' fighting, although McDowell himself had protested against the administration strategy that had held him north of the Rappahannock and considered that his proper place was with the army on the Chickahominy.

Pope made McDowell his first lieutenant and leaned on him heavily, but cursed him behind his back ("God damn McDowell! He's never where I want him!" Pope had cried on the eve of the battle), and Pope ignored him when McDowell gave him the advice that might have saved him from the snare Lee and Jackson were setting. A staff officer in King's division wrote after his first meeting with him: "I liked McDowell's looks; he seemed to me strong, self-contained, ready for responsibility and able to sustain it. I had yet to learn how much his too frequent forgetfulness of the courtesy due even to a common soldier was to impair his usefulness and injure his popularity."[1] And a young officer of engineers who dined with McDowell late in 1861 left the following appraisal:

"He was at that time in the full flush of mature manhood, fully six feet tall, deep chested, strong limbed, clear eyed, and in every respect a fine and impressive soldier, but at dinner he was such a Gargantuan feeder and so absorbed in the dishes before him that he had but little time for conversation. While he drank neither wine nor spirits, he gobbled the larger part of every dish within reach, and wound up with an entire watermelon, which he said was 'monstrous fine!' . . . As we rode back to the city in the afternoon, McPherson"—later General James B. McPherson, commander of the Army of the Tennessee—"and I discussed him freely, and, allowing him every professional qualification, we agreed that no officer who was so great a gourmand as he could by any chance prove to be a great and successful leader of men."[2]

That, then, was Pope's army; some poor soldiers and some good ones, led by two corps commanders who ought to have been back in civilian life and a third who had neither the luck to win victories nor the touch to make men respond to his leadership. In addition, Pope had received two army corps from the Army of the Potomac. One was under the command of General S. P. Heintzelman, a stout old regular with an engaging, knobby-cheeked face surmounted by a fuzz of whiskers. He had plenty of energy—had gone up in one of the newfangled observation balloons on the peninsula to see for himself what the enemy was up to; was blunt in speech, with a nasal twang to his voice, and somehow just missed being an effective corps commander. Heintzelman brought two of the best combat divisions in the army with him. One was Joe Hooker's: Hooker was an intemperate man, in several senses of the word, and he never got along with any of his superior officers, but he at least liked to fight and had driving energy. The other division was led by Phil Kearny, who was all flame and color and ardor, with a slim, twisted streak of genius in him.

Kearny had probably seen more fighting than any man on the field. He had served in Mexico as a cavalry captain; had remarked, in youthful enthusiasm, that he would give an arm to lead a cavalry charge against the foe. He got his wish, at the exact price offered, a few days later, leading a wild gallop with flashing sabers and losing his left arm. He once told his servant: "Never lose an arm; it makes it too hard to put on a glove." When General Oliver Otis Howard lost his right arm in the fighting at Seven Pines, Kearny visited him in hospital and said consolingly: "General, I am sorry for it, but you must not mind it: the ladies will not think the less of you." To which sobersides Howard returned his one recorded wisecrack: "There is one thing we can do, General; we can buy our gloves together." Kearny smiled gaily and cried, "Sure enough," and the two men had shaken on it with the hands they had left.

Kearny had served in the French Army in Algiers and northern Italy and had fought at Magenta and Solferino. A French officer wrote that Kearny "went under fire as on parade, with a smile on his lips." It was reported that in some battle on the peninsula a colonel whom he ordered forward into action asked him just where he should put his men and received the reply: "Oh, anywhere, Colonel—you'll find lovely fighting all along the line." Winfield Scott had called him "the bravest man I ever saw, and a perfect soldier," and nobody who had followed him would dispute the point. He hated McClellan and he hated Pope, and he had the knack of making his troops feel that they were the finest soldiers on the planet. He had invented the "Kearny patch," a red lozenge of flannel which every man in his command wore on his cap, so that the outfit became known as the "red diamond division" and wore its badge with vast pride. When a new regiment joined the division, the soldiers looked on it with reserve until it had proved its bravery in combat; then, a survivor wrote, they agreed that this new regiment "was worthy of the red diamond division." Later in the war Kearny's device was taken up at headquarters, and a special patch was made for each army corps. The shoulder patches worn by American soldiers in subsequent wars were direct descendants of Phil Kearny's morale builder.[3]

Kearny and Hooker might be hard to manage, and Heintzelman
might offer negligible qualities of leadership, but those two divisions
would fight furiously wherever they were put: Pope could be sure of
that. The same thing was true of the army corps brought in by Fitz-
John Porter: two divisions, one of regulars, one of volunteers, superb
soldiers who had fully proved their fighting qualities, with a corps
commander who might well have been the best officer then in the
army. Porter was well-born—a New Hampshire man, nephew of the
Commodore David Porter who was a hero of the War of 1812, and
a cousin of the Captain David Dixon Porter who was Farragut's
right-hand man on the Mississippi—and he was an intimate friend of
McClellan, who let him fight both Gaines's Mill and Malvern Hill in
his own way. He was handsome, soldierly-looking, perhaps just a
shade arrogant. He had nothing but contempt for Pope and he expressed his contempt freely, both verbally and in writing, a fact which
later had tragic results. He was one of the few soldiers of that bewhiskered era who could wear a full beard and still look trim and
dapper.

Lastly, Pope had just been joined by General Jesse Reno, a stocky,
capable soldier who brought one slim division and two brigades of
another from Burnside's corps; men who technically belonged to
McClellan but who had been on an expedition along the Carolina
coast and had not fought in front of Richmond. They had done well
in the Carolinas, and Burnside was not at the moment with them—a
considerable advantage, though no one realized it at the time.

All of these troops Pope was frantically summoning to overwhelm
Jackson. If battles were fought on a simple basis of counting numbers, he had more than enough to do the job, but battles aren't settled
that way. Pope's handicaps outweighed any conceivable advantage
numbers might give him. Pope's own men were discouraged because
they had never had good top leadership and saw no reason to believe
they were getting it now. The men from the Army of the Potomac
were battle-tried and considered themselves fighters every bit as good
as any Confederates they were apt to meet, but they were deeply
dejected by their transfer to Pope, and they had no higher opinion of
him than McClellan had. This was largely Pope's own fault. He had
celebrated his assumption of command by issuing an incredibly bom-
bastic address to the troops, announcing that out West where he came

from he was used to looking upon the backs of his enemies, and asserting that the army would henceforth stop worrying about bases of supply, lines of retreat, and so on, and simply go ahead and win battles. This was just asking for trouble and everybody knew it, and the Federal soldiers jeered at the message quite as much as did the Confederates. After the war Pope told a friend that Secretary Stanton had written the address and induced him to issue it. Even if that explanation is true (and Pope makes a poor witness) it doesn't exculpate him: the difference between the stupidity of a man who would write such a screed in the first place and the stupidity of a man who would issue it in his own name after someone else wrote it is a difference only in degree.

So the men Pope brought up to the Warrenton turnpike on the twenty-ninth of August were men who expected the worst and knew they were entitled to expect it. Whatever bravery and endurance could do to redeem the mistakes of the general in command would be done, but unless the soldiers' luck was in, for a change, it would not be enough. And their luck was not in. From first to last the Army of the Potomac was unlucky. It fought for four years, and it took more killing, proportionately, than any army in American history, and its luck was always out; it did its level best and lost; when it won the victory was always clouded by a might-have-been, and when at last the triumph came at Appomattox there were so very, very many of its men who weren't there to see it.

Pope fought his battle about as one might expect: with great energy, but defective judgment. Jackson, whose position he had finally discovered, was lined up behind an unfinished railroad embankment north of the turnpike, a position as good as a fort; and Jackson was quite happy to let Pope wear the Federal army out while he waited for Lee to join him. As soon as it was light enough to fight Pope began to oblige him. Sigel's Germans attacked first and were repulsed. Then Hooker drove for the center of the line and got a brigade up on the embankment, where Northern and Southern boys fought desperately with bayonets and clubbed muskets before the Northerners were driven down. Now Phil Kearny came in through the woods to smash at A. P. Hill, at the left end of Jackson's line—bent him back and forced him to call for reinforcements, but, like Hooker, found the task too much for him and had to pull out. Kearny sat his horse

in the woods and watched his beaten boys returning; saw the 3rd
Michigan, which had had ruinous losses, and wept as the regiment
went by, crying, "Oh, what has become of my gallant old Third?"[4]
Reynolds sent his Pennsylvanians in, but Jackson had too much artillery for them and they, too, were rebuffed; and after twilight Hatch's
division collided with Hood's Texans along the highway and had to
retreat in the darkness after a savage and confused encounter. A
major in Hatch's 76th New York, unhorsed and wounded, came
limping back and met disorganized troops in the dark and tried to
rally them, only to find himself a prisoner of war: the men belonged
to the 2nd Mississippi and wore the Rebel gray.

Meanwhile, off to the left, Porter was coming up with his men.
Pope thought Porter had a clear road ahead that would put him on
Jackson's flank and roll up his lines for keeps, and ordered him to
attack and win the day. But Porter discovered that his clear road was
most effectively blocked by thirty thousand sinewy Confederates under
James Longstreet, who had silently filed into line of battle around
noon, all unseen, and who were now lying in wait, fairly aching to be
attacked. Longstreet was a counterpuncher, and a deadly one, and
he wanted nothing on earth that day quite so much as to receive an
attack by Porter, whom he outnumbered three to one. Porter, sensibly
enough, notified Pope of this obstruction and sat tight. But Pope
simply refused to believe him. His calculations (made God knows
how) had convinced him that Longstreet couldn't possibly reach the
field for another twenty-four hours, and he sent back word that Porter
was wrong—there was nothing whatever in front of him, the way to
Jackson's unguarded flank was wide open, Porter must attack at once.
In the end, the attack was not made—to the salvation of the army
and the personal ruin of Fitz-John Porter—and long after dark Pope
sullenly recalled Porter and his men and brought them up to the main
line along the highway.

When morning came Pope gave way to his final, most disastrous
delusion. The Texans whom Hatch had bumped into the night before
had withdrawn along toward midnight, and Jackson had pulled back
his own men in one or two places to make his alignment more compact and had his troops snugly concealed in the woods back of the
railroad embankment. Pope was persuaded by all of this that Jackson was in full retreat, and he triumphantly notified Washington that

he had won a great victory, and ordered an immediate pursuit, horse, foot, and guns. He had his headquarters on an open knoll and he stood there this morning with his generals, puffing a cigar, overflowing with good humor, exchanging jokes and congratulations, while a small regiment of orderlies stood in the background holding the generals' horses and the breeze whipped the flags and pennants. McDowell was to be in general charge of the pursuit, and Porter, whose troops were fresh, was to lead; Hatch and Reynolds would follow him, while Hooker and Kearny would go along on a parallel road a couple of miles to the north. Orders were to press the enemy vigorously all day. In vain Porter tried to convince Pope that there was an ominous congregation of Rebels off to the south of the highway, with nothing to indicate that they had departed. When Pope made up his mind it stayed made up, and there was no room in it this morning for anything but the conviction that the enemy was in flight. So the troops were wheeled around and got into formation, the artillery came rumbling up, and the pursuit began.

It was probably the briefest pursuit in history. The skirmish lines that went combing through the meadows and groves very quickly discovered that something was still waiting behind that railway embankment. Under Pope's concept of things, that could be nothing more than a rear guard, left there to fight a delaying action while the main body got safely away. So Porter, with deep misgivings, pulled his men out into a battle line on the north side of the road and sent them forward, through a tangle of little hillocks and gullies, across a quiet country road, and on up a gradual rise toward the embankment and the silent woods behind it. Reynolds was under orders to follow him, fanning his troops out on the south side of the turnpike just in case there should be a few Rebels in that area, but now it looked as if Porter might need help, so Reynolds was called in to lend a hand on the right, and Porter's left was quite exposed. To give it a little protection, Porter pulled the 5th and 10th New York out of Sykes's division and sent them, with a battery of regular artillery, to a little hill south of the highway. His men went on, while Hatch formed line farther to the right, and the generals on the hill waited in quiet confidence.

A few Confederate batteries were in sight (part of the rear guard, judged Pope; harbingers of coming trouble, thought Porter) and they opened on Porter's lines, Union batteries replying immediately. The staccato bursts of fire from the skirmishers came more frequently as the advance continued, and the artillery fire on both sides became heavier and heavier. Then suddenly the whole railway embankment sparkled and glistened as the sunlight was reflected off polished rifle barrels, and Stonewall Jackson's massed troops came out of the woods to take their places on the firing line. A gigantic tumult of musketry filled the air, and Federals and Confederates exchanged long, crashing volleys at close range, and instead of a rear-guard action there was a full-dress battle. Jackson's men burned the slope with rifle fire, and on a hill to the southwest new batteries unlimbered, to rake Porter's battle lines with heavy salvos—a deadly enfilade fire that cut the support lines to pieces and left the advance isolated and helpless. The troops in front crumbled and fell back, rallied on the fragments in the rear, and went forward again, drifted back anew, and then drove ahead a third time.

It came to hand-to-hand fighting in places, and at one spot the Confederates ran out of ammunition and threw heavy stones down the bank on the heads of the Federals who were scrambling up. Everywhere there was a smother of battle smoke, the yells of the soldiers, and a tremendous uproar of gunfire. One Northern column came up led by an officer on horseback who rode two dozen paces in front, in defiance of regulations (mounted officers were supposed to ride in rear of the troops in all columns of assault). He rode straight for the embankment, looking neither to the right nor the left, sword held high, the storm of bullets somehow missing him, and put his horse up the steep slope and got clear to the top. For one agonizing, dramatic moment he was poised there, still facing to the front, all alone on the deadly sky line that his men could not reach, central figure in an unbelievable tableau. From the hard Southern fighters to the right and left there went up one spontaneous cry— *"Don't kill him!"* Then the smoke-fog covered the bank, and the crash of the rifles swept along the line, and when the smoke drifted away the horse and rider were dead at the top of the bank.

Off to Porter's right Hatch sent in his brigades in a deep column. The first line got to the embankment, broke, and came flying back. Gibbon was dashing about on foot, his revolver out, shouting: "Stop those stragglers—make them fall in—shoot them if they don't!" while a Wisconsin regiment crouched with fixed bayonets, ready to impale the fugitives if they went any farther. The rout was stopped, the attack went ahead again, and a skirmish line, strengthened almost to the weight of a line of battle, got on the embankment but could not stay there. From the left, Rebel artillery sent solid shot straight along the front. "A solid shot will plow into the ground, spitefully scattering the dirt," a survivor recalled afterward, "and bound a hundred feet into the air, looking as it flies swiftly like an India-rubber playing ball."[5]

Abner Doubleday brought his brigade into action. He had heard the first shot of the entire war—indeed, it had been fired at him personally, in a manner of speaking, since he had been a captain of artillery in Fort Sumter in the spring of 1861—and it was reported that Doubleday himself had sighted the gun which fired the first Union shot in reply. He had got his star when the Sumter garrison came north after the surrender, and now he was leading his troops in a desperate fight. One has to chuckle, just a little, thinking about Doubleday. The generals of that army, the good ones and the bad ones alike, were intensely jealous of fame and distinction. Here was Doubleday, strictly an average general, never making any great mistakes but never winning any great laurels either—when Reynolds was killed at Gettysburg the following year Meade took good care not to turn his corps over to Doubleday, the ranking division commander. It is fascinating to wonder what the other generals would have said if they could have known that in the end Doubleday was going to be one of the most famous of them all—not for his war record, but for his alleged connection with the origin of the game of baseball, which the soldiers were just then beginning to play in their off hours.

"Our lines were in the open fields in front of a strip of woods," a Wisconsin soldier wrote. "The Rebel musketry fire was pouring from the woods upon our men who were closing together and rallying under the attack. Regiments would sweep splendidly forward into the front line, fire a crashing volley into the woods, and then work with great energy. But they quickly withered away until there would appear to be a mere company crowding around the colors."[6]

Joe Hooker, who seemed to be ranking officer on that part of the field, trotted up at last on his white horse, looked the hopeless situation over, and ordered a retirement. The blue line drew back, step

by step, still facing to the front; and as it did so the Confederates
came out from behind the embankment and followed them, step by
cautious step, neither side firing. When the Federal line halted, the
Confederates would halt and lie down, holding their muskets ready;
when the Federals stepped back again, the Confederates would get
up and step after them—a strange, silent, queerly ominous advance
and retreat, with the crash of battle sounding loudly beyond the
woods to right and to left.

Porter's men were beaten and fell back, and Hatch's troops were
beaten and fell back. Longstreet brought his men out of their con-
cealment—it was time to disillusion John Pope at last—and drove
them forward in a long charge along the turnpike and over the hills
and fields to the south. And Reynolds's Pennsylvanians had been
taken off to the right, so that there was nobody in front of Longstreet's thirty thousand but one battery of regular artillery and Porter's
two volunteer regiments of infantry, isolated on a knoll behind a
farmhouse, and they were not nearly enough.

These two regiments belonged to Sykes's division. Except for
them the division was composed solidly of regulars, and when they
had first been brigaded with it the volunteers had not known quite
how to act. They remembered how General Sykes, cold and unemo-
tional, with a fine bushy beard and a crusty regular-army manner,
had greeted them when they had joined his command. He had them
lined up on parade and read to them McClellan's order which made
them part of his division. Then he said: "You have heard what our
commander-in-chief General McClellan says. I only add that if there
is any hard work to be done you have got to do it." The soldiers
gulped, then gave three cheers, and after that they belonged to the
family.[7]

Right now they belonged to a forlorn hope. The 10th New York
had been placed in front as a heavy skirmish line, and Longstreet's
advance rolled over it and crumpled it and ground it aside (one participant remembered "a fat little major" in the 10th whacking the
Federals with the flat of his sword to hold them to their work) and
came on up the hill to capture the battery. The 5th New York were
dressed as Zouaves—bright red baggy pants, white canvas leggings,
broad red sash at the waist, short blue jacket, tasseled red caps; it
appears that they were the soldiers who had taunted Gibbon's boys

the day before. They hung on now long enough to let the regulars get the guns away, and then they retired—what was left of them, anyway. In their brief fight they had lost 124 men killed and 223 wounded out of 490 present—the highest percentage of loss, in killed, suffered by any Federal regiment in one battle during the entire war. As they pulled out they could see Sykes's regular battalions, north of the pike, wheeling out of line and into column under a merciless fire as only the regulars could do. Whatever else might happen, Porter's men had lived up to the boast they had made to the Black Hat Brigade: they had shown any and all straw-feet how to fight.

Pope and McDowell saw the danger now and worked frantically to get protection over on the left. Some of Sigel's men were sent there, and they took with them a battery of mountain howitzers—funny little guns that were carried into action on the backs of mules, to be taken down and assembled on diminutive gun carriages when it was time to fight. Some of Hooker's boys saw these howitzers for the first time that day as Sigel's Germans took them forward into action, and they jeered loudly and asked what in the world sort of battery that was. "The shackass battery, by Gott—get out mit der way or we blow your hets off!" cried the Germans.

Ricketts sent a couple of brigades over from the far right, and they took possession of a little swale beside the Germans and slugged it out with Hood's Texans. In one of these brigades was the 12th Massachusetts, a kid-glove regiment commanded by Colonel Fletcher Webster, son of the great Daniel. This outfit had left Boston a year earlier amid impressive ceremonies, carrying an elaborate flag of white silk presented by "the ladies of Boston," the silk being edged in blue and gold and bearing the coat of arms of Massachusetts on one side and on the other a quotation from the famous orator—"Not a stripe erased or polluted, not a single star obscured."

In addition to a fancy flag and the admiration of the ladies of Boston, the 12th Massachusetts had brought a song to war—a fine, swinging song with a deep roll of tramping feet and ruffled drums in it, a song to which a woman later gave tremendous words, so that it lives on as the nation's greatest battle hymn, with something in it that goes straight down to the deepest emotions of the country's heart. During its training-camp days the 12th had been stationed at Fort Warren, in Boston Harbor, where the 2nd U.S. Infantry was also stationed; and the regulars had picked up a snappy tune—a camp-meeting revival hymn, written in Charleston, South Carolina, around 1850, entitled "Say Brothers Will We Meet You Over on the Other Shore?" What a battalion of U.S. regulars was doing knowing a gospel hymn is beyond imagination, but they did know it, and because it was a fine song to march to they had fitted new words to it: "John Brown's body lies a-mouldering in the grave . . . and we go marching on." The 12th liked the song and learned to sing it, and they had a fine band to provide the accompaniment. There was a big review on Boston Common on a bright summer afternoon, with Edward Everett delivering an oration, and a feminine committee presenting the silk flag, and an open-air dinner on the Beacon Street mall afterward. When the dinner had been eaten the regiment paraded back to Fort Warren, going down State Street singing the John Brown song with the band at the head of the column, and the war was all youth and music and bright flags and heroism.

A few days later they marched through Boston to take the train for Washington, and again they sang the song. When they got to New York they had a big parade up Broadway, and thousands of people lined the sidewalks and leaned out of the windows and heard the John Brown song for the first time—1,040 young men singing it, with a brass band playing and a great roll of drums and all the feet rhythmically tramping on the pavement. And in Washington they sang it again, and in no time at all the song was famous from the seacoast to the Mississippi Valley, and all the troops around Washington were singing it. Then one afternoon Julia Ward Howe sat in a carriage, heard a marching brigade singing it—the Black Hat boys claim it was their brigade, which is as it may be—and regretted that so fine a tune did not have better words. Early next morning she sat by an open window and wrote the mighty battle hymn, which has been a heritage of Americans ever since. And the 12th Massachusetts had started it all—or, if one goes back farther, the workaday 2nd regiment of regulars, aided by a pious hymnographer from the deepest south.[8]

But the dandy 12th was a long way from the ladies of Boston now, and Colonel Webster was killed, and the 12th was finally forced back, along with the rest of Ricketts's men and the Germans.

For whatever it might be worth to them, they had at least made Confederate John B. Hood pause and call for help before they retreated—a thing not too many Union troops were able to do, then or at any other time.

Dusk came, and the field dissolved in a blur of retreating regiments, bewildered stragglers, defiant batteries firing canister to stay the advancing Confederates, and heavy waves of assault crashing against the last hills this side of Bull Run Bridge, over which the entire army had to retreat. John Gibbon found himself on one of these hills, bringing his brigade and steady old Battery B back step by step in such fine order that General McDowell, riding up, told him to take charge of the whole rear guard and be last man over the bridge. McDowell rode away and Phil Kearny came up, furious with the shame of defeat.

"I suppose you appreciate the condition of affairs here, sir?" said Kearny savagely. Gibbon looked at him inquiringly. "It's another Bull Run, sir, it's another Bull Run!"

Gibbon hoped it was not as bad as that.

"Perhaps not," said Kearny. "Reno is keeping up the fight. He is not stampeded. I am not stampeded. You are not stampeded. That is about all, sir, my God, that's about all!"[9]

The sun went down, and in the twilight the air was so full of smoke that the Union Army could not see the men who had beaten it. But the bullets and the shell kept coming, and the rear guard hung on and let the wreckage stream back across the bridge, and the Pennsylvanians and Sykes's regulars and some of Sigel's Germans stayed grimly on the Henry House Hill, where Stonewall Jackson had won his nickname the summer before, and at last it was time to go. Gibbon's men got across, finally, and formed line of battle along the far side of the stream, but there was no further pursuit. The battle was over. Hungry Federals scrabbled among the wreckage of overturned wagons near the bridge to collect hardtack.

Late that night Phil Kearny overtook his headquarters wagon and sat down to write out his report. He had a writing pad on his knee, and since he had but one arm an aide stood by, steadying the pad with one hand. The aide was young, and what he had been through that day had shaken him, and he trembled, making the pad quiver.

Kearny looked up and asked him what was the matter. Frankly the youngster confessed that he was afraid.

Kearny gave him a long, sober look.

"You must never be frightened of anything," he said.[10]

4. Man on a Black Horse

The stone bridge and the road leading across it were a tangle of lost soldiers, sutlers' wagons, jolting guns and caissons, and weary regiments and brigades striving to keep some sort of formation as they forced their way through the confusion. A dozen long wagon trains were trying to get on the road simultaneously—some of them had been called from Centreville that morning, when the army thought it was going to pursue someone, and they arrived just in time to turn around and join in the flight—and there was a huge traffic jam. The sutlers' wagons seemed to be an especial problem; their drivers were almost frantic in their desire to get on the road and be gone, for in a jam like this, with discipline loosened, everybody hungry, and pitch-darkness prevailing, the soldiers were all too likely to consider them fair game and start indiscriminate looting. Now and then one of these wagons would succeed in getting on the highway and the driver would force his distracted horses to a gallop, careening ahead through infantry detachments and sending the men flying, and winding up, as likely as not, in a ditch.

In the grass and briars off the road there were little groups of men gathered about flags—each group the nucleus of some lost regiment trying to reassemble—and over all the noise of the retreat could be heard the cries of these men, plaintively chanting their regimental numbers: "Twenty-fourth New York! . . . Third Maine—Third Maine! . . . Bucktails!" Acrid smoke tainted the night air, and as the darkness deepened a steady rain set in. A soldier in the 27th New York remembered that his regiment was drawn square across the road with fixed bayonets to halt the flood; but blows, bayonets and threats were of no avail—"the disorganized and demoralized mob rushed recklessly around our flanks."[1] Later, he added, the disorder subsided, and the regiments marched by in more regular order. A war correspondent who had witnessed the headlong departure from the field after the first battle of Bull Run insisted that there was "little or none" of the panic that attended the first retreat, and felt that, all things considered, this retreat was fairly orderly; but it stood out in the memory of the men who had to live through it as one of the gloomiest, most miserable nights of the war.

And if there was no sustained panic there was a smoldering, unreasoning anger, and there was ugly talk. Luckless General McDowell sat his horse and watched the army struggle past, and as they went by men called out "Traitor!" and "Scoundrel!" A private in the 11th Massachusetts, from Hooker's division, turned to another and growled: "How guilty he looks, with that basket on his head!" This was in reference to poor McDowell's fancy summer headpiece. In the surviving photographs it does look somewhat like a battered coal scuttle, but the men's objections were not based on aesthetic grounds; somehow the army had acquired the remarkable conviction that for an obscure and traitorous purpose McDowell had designed this hat as a distinguishing mark for the enemy to see and recognize. As they trudged along the road the men of the 11th told each other how a brigadier in Hooker's division, meeting a non-com who was staggering wounded to the rear during the heat of the day's combat, had asked how things were going up front.

"We're holding our own now, but McDowell has charge of the left," said the non-com.

"Then God save the left!" said the brigadier bitterly.

At one stage during the battle, the men insisted, one of McDowell's regiments fired a random volley and then turned and ran for the rear, shouting to its officers: "You can't play it on us!" A diarist explained: "General McDowell was viewed as a traitor by a large majority of the officers and men . . . and thousands of soldiers firmly believed that their lives would be purposely wasted if they obeyed his orders in the time of the conflict." A stout partisan of Joe Hooker, this writer added: "General Pope acted like a dunderpate during the day, and scorning the wise advice of abler generals like Hooker and Kearny allowed General McDowell to maneuver the troops upon the field." One man was heard to say during the retreat: "I would sooner shoot McDowell than Jackson." Some uniformed reader of Horace Greeley, passing General Pope, sang out: "Go west, young man, go west!" A member of the Black Hat

Brigade noted that "open sneering at General Pope was heard on all sides," and a veteran of the 3rd Wisconsin, in Banks's corps, wrote that "the feeling was strong in the army against Pope and McDowell," adding: "All knew and felt that as soldiers we had not had a fair chance."[2]

The one chuckle anyone recorded for that dreary evening came early in the proceedings, when a pallid artillery officer, groaning with pain from a wound, was being carried to the rear on a stretcher. Suddenly a covey of shells sailed low overhead and burst a few yards beyond. With one bound the disabled officer leaped from the stretcher and ran to the rear on nimble and undamaged legs, his stretcher-bearers running after him but quite unable to overtake him, while the troops along the road whooped derisively.

Somehow the army got back to Centreville and began to sort itself out behind the entrenchments there in the cheerless dawn of a chilly, rainy morning. Franklin's corps came up from Alexandria at last and moved down the road to form line of battle along Cub Run, a small stream that cuts across the highway halfway between Centreville and Bull Run Bridge. Pope recovered his powers of undaunted speech and wired Halleck that the enemy was badly whipped, concluding bravely: "Do not be uneasy. We will hold our own here." But this was too obviously a whistle to keep up his own courage to be believed, and anyway, General Lee had no intention whatever of attacking him behind his entrenchments. Instead, Lee sent Jackson's men slipping around to the north through the drizzle, striking for a road that would put them once again in Pope's rear. The exhausted Union cavalry detected the move and notified Pope, and Kearny and Reno hauled their men out of the muddy camp and started back toward Washington, turning sharply to the left when they reached the Little River turnpike, to thwart the move.

Next afternoon there was a wild, brief, and bloody fight near the country house of Chantilly, with a mad, gusty wind and a driving rain, and an overpowering thunderstorm which made so much noise that the gunfire itself could not be heard at Centreville, three miles away. Jackson was repulsed, and Phil Kearny—galloping through the dark wood with the lightning gleaming on the wet leaves, his sword in his hand and the bridle reins held in his teeth—rode smack into a line of Confederate infantry and was shot to death. The Confederates took his dead body to a farmhouse and laid it out with decent care, and A. P. Hill came to pay his tribute to the stout warrior his men had killed. Lee later sent the body through the lines in an ambulance under a flag of truce, "thinking that the possession of his remains may be a consolation to his family." The boys of Kearny's battle-torn 3rd Michigan Regiment wept unashamedly when they heard the news.

Also killed in this fight was General Isaac Stevens, division commander under Reno: a little swarthy man who had come out of West Point years earlier to be an engineer officer, left the army to become governor of Washington Territory, and was beginning to be recognized as a soldier of more than ordinary ability and promise.

This fight might have developed into something fairly big if it had not been for the storm. Pope had two fresh army corps at hand—Franklin's, and Sumner's, which had arrived this day—and an opportunity to handle Jackson's men pretty roughly appears to have been developing. But it was just naturally too stormy to fight that evening. Most of the men's cartridges were wet ("If your guns won't go off, neither will the enemy's," Jackson sternly told a brigadier who wanted to leave the line), and the rain was coming into the men's faces so hard they couldn't see each other, and anyway, Pope had finally been persuaded that he was licked. So the armies drew apart, and the Federals evacuated the bleak bivouac at Centreville—leaving fires burning smokily in the rain to deceive lurking Rebels—and moved back toward the lines around Alexandria.

This was the final, formal admission that the campaign had ended in flat failure. The rain kept coming down, the men knew Phil Kearny was dead, and the mood of hopeless depression deepened.

The 55th New York, just up from the peninsula—the same whose colonel, landing at Alexandria, had heard much talk of treason—was sent up against the tide on some obscure mission requiring its presence at Fairfax Courthouse. The colonel left his record of what they got into on the day of the action at Chantilly:

"Soon the road became a mud hole, in which one could with difficulty direct his steps by the flashes of lightning. Disorder began to affect the ranks. The soldiers advanced painfully through the sticky earth, from which they could hardly lift their feet. The middle of the road was soon monopolized by an interminable file of wagons, re-

treating toward Alexandria. Mingled with them were batteries of
artillery, which, endeavoring to pass by the wagons, blocked the
road. The orders of officers, the cries of the teamsters, the oaths of
the soldiers, were mingled with peals of thunder. All this produced
a deafening tumult, in the midst of which it was difficult to recognize
each other, and from the confusion of which we could not free ourselves without leaving behind us a large number of stragglers."

At Fairfax Courthouse it was a great deal worse, and there was a
miserable, rain-soaked confusion: "By the light of the fires kindled
all around in the streets, in the yards, in the fields, one could see a
confused mass of wagons, ambulances, caissons, around which thousands of men invaded the houses, filled up the barns, broke down the
fences, dug up the gardens, cooked their suppers, smoked, or slept
in the rain. These men belonged to different corps. They were neither sick nor wounded; but, favored by the disorder inseparable
from defeat, they had left their regiments at Centreville, to mingle
with the train escorts, or had come away, each by himself, hurried
on by the fear of new combats; stragglers and marauders, a con-
temptible multitude, whose sole desire was to flee from danger."

Nor was this the worst. What the colonel had run into so far was
simply what might be called the advance guard of the retreat: the
walking wounded, the fainthearts, and the honestly bewildered,
pushed ahead by the army as it made its own progress to the rear.
Next day the main body began to come through. During the daytime
it was fairly orderly, but when evening came everything seemed to
disintegrate.

"Those who for eight days had done nothing but march and fight
were worn out with fatigue," the colonel noted. "Everyone knew
that the enemy was no longer at our heels. No salutary fear kept
them in the ranks and many gave way to the temptation to take a
few hours rest. They lighted great fires, whose number became greater
and greater, so that at a few leagues from Alexandria the whole country appeared to be illuminated. There was everywhere along the road
the greatest confusion. Infantry and cavalry, artillery and wagons, all
hurried on pell mell, in the midst of rallying cries of officers and calls
and oaths of the men."[3]

One-armed General Howard, rejoining the troops after recovery
from his wound just in time to take part in the retreat after Chantilly,

wrote dolefully: "Who will ever forget the straggling, the mud, the rain, the terrible panic and loss of life from random firing, and the hopeless feeling—almost despair—of that dreadful night march!"[4]

An Irish private, clumping through the mud, growled an all-inclusive complaint at the hardships of army life. A comrade scoffed at him: "You're just sore because you aren't a general and can't ride a horse."

"No," said the Irishman stoutly. "It's because it's meself that is obliged to associate with such fools as yourself and Gineral Pope."

An officer of Porter's regulars noted that "everyone you met had an unwashed, sleepy, downcast aspect, and looked as if he would like to hide his head somewhere from all the world." At each halt men would drop by the road and fall sound asleep, and each time it became harder and harder to rouse the men and get them to take their places in the ranks when the march was resumed. Some stragglers were still trying ineffectually to find their regiments; others had given up and were slouching along without their weapons, neither knowing nor caring where their regiments were. Men who went into bivouac around Fairfax Station found that the fields had turned into marshes, although the rain, fortunately, had stopped at last. Far away to the northwest there was heard the rumble of gunfire as some collision of outposts brought isolated batteries into action. Closer at hand Jeb Stuart's troopers were harassing the rear guard—Banks's corps, which had been guarding stores at Bristoe Station during the Bull Run fight and which had been ordered to destroy locomotives and cars, burn all supplies, and come hiking back to Alexandria. It came up to take position in rear of the army, its spirits sagging to zero. General George H. Gordon, commanding a brigade in this corps, noted that when supplies were issued at Fairfax on September 2, the divisions of Hooker and Kearny together drew only 5,000 rations. Between them they had taken more than 10,000 men into action at Bull Run and had suffered a joint total of 1,500 casualties; fully 3,500 men, then, had gone absent without leave—and this from two of the crack divisions of the army. Gordon also noted an Ohio cavalry regiment numbering just under 600 men which was short 448 horses.

In all the accounts of this retreat there is a great deal about the mud, the hunger, and the weariness of men who had marched and

fought until they were utterly exhausted. Yet those were not in fact
the really important troubles. A few miles away to the north and
west, taking a day's rest in the fields near the Potomac before striking across the river for further adventures, was Lee's Army of Northern Virginia. It had marched just as far and just as hard, and had
gone just as hungry, and had fought just as much. In proportion it
was even beginning to suffer as much from straggling, owing to a
complex of reasons ranging all the way from lack of shoes to inability
to understand the rationale of invasion. But this army was lighthearted and full of enthusiasm. It was well led and knew it, and it
had absorbed the notion that there were no Yankees anywhere whom
it could not whip. While Pope was sadly wiring Halleck that "there
is an intense idea among [the troops] that they must get behind the
entrenchments," and one of Colonel Haupt's aides was sending back
word that "the volunteers are much demoralized and ready to stam-
pede," the Confederates were looking ahead to new campaigns with
high confidence.

It wasn't hardships that had got the Federals down, although they
had had hardships and to spare. It was what had seeped down to
the men in the ranks from the hatred, suspicion, and confusion in
high places, the wastage which the men had seen for themselves and
had themselves been a part of, the heart-numbing realization that
what ought to be the Republic's finest army had been shockingly and
irretrievably mishandled. The very best that ardent young spirits could
give of bravery and endurance had been given, and it had all been
to no purpose. Porter's men, teaching the straw-feet how to fight;
Gibbon's young Westerners, proving their manhood by standing up
toe to toe with their enemies until night came down to make fighting
impossible; the Pennsylvanians and the regulars and the Germans,
hanging on in the dusk around the Henry House Hill to keep open
the last line of retreat—all of these had done as well as any soldiers
could do on any field, and all of them knew that it had been futile.
They were learning the reality of war, these youngsters, getting face
to face with the sickening realization that men get killed uselessly because their generals are stupid, so that desperate encounters where
the last drop of courage has been given serve the country not at all
and make a patriot look a fool.

And then, at the last minute of despair, the unbelievable happened.

The head of the leading column of the retreat was coming in on the Fairfax road, near the forts on Munson's Hill, on the afternoon of September 2. The sun had finally come out, and the roads had dried enough so that a long, lazy cloud of dust hung in the air above the marching men. Pope and McDowell rode in the lead, their uniforms gray with the dust, their beards powdered. Their mounted staff officers and orderlies followed them, and after a brief interval came Hatch's division with an endless shuffle-shuffle of dragging feet, each man staring dully at the back of the man in front, nobody saying a word. Out into the road ahead, coming toward them, rode a little knot of horsemen, trotting forward confidently; the man in front rode a great black horse and had a bright yellow sash about his waist and was erect and dapper in the saddle, and as he came up to the two generals his hand flipped up to the visor of his cap in a salute that had all the gaiety and snap of the youthful, confident army these men had once been and had all but forgotten. General Hatch, looking ahead, stiffened as he saw it—there was only one man in the army who saluted in just that way—and he cantered ahead suddenly to see and hear for himself. He got there just in time to listen as General McClellan told Pope and McDowell that by order of the President he was assuming command of the troops.

The two generals impassively returned the salute. McClellan gave a few directions about the positions the troops should take when they reached the fortifications. On the horizon there was a dull bump-bump of gunfire, and McClellan asked what that might be. Pope answered that it was probably some attack on Sumner's corps, coming up as flank guard; meanwhile, did General McClellan object if Pope and McDowell rode on in to Washington? McClellan replied that he had not an objection in the world, but for himself he was going to ride to the sound of the firing and see what was going on in the way of fighting. . . . One gathers that the interchange did McClellan a great deal of good.

Hatch had heard all that he needed to hear. He had a score to settle with Pope, whom he hated. When Pope had first come east, Hatch had been in command of the cavalry attached to Banks's corps, and when Pope had made his first thrust down to the Rapidan, Hatch had been ordered to go in advance to seize the important railroad junction of Gordonsville and destroy Rebel supplies and connections there. The march had been delayed; while Hatch waited for infantry and artillery to go with him, the delay gave the enemy time to occupy Gordonsville in force, and the move had been a failure. A few days later Pope ordered him to try again, this time taking cavalry alone and cutting the railroad line from Gordonsville to Charlottesville. Hatch crossed the Blue Ridge in a pelting rain, got mired in muddy mountain roads, and came stumbling back a few days later, his mission unaccomplished; Pope gave him an angry dressing-down, relieved him of his command, and sent him to King's division to lead a brigade of infantry. Hatch felt that he had been unfairly treated. Now was his chance to get even.

He trotted back the few yards that separated the generals from the head of his own infantry. In a loud voice—easily to be heard by Pope and McDowell—he shouted: "Boys, McClellan is in command of the army again! Three cheers!"[5]

There was a brief, stunned silence; then a wild, hysterical yell went up from the soldiers. Hats, caps, and knapsacks were tossed into the air. The roar swept back along the column as men to the rear heard the news, and the men still farther back joined in without waiting to be told: they knew there was only one man alive who could make the army cheer like that. The cheering did not stop; men capered, thumped each other on the back, yelled themselves into hoarseness. Far back down the highway, out of sight, went the noise, officers joining with the men. One of Hatch's staff came spurring back to John Gibbon and gave him the news. As an old regular, Gibbon took it as just another camp rumor and said so. No, insisted the officer, this time it was true: he himself had *seen* McClellan, just up the road, giving orders to Pope and McDowell. Gibbon swung in his saddle and raised his own voice: "Men, General McClellan is in command of the army!" The air was filled with tumult. Men broke ranks, danced, howled, laughed hysterically, wept; and, Gibbon wrote later, "the weary, fagged men went into camp cheerful and happy, to talk over their rough experience of the past three weeks and speculate as to what was ahead."[6]

It was a big army and it covered a lot of ground, and it took time for the word to get around. Sykes's regulars, pushing on to get into the lines before midnight, were still on the road by starlight. They had fallen out for a short breather, and the dead-exhausted men had dropped in their tracks and were dozing. Two officers stood by their horses, looking ahead in the darkness, and saw a few horsemen approaching. One of the officers gaped: if he didn't know better, he said, he would say one of those riders was McClellan. This, said the other officer, was nonsense. McClellan had been relieved days ago, and anyhow, what would he be doing out here, at this time of night, without an escort? The first officer continued to stare, hope rising. Then some other officer saw, and recognized; and over the silent roadway, where men slept in the dust under the stars, he raised a strong, clear voice that could shout orders above the din of battle: "Colonel! Colonel! General McClellan is here!"

Ten seconds later every man was on his feet, sending a long cheer up to the night sky; "such a hurrah," a participant wrote later, "as the Army of the Potomac had never heard before. Shout upon shout went out into the stillness of the night; and as it was taken up along the road and repeated by regiment, brigade, division and corps, we could hear the roar dying away in the distance. The effect of this man's presence upon the Army of the Potomac—in sunshine or rain, in darkness or in daylight, in victory or defeat—was electrical, and too wonderful to make it worth while attempting to give a reason for it."[7]

The men who were there that night seem to have spent the rest of their lives trying to make people who were not there understand what it was like. About all they could say was that there was mad cheering and hysterical happiness and a sudden feeling that everything was going to be all right, so that every man forgot that he was tired and hungry and dirty, forgot that he had been miserably beaten, and looked forward with a bright certainty that all mistakes would presently be redeemed. And it is clear that some sort of miracle had happened; the most amazing and dramatic one, perhaps, in American military history, with an entire army completely transformed between the hot dust of midafternoon and the quiet coolness of starlight. But exactly why this miracle took place, and precisely what it was that this man did to make the soldiers love him as no general in the army's history was ever loved—this they could not seem to tell, probably because they did not quite know themselves. One veteran, trying to explain, finally let it go by saying: "The love borne by soldiers to a favorite chief, if it does not surpass, is more unreasoning than the love of woman."[8]

Whatever it was, there it was: an intangible, like so many of the important things in the life of an army, or a nation, or a man, indefinable but of tremendous power. The men who cheered and exulted and went gladly forth to the bloodiest field of all because they saw this man at the head of the column are all gone, and the man himself, with the hatred and the adoration that he inspired, is gone with them, and the cheers and the gunfire of that army echo far off, in old memories, unreal and ghostlike, the passion and the violence all filtered out, leaving the inexplicable picture of an army transfigured. And it seems that this man, with his yellow sash and his great black horse and his unforgettable air of parade-ground trimness and dash, somehow was in his own person the soldier every soldier had longed to be, the embodiment of the gaiety that had been lost and the hope that had been given up. He was what the army and the impossible, picture-book war itself had meant back in the army's youth when innocence had not yet died. And when he came back men split their throats with cheering, and tilted their battle flags proudly forward, and forgot that they had been starved and misused, and became a great army once more and went off to define the shape and purport of the war on the sunlit fields and glades that were waiting for them around a little Dunker church in the Maryland hills.

TWO

The Young General

1. A Great Work in My Hands

He was trusted to the point of death by one hundred thousand fighting men, but he himself always had his lurking doubts. The soldiers firmly believed that where he was everything was bound to be all right. They would gladly awaken from the deepest sleep of exhaustion to go and cheer him because they felt that way. After Malvern Hill an entire division, underfed for days, deserted the sputtering campfires where in a gloomy rain it was cooking the first hot meal of the week, in order to splash through the mud and hurrah as he galloped down the road, and felt satisfied even though all the fires went out and breakfast was sadly delayed. But it seems that McClellan was never quite convinced. An uncertainty tormented him. It was almost as if some invisible rider constantly followed him, in the brightly uniformed staff that rode with him, and came up abreast every now and then to whisper: "But, General, are you *sure?*" Every man tries to live up to his own picture of himself. McClellan's picture was glorious, but one gathers that he was never quite confident that he could make it come to life.

Perhaps this was partly because too much had happened to him too soon. Long afterward he remarked: "It probably would have been better for me personally had my promotion been delayed a year or more"; and he was probably quite right. Fame came early, and it came like an explosion, touched off before he had had a chance to get set for it. He found himself at the top of the ladder almost before he started to climb, and the height was dizzying. One day he was leading a diminutive army of volunteers in an obscure campaign far back in the wild mountains; the next day—almost literally, the next day—he was the savior of his country, with President and Congress piling a prodigious load on his shoulders, and with every imaginable problem arising from the most confusing and pressing of wars seemingly coming straight to him, and to him alone, for solution. He bore himself with a confident air and he said calmly, "I can do it all," but somewhere far down inside there was a corroding unease.

He was thirty-five when the war started. A West Point graduate, he had done well as a young subaltern in the Mexican War, and later he had been sent to the Crimea by the War Department to watch the British and the French fight the Russians. Then, with the rank of captain, he had resigned from the army to go into business. A capable engineer, by the spring of 1861 he had become a ten-thousand-dollar-a-year railroad president, and he was working in Cincinnati when Fort Sumter fell and the war began. The war reached out for him without delay.

It began with the governors. State governors were of great importance in the war machinery of that era—considerably more important than the War Department itself, at first. Under the law, all volunteer regiments were raised, officered, and trained by the state authorities, and the regiments were sworn into Federal service only after they had been completely organized in the states. This threw a heavy load on the governors—men of peace and politics, whose military staffs consisted of militia colonels and brigadiers, ardent persons but utterly ignorant of any warlike activity beyond a peacetime militia muster. The governors, as a result, were frantic to get a few West Pointers around them, and a retired army officer with an excellent record, like McClellan, was an obvious prize. So by mid-April, McClellan, who was a Pennsylvanian by birth, had received a message from Governor Andrew G. Curtin of Pennsylvania, inviting him to come to Harrisburg at once and take charge of the Pennsylvania troops. He wound up his business affairs in Cincinnati as quickly as he could and took off for Harrisburg, stopping at Columbus en route to see

Ohio's Governor William Dennison, who wanted his advice. The stopover made all the difference.

McClellan appeared at Dennison's office, wearing civilian garb and a soft felt hat, impressing the governor and his advisers as a quiet, modest, self-possessed man and looking, as one of them remarked, exactly like what he was—"a railway superintendent in his business clothes." The governor explained what he was up against. He had what looked like the impossible job of getting ten thousand men ready for the field, and there was no one around who knew the first thing about the military arts. The state arsenal contained nothing in the way of equipment but a few boxes of ancient smoothbore muskets, badly rusted, plus a couple of brass six-pounder fieldpieces, somewhat honeycombed from the firing of salutes and devoid of any auxiliary equipment except for a pile of mildewed harness. The recruits were already beginning to show up—a few companies, gaudy in old-style militia uniforms, had got to town and were sleeping in uncomfortable elegance in the legislative chambers in the statehouse—and so far the state had not even picked a site for a training camp. Under these circumstances the governor had no intention of letting a good West Pointer slip through his fingers, and he then and there offered McClellan the command of Ohio's troops—the command of them, plus the task of getting them housed, fed, clad, trained, and organized. McClellan promptly accepted, moved into an office in the statehouse, and got down to work, a major general of volunteers.[1]

It is interesting to speculate about the difference there would have been in McClellan's career had he gone on to Harrisburg and taken command of the Pennsylvania troops instead of staying in Ohio. Fame would have come much more slowly, and he would have had a chance to adjust himself to it. Pennsylvania sent a solid division down to Washington shortly after Bull Run. It was the division McClellan would have commanded had he gone to Harrisburg; it contained good men and had some first-class officers, and it was just the right organization to build a solid reputation for its commanding general—it brought George G. Meade up to the command of the Army of the Potomac in 1863, after giving him plenty of time to prove himself and to find himself in battle. What would McClellan's luck have been with that division? No immediate limelight, comparative obscurity during the army's early days—what would have become of him, anyway?

(Another might-have-been: there came to McClellan's Ohio headquarters one day that spring a former infantry captain, somewhat seedy, presenting himself as a one-time acquaintance of the general looking for work; name of U. S. Grant. Was there a place for him, perhaps, on McClellan's staff? The general was away that day, and Grant was told to come back later. Instead of coming back Grant went west and finally wangled command of a regiment of Illinois volunteers. McClellan would have given him a staff job if he had seen him. What, one wonders, would Grant's future have been in that case?)

Well, the might-have-beens didn't happen. McClellan never did go to Harrisburg, command of the Pennsylvanians went to someone else, and if McClellan himself ever mused about it in later years there is no record of it. What did happen was that as soon as he got his Ohio regiments mustered into United States service he found himself holding one of the key jobs in the whole army. Ohio was on the frontier. The western part of Virginia was just across the river and the Confederates had sent troops deep into the mountains. It was correctly supposed in Washington that this part of Virginia was strongly Unionist—the Confederate commander, getting no recruits, complained that the inhabitants were full of "an ignorant and bigoted Union sentiment"—and it seemed important to drive the Confederates out. Also, the Rebels were cutting the Baltimore and Ohio railway, main traffic artery from the capital to the West. So McClellan, by the end of May, found himself across the Ohio River, commanding a substantial little force of sixteen Ohio regiments, nine from Indiana, and two newly organized regiments of Unionist Virginians from Parkersburg and Wheeling, together with twenty-four guns. He moved carefully up into the mountains, found two Confederate detachments drawn up in the passes, attacked one and caved it in, causing the other to retreat posthaste, and moved on to the town of Beverly, taking prisoners, securing everything west of the Alleghenies for the Union, and making possible the eventual formation of the state of West Virginia.

It had been neatly done, it was the North's first feat of arms, and the country rejoiced at the news—the more so, perhaps, because it looked like a good deal more of an achievement than it actually was. McClellan always knew how to make his soldiers take pride in their own deeds, and he gave it to them strong after they marched into Beverly, congratulating them in an official order which told them that they had "annihilated two armies, commanded by educated and experienced soldiers, entrenched in mountain fastnesses fortified at their leisure." This was all right, and it was the sort of thing that built up morale; but the "two armies" had in fact been separate parts of one ill-equipped, untrained force that hardly numbered forty-five hundred men all told, and the "annihilation" consisted in the retreat of this force and the loss by it of about a thousand men. The order was reprinted in the North, together with McClellan's dispatches to the War Department, which were somewhat less flamboyant but which still made the conquest look like something out of Napoleon's campaign in northern Italy. Also reprinted, and widely admired, was the address McClellan had issued to his soldiers just before the battle: "Soldiers! I have heard that there was danger here. I have come to place myself at your head and to share it with you. I fear now but one thing—that you will not find foemen worthy of your steel. I know that I can rely upon you."

All of this, remember, was happening in the early summer of 1861, when the war was still spanking new and people were hungry for heroes and for victories, and when the country was ready to take a general at his own evaluation. Some of McClellan's officers, to be sure, were just a bit baffled. One of his brigadiers wrote that McClellan's dispatches and proclamations seemed to have been written by "quite a different person from the sensible and genial man we knew in daily life and conversation" and remarked that the young major general appeared to be "in a morbid condition of mental exaltation."[2] But in the country at large it went over big; and just then, before anybody had forgotten about it, the news came in of the humiliating disaster at Bull Run, with untrained regiments legging it all the way back to Washington, and carriageloads of distinguished sight-seers contributing to the rout. Everybody had been chanting, "On to Richmond"; now came the realization that the war was not going to be a gay parade of triumphant militia regiments, whose bright uniforms and martial bearing would make up for any defi-

ciencies in military experience and leadership. The war was going
to be long, mean, and bloody, and above all else there was needed a
really competent general who could turn the volunteer forces into an
army.

To be sure, Lincoln had at his elbow Lieutenant General Winfield
Scott, the hero of two wars; but Scott was old and nearly senile, he
was too fat and infirm to mount a horse or even to review his troops,
let alone lead them into action, and his great reputation and his stout
old heart were all he could place at the government's disposal. Inevitable, then, that everyone should look at McClellan. His achievement in western Virginia took on an added shine when measured
against Bull Run. His troops had not fled in terror after a few
random volleys; they had gone into action coolly, scaling lofty mountains and annihilating two armies. This man knew what he was
doing, and knew how to make people believe that he knew what he
was doing, which was even more important just then; and the very
depth of the country's shame and disappointment at Bull Run helped
to lift McClellan to the peak. Overnight he was called to Washington and invested with the command.

No American general ever came to high command under circumstances quite like these. He was thirty-five, and it was just three
months since he had sat in Governor Dennison's office and received
the tender of command of Ohio's volunteers. Now he was in Washington, with the safety of the entire nation on his shoulders; and
before he had even started on this new job he was being universally
acclaimed as a genius, with a fanfare that built his brief Virginia
campaign up into an achievement that would stand comparison with
the records of the great captains of history. He was "the young
Napoleon" to one and all—even to himself, apparently, for he permitted himself to be photographed in the traditional Napoleonic
pose, one arm folded behind his back, the other hand thrust into his
coat front, a look of intense martial determination on his face. In a
letter home, written the day after he reached Washington, McClellan
sounds like a man who can hardly believe that what is happening to
him is real: "I find myself in a new and strange position here:
President, cabinet, Gen. Scott, and all deferring to me. By some
strange operation of magic I seem to have become the power of the
land." A few days later he went to Capitol Hill, to argue for a new

law permitting him to appoint aides to his staff from civil life if he
chose. The experience among the lawmakers was giddying—all experiences were, from the height he occupied just then—and he unbur-
dened himself in another letter to his wife:

"I went to the Senate to get it through, and was quite overwhelmed
by the congratulations I received and the respect with which I was
treated. I suppose half a dozen of the oldest made the remark I am
becoming so much used to: 'Why, how young you look, and yet an
old soldier!' It seems to strike everybody that I look young. They
give me my way in everything, full swing and unbounded confidence.
All tell me that I am held responsible for the fate of the nation,
and that all its resources shall be placed at my disposal. It is an immense task that I have on my hands, but I believe I can accomplish
it."

And he added, bemused: "Who would have thought, when we
were married, that I should so soon be called upon to save my
country?"

He *was* young, for a conquering hero, and it was only natural
that he himself should have been impressed by his own eminence.
And yet, in these letters to the young wife he had married little more
than a year earlier, one presently begins to find something more than
the natural blinking of a man who is dazzled by his own good
fortune; something more than the artless self-congratulation a man is
entitled to indulge in when he brags innocently to the wife of his
bosom. It gets said too often. There is too much lingering on the
adoration other men feel for him, on the wild enthusiasm he arouses,
on the limitless power and responsibility that are his. The perplexity
of the brigadier in western Virginia becomes understandable: this
man, utterly winning and modest and soft-spoken in all his personal
contacts, simply could not, down inside, look long enough at the
great figure he was becoming, could not get enough of the savor of
admiration and love that were coming to him. Over and over, from
the day he left Ohio for the expedition into the lonely mountains to
his final days in the army, there is this same note. What buried
sense of personal inadequacy was gnawing at this man that he had
to see himself so constantly through the eyes of men and women who
looked upon him as a hero out of legend and myth?

Early in June, before the great weight of national command had

been placed upon him, he was writing his wife of the huge crowds
that met him at every stop in Ohio—"gray-haired old men and
women, mothers holding up their children to take my hand, girls,
boys, all sorts, cheering and crying God bless you! . . . I could hear
them say, 'He is our own general'; 'Look at him, how young he is';
'*He* will thrash them'; 'He'll do,' etc., etc., ad infinitum." In western
Virginia there was more of the same: "It is a proud and glorious thing
to see a whole people here, simple and unsophisticated, looking up to
me as their deliverer from tyranny." The weight of his own duties
impressed him while he still commanded this detached force on the
slope of the Alleghenies: "I realize now the dreadful responsibility
on me—the lives of my men, the reputation of the country, and the
success of the cause." And he himself must do it all. From Grafton
he wrote that "everything here needs the hand of the master and is
getting it fast"; and, a little later, "I don't feel sure that the men will
fight very well under anyone but myself; they have confidence in me,
and will do anything that I put them at."

On his first day in Washington he was saying confidently: "I see
already the main causes of our recent failure; I am sure that I can
remedy these, and am confident that I can lead these armies of men
to victory once more." He had already, in less than twenty-four
hours, had to refuse dinner invitations from General Scott and from
four cabinet ministers; a few days later he dined at the White House,
guest of the President, with the British and French ministers and assorted senators present, reported that the dinner was "rather long
and rather tedious, as such things generally are." Scott, the aging
general-in-chief, had become a nuisance within a week and would
have to be quietly by-passed. "I am leaving nothing undone to increase our force; but the old general always comes in the way. . . .
I have to fight my way against him. Tomorrow the question will
probably be decided by giving me absolute control independently of
him. I suppose it will result in enmity on his part against me; but
I have no choice. The people call upon me to save the country. I
must save it, and cannot respect anything that is in the way."

Undeniably, Scott was an obstacle, a querulous fuss-budget, his
greatness only a memory. It would be inadvisable, he held, for the
young general to organize the forces about Washington as an *army:*
the regulations said McClellan commanded the departments of

Washington and northeastern Virginia, with all the troops that lay therein, and that was sufficient. Inadvisable, too, to organize the new levies into divisions. He, Scott, had simply had brigades in the army he took to Mexico City, and what was adequate then would be adequate now. Nor should regular-army officers be encouraged, or even permitted, to leave their own assignments in order to command volunteers; the hard core of regular troops was needed and the volunteer army must be grouped around it, and the strength of the regulars could not be diluted by sending the officers out into the new regiments and brigades. And so on and on; McClellan was entirely right—the job could not be done unless he could find a way around the old gentleman.

Furthermore, McClellan's boast was justified: the people *were* calling upon him to save the country, and he *did* see "the main causes of our failure" very clearly and was moving effectively to cure them. He began, simply enough, by getting the disorganized officers and men off the streets and into camp. The regulars who were available he formed into a provost guard, with a tough colonel to take charge of scouring out the bars and herding the uniformed wanderers back to their regiments. On the Washington side of the river, camps were set up to receive the new levies as they came in from the states, and provisional brigades were established to complete their training and discipline. More seasoned regiments were sent across to camps on the Virginia side, where they could help protect the capital while they were being turned into fully disciplined troops. Lines were traced for a complete ring of fortifications encircling Washington in a line thirty-three miles long; enclosed forts on commanding hills, protected batteries covering the intervals, chains of rifle pits in between, with particular attention to the approaches on the Virginia side. Confederate Joe Johnston had pushed his outposts up to within half a dozen miles of the river; McClellan had no intention of trying to push him back just yet, but he made certain that the enemy could not get any closer.

After a week he was able to report proudly: "I have Washington perfectly quiet now; you would not know that there was a regiment here." No soldier was allowed to leave his camp without a pass, and passes were made hard to get. Similarly, civilians were prevented from visiting the camps without passes and were kept from crossing the bridges to the Virginia side unless they had legitimate business there. The bewildered men in uniform who had been disconsolately idling on the streets and in their tents suddenly discovered that they were going to be soldiers after all; they were kept busy, things moved with snap and order, there seemed to be a reason for the routine that had descended upon their lives.

The most incompetent and unfit of the regimental officers were weeded out by hastily organized selection boards. These selection boards were badly needed. The great weakness of this army lay in its officer corps, and the big problem of the high command always was to find officers who were worthy of the men they were leading. Later, as the test of battle helped to weed out the obvious misfits, and as hard experience developed qualities of natural leadership in others, this problem became simpler, but in the beginning it occasionally seemed beyond solution. The officers were in most cases as ignorant as the men they led, and they were usually ten times harder to handle. A few of them saw their own inadequacy and eliminated themselves, like the sixty-year-old Maine colonel who, learning that a selection board had been set up, came before it voluntarily and asked to be relieved. He had enjoyed militia work for forty years, he said artlessly, but he was finding actual warfare a different proposition and he felt that he was too old to learn; he would send in his resignation at once if they would suspend proceedings and spare him the humiliation of being officially weeded out.[3]

An idea of the size of the officer problem can be had from a glimpse at the diary of a member of the 75th New York, which regiment stopped over in Baltimore while on the way to Washington that summer. This man wrote despondently: "Tonight not 200 men are in camp. Capt. Catlin, Capt. Hulburt, Lt. Cooper and one or two other officers are under arrest. A hundred men are drunk, a hundred more are at houses of ill fame, and the balance are everywhere. . . . Col. Alford is very drunk all the time now."[4]

A diarist in the 11th Massachusetts told of one colonel who put the regimental chaplain in charge of his cooking arrangements and held him so strictly accountable for the quality of the meals that the poor man had no time for his priestly duties. After one particularly bad meal the colonel called the chaplain before him and barked: "If you don't cook a better dinner than this tomorrow, I'll have you tied to the flagstaff next Sunday and make you preach to the regiment for two hours!" As a result, the chaplain spent so much time in the kitchen next day that he was unable to officiate at a funeral, and the services had to be read by the regimental surgeon. The diarist added sadly that colonels who didn't insist on having regular devotional services usually failed to hold the respect of their men.[5]

There was a happy-go-lucky informality about the men in charge of some of these new regiments. The 19th Maine, being Yankees, sought to turn an honest penny by laying in a stock of fruit and flour and baking pies, which the regiment sold in surrounding camps. A sergeant in a Massachusetts regiment, being offered a pie by one such, asked the price. Twenty-five cents, he was told. "I won't pay it," he said promptly, being a Yankee himself. "Your colonel was just through here selling them for twenty cents."[6]

Somehow these officers were either taught their business or eliminated. The selection boards weeded out more than three hundred, but they couldn't begin to reach them all, deep questions of local politics being bound up in most of the original appointments; state governors were touchy, and the administration hated to offend them. But what a selection board couldn't do a good brigadier general could. Phil Kearny, for instance, got his regiments up to snuff in short order. The day he was assigned to his brigade he found most of the men lawlessly stripping an adjacent apple orchard. He immediately called in the field officers of his regiments and gave them a terrific blowing up in his crispest regular-army style. The officers, as freeborn Americans who weren't used to being talked to that way, answered back with heat; so Kearny switched his tactics, turned on the charm instead, took all the officers to an elaborate dinner party, transformed them into a little band of brothers before they knew quite what was happening, and by midnight had them all agreeing that for the honor of the brigade and their own heroic souls they would thereafter enforce discipline in the strictest military style. They did, too.

All up and down the line the volunteers began to find that this was an army, not just a disorganized aggregation of soldiers. Someone took the trouble to inspect the camps and teach the colonels how to lay them out so they were neat, tidy, and sanitary. The supply system was reorganized and the men ate regularly; regimental sick lists declined as sanitation and meals improved and soldiers were taught how to pitch their tents so that the first shower would not flood everything they contained, and the dreary discouragement that divitalized homesick boys began to lift. Regimental commanders found themselves answerable to brigadiers who inspected camp and drill ground and insisted on good performance—and who, when performance was not good, knew enough about their jobs to show how it could be improved. Brigades, in turn, were formed into divisions, with regular-army officers riding herd on them. The War Department was still buying quantities of amazingly shoddy goods—the tents were skimpy and leaky, many of the fine new uniforms lost their shape and color almost overnight, the New England boys noted that the shoes were poorly made and would never last, and the arms that were issued were sadly imperfect—but at least the stuff was coming in and being distributed. The air of the holiday militia outing was gone.

Then there were the reviews—reviews of regiments, of brigades, of divisions—with regimental officers nervously inspecting arms and equipments beforehand, with the bands zealously blaring out marching tunes, and with the new soldiers proudly performing their recently learned maneuvers on the smooth turf, while the flags streamed in the breeze and admiring civilians stood about the reviewing stand, the ladies bright with their hooped skirts and sunshades . . . and always, as the crowning feature, the young general himself, galloping down the lines on his great black charger at a pace his staff could never quite maintain, seeing everything, demanding good performance, and then glowing with happy pride when it was given. They cheered as he went by—how could they help it, when he was the living symbol of their regained self-respect?—and they cheered afresh when he acknowledged their cheers. Wrote one of his officers:

"He had a taking way of returning such salutations. He went beyond the formal military salute, and gave his cap a little twirl, which with his bow and smile seemed to carry a little of personal good fellowship even to the humblest private soldier. If the cheer was repeated he would turn in his saddle and repeat the salute. It was very plain that these little attentions to the troops took well, and had no doubt some influence in establishing a sort of comradeship between him and them."[7]

Not that there was any familiarity or easygoing softness in the relations between general and soldiers. There was a vast gulf fixed, then as now, between the major general commanding and the humble private, and McClellan did not narrow it. He did not live in camp, but stayed in the heart of Washington, in a fine big house where he gave elaborate dinner parties to glittering people, and wherever he went he was trailed by his staff, including two genuine French princes, and a trim cavalry escort. The troops did not see him during their workaday routine; when he came on the scene it was always a special event, surrounded by all of the formalities. He could apply a severe discipline when it seemed necessary. The 2nd Maine Regiment refused to turn out for duty one day in August. Camped near it were some ninety-day regiments whose time had expired, and they were going home, and the boys in the 2nd Maine, although they had enlisted for three years, felt that they ought to go home too—the war was going to last much longer than they had expected; if it was fair for one regiment to leave, why wasn't it fair for all? McClellan came down on them quietly but hard, and sixty-three men were presently shipped off to the dreaded fortress of Dry Tortugas—a frowning pile of masonry on a desolate sand key in the Gulf of Mexico, originally built as "the Gibraltar of the new world" but now used as a disciplinary barracks for hard cases—to break rocks for the rest of the war.

With another somewhat similar case McClellan tried a different tack. The 79th New York was a former militia regiment; called itself the "Highlanders," came to Washington in the bare-kneed glory of kilts, and had a crusty Scottish colonel named Cameron. It had been at Bull Run, where its colonel had been killed; it had long since abandoned kilts for the regulation sky-blue pants, and it was fed up with military life. Also, it was brigaded under William Tecumseh Sherman, who was a hard man and who at that time seems to have had something to learn about the way to handle volunteer troops. So one morning the 79th refused to do duty and demanded an adjustment of its grievances. McClellan rounded up a battalion of regular infantry, plus a squadron of regular cavalry and a battery of regular artillery—hard-boiled Indian fighters from the plains, filled with strong disdain for volunteer soldiers—and lined them up facing the 79th, firearms loaded and ready for use; whereupon the 79th was invited to stop being mutinous and return to duty. The New Yorkers blinked at the ominous array in front of them. These regulars, clearly, were perfectly willing to shoot volunteers if ordered, and the officer in charge had a frosty glint in his eye. The 79th had had no notion that it was committing mutiny; it was just exercising its democratic right of protest, as American citizens always did; but if the major general commanding saw it differently, what with all those regulars, why . . . So the 79th returned to duty, and nobody was shot, and McClellan took the regimental colors away and kept them in his own office, restoring them a month later with a neat little flourish and the comment that the Highlanders had redeemed themselves by good conduct.

So McClellan was able to write to his wife truthfully: "I have restored order very completely already." Things were looking up, and the young general wrote, "I shall carry this thing *en grand* and crush the Rebels in one campaign. I flatter myself that Beauregard has gained his last victory." And how could he help feeling that way, when he drank daily of the adulation of his men? "You have no idea how the men brighten up now when I go among them. I can see every eye glisten. Yesterday they nearly pulled me to pieces in one regiment. You never heard such yelling."

Yet the Rebels were menacing, and there was cause for deep worry. Behind their fortified lines at Centreville and Manassas, who knew what dark plans were afoot? Washington was ill defended: "If Beauregard does not attack tonight I shall regard it as a dispensation of Providence." And in mid-August: "I cannot get one minute's rest during the day, and sleep with one eye open at night, looking out sharply for Beauregard, who, I think, has some notion of making a dash in this direction." Next day the danger seemed even worse: "I am here in a terrible place; the enemy have from three to four times my force; the President, the old general, cannot or will not see the true state of affairs."

It was very disturbing; especially so since the danger actually existed almost exclusively in the mind of the commanding general. The Confederates were well dug in near the site of their old Bull Run victory, but Joseph E. Johnston, their commander, and his flamboy-

ant second-in-command, the famous Pierre Gustave Toutant Beauregard—something of a young Napoleon himself, in ardent Southern
esteem—were asking nothing more than that the Yankees would
leave them alone for a few months. They had perhaps thirty thousand
men with them—about a quarter of the number McClellan believed
them to have—and their troubles in respect to organization, discipline,
and leadership were quite as pressing as those of the Federals, if not a
little more so, the Southern private being a rugged individualist not
readily amenable to military rule. The lone Southerner who was talking in terms of an offensive in those days was the dour and warlike
Stonewall Jackson, who figured that the North was still badly off
balance and could be had even by untrained troops; but Jackson
had not yet become famous, and his voice went unheard, and neither
Johnston nor Beauregard was even dreaming of offensive action.
Not until October would Johnston suggest an advance, and then he
conditioned the suggestion with the stipulation that he be heavily
reinforced. Reinforcements being denied, he dropped the idea. He
was heavily outnumbered and he was perfectly well aware of it, even
though McClellan saw him as having "three or four times my force."
While Johnston was trying to get his own disorganized battalions into
something resembling military shape, McClellan was anxiously writing: "I have scarcely slept one moment for the last three nights,
knowing well that the enemy intend some movement and fully recognizing our own weakness."

But if there were anxiety, unease, and a deep awareness of weakness at GHQ in Washington, there was also that dazzling glimpse of
greatness, the echo of strange promises of future fame loftier than
any other American had ever had, mysterious whispers that could
hardly be described even in the privacy of a letter to the general's
own wife. On the ninth of August, 1861, McClellan was writing
home:

"I receive letter after letter, have conversation after conversation,
calling on me to save the nation, alluding to the presidency, dictatorship, etc. As I hope one day to be united with you forever in Heaven,
I have no such aspiration. I would cheerfully take the dictatorship
and agree to lay down my life when the country is saved. I am not
spoiled by my unexpected new position. I feel sure that God will
give me the strength and wisdom to preserve this great nation; but

I tell you, who share all my thoughts, that I have no selfish feeling in this matter. I feel that God has placed a great work in my hands."

To which one can only remark that for a newcomer this young general had certainly been getting around. He had been in Washington less than a fortnight, and barely four months ago he had been an obscure Ohio civilian; but already there was talk of the presidency, and people were telling him he should become a dictator. It was a moment of infinite possibilities, the entire country was at his disposal, he could do as he liked with it: he would spurn the dictatorship, he would gladly lay down his life after taking the dictatorship, with God's help he would preserve the nation; and all the while, never to be forgotten, he could get those dark glimpses of unfathomable Rebel strength and schemings across the river, coiling and uncoiling in the dim light in movements of infinite menace. Secure in his own nutshell, he was king of infinite space. But there were those bad dreams.

2. Aye, Deem Us Proud

The war was very pleasant for a while, in the fall of 1861, for the soldiers who were guarding the line of the Potomac above Washington. The Maryland countryside there is open and gently rolling, with blue mountain ranges breaking the sky line to the west and with long vistas of cornfield and pasture and wood lot stretching away south to the river and beyond. The weather was mild and bright, and the business of learning how to be a soldier was engrossing and even rather exciting. Across the river there were unknown numbers of Confederates, whose pickets were often seen and frequently heard from in exchanges of long-range rifle fire. The 15th Massachusetts, picketing the shore near Edwards' Ferry, some fifteen miles upstream from the capital, felt that it was well acquainted with the Mississippi outfit on the other side. Northern boys and Southern boys used to exchange gossip across the river, and they finally agreed that "the shooting of pickets is all nonsense"—an agreement to which the Massachusetts soldiers came the more readily, as one of their number admitted, because they were armed with old smoothbore muskets which would barely carry across the stream, while the

Southerners had rifles. One day a Mississippian crossed the river in a leaky skiff and had dinner with a knot of Massachusetts soldiers on the bank.[1]

Permanent camps were laid out, and soldiering was not too uncomfortable most of the time. There was a great deal to learn—about the war, and about the people who lived in a state where human beings were owned as slaves. Boys in the 27th Indiana felt that they had come to a foreign land; styles of architecture and methods of farming were different, here in Maryland, than they were back along the Wabash, and even the language seemed strange. The money, for instance, was spoken of in terms of sixpences and shillings, and the Hoosiers learned they weren't understood when they said "quarter" and "dime." The 21st Massachusetts found that the thrift and neatness of New England farms were not visible here, and the colored field hands seemed shockingly ragged, ignorant, and shiftless. To this abolitionist regiment, slavery seen at first hand was abhorrent. A little earlier, at Annapolis, a fugitive slave came into camp and was hidden, and after dark the soldiers stole a rowboat, fixed the slave up with hardtack and salt pork, and helped him steal off north by water. It developed that the slave was owned by the governor of Maryland, no less, and there were repercussions—Lincoln and the governor being engaged just then in a delicate game to keep Maryland in the Union, and the governor's good will being important.[2] The slavery issue, indeed, was beginning to disturb a number of the Northern soldiers. By the end of September, Brigadier General Charles P. Stone, commanding the division which held this part of the Potomac, felt it necessary to issue general orders admonishing all hands "not to incite and encourage insubordination among the colored servants in the neighborhood of the camps."

In general, the Western troops were less disturbed than the New Englanders. To the Westerners, this war was being fought to restore the Union; to the New Englanders, the abolition of human slavery was mixed up in it too, and freedom was an all-embracing idea that included black men as well as white. Sentiment back home was strongly abolitionist, and it was felt in camp. Shortly after General Stone issued his warning, two fugitive slaves sought refuge within the lines of the 20th Massachusetts. Obedient to the general's orders, a young officer took a squad, hauled the slaves out of hiding, and returned them to their owner. The regiment was a bit upset, and some of the men wrote home about it. Shortly afterward the colonel of the regiment received a stern letter from John A. Andrew, the governor of Massachusetts, officially reprimanding the young officer for returning the slaves and rebuking the colonel for countenancing it.

The colonel was William R. Lee, a doughty old West Pointer, one of whose classmates at the Academy had been a brilliant, ramrod-straight young Southerner named Jefferson Davis. Lee had simply been obeying orders, and he passed the governor's rebuke along to General Stone, who wrote the governor a sharp letter: this regiment was in United States service now and the governor had no business meddling with discipline, the young lieutenant and the colonel had properly done what they were told to do and were not subject to reprimand from any governor, and would the governor in future please keep his hands off? Governor Andrew, an executive whose strong support of the administration's war program in the dark days just after Fort Sumter fell had been an extremely important factor, was the last man in America to take a letter like that meekly, and he replied with some heat. The correspondence became rather extensive and passionate, and Governor Andrew finally passed it all along to the senior senator from Massachusetts, Charles Sumner, who denounced General Stone on the floor of the Senate. The general, in turn, wrote to Sumner in terms so bitter that it almost seemed as if he were challenging the senator to duel.

General Stone was getting in a bit over his head here, with the war still in its swaddling clothes, and with both of these Massachusetts statesmen being men of vast influence with the administration. As a soldier, General Stone felt that he was on solid ground—as, in fact, he unquestionably was. Stone might have been influenced, too, by the fact that he himself had more or less of a stand-in at the White House. Early in 1861 he had been commissioned as a colonel by James Buchanan, made inspector general of the District of Columbia, and given responsibility for maintaining order and preventing any secessionist putsch before and during the inauguration of Abraham Lincoln. He used to remark that he was the very first man mustered in to defend the country against rebellion. Lincoln had seen a good bit of him and had learned to trust him; indeed, if there was any substance to the story of secessionist plots to prevent the inauguration—and to the end of his days Stone believed that there was a great deal of substance to it—Lincoln had trusted him with his life. Now Stone was a brigadier commanding a division, he had the strong support of General McClellan, and he was quite willing to bark back at a senator, a governor, or anyone else if he had to do it to maintain discipline.

The flare-up over slavery, however, was not yet ready to come to a head. What was important now was perfecting the drill and training of the troops and guarding the line of the Potomac. Joe Johnston had a substantial outpost at Leesburg, over on the Virginia side, just a few miles away, and the commanding general was suspicious and wanted a good watch kept. Meanwhile, the boys still had a good deal to learn. There was a little trouble in the 15th Massachusetts over ambulance drill. The 15th had a nice twenty-four-piece band, and the bandsmen discovered that when they weren't tootling on their instruments they were ambulance men, required to put in at least one hour every day learning how to apply tourniquets, how to carry stretchers so as to give a wounded man the minimum of discomfort, how to get a casualty from a stretcher into an ambulance, and so on. They objected bitterly, refusing to turn out for drill and announcing, somewhat vaingloriously, that they would die before they would do any such duty. The colonel took them at their word; he had them locked in the stockade under guard and informed them that they would get food and water when they decided to obey orders, but not before. The bandsmen presently recanted.

In their sister regiment, Colonel Lee's 20th, it was discovered that city-bred Bay Staters had got a long way from the old tradition of the minuteman with his ever-ready rifle. The regiment was turned out for target practice and the colonel found that most of the boys simply pointed their rifles in the general direction of the target, shut both eyes tightly, and hauled back on the trigger. This had to be fixed, and was. . . . The artillery needed teaching too. Here and there, on hills commanding the river, was a battery posted to foil Rebel cavalry, which was believed to be exceedingly daring and dangerous, and the battery commanders took alarm easily, smiting the Virginia hills and fields with solid shot whenever anything suspicious appeared. It is recorded that one battery gleefully reported that it had bombarded and gloriously routed a whole regiment of Rebel cavalry, only to find a bit later that it had been disrupting a colored funeral procession.

There were practice marches to be made, too, by troops which were full of enthusiasm for war but which did not quite see the point of some of war's training-camp maneuvers. The 55th New York, for instance, a regiment composed largely of Frenchmen recruited on Manhattan Island, with non-coms who had served in the French Army, had a comfortable camp at Tennallytown, on the edge of Washington, and hiked far upriver in a cold, drizzling rain. The regiment countermarched, at last, and finally took position on a comfortless hilltop in plain sight of its own snug camp, which was no more than a mile away; and here, with the rain coming down harder and colder, the men were ordered to bivouac for the night. They muttered angrily: What point in sleeping here, shelterless, in the rain, when they could regain their own camp in another half-hour? A sergeant, veteran of the Crimea and Algiers, ruffled his Gallic mustachios and spoke soothingly. "Bah!" he said. "This is but to season the conscripts. We shall see many worse days than this." (He was quite right about seeing worse days; the 55th New York was to get so badly shot up that within a year it had to lose its independent existence and be consolidated with another regiment.)[3]

So the boys learned the ways of soldiering, and bumped against the hard edges of the slavery problem, and enjoyed the lovely landscape and the good weather and the relatively harmless thrills of long-range picket firing at Johnny Reb. The New Englanders discovered that the 1st Minnesota, posted near them along the river, made good neighbors; the Minnesota regiment had several companies of lumberjacks from the north woods and the lumberjacks were mostly recent migrants from the forests of Maine, so that the outfit had something of a down-East flavor. The Minnesotans were enjoying the war at the moment; had built bake ovens so that they could have soft bread instead of hardtack, bought fruit and sweet potatoes from the Maryland farmers, and wrote home that they were living "like princes and fighting cocks." Their picket post was on a tree-shaded hill overlooking the Potomac, and they got rope and put up a swing there and swung in it while keeping an eye open for invaders, and made friends, long-range, with the Rebels on the opposite shore. Their colonel, just then, was a man with the surpassingly warlike name of

Napoleon Jackson Tecumseh Dana, soon to be promoted to a brigadier's commission.[4]

The 20th Massachusetts considered itself tolerably well seasoned.
It could laugh, in mid-October, at its greenhorn nervousness of early
September, when it marched up from Washington, bivouacked dead-
tired in the dark, and sprang to arms in a wild panic because of a
sudden, unearthly noise that shattered the midnight stillness: the
braying of teams of army mules tethered in the next field. Colonel
Lee was happily writing to Governor Andrew that General Stone
(whatever his defects might be on the slavery issue) had promised
the 20th that "we would not be deprived of our due share of active
service." He related, too, the great pride the regiment felt in the fine
equipment its state had provided. The general had asked if the regiment had everything it needed, and Colonel Lee had replied: "My
regiment, sir, came from Massachusetts!" The governor could take
a bow on that one; right after Fort Sumter he had sent an agent
to England to buy arms, and the 20th had been equipped from the
start with Enfield rifles, the regulation British army musket.[5]

Along toward the end of October the general was able to make
good his promise to the 20th Massachusetts. A colored teamster
who had deserted the 13th Mississippi at Leesburg was brought into
camp with a tale to tell, which was that the Confederates at Leesburg
had sent all their baggage back to Joe Johnston's lines at Manassas
and expected to retreat very soon, fearing that the Yankees over in
Maryland heavily outnumbered them and planned aggression. Right
at this time McClellan sent a division up the river on the Virginia
side, halting it at Dranesville, a village some ten miles southeast of
Leesburg, to see what the Rebels might be up to; and to General
Stone he sent word of this move, suggesting that the general might
make a small reconnoissance of his own. The suggestion was a bit
vague, and General Stone interpreted it liberally; crossed a regiment
or two at Edwards' Ferry and sent others three miles upstream to
make a crossing at Harrison's Island, figuring that a slight demonstration there might make the enemy evacuate Leesburg.

The 20th Massachusetts thus found itself making a night march,
and at midnight it was down on the bank of the dark river, the
men waiting their turn to get into three small boats to be ferried over
the water. There was much confusion and waiting; nobody in par-

ticular seemed to be in charge of anything, and the boats were
ridiculously inadequate, having a combined capacity of only twenty-
five men. But by the time the sky was beginning to get light in the east,
most of the 20th was roosting on the flat, uninteresting length of
Harrison's Island, peering at the 150-yard channel that separated
the island from the Virginia shore. There was a high, wooded bluff
over there—Ball's Bluff, it was called—and the boys of the 20th learned
that five companies of the 15th Massachusetts had crossed the evening before and were up to something beyond the rim of the hill.
At dawn two companies of the 20th, accompanied by Colonel Lee
himself, went across, found their way up the bluff by a roundabout
cow path, and joined the 15th in an open glade on the heights. During the morning the rest of the regiment joined them.

Nothing much appeared to be happening, nor did there seem to be
any especial point to the proceedings. Colonel Charles Devens, the
Boston lawyer who had become colonel of the 15th and who was
ultimately to develop into quite a soldier, had taken a few of his men
nearly to Leesburg, in the early dawn, without discovering any Rebel
camp. Then, a little later, he had brushed into some Confederate
outposts, and there had been a desultory exchange of random shots.
Now he was back in the glade, reinforcements were coming up, and
it looked as if there might be a fight sooner or later. The Confederates were off in the woods; nobody knew just where they were or
how strong they were, but the pickets were doing a little shooting.
Devens had sent back all the news he had to General Stone, who had
messaged him to hang on: he was sending Colonel Edward D. Baker
over to take charge, with additional troops.

Presently Colonel Baker appeared. He was a man of some fame,
with a streak of romance in him, an intimate friend of President
Lincoln, a man who had roamed to far places and loved the swing
of poetry and the ring of great words. A veteran of the Mexican
War, he had gone to California and had become a man of considerable note in gold-rush San Francisco. In 1860 he had moved to
Oregon, winning election there to the United States Senate, and he
had introduced Lincoln to the crowd at the inauguration ceremonies
in March, riding with him in his carriage as his chosen companion.
He told the Senate that spring: "I want sudden, bold, forward, determined war," and he set out to get it personally, raising and be-

coming colonel of the 71st Pennsylvania—a Philadelphia regiment which, as compliment to its colonel, was then known as "the California regiment," although Baker by now was officially an Oregonian. He went off to war gaily, and to a friend he quoted: "Press where ye see my white plume shine amidst the ranks of war." Now he was here on Ball's Bluff in charge of an advance against the enemy. He had been delayed getting here; bringing his regiment up on the Maryland side, he had been dismayed by the lack of boats and had spent an hour or more getting an old flatboat out of the canal, nearby, into the river so that more men could be carried. He had a couple of guns coming up, and he was ready for a fight.

The fight was beginning to develop. The Confederates were gathering in the surrounding woods in some strength, and when Baker came up to the 20th Massachusetts he shook Colonel Lee's hand and said briskly, "I congratulate you, sir, on the prospect of a battle." Turning to the soldiers, he called out, "Boys, you want to fight, don't you?" Quite sincerely the boys cheered, and yelled that they did. Baker hurried back to the edge of the bluff, where there was a great deal of trouble getting the guns up, and the boys of the 20th peeled off their overcoats—fancy gray coats with brilliant linings of red silk: the Bay State had equipped them nobly—and hung them on the trees and got ready to fight. From the woods in front of them there came a ragged volley, which hurt no one—in the uncertain shadows the Rebels seem to have mistaken the line of hanging overcoats for soldiers, and the empty coats were liberally peppered. Then there began a noisy uproar of earnest file firing and the battle was on; the heavy smoke drifted across the little clearing like a rank fog, and the 20th Massachusetts began to fire back. Men were hit now, and there was a high nervous tension in this green regiment. The Rebels began to be visible through the trees and the smoke. A Massachusetts private saw a Confederate officer on a big horse and drew a bead on him. Unaccountably, when he tried to pull the trigger nothing happened. He lowered his musket and stared stupidly at his right hand; the trigger finger had been neatly removed by a bullet, and he had not even felt it. Off to the left the two guns were finally put into position and began to bang.

Colonel Baker went back to the edge of the bluff. His own regiment had come up and was in line, and another one was scrambling up—the 42nd New York, widely known as the Tammany Regiment, led by Colonel Milton Cogswell. Baker waved to him and came close enough to sing out an adaptation of a couple of lines from Scott's *Lady of the Lake*—

> *"One blast upon your bugle horn*
> *Is worth a thousand men"*—

and asked Cogswell how he liked the looks of things. Cogswell, who was a West Pointer, didn't like it much. The confusion around the river crossing seemed inexcusable, with no one in charge of the boats and no sort of order being maintained; a knack for quoting poetry while under fire seemed a poor substitute for executive ability, and it struck him that the force on the bluff was in a desperately bad spot, with the Confederates shooting down at them from higher ground in the woods and with no intelligent plan of battle being followed. The two guns were silent, sharpshooters having knocked off the gunners; Colonel Lee himself was helping with the loading for a time. On its final discharge one gun recoiled back to the edge of the bluff and toppled over. Baker hurried to the right of the line, exhorting everyone to hold on. A swift mental calculation had shown him that with the few boats available it would take three hours to get everybody back across the river, and it seemed better to stay and fight. Nobody knows what sort of tactics he might have devised to continue the battle, because just at that moment he fell dead with a Rebel bullet in his heart.

After that everything began to go to pieces. Cogswell led an abortive assault off to the left, in an attempt to cut an opening so that the command could go downstream on the Virginia side to join the troops that had crossed at Edwards' Ferry. The assault crumbled almost before it began, and there was nothing left but to try to get down the bluff and cross the river.

So there was a wild scramble down the steep hill in the dusk, with exultant Confederates following closely to the brow of the hill and shooting down at the fugitives. The 15th Massachusetts held them off for a while with a skirmish line, but finally they had to go, and a detachment from the Tammany Regiment which tried to take their place fared no better. Pretty soon everyone was on the beach, and it was almost dark, and musket fire was coming down heavily from the bluff, and there were only four boats—two of them the merest skiffs—to carry upward of a thousand men across a wide river. The big flatboat that Colonel Baker had horsed out of the canal earlier in the day was loaded down until it was almost awash, and then it set out, with men standing on each side to pole it along.

Rifle fire followed it—so many bullets were splashing in the water, a soldier wrote, that the river was "as white as in a great hail storm" —and presently a couple of the men who were poling were shot and fell heavily on the gunwale, tilting the overloaded boat so that water came rushing over the side and it capsized. Thirty or forty men were drowned, and the boat floated away in the darkness, bottom-side up. The two skiffs disappeared and were seen no more. The one remaining craft, a sheet-metal lifeboat, was punctured by bullets and sank in midstream, and all hands were marooned. A few men found a neck-deep ford to Harrison's Island and made their escape that way. Others took off their clothing and swam, an officer warning them to throw their rifles into the river so that the Rebels couldn't have them. The rest were taken prisoner.

Next day, when what was left of the command assembled on the Maryland side and counted noses, they found that more than nine hundred men had been lost—some two hundred or more shot, the remainder captured. Colonel Lee, Colonel Cogswell, and the major of the 20th Massachusetts, Paul Joseph Revere, descendant of the Revolutionary rider, went off to Libby Prison in Richmond. Among the wounded left on the Virginia shore was a young first lieutenant of the 20th's Company A, Oliver Wendell Holmes, Jr. And Colonel Baker, the friend of Abraham Lincoln and the hero of the United States Senate, was dead.

Which meant that there was going to be a post-mortem, and a big one. If the nation had known as much then as it knew two years later about war and loss and the mischances of the battlefield, the dark little tragedy might not have aroused such an uproar. But the war was still new, and Baker's death meant that a bright flame had suddenly been snuffed out, and the confusion and mishandling that had caused the defeat seemed to cry aloud for investigation. This was no Bull Run, where defeat had obviously been due to the greenness of the troops. The men who fought here had fought well enough, but it

was inescapably clear that there had not been any very good reason
for their crossing the river in the first place, and that, once they had
gone across, no one had known what to do with them. Baker was
dead, and his own brave but incompetent efforts were not to be criti-
cized, but there was angry criticism and to spare piling up for somebody.

Somehow the spotlight stayed on this affair. The papers told how
Colonel Devens paraded what was left of the 15th Massachusetts a
few days after the fight and gave them a brief pep talk, asking them
if they were ready to meet their "traitorous foes" once more: "Would
you go next week? Would you go tomorrow? Would you go at this
moment?" To which, of course, the emotional youngsters replied
with a wild shout of "Yes!"[6] From beyond the enemy lines it was
reported that the Confederates had said that fewer of the Massachusetts officers would have been killed had they not been too proud
to surrender—which inspired Union Brigadier General Lander, a
regular-army officer to whose brigade the Massachusetts regiments
actually belonged, to write a poem, beginning:

> *Aye, deem us proud, for we are more*
> *Than proud of all our mighty dead . . .*

It went on for eight full stanzas. The anthologies no longer carry
it, but it must come close to winning the distinction of being the best
threnody ever written by a brigadier general in the United States
Army; and it drew plenty of attention at the time.

Furthermore, public attention was painfully focused on Colonel
Lee and Major Revere. The United States Navy had just captured
a Confederate privateer, and it was announced that since the Confederacy was not a legitimate nation her so-called privateersmen
were in fact pirates and would be hanged as such; and the government
at Richmond promptly replied that if these privateers were hanged
an equal number of Federal army officers, chosen by lot from among
the prisoners at Richmond, would be hanged in reprisal. The lot fell
on Lee and Revere, among others, and they were lodged in condemned cells. A captured sergeant from the 20th Massachusetts
talked to Lee just before he was locked up: did the colonel have
any message for his old regiment? Colonel Lee was reputed to be

the oldest officer in the army, except for General Sumner, and he was deeply affected by emotion. "Tell the men——" he began. He stopped and cleared his throat heavily; when emotion takes an old soldier it usually takes him hard. "Tell the men their colonel died like a brave man." The message got back and was printed. Agonized attention fell on the officers waiting for death—until at last the Lincoln administration decided that nothing was to be gained by getting into a hanging contest with Jefferson Davis, and let it be known that the privateersmen would be treated as regular prisoners of war, after all. In time Lee and Revere were exchanged and came north, and Lee later became a brigadier.

But if concern over the possible hanging of prisoners was ended, there was no quick ending for the concern over the tragedy of Ball's Bluff. The state of Massachusetts had seen her sons sacrificed to no purpose and had influential spokesmen in Washington; also, the state of Massachusetts—through her governor and her senior senator —had already had trouble with this General Stone who was responsible for the whole Ball's Bluff business in the first place. Stone was a pro-slavery man—or at least he was not anti-slavery, and that might be much the same thing—and there were queer stories afloat. He went out of his way to protect Rebel property—*Rebel* property, the property of men who were trying to destroy the government. There had been flags of truce between his headquarters and Confederate headquarters across the river. Mysterious messengers had been seen going and coming; there was a question about passes that had been issued, allowing Southern sympathizers to go through the lines: was not this general actually in league with rebellion? Might it not be that the regiments sent across the river into a deadly trap had been designedly sacrificed? Should not Congress look into it: Congress, whose own hero had been slain in this affair? Should not Congress be alert to make sure that there was no sympathy with treason in high places in the army?

Congress should. Congress acted accordingly. And there grew out of all of this a new force in government, a force which was to have a great effect, for good or for evil, on the way the war was run and on the men who ran it: the Joint Committee on the Conduct of the War, with the bitter-end anti-slavery radical Republicans in complete control and with Senator Ben Wade of Ohio as chairman. Wade was as tough as Allegheny nails, and he hated slavery and all of slavery's spokesmen; had brought his rifle to Washington when he was elected to the Senate, daring the fire-eating Southerners to challenge him to duel, and had given back bitterness for bitterness, hatred for hatred, on the floor of the Senate, doing all that one man might do to make the coming conflict a war to the knife, utterly determined now that it should be a war to end slavery and destroy the slave-owning class as well as a war to save the Union.

The committee held hearings and broke General Stone. A mass of vague and mysterious evidence was collected—indefinite, unanswerable, and damning—and it was passed along to the War Department, accompanied by strong subsurface pressure. The evidence was just strong enough so that McClellan himself could not save Stone, just strong enough to make Lincoln, who had trusted Stone so deeply, admit that there seemed to be grounds for action; and Stone was removed from his command and locked up for long months in Fort Lafayette in New York Harbor. No formal charge was ever placed against him. He could not answer his accusers because he never knew quite what he was accused of; he could not be brought to trial because nobody else knew either. He was simply encased in a cloud of doubt and suspicion. One day he was a general in charge of a division, honored among men, and the next day he was a prisoner in a cell, walled away from the world. Months later he was quietly released; many months after that, when Grant came to the top command, he was given a combat assignment again, heading a brigade in the Army of the Potomac. But for the moment he was completely ruined.[7]

And this, if anybody had bothered to see it that way, was more than just a rough deal for General Stone. It was a flaming portent in the sky for all soldiers who might come to command in the armies of the Union: the civil authority was going to ride herd on the generals, and woe unto the man in shoulder straps who failed to please it. A new and unlooked-for complication was entering the ancient science of war. It was not going to be enough for a general simply to have military ability. He would have to show that his heart was in the cause, and the definition of "the cause" was going to be in the hands of men who had ideas never taught at West Point.

3. I Do Not Intend to Be Sacrificed

That was the point General McClellan never quite understood. How could he? No general had ever had to understand anything of the kind before. He was not merely the commander of an army in a nation at war; he was the central figure in a risky new experiment which involved nothing less than working out, under fire, the relationships that must exist between a popular government and its soldiers at a time when the popular government is fighting for its existence.

Nothing in the country's previous history shed any light on the problem. The Revolution itself had simply been a great act of creation—an inspiration, from which both sides could draw equally, but not an object lesson. Eighteen-twelve and Mexico had hardly been more than episodes—sudden, angry outbursts of the energy of growth and development, absorbing enough but bringing no problems that could not for the most part be left to the regular military establishments. But this war was different. It went all the way to the heart and it could not be left to the regulars. Nobody had yet discovered how a democracy puts all its power and spirit under the discipline of an all-consuming war and at the same time continues to be a democracy. Here was where everybody was going to find out, and the only safe prediction was that it was going to be a tough time for soldiers.

One thing, to be sure, had been made clear: no simple outpouring of undisciplined and untrained men was going to win. Bull Run had taught that much. The tradition of Lexington and Concord no longer applied. The embattled farmer, leaving his plow in the furrow and taking his musket from the wall to go out and whip the King's soldiers, had to sign up for three years now, and the bark of the drill sergeant—heard all day long on every field around Washington —was the audible symbol of the fact that until the war ended the freeborn American was going to be taking orders. That fact had been accepted, the young general had it well in hand, and everybody was happy about the way he was doing the job. But what came next?

What came next was the fact that nobody trusted anybody, which put a terrible new factor into the military equation: an unknown, packed with explosive force.

By all standards of military common sense, General Stone had been quite right in squelching Governor Andrew, and the governor had been absurdly wrong. But military common sense wasn't enough now, unless it was linked to an understanding of the overwhelming pressures which could be created by purely political considerations. Right though he might have been, according to the books, General Stone had in fact been wrong. By the purely pragmatic test—how does a general act so that he can get his job done?—he had made a huge mistake. He might have been perfectly correct in insisting that the civil authority must not reach inside the military machine to interfere with the discipline, but in the end the civil authority did reach into the machinery long enough to pluck General Stone out of it. That was doubtless very unjust, but it was the way things were and it behooved every general to take the fact into account. The war could be won without generals like General Stone, worthy as the man was, but it could not be won without war governors like John Andrew, wrongheaded and obstreperous though such men might frequently be.

There was also the Cabinet. Specifically, there were men like the honorable Salmon Portland Chase, Secretary of the Treasury and a power in the land. Secretary Chase was not a particularly lovable character; he was humorless and more than slightly sanctimonious and he was cursed with a burning, self-centered ambition which he could always justify somehow, to himself, as a simple passion for God's own righteousness, with which he identified his every motive. He was away outside the field of military operations, his concern being—in theory, at least—exclusively with currency and loans and taxation and the ins and outs of wartime finance. But he was also a man the generals had to reckon with. He was not in the Cabinet because he was a genius of finance; he was in there because he was a power in politics, leader of a certain group in the electorate, spokesman for an important number of the American people. He concerned himself directly and immediately with military matters, and when he raised his voice on those subjects it was listened to. So McClellan found himself, rather against his will, closeted with the Secretary of the Treasury now and then, explaining military plans to him and listening, with such grace as he could muster, to the military ideas the Secretary had evolved.

There is something almost grotesque, to modern eyes, in the recorded spectacle of Chase solemnly bending over a map of Virginia and with pudgy forefinger tracing the proper line of operations for the Army of the Potomac. But it is quite beside the point to say that Chase should not have been bothering his head about such matters. There he was, one essential element in the government of the country, embodying a popular voice which might indeed be tragically confused but which had to be heard if the country was to be held together. He was a part of the unknown new factor in the problem which the young general had to solve, and there was no sense in simply complaining that he ought not to be in it at all: he *was* in it and he was going to stay in, and that was that.

Then there was such a man as Edwin M. Stanton, the prominent lawyer and Democratic politician, recently Attorney General in the dying months of Buchanan's administration, who was entering the intimate circle around the young general as a species of unofficial legal counselor, and who a little later was to become Secretary of War. Mr. Stanton was irascible, with a nature which was a singular blend of a habit of blunt speech and a fondness for devious intrigue. He had hard eyes behind steel-rimmed spectacles and he had a talent for savage criticism—a man who could plunge into sudden pessimism so deep as to resemble abject panic, but who could also drive for a chosen goal with uncommon ruthlessness. Right now he was deeply disgusted with everything the Lincoln administration was doing—with Lincoln himself, whom he spoke of bitterly as "the original gorilla," and with all of Lincoln's official family, which he suspected would be turned out of office before long by the arrival in Washington of Jefferson Davis and his minions. He was complaining that the administration was trying to give a strict Republican-party cast to the war; a complaint which comes very strangely from the man who, a few months later, was bending every effort to have the war conducted by the most extreme Republican principles. He was also urging McClellan to ignore the cackling politicians and make himself dictator. Of McClellan he wrote despondently to Mr. Buchanan: "If he had the ability of Caesar, Alexander or Napoleon, what can he accom-

plish? Will not Scott's jealousy, cabinet intrigues, Republican interference, thwart him at every step?"[1]

With this McClellan unquestionably would have agreed; most particularly with reference to General Scott. Scott was in the way, and
it was clear that he would have to go. He belonged to an earlier day,
and he was now hardly more than a great reputation bearing up a
showy uniform. McClellan was pointedly keeping him in ignorance
of the number and assignments of the new troops that were arriving,
even though the old general was, at least nominally, the commander
of the country's armies. McClellan also was conferring with senators
and cabinet members about matters which legally fell within Scott's
purview. Painfully Scott confessed that "I have become an incum-
brance to the army as well as to myself"—for he was, as he wrote,
"broken down by many particular hurts, besides the general infirmi-
ties of age"—and he could see that it was time for him to leave and
let a younger man take over. He hoped that the younger man might
be Henry Halleck, who had written military textbooks and who could
put down on paper elaborate and beautifully reasoned treatises on
strategy, and who was casually but on the whole respectfully known
in the army as "Old Brains." But the White House was cool to the
idea. General Scott had to admit that McClellan seemed to be in line
for the place; had to admit, also, that he unquestionably had "very
high qualifications for military command"; and so in mid-August the
old general finally requested that he, Winfield Scott, be placed on the
retired list.

The President went to him and tried to talk him out of it, and
when he failed the application was simply pigeonholed, and Scott
stayed on for a time as a pathetic supernumerary, ignored and absent-
mindedly honored for what he used to be. It hurt the old man
acutely, for he was intensely vain; but Scott wrote that no matter
how or where he spent the rest of his life, "my frequent and latest
prayer will be, 'God save the Union.'"[2] And at last, in November,
a couple of weeks after the Ball's Bluff disaster, Scott's plea for retirement was accepted, and McClellan got up in the half-light of a
rainy morning to go clattering down to the station with his mounted
escort to see the old man off. There they stood on the wet platform,
formally bidding each other Godspeed, the worn-out old soldier,
grotesque with his feeble fat body bulging in its uniform, and the

dapper youngster, erect and confident, with the lesser brass standing at attention all around; and McClellan himself felt the force of the contrast. "It may be," he wrote to his wife, "that at some distant day I, too, shall totter away from Washington, a worn-out soldier, with naught to do but make my peace with God. The sight of this morning was a lesson to me which I hope not soon to forget. I saw there the end of a long, active and ambitious life, the end of the career of the first soldier of his nation; and it was a feeble old man scarce able to walk; hardly anyone there to see him off but his successor. Should I ever become vainglorious and ambitious, remind me of that spectacle."

It was to be just a year, plus three or four days, before McClellan himself would take the train out of Washington to retirement. But for the moment that day was deeply hidden in the future, and there were the problems of the present to worry about. And while McClellan took Scott's high place and became general of all the country's armies, his most pressing problems seemed to be chiefly two: the presence of General Joe Johnston's army in Centreville and Manassas, with outposts so far north that Confederate pickets could see the unfinished dome of the Capitol, and the existence along the Potomac River of highly effective Rebel batteries of artillery.

These latter created an immediate pinch. During the weeks before Bull Run the Confederates had edged forward to the river below Washington and had put up fortifications at three places—at Quantico, at Mathias Point, and at Aquia Creek, northern terminus of the Richmond, Fredericksburg and Potomac Railroad. In addition, they had removed all lights, buoys, and channel markers from the stream. Nobody much came down to molest them, and they had plenty of time that summer to make the positions strong and to mount heavy guns; and by early autumn the Lincoln administration was forced to realize that the capital was effectively blockaded as far as its water approach was concerned. To be sure, the railroad line was open, and troops and supplies could come in freely; but the water route was closed—warships could run the gantlet without too much trouble, but merchant vessels couldn't—and this was not only a big nuisance but a flaming humiliation as well. While Secretary Seward was assuring European nations that the Federal government was getting the insurrection well under control, the uncomfortable fact remained that the government could not open the waterway to its own capital.

The navy did what it could to restore the situation, without effect. It simply had no good ships to spare for operations on the Potomac. Practically everything that would float and carry a gun was needed on the blockade, or on the inland rivers, or on the high seas hunting commerce destroyers. At the beginning of the summer the navy's Potomac flotilla consisted of one small side-wheel steamer and two converted tugs, the three mounting a total of seven light guns. In June this hopeful little squadron steamed down to attack the works at Aquia Creek, retiring after a five-hour bombardment in which a good deal of powder was burned and a grand racket created but in which nobody on either side was hurt. Later in the month, stiffened by the arrival of the U.S.S. *Pawnee*—which was at least a regular warship, although only a second-class sloop—the navy returned to the fray, going down to Mathias Point and sending a landing party ashore, under the cover of gunfire, to seize the works and spike the batteries. This was playing into the Rebels' hands; they had infantry there, brought it up, drove the landing party off, and killed Commander James H. Ward, who had charge of the venture. After that the batteries were allowed to stay there undisturbed. In February of 1862, when the navy began mounting the expedition that was to capture New Orleans, David Dixon Porter came under fire while going downstream in the ex-revenue cutter *Harriet Lane,* which took a round shot through one of her paddle wheels.[3]

Clearing the Potomac, then, was up to the army—which of course meant that it was up to McClellan. McClellan pointed out, sensibly enough, that the existence of the Rebel batteries along the Potomac depended on Johnston and his army at Centreville and Manassas; as long as Johnston stayed there they would remain, but they would go automatically when he retreated. The Manassas-Centreville stronghold was the real objective, then. The young general would presently put his army in motion and clear this stronghold out?

He would. Riding out in the Virginia countryside with McDowell, McClellan used to gesture toward the eastern end of the Confederate line at Manassas and say, "We shall strike them there." He eased some troops forward a few miles "by way of getting elbow-room" and wrote confidently to his wife: "The more room I get the more I want, until by and by I suppose I shall be so insatiable as to think I cannot do with less than the whole state of Virginia." Joe Hooker, who had his division in training over on the eastern shore of Maryland, was lined up to prepare for a river crossing that would clear the Virginia shore of all graycoats. But McClellan refused to be precipitate about it. The lines around Centreville and Manassas were strong. The army's secret service assured McClellan that Johnston had something like ninety thousand men behind those entrenchments—men well drilled and well armed, and all athirst for Yankee blood The more McClellan thought about it, the less did a frontal assault on those lines appeal to him

He was in this mood when he took over Scott's job and became responsible for the strategy of the entire war; and a day or so after that he attended a cabinet meeting, sitting alone and somewhat silent at one end of the long council table At the meeting this day was a young colonel of the 9th New York, one Rush Hawkins, who had just come back from the expedition which had seized Hatteras Inlet on the Carolina coast, and who was making a report on the situation there. When the meeting ended McClellan beckoned Hawkins to his side and began to ask questions, not about Hatteras but about conditions around Norfolk and Hampton Roads Hawkins was all primed; he had been telling old General Wool, who was in command at Fortress Monroe, that what the government ought to do was land an army at the tip of the Virginia peninsula and move on Richmond from the east, and he quickly sketched out a rough map of the terrain, showing where the roads led and pointing out how gunboats could provide transportation and flank protection for an invading army by steaming up the York and James rivers.

McClellan pumped him dry and pocketed his sketch map. The young colonel's idea meshed with an idea of his own—was it really necessary to attack the Confederate fortifications at Manassas at all? The North had sea power and the South did not; despite the batteries along the Potomac, a properly convoyed fleet of transports could ascend and descend the river at any time. Why not take the army down the bay by water, land somewhere east of Richmond just as Hawkins was suggesting, and move in on the Confederate capital from that direction, completely by-passing Joe Johnston and his defensive works? The move would compel Johnston to retreat at once. Unless he retreated swiftly, the Federal army might even get to Rich-

mond before he did. In any case, it could get clear to the gates of
the Rebel capital without a contest and could fight its great battle
there where victory would be decisive.

McClellan developed this idea. The President, the Cabinet, and
the newspapers were calling for action—open the Potomac, drive
Johnston out of northern Virginia—but McClellan at length concluded that his new plan was sounder; and by early December, in
reply to a note from Lincoln, he wrote that "I have now my mind
actually turned toward another plan of campaign that I do not think
at all anticipated by the enemy nor by many of our own people."

This meant delay. It would take time to round up enough shipping
for an amphibious venture of this magnitude—for McClellan proposed to move on Richmond with an army of at least 150,000 men—
and there were innumerable details to get in shape. McClellan began
to see that it would be spring, at the earliest, before he could move.
This meant that the people and the administration would have to
be patient. It was a bad time to call for patience. Ball's Bluff seemed
to call for action—not merely for revenge, although that would be
welcome, but for an advance that would relieve the North of the
shame of having impudent Rebel hordes camped almost within gunshot of the capital, ready to gobble up any detachment that ventured
to cross the river. By the end of October the navy had formally reported that the Potomac would have to be considered closed to water
traffic, except for movements made under the protection of heavy
warships.

And this, in turn, meant that the young general's place was beginning to be difficult. He was still the predestined hero chosen to save
the Republic, and the cheers of his men continued to echo across
the hills when he rode about the lines; but he was learning that much
is expected of the man to whom much has been given, and his temper
was beginning to wear ragged. There was a flaw in the arrangement
somewhere. He saw the problem so clearly, and he had promised the
country that the war would be "short, sharp and decisive," and he
had worked a great transformation in the capital and in the army
that protected it; yet there was a growing note of criticism, the President and his Cabinet seemed to be more and more impatient, and
the clear strategic plans that were so simple to a trained soldier had
to be explained, and justified, and explained afresh to men who did

not understand what he was talking about and who could by no means be trusted to keep their mouths shut when they were entrusted with classified information.

This fall the young general was writing to his wife: "I can't tell you how disgusted I am becoming with these wretched politicians," and "this getting ready is slow work with such an administration. I wish I were well out of it." The note recurred, as the months wore away: "I am becoming daily more disgusted with this administration —perfectly sick of it. If I could with honor resign I would quit the whole concern tomorrow; but so long as I can be of any real use to the nation in its trouble I will make the sacrifice. No one seems able to comprehend my real feeling—that I have no ambitious feelings to gratify, and only wish to serve my country in its trouble." He was no longer telling proudly about multiple dinner invitations from members of the Cabinet. Instead: "When I returned yesterday, after a long ride, I was obliged to attend a meeting of the cabinet at eight p. m., and was bored and annoyed. There are some of the greatest geese in the cabinet I have ever seen—enough to tax the patience of Job."

There was never-failing consolation in the adoration of the army: "'Our George' they have taken it into their heads to call me. I ought to take good care of these men, for I believe they love me from the bottom of their hearts; I can see it in their faces when I pass among them." But the army, unfortunately, was not all: "I appreciate all the difficulties in my path: the impatience of the people, the venality and bad faith of the politicians, the gross neglect that has occurred in obtaining arms, clothing, etc." There were matters of state to worry about also: "This unfortunate affair of Mason and Slidell has come up and I shall be obliged to devote the day to endeavoring to get our government to take the only prompt and honorable course of avoiding a war with England and France. . . . It is sickening in the extreme, and makes me feel heavy at heart, when I see the weakness and unfitness of the poor beings who control the destinies of this great country."

Something—it may be remarked—seems to have been going to the young general's head right about then. The famous Mason and Slidell incident had indeed created a regrettable moment of crisis, and the country could have had a full-dress war with England just by asking for it, in December of 1861. But neither Lincoln nor Seward had the remotest notion of letting the dispute boil over into war—"One war at a time," Lincoln kept saying—and the dispute was settled smoothly, at some cost to inflamed national pride. McClellan was simply deluding himself if he thought that it was at any time necessary for him to needle either the President or the Secretary of State into sensible behavior.

For that matter, if McClellan felt obliged to guide the President on foreign policy he was hardly taking the most tactful path to gain his end. It was just at this time—when the danger of war with England had suddenly become real and imminent, when the administration was irritably asking when the army would take the offensive, and when the Potomac River shipping was stagnating at the wharves because of the defiant Rebel batteries downstream—that McClellan chose to deliver his famous snub to the President: came back to his house one evening, was told the President was in the parlor waiting to see him, and calmly went upstairs and got into bed, leaving the President to cool his heels as he might please. At about the same time he was writing to his wife: "I have not been at home for some three hours, but am concealed at Stanton's to dodge all enemies in the shape of 'browsing' presidents, etc." A few months later, when the unpredictable Stanton had become Secretary of War and great enmity had arisen between general and Secretary, McClellan was to complain that Stanton insulated him from the White House and kept him from seeing the President. If Stanton did do that when his time came, he at least had something to work on.

Not that McClellan did not have many things on his mind. The whole load had been placed upon him. He had said confidently, "I can do it all," and he was overworking himself with relentless energy, but the load was crushing. He saw himself at times as a man held back by civilian incompetence: "The people think me all-powerful. Never was there a greater mistake. I am thwarted and deceived by these incapables at every turn." And while Lincoln had the impression that an advance on Manassas was prevented only by McClellan's hesitation, McClellan was writing: "I am doing all I can to get ready to move before winter sets in, but it now begins to look as if we were condemned to a winter of inactivity. If it is so the fault will not be mine: there will be that consolation for my conscience, even if the world at large never knows it."

McClellan was beginning to realize, too, that as general-in-chief of the armies he had some sort of responsibility in regard to the slavery issue. He was moved to deep reflections on the evils of slavery when he read the reports from the expedition that had captured Port Royal, South Carolina, late that fall. As the troops seized portions of the Carolina coast, great numbers of slaves came wandering into the Union lines with their simple possessions tied up in bundles—infinitely wistful and confused, not knowing what was happening but sensing, somehow, that a great day of change had arrived. There was something in this spectacle "inexpressibly mournful" to the young general as he sat at headquarters late at night and poured out his inmost thoughts to his young wife. He wrote: "When I think of some of the features of slavery I cannot help shuddering. Just think for one moment, and try to realize that at the will of some brutal master you and I might be separated forever! It is horrible; and when the day of adjustment comes I will, if successful, throw my sword into the scale to force an improvement in the condition of these poor blacks." And then the young general, so deeply moved with a sincere, fundamental emotion, added the towering anticlimax: "I do think that some of the rights of humanity ought to be secured to the negroes. There should be no power to separate families, and the right of marriage ought to be secured to them."

But these moments of self-communion, bringing the bright vision of an all-powerful young conqueror using his great victory to right profound wrongs, were after all relatively few. The more immediate concerns left little room for them. Washington had become antagonistic to him. There was afoot a subtle, implacable hostility, born of villainy, moving below the surface to thwart the man who would save the country. Matters were not going right, and it was because there were men in high places who did not want matters to go right. Very late at night, worn by a hard day, McClellan told his wife: ". . . the necessity for delay has not been my fault. I have a set of men to deal with unscrupulous and false; if possible they will throw whatever blame there is on my shoulders, and I do not intend to be sacrificed by such people. I still trust that the all-wise Creator does not intend our destruction, and that in His own good time He will free the nation from the men who curse it, and will restore us to His favor." Specifically who might these men be? They are not named, they are just there, the men who try to talk strategy to a soldier, who insist on a quick stab at Manassas (where overwhelming foes lie in wait) instead of easily agreeing that it is more sensible to wait and go round by the peninsula; the men who want the Potomac opened at once; the frock-coated politicians who think they are somebodies even though there is a great war to be fought, who commission ignorant civilians like themselves as generals and entrust troops to them, who sometimes quite openly do not want or expect a soldier to succeed unless he sees political issues as they do.

The effect of all this was to drive McClellan deeper in on himself—this sensitive, immeasurably introspective man, whose high confidence rested on a dark substratum of doubt, where every problem, every venture, had to be given prolonged study to make sure that inexplicable dangers were not attached to it. The army was not only the instrument he had created and was ready to use; it was his refuge as well, ready with cheers and understanding to dispel those queer twinges of self-distrust that could come up even without the nagging criticism of ignorant politicians. To this nagging he could oppose obstinacy. He would handle the army according to purely military principles, and he would not be hurried.

He presented at last his plan for taking the army down the river by water (in the spring, when warm weather and the end of winter damp had made passable the execrable unpaved roads of Virginia), and there was endless to-do about it. Typhoid fever laid him up for a while. Lincoln came to see him while he was convalescing, and once again couldn't seem to get admitted to the presence; Lincoln then called into council General McDowell and General William Franklin, explaining that he had to talk to somebody, and remarking that if General McClellan did not intend to use the army he would like to borrow it for a time. Recovering, McClellan found himself involved with a good part of the Cabinet, plus the two generals, discussing matters of strategy. He froze McDowell with icy politeness when McDowell tried to express his embarrassment at having been called into consultation over the head of the army commander, and listened in noncommittal silence while Secretary Seward, slouching in his chair, said he didn't particularly care whether the army beat the Confederates at Manassas or at the gates of Richmond, just so long as it beat them somewhere. When Secretary Chase asked him bluntly if he actually did plan to do anything definite with the army, and if so when he proposed to do it, McClellan was equally blunt: said that he had a plan, with a perfectly good time element in it, and if the President ordered him to spill it in public he would do so, but that if he were not so ordered he would prefer to keep quiet, feeling that it would be well to have as few civilians as possible know about secrets of strategy. Whereupon, amid some hemming and hawing, Lincoln adjourned the meeting.

They had come quite a distance now from the day when Republican senators were flocking around the general with throat noises of admiration, saying, "How young he is!"; quite a distance from the day when four separate cabinet ministers craved the general's presence at dinner, and all criticism was suspended while the young soldier had a free hand. And it was all dreadfully complicated by the fact that suspicion and fear—perfectly natural, considering that the country was at war with itself—had been turned loose in the capital. That operated to intensify the handicap which, under any circumstances, must rest on the shoulders of a democracy's general. Of necessity, a democracy deeply distrusts its army, and in all ordinary times it wears its distrust openly on its sleeve—especially a democracy like that of 1861, which was still brash and crude and wore its hat in the parlor. But when a democracy goes to war in a big way it is suddenly compelled to rely on its army for its very existence. Then its instinct for self-preservation forces it to watch the army very carefully, to be excessively critical, to demand illogical and sometimes impossible things, and to be savage if they are not quickly done. And it is up to the general in command to realize all of this. A capacity for getting along with the civil authorities is just as essential a part of his equipment as is the ability to plan campaigns and win battles. (McClellan's opposite number, Robert E. Lee, could have told him about that: Lee had this capacity to his very finger tips.)[4]

And this capacity for getting along with the civilians does not consist merely in an ability to butter people up gracefully, to suffer fools in council with patience, and to yes the ignorant officeholders along. What it really means is that the general must understand that he is not a free agent and cannot hope to become one. He has to work within the limitations imposed by the fact that he is working for a democracy, which means that at times he must modify or abandon the soundest military plan and make do with a second-best. McClellan's experience in that difficult autumn and winter of inaction provides an illustration.

The administration desperately wanted him to drive the Confederates out of northern Virginia and open the Potomac waterway. For perfectly sound military reasons McClellan refused. What never entered his head was the fact that his own ability to command the army and to control the war was going to depend, at least in part, on the readiness with which he satisfied the administration's demands. In the long run this civilian voice was going to be heard, whether or no; if the general would not listen, there would eventually be a general there who would.

It was the same in the matter of appointing corps commanders. An army as big as the Army of the Potomac could not operate very well with the division as the largest administrative unit. The divisions had to be grouped into army corps, and generals had to be named to command those corps. Lincoln and his Cabinet, spurred by a bookish understanding of this, kept pressing McClellan to set the corps up and appoint the commanders. McClellan kept refusing; he would name corps commanders, he said, only after the test of battle had shown him which generals were best qualified for those important jobs. Which was all right—except that one morning he came down to work and found that the President had officially appointed the corps commanders himself. McClellan complained bitterly about it, as well he might; but he never saw that he really had himself to blame. The administration's insistence on having corps commanders appointed meant that corps commanders were going to be appointed —if not by the major general commanding, then by someone else. This was probably wrong, but it was one of the facts of life which the major general commanding needed to assimilate.

But by midwinter, in spite of all disputes and misunderstandings, the War Department was collecting steamers, ferryboats, tugs, canal barges, schooners—anything that would carry men or supplies—and making ready for the great descent of the Potomac, for McClellan had finally made his point. Richmond was to be attacked from the east, and a tremendous amphibious operation was to be launched.

There was a stir in the far-flung camps. Discipline was good, spirits were high; the new system of corps command was creaking somewhat, but it was working. With profound relief McClellan looked forward to getting out of the capital, away from the scheming politicians, out into the field with his soldiers. To his wife he wrote: "If I can get out of this scrape you will never catch me in the power of such a set again."

And a young officer in the 7th Maine wrote home: "We have no baggage with us but our blankets. I enjoy this kind of life immensely. We expect to be in Richmond in a fortnight."[5]

THREE

The Era of Suspicion

1. But You Must Act

The point that is so easy to overlook nowadays is that the men of the 1860s were living in the center of a fiery furnace. It was not a tidy, clear-cut war against some foreign nation that was being waged. It was a *civil* war, a war not between men of two nations but between men of two beliefs, two philosophies, two ways of considering human society and its structure and purpose. The opposing beliefs were not sharply defined and clear so that no man could mistake which camp he belonged in. On the contrary, there were a dozen gradations of belief leading from one to the other, and a man might belong in one camp on one issue and in the other camp on another; and the very word "loyalty" might mean loyalty to a flag, to a cause, or to a belief in some particular social and political theory, and "treason" might mean disloyalty to any of these. Indeed, the war was peculiarly and very bitterly a war of the tragically modern kind, in which loyalties and disloyalties do not follow the old patterns even though those patterns may be the only ones men can use when they try to formulate their loyalty. And so that generation was deprived of the one element that is essential to the operation of a free society—the ability to assume, in the absence of good proof to the contrary, that men in public life are generally decent, honorable, and loyal. Because that element was lacking, the wisest man could be reasonable with only part of his mind; a certain area had to be given over to emotions which were all the more mad and overpowering because he shared them with everyone else.

Hence the Civil War was fought and directed in an air of outright melodrama. It was stagy and overdone, and the least inhibited theatrical director nowadays would throw out large parts of the script on the simple ground that it was too wild to be credible—but it was all real, the villainies and dangers were all visible, and the worst things anyone could imagine seemed quite as likely as not to be completely true. The confused soldiers who imagined that General McDowell wore a fancy hat in order to have traitorous communion with the Rebels were not out of their minds; they were simply applying, on their own level, the same sort of panic suspicion that was besetting their elders. All the way through there were two lines of action going on: the visible one, out in the open, where there were flags and rumbling guns and marching men to be seen, and the invisible one which affected and colored all the rest. Sunlight and death were upon the earth in the spring of 1862, and no one was wholly rational.

On the surface, everything was fine. Nearly two hundred thousand young men had been drilled, disciplined, clothed, armed, and equipped. They innocently thought themselves veterans. They had roughed it for a whole autumn and winter under canvas, knew what it was like to sleep on bare ground in the rain, had learned the intricate, formalized routines by which marching columns transformed themselves into battle lines, and they had been brought to a razor edge of keenness. The great unpredictable that lay ahead of them seemed a bright adventure, for in the 1860s cynicism was not a gift which came to youth free, in advance; it had to be earned, and all illusions had to be lost the hard way. Day by day the new divisions got ready for the great move southward, discarding surplus gear, preparing wagon trains for cross-country movement. The roads and docks and warehouses along the Potomac were full of bustle and hustle, and the empty transports lay waiting on the bright water.

But beneath this enthusiasm and eager hope there were doubt and bickering, and the men who knew the most were the men who worried the most. A cloud somewhat larger than a man's hand lay upon the sky: symbolized, as winter died, by a very literal cloud of black, oily smoke rising from the burning supply depots of the Confederate encampments around Centreville and Manassas. Confederate Joe Johnston, meditating on the fact that McClellan had three times his numbers, had decided not to wait to be pushed. He put the torch to all the goods he could not move—a million pounds of bacon, along with much else, went to the flames—and he pulled his army out of its entrenchments, marching back to a safer post behind the Rappahannock River. And while this retreat was, in a way, what everybody had been hoping for—Rebel vedettes could no longer gaze insolently down on the capital city, and the troublesome batteries along the Potomac were all evacuated, leaving the waterway clear—the move took the high command by surprise. It might be cause for joy, but it was also very disturbing.

To General McClellan, among others. In the elaborate chess game that was just beginning he had worked out a clever sequence of moves, and this retreat joggled the board and displaced the men. McClellan had planned to float his army down to the mouth of the Rappahannock, landing at a town called Urbanna, some sixty miles due east of Richmond. That would put him in Johnston's rear, the Confederate Army would have to retreat in hot haste—and, being so hasty, very likely in considerable disorder—and the Federal army would be where it could cut off this retreat and bring on a battle under highly favorable circumstances. But now Johnston was not where he had been, and the Urbanna move was no good. Committed to the water route, at the cost of long, infinitely difficult wrangles with President and Cabinet, McClellan realized that he would have to go to Fortress Monroe and make his way up the long peninsula between the York and James rivers.

In a way, that was all right. His flanks and his supply line would be protected, and he had been informed that the peninsular highways were sandy, and hence readily passable in wet weather—a thumping bit of misinformation, if ever there was one. But it meant a slow, slogging drive, no chance to cut off the Rebel army, and a big, stand-up fight before Richmond was reached. He had written earlier that the move via the peninsula was "less brilliant." Still, he greatly preferred it to the overland route, which was what Lincoln and his Cabinet wanted: the route straight down the railroad track, supply line getting longer each day and cruelly tempting the Rebel cavalry raiders, and all sorts of mischance possible as the army got deeper into enemy territory.

There had been trouble about that; much trouble, the end of which was not yet. Out of it had come a singular episode—fantastic, reflecting the temper of the times and the strange character of the war they were fighting. It happened, oddly, on the very day General Johnston started his gray columns south out of Manassas, when Lincoln sent for McClellan early in the morning and asked him to come to the White House. When McClellan got there he found the President sober, somewhat distraught. There was, said Lincoln, an ugly matter to talk about. It seemed to be so ugly that Lincoln hardly knew how to begin; McClellan finally had to prompt him by suggesting that, the uglier the matter was, the better it would be to speak about it frankly and openly. So Lincoln got into it.

People had been telling him, said the President, that there was much more to McClellan's plan of campaign than met the eye. The big objection to taking the army down the bay by water had always been the fear that Washington would be left uncovered, defenseless against a sudden Rebel stab—and a successful stab into the heart of the capital would mean the end of everything, the Southern Confederacy a real nation, the mystic union of the states dissolved forever. Now, the President went on, it was being alleged, by men whose suspicions had to be taken into account, that McClellan was planning to leave the capital unprotected on purpose—that he was inviting the Rebel stab, that he wanted the Confederacy to win, that he was moving according to stealthy and treasonous design.

McClellan sprang to his feet. He could permit no one, he said, to couple his name with the word "treason." Years later he wrote that he spoke "in a manner not altogether decorous toward the chief magistrate." The President, said the general hotly, would have to retract that expression. Lincoln tried to soothe him; the expression was not his, he was merely telling McClellan what others were saying. For his part, he did not for a moment believe that McClellan had any traitorous intent. (Which should have been fairly obvious; otherwise, he was simply an imbecile to retain him in command of the army.) McClellan's feathers, having been thoroughly ruffled, were slow in settling back into place. He remarked that the President might well be careful thereafter in his use of language. Again Lincoln insisted that the offensive accusation was not his; according to McClellan, Lincoln apologized, and the general finally took his leave, wondering how "a man of Mr. Lincoln's intelligence could give ear to such abominable nonsense."

Abominable nonsense it surely was. Lincoln was no fool and Mc-Clellan was no knave, but they sat in the White House and this monstrous accusation that the commander of the nation's armies was a traitor had to be taken up and considered, dark suspicion being the order of the day. What a change had taken place since the great days of the previous July when all anybody wanted was to entrust the country's fate to the young general from the West; what an unendurable tension must have been in the air, to make such an interview possible!

Yet McClellan seems to have missed the real point. He left the White House feeling that Lincoln himself more than half believed the charge, and he was naturally full of deep resentment. But somehow he never realized that the mere existence of this calumny must profoundly affect his own course of action. Here again was that unknown quantity in the military equation he had to solve, and there was nothing in the West Point textbooks to prepare him for it. How does a general beginning a great campaign act, when the men he must report to suspect that he wants to lose rather than to win?

The one thing that is obvious is that such a general does not act the way generals ordinarily act. For McClellan was not a general out of the military histories, solving according to the best scientific principles the problem which the civil power had handed him; he was a man living and working in an era so desperately beset that "abominable nonsense" could be believed by responsible public officials. What might be permitted to a general in another era would not be permitted to him. The existence of the deep and terrible suspicion and uncertainty which lay back of Lincoln's summons to the White House would have to be as much a factor in McClellan's calculations as would the strategic plans of General Joseph E. Johnston. Lincoln had tried to tip him off, and McClellan could see only that a great injustice was being done.

Events were not kind to him in the days immediately after the interview. Johnston's retreat became known. McClellan marched his troops down to Centreville and Manassas, partly for pursuit, in case

the Confederate withdrawal offered an opening to strike, and partly
to give the army practice in cross-country movements. Viewed by a
military eye, the defensive works which Johnston had evacuated
were indeed strong; but in the gun emplacements there remained
large numbers of harmless wooden cannon—trimmed logs, painted
black and upended over wagon wheels, menacing-looking from a
distance but incapable of killing Union soldiers. Whether these
Quaker guns had been there all the time or had simply been put in
place by the wily Confederate leader (a man fertile in deceptive ex-
pedients) to cover the withdrawal, no one knew—or much cared:
for the obvious fact was that in nearly eight months of command
McClellan had never got his troops close enough to Johnston's lines
to find out whether Johnston's guns would shoot or not. The story
of the wooden guns went all across the land, and there was an uproar: so *this* was the danger that had kept the great Federal army
immobile all fall and winter. Proper military caution was made to
look like plain timidity. It was unfair, but there was no help for it;
and the men who doubted McClellan's desire to win a victory had
one more item to record against him.

None of this depressed the army itself. The boys enjoyed the
march, even though they had strong remarks to make about the
depth of the Virginia mud; and while they were innocently eager
to go into action they were willing to agree that the general who kept
them from assaulting the wicked entrenchments around Manassas
had done them a good turn. McClellan deftly reminded them of this
in a spirited address issued at Fairfax Courthouse in mid-March.
After telling the soldiers that he was about to take them "where you
all wish to be—the decisive battlefield," and remarking that the time
of inaction was over, he declaimed:

"I am to watch over you as a parent over his children; and you
know that your general loves you from the depths of his heart. It
shall be my care, as it has ever been, to gain success with the least
possible loss; but I know that, if it is necessary, you will willingly
follow me to our graves for our righteous cause. . . . I shall demand of you great, heroic exertions, rapid and long marches, desperate combats, privations perhaps. We will share all these together;
and when this sad war is over we will return to our homes, and feel

that we can ask no higher honor than the proud consciousness that we belonged to the Army of the Potomac."[1]

The army was definitely going to move. With the Manassas line evacuated, it was going to go to the peninsula rather than to Urbanna, and the transports had been assembled. Lincoln was deeply dubious about the move, and he laid down as the unalterable guiding principle that, no matter where the army went or what it did, Washington must not for one minute be left unprotected. The steps he took to make certain of that point were not especially pleasing to McClellan. He first removed McClellan from command of all the armies and limited him to command of the Army of the Potomac. (There may be some reason to suppose that this was simply a precautionary measure—that Lincoln intended to have a long look at McClellan in actual field operations and was ready to restore him to supreme command if everything went well. No one was named to the vacated job for some months. McClellan, of course, could see it only as a demotion, and it rankled.)[2] As a second step, having stipulated that the capital must at all costs be left secure, Lincoln called a council of McClellan and his corps commanders—those new corps commanders, in whose selection McClellan had had no voice—and asked them what force they, as military men, thought adequate to insure such security.

The assembled generals, after taking thought, reported that forty thousand men "in and about Washington" would be adequate. Lincoln accepted this figure, stipulating in addition that a substantial guard must also be left in the neighborhood of Manassas, to keep the Confederates from reoccupying their abandoned works. This was agreed to. There were men enough to provide this force and still leave McClellan ample means for his campaign on the peninsula. But while the men were going aboard ship and the first of the transports were dropping down the Potomac, high strategy began to get all snarled up in a question of arithmetic, and the way was paved for failure.

The plan was somewhat complicated. McClellan was going to take upward of a hundred thousand men down to Fortress Monroe for the march up the peninsula. In addition, McDowell, commanding one corps of the army, was to assemble thirty thousand-odd at Fredericksburg, whence he could take them down to join McClellan

whenever McClellan summoned him. Up in the Shenandoah Valley
there was General Banks, whose primary function was to keep the
Rebels from cutting the line of the Baltimore and Ohio and erupting
into Pennsylvania. Banks had more men than he needed, the situation
in the valley being quiet, so he was instructed to leave part of his
men there and bring the bulk of them over to Manassas. Farther
west, in the mountain country where McClellan had made his first
reputation, there was General John Charles Frémont, the famous
"Pathfinder" of California, the darling of the abolitionists, and a hero
to all ardent Republicans.

Lincoln was already aware of Frémont's irritating eagerness to
make high policy for the administration, and he knew that he was
hopelessly inept as an administrator, but he had not yet discovered
that the man was also completely incompetent as a soldier; and
Frémont's mission was to slide southwest through the mountains in
the general direction of eastern Tennessee, where there was strong
Unionist sentiment that seemed worth cultivating and where there
was also an important Confederate railway line that might profitably
be seized. To give Frémont added strength, and also to put under
his congenial command more of the German regiments in which anti-
slavery sentiment ran so strong, Lincoln detached Blenker's division
from McClellan and sent it west; he admitted to McClellan that
political pressure which he felt unable to resist was chiefly responsible
for this, and McClellan bitterly wrote it down as a sign that the
President was weak-willed.

Everybody was beginning to move. Banks was bringing the larger
part of his force east over the Blue Ridge, to take station at Manassas;
McDowell was grouping his own divisions and preparing for the
advance; the leading elements of the Army of the Potomac were
going ashore at Fortress Monroe—going down from the ships on
long, floating bridges and jumping into waist-deep water to wade the
last few yards—and if the administration was making things difficult
for McClellan, it was at least satisfied with the layout. And just then
Stonewall Jackson upset the entire schedule.

What Jackson actually did, measured by any quantitative standard, was not really very important. He commanded fewer than four
thousand men at that time, and he had them camped in the Shenandoah Valley to keep an eye on the Yankee invader. He got wind of

Banks's move eastward, underestimated the numbers Banks was leaving behind, and moved boldly forward to the attack, hitting Shields's division at Kernstown, a few miles south of Winchester, one afternoon late in March. Since Shields had twice as many men as had been supposed, Jackson was roundly whipped and he had to retreat up the valley after a savage little battle which Shields's boys recalled later with vast pride—theirs was the only outfit in the Union Army which could say it had licked Stonewall Jackson in open fight. As a military spectacle this battle of Kernstown was notable chiefly because it showed what an iron-hard man Jackson was: he cashiered his best general afterward for withdrawing his men without orders. To be sure, the men were totally out of ammunition and were badly outnumbered, and the withdrawal was just plain common sense, but that made no difference: the retreat hadn't been ordered at headquarters, and anyhow, as Jackson sternly remarked, the men could have stayed and used their bayonets. This was rough on the general who got cashiered, but it had a notably stimulating effect on all other generals who served under Jackson thereafter.[3]

Seemingly, all that had happened was that Jackson had made an ill-advised attack and had been beaten. But the effects, by a roundabout route, were felt afar off. Both McClellan and Banks agreed that if Jackson was strong enough to attack Shields he had better be watched pretty carefully, since the Rebels obviously had more men in the valley than had been supposed—neither general dreaming that Jackson had made his attack with so small a force. So it was decided that Banks must keep his entire command in the Shenandoah Valley, a strategic area of considerable sensitivity; and troops were drawn from the fortifications around Washington to occupy the Manassas-Centreville line which had originally been designated for Banks. That done, McClellan took a last look around, concluded that everything was under control, wrote a final note to the War Department showing how the troops which he was not taking with him were disposed, and set off for Fortress Monroe.

Now the dispositions he had made, as revised because of the battle of Kernstown, were certainly adequate to give Washington the protection Lincoln had insisted on. As a military man McClellan could honestly feel that he had done all that was required. But he wasn't called on to satisfy military men on this point; he had to satisfy politicians who were more than ready to see spooks under the bed, and from their point of view he had left himself wide open to the charge of ignoring his instructions—this general whom the Secretary of War and the administration leaders on Capitol Hill had already accused of treasonous intent. The actual figures are a bit dull, but they need to be looked at for a moment:

McClellan had left some seventy-three thousand men behind, as his note showed. Banks in the Shenandoah had slightly more than thirty-five thousand, some eighteen thousand were at Manassas and Warrenton, thirteen hundred or so were along the Potomac downstream from Washington, and there were approximately eighteen thousand in the Washington garrison. Total, seventy-three thousand and odd—enough, surely, to carry out the letter of his instructions?

Not to Lincoln's eyes, which were the eyes that had to be satisfied. To begin with, some ten thousand of these men were Blenker's Germans, bound west to serve with Frémont and hence out of calculation as far as the defense of Washington was concerned. In addition, when he figured the strength of Manassas and Washington, McClellan had included certain troops which were due to come in soon from the state capitals but which had not yet arrived; what Lincoln soon discovered was that there were actually less than thirteen thousand in the Washington garrison, almost all of them untrained men. As far as he could see, instead of the forty thousand men who were to be left "in and about Washington" there were only these almost useless thirteen thousand, plus the handful downstream, plus the troops at Manassas and Warrenton. All in all, after carefully counting heads, Lincoln could find fewer than twenty-eight thousand soldiers in and near the capital.

To this, of course, McClellan would have replied that the thirty-five thousand under Banks in the Shenandoah should properly be added, since they were near enough and strong enough to make their presence felt. But it was asking a little too much to expect Lincoln and the Cabinet to see it that way under the conditions then prevailing. To civilian eyes the force in the Shenandoah was a long way off. No one in Washington could forget that the Union had had a fairly strong army in the Shenandoah when McDowell was beaten at Bull Run: its presence in the valley had not served to protect Washington in July 1861, and an unmilitary President and Cabinet could hardly be blamed for feeling that things might be no different in April of 1862. Add it up any way he tried, the President could only conclude that McClellan had not done what he had been told to do. The capital was not properly defended.

The reaction to this was immediate. McClellan had barely started up the peninsula when he was officially notified that McDowell's corps at Fredericksburg had been withdrawn from his command and would get its orders hereafter direct from Washington.

Which meant that his campaign started under a great handicap. McClellan himself got off the boat at Fortress Monroe on April 2 and found that he had on hand—disembarked, equipped, and ready to go—some fifty-eight thousand men: five infantry divisions, a scattering of cavalry, and a hundred guns. He at once started them up the roads toward Yorktown, with instructions that the rest of the army was to follow as soon as it arrived. The first thing he discovered was that someone had steered him wrong about those sandy roads on the peninsula. Instead of being sandy they were uniformly of pure gumbo mud, with hollow crowns so that they collected whatever water might be coming down; and the weather turned rainy, so that the roads quickly became bottomless beyond anything in anybody's imagination. Guns and wagons sank to the axles and beyond. One officer wrote later that he saw a mule sink completely out of sight, all but its ears, in the middle of what was supposed to be a main road. He added that it was a rather small mule.[4]

McClellan's next discovery was that the Rebels had dug a line of entrenchments running completely across the peninsula from Yorktown, on the York River, to the mouth of Warwick Creek, on the James. Emplaced in these lines they had several dozen heavy naval guns (acquired a year earlier through capture of the United States navy yard at Norfolk) plus a number of fieldpieces, and they appeared to have all the infantry they needed. The approaches to this line led through swamps and tangled woodlands, and every foot of road would have to be corduroyed before guns could be brought up. Bewiskered old General Heintzelman, leading the advance, reported—somewhat hastily, it would seem—that a direct assault was out of the question. McClellan decided there would have to be a siege. Under his original plans he would simply have brought McDowell down from the north to take the Rebel works in the rear, thereby forcing their immediate evacuation, but McDowell was no longer his to command. To get past these lines McClellan would have to go straight over them, and that appeared to be a matter for the slow, methodical, step-by-step process of digging parallels, moving up heavy guns, and getting everything ready to blast the Rebel works off the face of the earth by sheer weight of gunfire.

Concerning which there was to be great argument, then and thereafter. When McClellan got his first look at the Yorktown lines, the Confederate force there was under command of General John B. Magruder, who had no more than twelve thousand men and who felt the lines to be faulty both in design and in construction. Magruder was never especially distinguished as a combat general, but in his idle moments he had considerable talent as an amateur actor, and he now called on this theatrical ability to help him. He marched a couple of regiments through a clearing, in sight of the Federal advance guard, double-quicked them around a little forest out of sight, and then marched them through the clearing again— over and over, like a stage manager using a dozen adenoidal spear carriers to represent Caesar's legions. The device worked, and Heintzelman reported the Rebels present in great strength with many more coming up.

Joe Johnston, hastening down in advance of his own troops to have a look at the situation, appreciated the dodge but felt it could hardly be relied on forever. He galloped back to Richmond in dismay to report that the lines were quite untenable: McClellan could get through or around them any time he wanted to make a real push, to put the whole Confederate Army there would simply be to put it in a trap, best to evacuate at once and prepare to fight near Richmond. Davis and Lee overruled him, on the ground that McClellan's advance must be delayed as long as possible. Evacuation would mean the fall of Norfolk, and that would mean the loss of the famous ironclad *Virginia* (ex-*Merrimac*), which drew too much water to come up James River to Richmond and was too unseaworthy to go out beyond the Virginia capes into the open ocean. Also—and far more important—the entire Confederate Army was about to undergo complete reorganization. The men had originally enlisted for twelve months, and their terms were just now expiring. Conscription was going into effect and none of the manpower would actually be lost, but for some weeks there would be complete turmoil, not to say chaos, with officers being shifted or replaced all over the lot and with every regiment having a grand reshuffle. It would be almost impossible to maneuver or to fight in the open until that was over. So Johnston, much against his will, took his army down to Yorktown to stave off the advance as long as he could. When he got it there his pessimism deepened; to Lee, in Richmond, he wrote that "no one but McClellan could have hesitated to attack." But the attack was not made. Instead there was a gradual, painstaking building up of Federal strength in preparation for a final, overwhelming artillery bombardment. Johnston knew that when this assault came he would have to leave, but mercifully (to his eyes) the assault was long in coming.

Lincoln and his Cabinet knew nothing of Johnston's trepidation or of the disorganized condition of the Confederate Army. What they did know was that McClellan's army was simply sitting down before the enemy's works, waiting. They had already begun to suspect that McClellan was a general who moved very slowly; now, knowing little or nothing of the obstacle in front of him, knowing only that weeks were passing without an advance, they found suspicion hardening to certainty. This was hard to bear; for men who already doubted McClellan's good faith and loyalty it was quite impossible to bear in silence. The clamor against McClellan deepened, became a clamor against Lincoln for keeping him in command. Lincoln tried to give McClellan an understanding of this increasing pressure as a factor which McClellan would have to keep constantly in mind when he made his plans; tried to show him that it was a pressure which, political conditions being what they so regrettably were, even the President of the United States might finally be unable to resist. On April 9 Lincoln wrote him: "And once more let me tell you, it is indispensable to *you* that you strike a blow. I am powerless to help this." He concluded the letter by assuring McClellan that he would sustain him as far as he could: "but," he added, "you must act."

This was easy enough to order from Washington. McClellan might be pardoned for feeling that he was being second-guessed in an unconscionable manner by men who knew nothing about what he was really up against. To say "Strike a blow!" was simple enough; actually striking it meant sending young men through swamps and almost impassable second-growth timber against enemies amply protected by heavy earthworks, and even at this date it is not easy to say that such an attack would have won. The men of the Army of the Potomac were to learn that when the Army of Northern Virginia was once properly dug in, on ground where it proposed to linger, it could be uncommonly hard to move. Joe Johnston might have been wrong and McClellan might have been right. The trouble was that being right wasn't quite enough. Nothing was going to satisfy Washington except results, and Washington was not going to wait too long for them, either. Nobody was going to be reasonable about anything.

2. The Voice of Caution

In the end, the big show at Yorktown never came off. The army waited in front of the Rebel lines for a month, nerving itself for the great test; and then one morning the pickets sent back word that the enemy trenches were all empty. Patrols went groping forward and confirmed the news: nobody there, nothing left but a few dozen heavy guns which the Confederates had been unable to move—not wooden guns this time, as at Manassas, but sure-enough cannon of the navy model, too heavy and cumbersome to be taken along by an army that proposed to make speed on the retreat. McClellan had finally completed his approaches, and his siege guns and heavy mortars were all in position. In one more day he would have been ready to open a shattering bombardment, and Johnston had decided not to wait for him.

So instead of the great drama of a ten-mile cannonade and a mighty assault by storming battle lines extending beyond vision, what the army got was a floundering pursuit and a nasty, confused rear-guard action in damp thickets and flat, dismal fields, where reality was limited to the actions of the nearest dozen comrades, where men fell killed or maimed without seeing the enemies who struck them, and where it was quite impossible for most of the men to get any sort of idea of what was actually going on.

The troops got across the empty entrenchments and moved up the unspeakable roads, with a dull rain coming down, over a soggy level country of soaked fields and gloomy woods and scattered farms, none of them like the familiar green farms of home; and far up ahead the men heard the noise of fighting, and the roads were hopelessly clogged with mired wagon trains, and Phil Kearny came galloping up to force a way for his troops. He stormed mightily, put two officers of the train guard under arrest, demanded that the wagons be tipped over off the road or burned where they stood—he was ordered up to fight and he would have the road regardless. Admiring, the soldiers listened while he roared: "I will show you what fire *feels* like unless you set the torch to your goddamned cowardly wagons!"[1] And his men finally got by the tangle, passing open fields wherein huge bodies of troops were unaccountably standing quite idle, and went plodding unevenly forward until they got up within range; and there, in an obscuring haze of smoke, the boys formed line as well as they could and blazed away in the general direction of the bursts of rifle fire that were coming out of the woods and fields a couple of hundred yards away.

Some of them were formed out in the open and some in dense forest, full of fallen trees and bothersome underbrush; the enemy was a more or less invisible presence—an area, like a hazy, indistinct wood lot, or a smoky line of rail fence with briars grown up around it, from which came little spitting streaks of flame, and whistling bullets that made an unnerving noise. The 55th New York, with its baggy red French pants quite rain-soaked, got into a stretch of timber where the soldiers could hear the Rebels but could seldom see them. They stayed there for three hours, firing as fast as they could load, using up sixteen thousand rounds of ammunition, and—as the colonel discovered later, when he went out to examine the ground in front of them—killing just fifteen Confederates. The colonel made a rough calculation and figured that perhaps a hundred and fifty more of the enemy, at a maximum, had been wounded: where had all those bullets gone, anyhow?

Hooker's men discovered that the neat, formal battle lines of the training camp didn't seem to make their appearance in actual combat. Instead everybody got behind a tree or a stump or a boulder if he could possibly manage it. One private, thus protected, called out to a buddy: "Why don't you get behind a tree?" and heard the buddy shout: "Confound it! There ain't enough for the officers!" Men

of the 5th New York went up to the front through a little cemetery
where were buried Confederate soldiers who had died during the
preceding winter. The little burying ground was full of graves, but
over the gate someone had tacked a sign: "Come along, Yank,
there's room outside to bury you."[2]

The firing at last died down and the Rebels drew off. It was only a
rear-guard action, after all, and Joe Johnston had no intention of
keeping his men there to make a finish fight of it. Then the Federals
at the front heard a great cheering behind them, and they knew what
caused it and joined in it lustily; and there, spattering across the damp
fields, came General McClellan, blue coat all stained with mud, a
glazed covering over his cap, his staff riding furiously in a vain effort
to keep up with him. McClellan rode all along the lines, each regiment got a chance to cheer, and night came down on the army's first
battlefield.

Among the higher echelons the battle gave rise to grumblings.
Heintzelman, who had command of the advance, asserted that Sumner was on the field with thirty thousand men and failed to get any
of them into action, and the two generals argued the matter hotly.
McClellan, coming up as the fight ended, got the idea that most of
the fighting had been done by Hancock's brigade, which had indeed
done well, though it got into the action late. He built his dispatch
around that part of the battle, telegraphing Stanton that "Hancock
was superb," and thereby roused the anger of Hooker and Kearny,
whose troops had suffered far more than had Hancock's, and who
felt that the major general commanding was purposely slighting them.
But in the end that was straightened out, and the army went toiling
on up the peninsula, while Johnston pulled his own troops close to
Richmond and made ready for a finish fight.

The men were beginning to get their officers sorted out by now.
Hooker and Kearny were already known to the whole army. They
had fire, ardor, the quality which writers of that generation called
"dash"; like McClellan, they insisted that members of their staffs be
brightly uniformed and excellently mounted, and they made their
rounds as McClellan made his, with a fine brave clattering and show,
very martial and stimulating for young soldiers to see. They built
high morale in their troops. Hooker's division, going into action in
this rear-guard fight at Williamsburg, saw a regiment of cavalry

stringing out its mounted line in the rear, according to army custom, to check stragglers and round up laggards. Angrily the men set up the shout: "Hooker's men don't need any cavalry to make *them* stay in front!"

All kinds of stories were beginning to cluster about Kearny. His headquarters wagon carried a fancy carpet for his tent, a special camp bed imported from Europe, and a huge stock of imported wines and brandies; and he had a field kitchen on wheels, on the French army model, which always kept up with his headquarters so that he could have hot meals. (Kearny was independently wealthy and could afford such frills.) Officers of the New Jersey brigade claimed that he had happened along once just as they had taken over a planter's house for brigade headquarters. They found in the parlor a decanter of whisky which they hesitated to drink, fearing that it had been poisoned—army rumor said that was a favorite Rebel trick. Kearny listened as they explained their fears, then poured out a thumping major general's dose and drank it down. "If I'm not dead in fifteen minutes," he said, turning to mount his horse, "go ahead and drink all you want."[3]

The men were getting acquainted with Edwin V. Sumner, too; a tough old man with white hair and beard, who had been in the army since 1819 and had a tremendous booming voice. They called him "Bull Sumner," or "The Bull of the Woods," and liked him even though he was a great martinet, with old-army ideas about discipline. He was a formidable-looking general, now in command of an army corps, always erect and proud in the saddle, and he never quite realized that the army was any different now than it had been before the war, when he spent almost forty years in slow progress from second lieutenant to colonel. Youthful Major Thomas Hyde of the 7th Maine was sent to deliver some report to him one day; Sumner looked him over from head to foot and finally burst out: "You a major? My God, sir, you will command the armies of the United States at my age, sir!"[4] After one searing fight the 66th New York showed up under temporary command of a second lieutenant, who happened to be the senior surviving officer. Sumner looked at the boy and instead of seeing the frightfully cut-up regiment he saw only that a shavetail had a colonel's job. He shook his head and said: "If I had found myself, when a second lieutenant, in command of so fine a regiment, I would have considered my fortune made."[5] He was still the cavalry colonel of the Indian-fighting plains army, with all the defects and virtues which that implies; not qualified for proper corps command, but a fine old smoothbore for all that.

Then there was Heintzelman, another corps commander, very much like Sumner in many ways; an old-timer, an Indian fighter from the plains, rugged and stiff and hard, still a regimental officer at heart, brave enough for a dozen men but unfitted for any problem of leadership that extended beyond men he could reach with his own voice. Like Sumner, he could put Johnny-come-lately officers in their place. When Oliver Otis Howard first reported to him, proudly bringing in his new 3rd Maine Regiment, Heintzelman looked the men over and said to Howard: "You have a fine regiment; they march well and they give promise for the future; but they are not well drilled—poor officers but good-looking men!"[6] Heintzelman had been in the middle of the fighting at the first battle of Bull Run, where he had been badly wounded.

The Pennsylvania troops were beginning to know George Gordon Meade, even though he was as yet only a brigadier, and a new one to boot. He was a tall, grizzled man with a fine hawk's nose and a perfectly terrible temper, which would lash out furiously at any officer who failed to do his job. A war correspondent considered that Meade, on horseback, looked "like a picture of a helmeted knight of old"; one of his staff complained that he rode "in a most aggravating way, neither at a walk nor a gallop but at a sort of amble." He was notably cool under fire; sat his horse with his staff, one time, surveying the situation through glasses, while Rebel bullets whizzed wickedly all around and the staff earnestly wished the general would finish his reconnoissance so they could get out of there; lowered his glass at last, took in the staff's nervousness, and remarked sardonically that maybe they had better leave—"This is pretty hot; it may kill some of our horses." He lacked the ability to inspire troops; once remarked, without any rancor, that he had heard his men call him "a damned goggle-eyed old snapping turtle." He never drew the kind of cheers that Hooker and Kearny always got, but he kept his command in good shape and had a sharp eye for details. He was wholly admirable as a man, with no trace of self-seeking; would reach high place in the army, do his hard job to the best of his ability, and indulge in no argument or complaint when promotion and praise finally missed him.[7]

One by one the officers were beginning to stand out, for this virtue or that. Already noticeable was an extremely junior second lieutenant on McClellan's staff, to which he had recently graduated from Kearny's: a broad-shouldered six-footer with a slim waist and muscular legs, fresh out of West Point, known as one of the finest horsemen in the army—George Armstrong Custer, who was to survive hot actions of this war only to die under the guns of the Sioux on the Montana hills. Custer was familiarly known as "Cinnamon" because of the cinnamon-flavored hair oil he used so liberally; wore long glistening curls and a show-off uniform with a tight hussar jacket and black trousers trimmed with gold lace, and looked, as another staff member remarked, "like a circus rider gone mad." Like Confederate George Pickett, who also wore curls, and Jeb Stuart, who was also a show-off, he was all soldier. He first impressed himself on McClellan's attention when the general, accompanied by his gilded staff, rode up to the bank of the Chickahominy for the first time and remarked, "I wish I knew how deep it is." The staff exchanged glances, looked thoughtfully at the dark water, began to make estimates. Custer spurred up to the bank, muttering "I'll damn soon show him," and rode his floundering horse out to the middle of the river, where he turned in his saddle and called out, "That's how deep it is, General."[8]

But standing out above all of these, of course, was McClellan. He had become the general who could do no wrong, in the soldiers' eyes, and they blithely overlooked things that would have earned bleak hatred for any other general. Officers of an anti-slavery cast noted suspiciously that McClellan took uncommon pains to protect Rebel property from the moment the army landed on the peninsula. One of them complained bitterly that provost guards were to be found protecting every farmhouse, stable, kitchen garden, and well, and asserted that they stood guard even over the rail fences, regarded by soldiers as prime material for campfires. "I have seen our men," protested this officer, waxing warm, "covered with dust and overcome by the heat, try in vain to get water from wells overflowing, from which stringent orders drove them away because the supply of water for a Rebel family might be diminished. I have also seen them, covered with mud and shivering with the rain, prevented by orders of the general-in-chief from warming themselves with the fence rails of dry wood which were ready at their hands, because the cattle of a Rebel farmer might get out and eat the grass in his fields while he was rebuilding his fences."⁹ Another officer noted indignantly that the farmers admitted that McClellan protected their property against the men of his army better than Johnston had protected it against the Confederates.

But somehow all of this made no difference whatever. Up around Fredericksburg, at that time, General McDowell was winning the lasting enmity of his own soldiers by his care to protect civilian property; here was McClellan, right in the presence of the enemy, doing the same thing and rising even higher in popularity. How account for it? How, except by saying that one man had the magic touch and the other lacked it. But the magic touch is not entirely a mystery, even so. McClellan took extraordinary pains to make his men feel that they were good soldiers and that the commanding general knew they were good and was grateful to them for it. After the fight at Williamsburg he was prompt to visit the regiments which had been engaged and thank them for their fine work. In one newspaper dispatch we see him visiting, in succession, the 5th Wisconsin, the 7th Maine, and the 33rd New York, making a brief, graceful little speech to each: "I have come to thank you for your bravery and good conduct in the action of yesterday. . . . You acted like veterans! Veterans of many battles could not have done better!"

Then there was the time, a few days later, when the 4th Michigan, plus a squadron of cavalry and a few engineer troops, made a reconnoissance across the Chickahominy and collided with Rebel troops, driving them off and losing some eight men in killed and wounded while doing it. McClellan visited the regiment as soon as it got back to camp; in front of the men he shook hands with the colonel and congratulated him, shook hands also with a captain who had been mentioned for gallant conduct. Then he turned to the men themselves, not with a little speech this time but with an easy, friendly comradeship. "How do you feel, boys?" There was a quick chorus of "We feel bully, General!" Still casual, McClellan asked them: "Do you think anything can stop you from going to Richmond?" And the regiment yelled "No!" in a shout that Jefferson Davis might almost have heard, off beyond the swamps in the Confederate capital; and McClellan gave the men his gay little salute and galloped away, leaving the Michigan boys feeling almost as if they had married him.[10]

And if there is a mystery in the way McClellan's men could ignore his care to protect Rebel property while McDowell's men found the same care unforgivable when McDowell displayed it, there is equal mystery in the way those actions were regarded back in Washington. The anti-slavery Republicans, already suspecting that McClellan proposed to sell out the Union, found in his protection of Confederate civilian property strong corroboration of their suspicion. Yet McDowell, who was doing exactly the same thing, was the chosen hero of these men. They rejoiced when he was taken out from under McClellan's command and would have liked to see him in McClellan's place; to their minds he was the shining example of what a general ought to be. Again, the answer, to an extent, may be much the same in reverse: one general had the touch for dealing with political persons at the capital, and the other general did not.

Indeed, that queer riddle of what a general could and could not do goes even farther. At the time when McClellan was slowly pursuing Johnston up to the edge of Richmond, General Halleck, out in the Mississippi Valley, was pursuing General Beauregard, who was retreating down into northern Mississippi after the dreadful, mangling fight at Shiloh. McClellan was pursuing very cautiously. His reasons might have been good or they might have been bad; in any case, his pursuit was slow, which was a damning mark against him with Secretary Stanton and the radical group in Congress. Halleck, who had more of a numerical superiority over Beauregard than McClellan had over Johnston, was edging forward with a sluggish deliberation that made McClellan's advance look precipitate, averaging hardly a mile a day and entrenching up to the ears every evening. Yet Halleck, like McDowell, was a hero to Stanton and his crowd, rising in favor daily, destined before long to be brought to the capital as supreme commander. McClellan's hesitation was proof of his disloyalty; Halleck's hesitation, twice as pronounced and far less justified, was simply ignored—by everyone except Lincoln, who felt that both men ought to hurry a little more.

All of this proves nothing much except that the nation was running a high fever and had a touch of delirium now and then. But the effects were tragic, for in the end it was those amateur soldiers down among the Chickahominy swamps who were going to have to pay for it. The relations between a general and his superiors can't be poisoned in just one direction; the poison works both ways, and if the radicals believed McClellan to be a villain, McClellan returned the sentiment with interest. His letters to his wife no longer showed merely the irritation and nervous strain of a young general who was being crowded a little too hard; they reflected downright fury, coupled with a conviction that the civilians who were working against him were scoundrels. The detachment of McDowell's corps was "the most infamous thing that history has recorded." When the President urged McClellan to break the Confederate lines, "I was much tempted to reply that he had better come and do it himself." Long before the siege of Yorktown ended he was writing: "Don't worry about the wretches; they have done nearly their worst, and can't do much more. I am sure that I will win in the end, in spite of all their rascality. History will present a sad record of these traitors who are willing to sacrifice the country and its army for personal spite and personal aims." He spoke of his predicament—a man with "the Rebels on one side, and the abolitionists and other scoundrels on the other"—and a few days later wrote that "those hounds in Washington are after me again."

The main collision with the Confederate Army had not yet taken place. Yet already there had developed this amazing situation: the Secretary of War, plus leading administration senators, believed the general commanding the army to be a traitor who would rather lose than win, and the general, in his turn, believed that *they* were traitors who would rather see the country lose than permit him to win. That word "treason," so rare in American history, was dancing back and forth like a tennis ball. Misunderstanding between the home office and the man in the field had become complete; had developed a breach not to be healed, with hatred and anger and terrible suspicions that would be incredible were they not all part of the record. Like a steaming, choking fog, this atmosphere hung over the army, poisoning its chances, staining its banners. Whoever was most at fault, this heavy intangible lay across the army's path, ready to take the lives of boys who had had no part in it and who would die not knowing that it existed.

Now there could be only one road to salvation for McClellan, for his soldiers, and for the country itself. McClellan had to win. Victory in front of Richmond would swallow up everything, leaving the hot accusations and recriminations as dry bones which the historians might pick over at their convenience. The weight that rested on the broad shoulders of the young general was heavier than he knew. For if the war itself was the supreme test of democratic institutions— "testing whether . . . any nation so conceived and so dedicated can long endure"—the fighting of it was testing the qualities of democracy's leaders. The unfathomable strength of the country had been placed at these leaders' disposal. If that strength could be used properly, the war could be won quickly and the country would be spared much suffering. If it could not, if leadership failed to measure up, then the people themselves would have to carry the whole load, and everything they had hoped for in this bright land of promise would depend on their finding within themselves enough endurance and heroism and patience to meet the unimaginable agony which their leaders had been unable to spare them.

To which it may be said that McClellan did the best he could and that he worked under terrible handicaps, some of which he created himself. One of them—in some ways, considering his own inner nature, the most damaging of all—was a matter of detail: selection of the wrong man to run G-2, Army Intelligence—Army Secret Service, as they called it in those days.

G-2 was handled by a short, stocky, bearded man who was known around headquarters as Major E. J. Allen, and who in reality was Allan Pinkerton, famous head of a famous detective agency in Chicago. First of the country's great private detectives, Pinkerton had genuine talent, coupled with a certain flair for publicity; he had handled many jobs for railroads, as a railroad man McClellan had known him before the war, and when McClellan became a major general he called in Pinkerton and put him in charge of military intelligence, espionage and counterespionage alike. Pinkerton built up quite an organization, and in the long run what McClellan knew about the Confederate Army that was facing him was mostly what Pinkerton told him.

As it turned out, Pinkerton was a fine man for running down train robbers and absconding bank cashiers but was completely miscast as chief of military intelligence. He had energy, courage, administrative ability, and imagination—too much imagination, perhaps, for he was operating in an era when a fine hairline separated the ridiculously false from the frighteningly true. Early in 1861, while he was still in civil life, he had gone into Maryland at the bidding of the president of the Philadelphia, Wilmington and Baltimore Railroad, who had heard of secessionist plots to sabotage the railroad leading to Washington and wanted to find out about them. Pinkerton planted operatives in Baltimore, Havre de Grace, Perryville, and other places, and presently reported that he had discovered not merely a plan to sabotage the railroad but a widespread plot to kill Abraham Lincoln before his inauguration.

Pinkerton's men lived with this plot; after the war, in his memoirs, Pinkerton told how they got into secret societies, mingled freely with secession-minded Baltimore blue-bloods, cultivated beautiful friendships with Baltimore belles "under the witching spell of music and moonlit nature," and uncovered a far-reaching, elaborately detailed conspiracy for assassination. It is something of a comedown to find that the leader of this conspiracy was a barber in a Baltimore hotel —the build-up about Southern aristocrats leads one to expect a Virginia Carter, at the very least—but so it was. One of Pinkerton's men sat in on a secret meeting where men drew lots to see who would actually do the killing, another one came up with information about plans for cutting telegraph wires and destroying railroad bridges (presumably so that the North could neither learn of the assassination nor do anything about it after it had happened), and Pinkerton submitted a full report while Lincoln was on his way east.

The report caused much excitement, quite naturally: it was either a perfect script for a theatrical thriller or an astounding revelation of deadly plotting which simply had to be frustrated. As a final result Lincoln changed his plans: slipped quietly out of Harrisburg and came into Washington by sleeping car a day ahead of time, thereby arousing much derision and criticism.

Lincoln seems never to have been quite certain whether Pinkerton had saved his life or induced him to make a fool of himself, and nobody since then has been able to be quite certain about it either. The plot itself, as Pinkerton described it in his book, has a wildly improbable sound, with the conspirators behaving in an impossibly stagy manner; but just as one concludes that the thing simply could not have been true, there comes the recollection that when the 6th Massachusetts Infantry passed through Baltimore just after Fort Sumter there was precisely the kind of riot that Pinkerton's men had mentioned as a projected stage setting for the murder of Lincoln: a riot in which angry men fired real guns and in which both soldiers and citizens of Baltimore were killed. Also, in 1865, a plot quite as harebrained as anything Pinkerton's men reported did result in Lincoln's death. Men were living in the center of a lurid and improbable melodrama in those days, and if it was fantastic, it was very real; just as the tale strains credulity to the breaking point somebody is killed—by pistol or by knife or by hangman's noose. They might have exaggerated their stage effects in a most inartistic manner, but their guns were not loaded with blank cartridges.

At any rate, Pinkerton took over McClellan's military intelligence problem and applied real ingenuity to the job. His men went fanning out behind the Confederate lines to some purpose; one of them actually got in with Confederate Secretary of War Judah Benjamin, in the days before McClellan took his army down to the peninsula, and carried a pass signed by that official and became a member of a Rebel counterespionage outfit that was trying to catch Yankee spies. Each of Pinkerton's men carried a pass through the Union lines written in invisible ink which became visible only on exposure to sunlight. They got in touch with a secret organization of colored men in Richmond, the Loyal League, who met in cellars and attics and whose password was "Friends of Uncle Abe," and who helped the Union operatives in and out of the Rebel capital. One agent even joined a Confederate spy team and became a courier, carrying messages back and forth between Richmond and Baltimore—the messages, of course, all being copied for McClellan before delivery. Timothy Webster, the greatest of Pinkerton's spies, was finally caught and hanged. Other spies disappeared, as spies do in wartime; but all in all they had perfected a genuinely remarkable system for getting forbidden information out of Richmond.

But the incomprehensible part about it all is that with this elaborate espionage network, operated by experts and staffed by brave and intelligent men, the information that was brought to McClellan was so disastrously wrong. Disastrously, because it made the Rebel armies appear more than twice as large as they really were and because McClellan believed it and acted on it. Pinkerton's spy system was well organized, bold, successful—and McClellan would have been infinitely better off if he had had no spy system whatever.

While McClellan was waiting in front of Yorktown, Pinkerton proudly gave him a report showing that Joe Johnston had from 100,-000 to 120,000 men in line against him. This information, he said, came from "officers of their army and from persons connected with their commissary department," where they were issuing 119,000 daily rations—the only instance in history, probably, where the Confederates were accused of overfeeding their men. Pinkerton added that it was safe to assume that his estimate was under rather than over the real figure. Now the only trouble with that was that Johnston at the time had barely 50,000 men on the peninsula. He was shockingly outnumbered and he knew it, and the only hope that he could see was for Davis to strip the Southern coast line bare of troops, no matter what the cost locally, and reinforce him with every available man so that he might be brought near enough to McClellan's numbers to have some chance of fighting a successful battle.

Some six weeks later, on the eve of the fateful Seven Days' Battles in front of Richmond, Pinkerton assured McClellan that Lee had more than 180,000 men facing him; probably many more, since the agents had actually identified 200 regiments of infantry and cavalry, eight battalions of independent troops, five battalions of artillery, twelve companies of independent infantry and cavalry, and forty-six additional companies of artillery, and the Rebels undoubtedly had many other outfits present whose designations could not be learned. After the fighting was over, Pinkerton reported that he was satisfied the Rebels had at least 200,000 men in the battles, of whom 40,000 were casualties. Long after the war Pinkerton continued to insist on the accuracy of his figures; he had obtained them, he said, "from prisoners of war, contrabands, loyal southerners, deserters, blockade-runners and from actual observations by trustworthy scouts."

So to all the other handicaps that beset him—distrust at the War Department, troops withheld, strategic plans countermanded—McClellan had this final, ruinous handicap to contend with: heavily outnumbering his opponent, he was led to believe that his opponent heavily outnumbered him. He and his staff took Pinkerton's word as gospel. This was hard to do sometimes; McClellan's headquarters had a fairly accurate count on the number of divisions in the Confederate Army, and that number could not conceivably account for the vast hordes of men supposed to be present. But instead of questioning Pinkerton's figures, headquarters simply assumed that those divisions were "grand divisions"—oversized groupings of two or more army corps, such as Burnside set up later at Fredericksburg—and continued to believe that from 180,000 to 200,000 armed Rebels were in front of them.

It was just tragic that this had to happen to McClellan, of all generals; for this man must always listen, at the last, to the voice of caution, the subconscious warning that action may bring unlooked-for perils, the lurking fear that maybe some contingency has not been calculated. Before he can act, everything must be ready, every preparation must be made, every possible mischance must be provided for. Now, with his own career and the nation's fate balanced on a knife's edge, with Lincoln quietly warning him that he must at all costs *do* something, there is this final deterrent: conducting an offensive campaign deep in enemy territory, he finds himself to be dreadfully outnumbered—so much so that only a very great daring would make an offensive possible at all. Almost everything he did and failed to do in this campaign can be explained by that one fact.

3. Tomorrow Never Comes

With all of these difficulties of espionage, counting numbers, and weighing risks, the men in the ranks had nothing to do. They never even saw their own army all in a mass, to say nothing of the enemy's. In this broken, wooded country the Rebels were usually visible, even in battle, only as small detachments. The men could see that they were edging up toward Richmond. Heintzelman's corps was close enough so that the men could hear the church bells ringing in the capital, and if progress looked slow to people back in Washington, it seemed fast enough to the men who had to tramp along the bottomless roads.

There had been too much rain, and in the lowlands the humid heat was an oppressive weight to boys from the North, and a general air of weather-beaten tarnish began to appear on brigades that had been natty and polished when they came off the transports. Officers who had been bright with gold-embroidered shoulder straps, red sashes, and plumed felt hats became more somber-looking; many of them bought privates' uniforms and sewed the insignia of rank on the shoulders, having learned that in a fight or on the picket lines the enemy believed in picking off the officers first. Regiments that had worn fancy leggings or gaiters began to discard them, the men finding that it was more comfortable to roll the trouser leg snug at the ankle and haul the gray regulation sock up over it. Paper collars had disappeared, and the men in the Zouave regiments, which wore gay red pants and yellow sashes, topped by Turkish-style fezzes, began to wonder if these uniforms were not both unduly conspicuous on the firing line and excessively hard to keep neat.

When the actual fighting came it was desperately confused, and even the generals seem to have had trouble understanding what was happening. Finding McClellan with part of his army south of the Chickahominy and part of it north, Joe Johnston waited for a heavy rain to swell the river and make passage between the two wings more difficult, and then fell hard on the part that was south of the river. The battle of Seven Pines, or Fair Oaks, which resulted was bloody enough, with five or six thousand casualties on each side, but it was indecisive. The diaries and memoirs of the men who fought in it cannot be put together to make a picture of anything but a series of savage combats in wood and swamp, where wounded Confederates drowned in stagnant pools and wounded Federals were burned when powder flashes set fire to dead leaves and underbrush insufficiently dampened by rain; and there seemed to be no tactical plans other than a simple urge to get the men up into places where they could shoot at each other.

Things went badly, and Bull Sumner was ordered to bring his corps over from the north side and get into the fight. He marched his men up to the flooded river to find that the makeshift bridge the engineers had built was ready to float off downstream—center part loose from its underpinning, foaming water all about, engineer officer coming up to tell him that the bridge was unsafe and it was impossible to use it. Sumner roared: "Impossible? Sir, I tell you I *can* cross! I am ordered!" And cross he did, too, although his men waded knee-deep in water that swirled over the planking. The muddy roads on the south side were so soupy that his artillery almost sank out of sight, and the gunners worked up to their waists in mud and water to inch the guns along. When they finally got them into action, each recoil drove the wheels down into the soft ground nearly to the hub caps.[1] Sumner sent the 5th New Hampshire in on a counterattack after a Confederate charge had been repulsed. The regiment's colonel, a former newspaper editor named E. E. Cross, who had lived in the Far West and had fought both Mexicans and Indians, exhorted the men: "Charge 'em like hell, boys—show 'em you *are* damned Yankees!" As the regiment advanced, Cross fell wounded. He propped himself up on an elbow, and when some of the men came over to help him he told them: "Never mind me—whip the enemy first and take care of me afterward."[2]

General William H. French, stout and apoplectic, with a face so red that he always looked as if his collar were choking him, set out to gallop boldly along the line of his brigade as it prepared to go into action, and dropped completely out of sight in muddy water when his horse bounced into what had been thought to be a mere surface puddle. The general came up blowing and swearing mightily, while the brigade shouted with laughter. A lieutenant in the 57th New York was told by his colonel to lead his company off through the wood to get an enfilade fire on a Confederate detachment in front. He did so, and the Rebels withdrew, new troops being, as Longstreet indelicately remarked, "as sensitive about the flanks as a virgin." When the metropolitan papers came to camp a few days later the lieutenant discovered that this modest little exploit had become a grand charge, led by a general, which had driven the enemy with great slaughter. Reflecting on the way a small story can become great, the lieutenant wrote: "If the history of past ages is as much tainted as the history we are now making—then alas poor Yorick!"[3] Toward the end of the battle, some anonymous Federal put a bullet through Joe Johnston's shoulder, and a moment later a shell fragment hit the general in the chest and unhorsed him: and thus the one significant result of the battle—its significance not guessed at the time—was that Robert E. Lee became commander of the Army of Northern Virginia.

After the battle things were about as they had been, except that a horrible stench hung over the whole broad valley. McClellan felt that the attack had been intelligently conceived—"It is the only smart thing Joe Johnston has yet attempted. It was *very* smart," he was quoted as saying—and he busied himself getting the roads improved so that heavy guns could be moved up, while he saw to it that his lines were protected by proper entrenchments, and he moved more and more of the army over to the south side of the river. He had each division lined up for dress parade a few days after the battle, and a stirring order from himself was read to the men:

"Soldiers of the Army of the Potomac! I have fulfilled at least a part of my promise to you. You are now face to face with the Rebels, who are held at bay in front of their capital. The final and decisive battle is at hand. Unless you belie your past history, the result cannot be for a moment doubtful." The proclamation went on and on, assuring the soldiers that they were better fighters than their enemies, and concluding: "Soldiers! I will be with you in this battle and share its dangers with you. Our confidence in each other is now founded upon the past. Let us strike the blow which is to restore peace and union to this distracted land. Upon your valor, discipline and mutual confidence the result depends."[4]

It is written that the soldiers cheered when they heard these fine words, and they probably did—although during the next fortnight or so there seemed to be very little in their general situation to cause much cheering. The weather was muggy and enervating, the mosquitoes were a trial, sick lists grew dolefully long as malaria and other complaints appeared, and there was no escape whatever from the frightful smell. Many dead had gone unburied in the swamps and thickets, others had been given a mere covering of earth which the rains quickly washed away, and anyway, nobody had warned these boys that one of the worst things about war is the way it stinks. All any individual soldier could see was the uninspiring acre or so in his immediate vicinity, and the adventure and excitement of war seemed to have shrunk to sullen endurance of boredom and acute physical discomfort.

But morale did not sag as much as might be supposed. McClellan's prose might be purple, but it did create self-esteem. The men felt that they had done well at Williamsburg, and Seven Pines had been twice as big a fight and they had got through it all right; they had passed the test of battle and nobody had ever licked them, and they began to feel that they were seasoned old soldiers. They had learned about artillery fire, which was so terrifying to new troops and, for that matter, not exactly pleasant even to old ones. Shell and solid shot fired by smoothbore cannon were perfectly visible in flight and always seemed to be coming right at the observer: a completely unnerving thing until one got used to it. Spent shot, rolling along the ground, was deceptively dangerous; it looked harmless but wasn't, and some of Hooker's men told how an officer had put his foot out to stop such a ball and had lost his leg thereby. Shells were unpredictable. One man had picked up a dud and it had exploded in his hands—yet by some freak he was not badly hurt; at other times one shellburst might kill half a dozen men. A boy in a New Jersey regiment wrote that going under fire for the first time was pretty terrible: some of the men in his company, he said, were so scared they simply fell to the ground as if shot, picking themselves up sheepishly a bit later as nerve returned. He recalled one boy who went up to the firing line like a man in a trance, moaning over and over: "O Lord, dear good Lord!"

Regiments which were still equipped with the old Harper's Ferry muskets were disgusted with these weapons: ancient flintlocks which had been altered to percussion firing, with a rifled tube inserted in the barrel. They had a tremendous kick and were considered almost as dangerous to the user as to his target. Members of the Pennsylvania Bucktails—the 13th Pennsylvania, recruited in the Northern mountains and used to good rifles—found that the kick arose from the fact that the original bore of the musket was deeper than the tube; they remedied matters by ramming two or three dimes solidly down the bottom of the barrel, filling the chamber and preventing "back action."

The Frenchmen of the 55th New York, who knew things about cookery that most of the American boys did not know, felt that there were worse places to camp than the Chickahominy Valley. The place was full of bullfrogs, and the regimental mess reveled in frogs' legs "as large as and more delicate than the legs of chicken." The venturesome Frenchmen also learned that the blacksnakes found in the swamps were good to eat, although the other regiments were slow to copy them. A number of the generals, gifted with some political awareness, took the trouble to write to the state governors, telling them how well their troops had behaved.

New troops came in. McDowell's corps was still an independent command, but McCall's division was detached from it and joined McClellan via Fortress Monroe, while a division under General William B. Franklin came along a bit later. McClellan got permission to form a couple of new army corps and name the commanders himself, Porter and Franklin getting the posts; now he at least had two corps commanders of his own selection, and he began to feel encouraged. Day by day he got his lines closer in toward Richmond, bringing up the heavy guns that were to have blasted Joe Johnston at Yorktown, defending himself every step of the way with earthworks.

Lee concluded that McClellan's attack would be a matter of regular approaches and siege guns, as at Yorktown, and confessed that the Confederates could not play that sort of game. Longstreet wrote long afterward that the Yankee plan was sound "and would have been a success if the Confederates had consented to such a program." McClellan kept Porter and his new corps north of the river—McDowell was under orders to march down from Fredericksburg and join him, and it was important to extend a hand to him. A little later Stonewall Jackson erupted again in the Shenandoah Valley, and McDowell was held back on panicky orders from Washington, and Porter's corps was left extending its welcoming hand into empty space. Once again McClellan felt betrayed; but the long rainy spell had ended, the sun was drying the roads, and the prospects for an advance looked good.

Indeed, McClellan was whistling quite a hopeful tune just then. A week after the Seven Pines fight he wired Secretary Stanton that he would be "in perfect readiness to move forward and take Richmond the moment McCall reaches here and the ground will admit the passage of artillery." Three days later he assured the Secretary: "I shall attack as soon as the weather and the ground will permit." Four days after that he wired: "After tomorrow we shall fight the Rebel army as soon as Providence will permit."

Nor was this just his official version. To his wife McClellan wrote with equal confidence. In mid-June, a few days after McCall's division had checked in, he assured her that he would begin his advance "on Tuesday or Wednesday," when the roads would be thoroughly dry and all the temporary bridges over the river would be complete.

He gave her a peek at his strategy; as Lee and Longstreet had suspected, he would try to get his heavy artillery far enough forward to blast an opening for his troops, driving the Rebels from their trenches by gunfire, moving his soldiers up to the abandoned works, bringing the siege guns up close again, shelling the city, and then making a final assault. He was confident because of the soundness of his plans and because of the ardor of his men: "I think there is scarcely a man in this whole army who would not give his life for me, and willingly do whatever I ask. . . . I think I can so use our artillery as to make the loss of life on our side comparatively small." Two days later he was writing that "we shall soon be on the move," and four days after that he confided that he would strike his first great blow "within a couple of days." Two days after this letter he wrote: "I expect to be able to take a decisive step in advance day after tomorrow."

Day after tomorrow was slow in coming. For more than a fortnight the opening of the grand assault was always just a day or two ahead; and always there were additional last-minute preparations to make, final repairs to be put on the roads and the bridges, new dispositions to be made in the arrangement of the waiting troops. He believed that he was outnumbered, even with the reinforcements; Pinkerton's reports on Lee's overwhelming strength were detailed and explicit. Everything must be completely ready before the army can move, the last perfecting touch must be added, when the fight begins there must be nothing left to chance. And this was not only because of the overmatching strength of the enemy. There was Washington to think of; men there were trying to wreck the country, and if anything went wrong in the army the nation's ruin would be complete.

McClellan went into detail on this subject in a letter to his wife. The grapevine told him that Secretary Stanton and Secretary Chase had quarreled, and that McDowell—whom, by this time, McClellan had written down as a conniving schemer who wanted the top command for himself—had given up his old alliance with Chase and was now cultivating the Secretary of War. Sadly (and, heaven knows, understandably enough) McClellan wrote: "Alas! poor country that should have such rulers." He added: "When I see such insane folly behind me I feel that the final salvation of the country demands the utmost prudence on my part, and that I must not run the slightest risk of disaster, for if anything happened to this army our cause would be lost." A day or two earlier he had written her that recent messages from Lincoln and Stanton had quite an amiable tone, but he added acidly: "I am afraid that I am a little cross to them, and that I do not quite appreciate their sincerity and good feeling. *Timeo Danaos et dona ferentes*. How glad I will be to get rid of the whole lot!"

From all of which it is clear that the whole miserable combination of sorry circumstances—estrangement from his superiors, false reports from his intelligence section, and dreadful suspicion and enmity clouding all the channels between army headquarters and Washington —had piled up too much of a load for this man's army to carry. The great assault on Richmond must be delayed to the last moment because caution, above all other qualities, is the one great essential: caution in the face of powerful foes in front, caution because of treachery and foul conspiracy in the rear. Everything that had been building up through nine long months of disillusionment, every paralyzing force created by the willingness of public men to believe the worst of their fellows, was pressing on him now to make him wary, to compel him to think twice and thrice before taking a step, to people the starless darkness of imagination with just-discernible dangers that must be prepared for in advance. One false move and the country itself is lost! No wonder that tomorrow never quite comes, that there is always a final safeguard to erect.

And while all of this was going on, Lee, half a dozen miles away, was exerting all his strategy to keep McClellan immobile, with Porter's corps extended helplessly north of the river, until by the use of every possible expedient the Rebel army could be made strong enough to hit that one weak spot. McClellan could not be attacked south of the river—his works there were too strong, Lee's numbers were too few —but at all costs he must be kept from asserting the initiative and beginning his remorseless siege-gun advance, for if that were once well begun Richmond would inevitably be lost. And so while McClellan waited and made ready (he was writing: "I have a kind of presentiment that tomorrow will bring forth *something—what*, I do not know"), Lee brought Jackson down from the valley and with an audacity that still looks breath-taking assembled three fourths of his outnumbered army on the north side of the Chickahominy to assault the troops of Fitz-John Porter.

Lee was barely in time. Even while he was grouping his forces for the grand attack, McClellan was at last beginning to move. Orders filtered downward, from army to corps to division; and on the morning of June 25, Kearny's and Hooker's men left their knapsacks in camp, formed line of battle, and started out toward the Rebel capital.

They passed the advance entrenchments along the old Williamsburg road, where the Seven Pines fighting had centered, and set out across the gloomy country in a drizzling rain. There was a broad open field, and on the far side there was a stretch of timber, with the ground all swampy underfoot, the black tree trunks coming up in damp twilight out of dead pools and spongy earth. At the near side of this wood the infantry halted, and the guns in the rear opened up and raked the timber. Rebel batteries off in the distance answered back, and for a time there was a spirited artillery duel, noisy but not doing much harm to either side. Then the gunfire died away, the soldiers moved forward into the wood, and the skirmish line began to shoot at the Rebel pickets and waited for the main line to come up; and there was a slow, mean fire fight in the wood, where wounded men had to be propped up against trees or stumps, while they waited for the stretcher-bearers, lest they drown. In the end the Rebels withdrew—they were not present in any great strength—and the Northerners cleared the wood and got to the far edge, where they looked out upon a broad clearing which held the dark earthworks of Lee's main line of defense. The drizzly afternoon wore away and word came to dig in; the new line was a mile or more in advance of the old one, and it looked as if the big push for Richmond had begun.

But next day everything slowed down. The Confederate Army seemed to be in a high state of nervous irritability. The Yankee picket line had to be strengthened until it had almost the weight of a regular skirmish line; here and there, up and down the front, little detachments of Rebels would attack in a rush, drawing off again when the fire got hot. All along the line, throughout the day, there would be sudden bursts of artillery fire as Confederate batteries sprang into unexpected activity, fired a dozen rounds, and then subsided into silence. Nothing ever quite developed into a real battle, but it was not what could be called quiet, either.

Through gaps in the trees, in the rare spots where one could get a look into the distance, lines of marching troops could be seen. There was an ominous sense that something was building up, as if

thunderheads were piling high on the horizon, about to break forth
with wild lightning. Off to the north, muffled by distance and dead
air, there was a steady rumble of gunfire during the afternoon and
evening, but three quarters of the army was south of the river and
the boys had their minds on what was right in front of them; what
was going on north of the river didn't sound much different from
what was going on right here, except that there were fewer breaks
in it. The men spent an uneasy night on the line; a number of regimental bands were kept playing long after dark, the brisk tunes
dying away in the somber pine flats. Some of the men heard vague
talk of a victory won north of the river.

Next day there was more of the same, with a slightly increased
tempo. The outposts in front of Hooker's division could hear a good
deal of frenzied activity beyond the Rebel picket posts. Southern officers were shouting constantly, apparently trying to get large bodies
of troops formed up and moved; the Northerners could hear repeated commands—"From the right of companies to rear in a column.
. . . Right face. . . . Don't get into a dozen ranks there. . . . Why
don't they move forward?" Something big was in the wind; yet afterward the outposts remembered that they had been mildly puzzled:
with all that shouting and maneuvering going on, they didn't seem
to hear the actual tramp of marching men.[5]

At the various headquarters the men noticed a good deal of coming and going, with aides and mounted orderlies constantly galloping
in and galloping out. To the northward, as the afternoon of June 27
wore away, a huge cloud of dirty white smoke went rolling up the
sky, and the men who saw it wagged their heads: lot of guns being
fired over there across the river, to make all that smoke. The atmosphere was heavy, and for some reason it affected the acoustics; in
places the roar of that battle could be heard plainly, in other places
there was no noise at all, even though the firing was abnormally
heavy and was taking place only a few miles away. Along in midafternoon Slocum's division of Franklin's corps was pulled out of
camp and was sent hiking along the miserable woods roads to the
Chickahominy bridges. In this division was the 16th New York, gay
and bright with a fancy touch to its uniforms; the colonel's wife had
sent down a huge bale of brand-new straw hats, one for each man,
and the whole regiment was wearing them. A few days later it was

noticed that every straw hat was gone. The men found that when they got into action—which they did, as soon as they crossed the river—the hats turned them into perfect targets, and they lost 228 men before they discarded them.

And still nothing much actually seemed to happen south of the river. When night came word trickled back that there had been a terrible big fight over on the north side; but on the south side, although they had been right on the edge of an all-out battle for two days, it never quite developed. The Rebel lines continued to bristle, and in one or two spots the Confederates came out with what looked like pretty serious assaults (although it did seem that they were repulsed rather easily) and the Rebel artillery was ready to make a nuisance of itself at a moment's notice all along the front. And then next morning there was more galloping and coming and going than ever, around corps and division and brigade headquarters, and great black clouds of smoke went up as men set fire to various supply dumps. While the boys were puzzling over this, they were marched up to wagon trains and told to load up with salt pork, hardtack, coffee, and the like; and they noticed that instead of having definite quantities measured out for them, the way it usually happened, they were simply given all they could put in their haversacks. The 5th New York was directed to wagons containing the brigade's knapsacks; instead of being allowed to look for their own, the men were told to take the first ones they came to and be quick about it, and as soon as every man had one, provost guards set fire to the rest. The 4th New Jersey, to its amazement, got sudden orders to dig pits and bury all knapsacks. Up and down the camps the men began to look at each other and mutter: "It's a big skedaddle."

It was. By a painfully narrow margin Lee had beaten McClellan to the punch. Leaving twenty thousand men on the south side of the river—twenty thousand to face some seventy thousand Federals—he had marched everybody else to the north side for a vicious attack on Porter's isolated corps. The first blow, struck at Mechanicsville on the afternoon of June 26, had been rebuffed, but the next day Lee threw fifty-seven thousand men at Porter's new lines back of Boatswain's Swamp, near Gaines's Mill, and after a crunching, grinding struggle in which some Confederate brigades were all but torn apart he broke

the lines in and drove Porter back across the river, forcing McClellan
to order a retreat.

The ominous noises which the Federals south of the river had
been hearing in their front throughout the two days were simply the
contribution of the Confederacy's distinguished amateur actor, General Magruder, who was having just the kind of time for himself he had
had at Yorktown. Magruder had been exceedingly nervous. His twenty
thousand men were all that stood between McClellan and Richmond
for forty-eight hours, and Magruder was very much aware that if
the Yankees once caught on there was little he could do to keep
them from rolling right over him and going into the capital. So he
had played the old Yorktown game with every variation he could
think of. Regiments had gone out into open spaces to march and
countermarch and look numerous; officers had stood in the woods,
shouting commands to completely imaginary brigades; picket lines
and patrols and advanced batteries had been kept effervescently
active, as if making final preparation for a huge attack. In the end,
it had worked.

It had worked, partly because Magruder skillfully imposed on the
Union commanders facing him—or on most of them, at any rate—
and partly because McClellan and his corps commanders were already convinced that Lee had close to two hundred thousand men
on the field, so that it was possible for him (as it seemed to them) to
use sixty thousand or more to crush Porter north of the river and still
retain overwhelming numbers on the south side. Pinkerton's fantastic
reports, believed like the writ of the true faith, were worth a couple
of army corps to the Confederacy that week. Heintzelman, under
whom the preparatory advance had been made on June 25, had
been worried all along; told McClellan that night that he hardly
thought he could hold his advanced position unless he could be reinforced, and when the attack on Porter was at its height and Mc-
Clellan messaged his corps commanders to see if they could possibly
spare any men, Heintzelman replied that in a pinch he could send
two brigades, "but the men are so worn out I fear they would not
be in a condition to fight after making a march of any distance."
Sumner had been imposed on equally; his messages back to army
headquarters told about "sharp shelling" all along his lines and predicted a heavy attack on his right. Franklin notified the commanding

general that the enemy was "massing heavy columns" in his front, and the remaining corps commander, Erasmus Keyes (who was to drop into military oblivion at the end of this campaign), reported it would take all the men he had to hold his position.

McClellan stayed in his headquarters tents, pitched under trees on a pleasant hill by a farmhouse a mile or more south of the river, his uniform coat folded over a camp chair, standing in the open now and then to listen to the firing, totting up the reports from his subordinates. The situation on both sides of the river, he wrote, was so ominous that he could not tell where the real assault was going to be made; at night he wired Stanton that he was "attacked by greatly superior numbers on this side."

He did not visit the battlefield. Indeed, in all of the great fights which the Army of the Potomac had while under his command, McClellan stayed close to headquarters. His physical courage was high enough—many of his soldiers have commented on his extreme coolness when making reconnoissance under fire—but there seems to have been in him a deep, instinctive shrinking from the sight of bloodshed and suffering, an emotional reaction to the horrors of the front lines that was more than he could stand. He wrote to his wife, about this time, that "every poor fellow that is killed or wounded haunts me," and the army's profound confidence that McClellan was anxious to spare his men's lives was solidly based on fact. He was anxious to spare them, and when he had to send them to their deaths he did not like to watch it. So, in any case, he remained at headquarters, where he took counsel of his caution: dangerous to send heavy reinforcements north of the river lest the lines to the south be broken; dangerous to strike boldly for Richmond, on the south side, lest disaster take place on the north; hold on, then, as well as may be, on both banks, make Porter's fight a holding and delaying action, withdraw to some good point on the James River, get reinforcements, refit, and prepare for a new offensive at a later date. On the night the Gaines's Mill fight ended McClellan called in his corps commanders and gave orders for the retreat.

The corps commanders agreed that this was the only thing to do. Not so the two firebrand division commanders who held the lines nearest Richmond, Phil Kearny and Joe Hooker. They were indignant at the news, for it appears that Magruder had not fooled them very much; they knew the Rebel lines in front of them were thin and they believed they could and should be broken at once. They pressured their corps commander, Heintzelman, and late in the evening dragooned him into taking them to see McClellan, accompanied by a few of their brigade commanders. At the headquarters tent Kearny demanded permission to make an attack at once. He and Hooker, he said, could march straight into Richmond: if the general felt that they couldn't stay there (the disaster north of the river had broken the army's supply line) they could at least free the fourteen thousand Union prisoners of war in the city, disrupt all of Lee's strategic plans, and get back safely. Hooker agreed; in his opinion one division could do the job, but to play safe they might use two—let Kearny make the attack with his division and let Hooker support him with his. Heintzelman, under pressure, said that he felt the generals' proposal was sound.

McClellan was unmoved and insisted that the retreat must take place as ordered. Fiery Kearny was indignant; a staff officer who was present wrote later that Kearny denounced McClellan "in language so strong that all who heard it expected he would be placed under arrest until a general court martial could be held, or at least he would be relieved of his command." That didn't happen, however, McClellan apparently feeling that the thing to do with Kearny was to let him blow off steam every now and then, and the officers went back to their posts.[6]

So the retreat was made. It was handled, the books say, with consummate skill. Lee never could quite find the opening he needed to turn the withdrawal into a rout, and if the general situation gave him a chance to destroy the invading army, McClellan prevented him from taking advantage of it. But to the soldiers themselves the picture was never clear. They had no maps; they only knew that after spending some weeks in their fortified lines they were on the march again, in a confused country where none of the narrow, winding roads appeared to lead anywhere in particular, and there seemed to be a good deal of fighting mixed in with all the marching.

A member of the 40th New York wrote that, when his regiment was pulled out of the line and marched off to become part of the rear guard, the men thought for quite a time that they were actually advancing on Richmond to capture the place and end the war. The

1st Minnesota found itself drawn up in a field near a country railroad station, supporting a Rhode Island battery. A Confederate battle line emerged from a wood a mile away and advanced to the attack. Old General Sumner came galloping up, his white head bare in the wind, his hat clenched in one fist; he put the 5th New Hampshire and the 88th New York in beside the Westerners, and they went out into the field and drove the Rebels back. A little later a brigade of New York troops charged and captured a section of a Rebel battery, spiking the guns when they found they couldn't get them away. Then, after dark, the Federals moved off down a road through a swamp. Long afterward they learned that they had had a part in the battle of Savage Station, in which the army's retreat was effectively protected, but at the time it was just a fight; and if the rest of the army was in retreat, the fact was not especially evident to the high private.

Indeed, old man Sumner himself got a little mixed up about it. When evening came he felt that he had won a victory, and when orders came to withdraw he cried: "I never leave a victorious field —why, if I had twenty thousand more men I could crush this rebellion." Staff pointed out that McClellan's orders to withdraw were explicit, and Sumner finally obeyed, complaining: "General McClellan did not know all the circumstances when he wrote that note. He did not know that we would fight a battle and gain a victory."[7]

The 15th Massachusetts knew a retreat was going on, but had fun anyway: their job was to destroy supplies that couldn't be moved, and they had a freight train of ammunition to get rid of. The railroad bridge over the river had been wrecked, so they simply set the train on fire, started it moving toward the ruined bridge, and sat back to enjoy a grand combination of train wreck, bonfire, and Fourth of July fireworks.

Night came on, and two weary batteries of regular artillery—Batteries A and C, 4th U.S.—went to sleep in a wood, dead-tired. Next morning the skipper of the two batteries, Captain George W. Hazzard, heard bugles sounding reveille from fields which he knew had been unoccupied the night before. He got up to look about—Rebels all around him, no sign of any Union troops anywhere. He gave hurried orders: hitch up quickly but quietly and get the guns away before the Rebels catch on, move at a walk so as not to make any more noise than can be helped. He finally rejoined the army, bringing with him a battalion of infantry stragglers who, like the artillerymen, had gone to sleep in the wood ignorant that the army was pulling out. A similar adventure befell three infantry regiments—104th Pennsylvania and 56th and 100th New York, which fought in front of Savage Station and weren't notified that everybody else was leaving. They were nearly captured, made an all-night march along bewildering roads, got entirely lost, and at last came stumbling into camp three days later, mad enough to bite the heads off nails. It was reported that they were the only regiments in the army which failed to cheer McClellan after the army was safely back on the James River.

That same night Colonel William Averell of cavalry came riding up to McClellan's field headquarters all excited: the roads between the army and Richmond were empty and the army might go there unopposed. McClellan smiled grimly and shook his head; the roads would be full enough tomorrow—which was entirely correct, since Lee was bringing every man he had to press the retreat, and the moment for a counterblow had passed. To Averell, McClellan added: "If any army can save this country it will be the Army of the Potomac, and it must be saved for that purpose."[8]

Next day there was bitter fighting late in the afternoon around a crossroads settlement named Glendale, where Lee led Longstreet's and A. P. Hill's divisions up to the middle of McClellan's long column and tried to break it in half. The worst of the fighting fell to McCall's Pennsylvania division, which met Longstreet's attack head-on, and there was deadly hand-to-hand fighting around a Union battery, with Northern and Southern boys savagely braining each other with clubbed muskets, driving bayonets into human flesh. A Confederate officer slew two gunners with his sword, went down when three Federals fell on him with bayonets. Captain Hazzard, who had been left behind the night before, was killed, and General McCall was taken prisoner, and the Pennsylvanians finally broke and went to the rear fast. Going back, they met Hooker's division coming up. A Pennsylvania colonel, riding to the rear faster than the soldiers thought necessary, tearfully implored the oncoming troops to "hurry up and save my poor men." Hooker's boys jeered at him, yelling:

"Dry up, you old fool—pull your eagles off—go home to your mother."[9]

The 1st Minnesota was one of the regiments sent in to repair the break. Sumner came riding up as they formed their battle line; reining up in front of them, he called out: "Boys, I may not see all of you again, but I know you'll hold that line." Then he waved his hat, and they moved forward. Kearny, holding on over to the right and looking for any help he could get—both Longstreet and Hill were attacking now, and the safety of the whole army was in the balance—sent staff officers back to bring up the first troops they found. These turned out to be General George Taylor's brigade—1st, 2nd, 3rd, and 4th New Jersey, which used to be Kearny's own: the same which had been lawlessly robbing an orchard when Kearny first took command, disciplined by his own hand, still famous foragers. (Kearny once told Lincoln, in effect: If you really want to capture Richmond, put a hen house and a peach orchard on the far side and the New Jersey brigade on this side—they'll get through all the fortifications of Richmond to get the hens and the peaches.)

Staff officers pulled up, all in a lather: General Kearny had lost a battery and wanted the old brigade to help him get it back—would they come? Brigade let out a yell and swung into line almost before the orders could be given; swarmed across a field, chased assorted Rebels out of a sunken road, and recaptured the guns, boasting afterward that they got there before Kearny's own men arrived. . . . It was this brigade's General Taylor, incidentally, who had been momentarily confused at Gaines's Mill a couple of days earlier. He had led his brigade up as reinforcement and was met by one of the French princes serving on McClellan's staff, loaned that day to Fitz-John Porter and riding to Taylor with Porter's orders. In the excitement of the fight the young prince began shouting the orders in French, of which Taylor knew not a word. Turning to his staff, Taylor demanded: "Who the devil *is* he, and what does he want?" A staff officer who could speak French finally showed up, and the puzzle was straightened out. . . . Somewhere in this Glendale fight was another Union battery which the Rebels attempted to capture. As the Southerners advanced, the battery commander told his men to stand firm; a grim Yankee gunner, looking at the tattered foe, remarked:

"I ain't goin' to git from no such ragged fellers as they be," and the battery held its ground.

After the Glendale fight there was more marching. The army was continuing its retreat to the James River, where gunboats and fleets of supply steamers promised safety; but to the soldiers it was just another night march rather than a retreat. They had been hurt badly at Glendale, but when the line was broken they had restored it, and at the end of the day the Rebels had been beaten back, and the men felt they had done well. They were confirmed in this opinion next day, when part of the army and most of the artillery lingered on Malvern Hill, where Lee's last attempt to destroy the Army of the Potomac was decisively repulsed. This fight was a field day for the gunners; Rebel artillery couldn't seem to get into position to do much damage, the roads being few and Lee's staff work defective, and solid rows of Union fieldpieces, lined up hub to hub at the top of a long slope, broke the charging Confederate infantry to bits. The Confederate General D. H. Hill noted after the battle that more than half of all the casualties Lee's army suffered that day were caused by artillery fire—an unprecedented thing for that war, where the infantry musket was the big killer.

Rain set in again during the night, and in the early morning Colonel Averell, who had the rear guard, found his little command alone on the broad hilltop. Behind him, in the low country where the muddy lanes led to the banks of the James, the army and its heavy wagon trains were struggling along to the most cheerless of camps, with the dark gunboats anchored offshore. In front of him there was a heavy mist, blotting out the terrible slope where the battle had been fought. In the mist he could see nothing, but out of it came a pulsating, endless wave of pitiful sound—the agonized crying and moaning of thousands of wounded boys who had been lying on the ground, unattended, all night long. By and by the sun came up and the mist thinned, and presently he could see the battleground, one of the most horrible sights of the war. Five thousand men lay there, covering the ground like a ragged carpet that lived and made incoherent sounds and, here and there, moved dreadfully. "A third of them were dead or dying," he wrote, "but enough of them were alive and moving to give the field a singular crawling effect." The ambulance parties came out to do what they could for the mangled men, and at one side of the field Stonewall Jackson had details out hastily burying the dead: he expected to have to fight over that ground and he felt it would hurt morale to make his men advance past so many corpses. And Averell finally recalled his rear guard and went down the reverse slope of the hill to join the rest of the army in the new camp at Harrison's Landing.[10]

4. *Pillar of Smoke*

It was either the end of everything or a new beginning. The fields by the river were sodden, and the sky kept dripping rain as if the bottom had fallen out of all the clouds, and the fine hopes of a year of unlimited promise had been ground under in mud and bloodshed and the nameless horrors of the battlefields. Weary with a week in the saddle and with the unutterable loneliness and weight of command, McClellan took over the house and grounds of Berkeley Plantation for his headquarters. The house was a fine one, spaciously built of brick in the colonial days, but he did not care to occupy it. Ambulance details had got there ahead of him, and it was filled with desperately wounded men—"a gruesome place," one officer confessed after visiting it—and the commanding general's tents were pitched on the lawn some rods away from the dwelling.

Lee had failed in his big effort to surround and demolish this army. It was safe here on the river, with gunboats on guard in the stream and with a fleet of transports and supply steamers ready to bring new men and equipment. Yet the army was isolated, just the same; in the war, but curiously out of it for the moment, as if it had been stranded here on the mud flats by some strange ebb tide, damaged by wind and wave, inert, its future wholly problematical. For it was an army which, by now, drew its spirit and its tone from its commander, and its commander was walled away from the world. It was not for nothing that he identified himself, in the purple prose of his army proclamations, with the lives and well-being of his men. The seven days of fighting which had torn the army so cruelly had torn him in the same way. The emotional tension thus created in him had led to a blind and angry reaction: the army had suffered; suffering, it had failed; the failure could only be due to betrayal by those who should have supported it. At any cost, its commander must show that the cause of this suffering was not himself. In the heat of this feeling he had sent Secretary Stanton a passionate telegram after the fight at Gaines's Mill—a strange, taut message, explaining how evil the fortunes of the day had been and bitterly disclaiming any responsibility for the defeat. With only ten thousand more men, he cried, he could yet gain the victory; the battle just fought would have been so different if Washington had not held back the few reinforcements he had asked for. He continued:

"I feel too earnestly tonight. I have seen too many dead and wounded comrades to feel otherwise than that the government has not sustained this army. If you do not do so now the game is lost."

And then the final, bitter sentences, calculated to burn all bridges —or, conceivably, not calculated at all, just slipping out like a cry of unendurable passion:

"If I save this army now, I tell you plainly that I owe no thanks to you or to any other persons in Washington. You have done your best to sacrifice this army."

Passionate or cold, McClellan was a man of clear intelligence and he knew as well as anyone that an army commander does not say that to the Secretary of War, and through him to the President, without forcing a showdown. Everything said and done in Washington, after this message, would be judged by McClellan in light of the fact that those words had been spoken. Presumably he would be cashiered; if not, it could only mean that Washington was knuckling under and was tacitly confessing its guilt as well—continuing him in command and leaving so flat an accusation unanswered! But what McClellan never knew was that neither Lincoln nor Stanton ever saw that bitter, accusing conclusion until many months later. A War Department functionary, decoding dispatches from army headquarters and preparing them for the Secretary, found his eyes popping out when he read those two closing sentences. Shocked to the bottom of his orderly governmental soul, he simply deleted them, and the general's dispatch went spiraling upward through the hierarchy with the damning charge omitted. Irascible Stanton did not see it until long after he and McClellan had ceased to be problems to each other.

Meanwhile, the general was more than ever thrown in on the army.

He might draw supplies from Washington, might even get reinforcements—he was telling the War Department that he needed fully a hundred thousand fresh soldiers—but he could not get emotional support from that source any longer. That could come only from the soldiers. To his wife, on the day the dejected army filed into the lines at Harrison's Landing, he wrote that "the dear fellows cheer me as of old as they march to certain death, and I feel prouder of them than ever," and he confessed that it was only among the troops that he felt at home. Describing the week of fighting and marching, he wrote: "You can't tell how nervous I became; everything seemed like the opening of artillery, and I had no rest, no peace, except when in front with my men. The duties of my position are such as often to make it necessary for me to remain in the rear. It is an awful thing." But the men never failed. He rode among them and "they began to cheer as usual, and called out that they were all right and would fall to the last man for 'Little Mac.'"

So he tried to give the army the reassurance which the army gave him. Independence Day came three days after the army reached the river. To the troops McClellan issued a stirring proclamation: "Under every disadvantage of numbers, and necessarily of position also, you have in every conflict beaten back your foes with enormous slaughter. That your conduct ranks you among the celebrated armies of history, no one will ever question; then each of you may always say with pride, 'I belonged to the Army of the Potomac.'"[1]

It must be admitted that when it first reached camp the army did not feel particularly heroic or distinguished. The flat fields around Harrison's Landing struck it as a poor place for a camp. Most of the ground was growing wheat, which was cut down and laid to serve as bedding under the shelter tents. It didn't work very well. The ground turned into semi-liquid mud, the tent pins wouldn't hold, the soggy straw either floated away or was mashed out of sight, and worn-out men awoke to find themselves lying in mud puddles with clammy canvas collapsed on top of them. (Some of them did, anyway: many others had had to abandon tent-and-blanket rolls during the retreat and had nothing whatever to sleep on or under.) The 8th Ohio, coming down from the north in a reinforcement brigade and reaching the landing the day after camp had been made, thought at first that the whole country had been flooded. "It was almost as muddy," wrote one soldier, "as if the waters of the deluge had just retreated from the face of the earth."[2]

Nobody had had much to eat for several days, what with the constant fighting and marching, and it was hard to find wood for fires here—or, while the rain lasted, to make fires burn if wood could be found. There was great confusion at first, with men separated from their commands, and brigades and divisions were all split up and intermingled. While they were trying to sort themselves out an obnoxious battery of Confederate horse artillery popped up on a low ridge north of camp and began flinging shells down on the plain. The men swore wearily, a brigade went up to drive the guns away, and the high command—almost as punch-drunk momentarily as the men themselves—got some field fortifications built along the ridge so that further disturbers of the peace could be held away.

It was right at this time, too, that the army as a whole made a horrifying discovery about itself. It was lousy.

The men were ashamed when they discovered it, until they found that everybody was in the same boat; then they accepted it as one of the miserable facts of army life and made jokes about it. One man declared that in the Glendale fight he had seen a high officer dramatically calling a brigade to the charge—posing bravely on his horse, his right hand holding his sword high, while with his left hand he busily and unconsciously kept scratching himself. The surgeon of the 57th New York would not believe it when the colonel told him the regiment was infested; said it must be just a few of the men, careless fellows, no doubt, who didn't bother to keep clean. The colonel, probably wondering how anyone could be expected to keep clean in a solid week of unbroken fighting and marching, exploded at him: "The whole army is lousy! I am lousy, you are lousy, General McClellan is lousy!"[3] The army got some relief as supply ships came up. New clothing was distributed, and details were formed to collect and burn verminous underwear and uniforms.

The heat was oppressive. Mosquitoes seemed even worse here than they had been around Richmond. The camp stank horribly: too many men were crowded into too small an area, the pits that were dug for refuse never seemed quite adequate, the latrines were an abomination. There was a plague of flies, and the drinking water (obtained, for the most part, by digging shallow wells) was unpleasantly warm and muddy, and was beyond all question tainted. A new surgeon arrived to join the 5th New Hampshire just at this time, and he wrote feelingly of the impression made by what he saw: "the bare-footed boys, the sallow men, the threadbare officers and seedy generals, the diarrhea and dysentery, the yellow eyes and malarious faces, the beds upon the bare earth in the mud, the mist and the rain." All of this, he confessed, instantly destroyed his "pre-conceived ideas of knight-errantry."[4]

Fresh provisions came down from the North, which was a help; cabbages, tomatoes, and potatoes were welcome, although the men were not entirely sure that fresh beef was much better than salt pork —the butchers were inexpert and hasty, carcasses were usually cut up while lying on the ground, and the meat had a way of being sandy by the time it got to the company cooks. In any case, the cooks rarely knew of any way to cook beef except by boiling it. The one good feature about the place, the men agreed, was that they could bathe in James River.

But even though Harrison's Landing was a miserable camp, where the regimental sick lists kept lengthening and tired boys had enough unwanted leisure to remember that they were homesick, the army was not altogether discouraged. It had learned things about war that it had never dreamed of, to be sure, but as the men compared notes on what they had been through it seemed to them that they had done very well indeed. They could not understand just why they had had to retreat, and it was a disappointment not to be in Richmond; but every battle, when they looked back on it, seemed to have been no worse than a draw, and Malvern Hill they rightly considered a distinct victory. If some of them felt that so fine a victory ought to have been followed up by an advance on Richmond, they concluded after talking it over that Little Mac knew what he was doing and that they could safely leave all such problems to him.

Had they known it, as stout a friend of McClellan as Fitz-John Porter himself believed that the retreat after Malvern Hill was a mistake; a determined advance next day, he thought, would have pushed Lee aside and opened the way to Richmond. Phil Kearny, who had long since come to dislike McClellan intensely—he still thought McClellan had slighted him in his dispatches describing the battle of Williamsburg, and anyway, McClellan just wasn't the type that hot-blooded Kearny could admire—was violent in his criticism. When the order to retreat reached him at the end of the battle, he cried out: "I, Philip Kearny, an old soldier, enter my solemn protest against this order for retreat. We ought instead of retreating to follow up the enemy and take Richmond. And in full view of all the responsibility of such a declaration, I say to you all, such an order can only be prompted by cowardice or treason."[5]

Kearny's remarks were to get back to Washington in time, but they did not circulate among the enlisted men. With them McClellan's name still had the old magic. The 3rd Michigan, which was one of Kearny's regiments, was making a despairing effort to boil coffee on one of the first mornings in camp. Fires wouldn't burn in the rain, and men were gathered around trying to hold blankets, overcoats, and what not over the smoldering embers, when McClellan came riding by. The men dropped everything and ran over to cluster around him and shout, and when he could make himself heard he quietly told them that he knew things had been tough but that everything was going to be all right from now on: they were fine soldiers, they had given the Rebels more than they had received, and they'd take Richmond yet. The boys cheered and went back to their fires, got them going somehow, drank their coffee, and felt better. Talking things over after they had finished their coffee and had their pipes lighted, they agreed that they were quite a regiment and the army was quite an army; they had marched all night and fought all day for a week, most of the time they had whipped the enemy—who could have done better than that? And as for McClellan: he was still the man.[6]

New uniforms were issued, and there were reviews: a grand series of reviews, presently, with President Lincoln himself on hand to sit on his horse, lanky and ungainly, beside McClellan to watch the men march past. A boyish lieutenant on the staff of General Taylor, of the New Jersey brigade, hadn't managed to get in on the issue of new uniforms. His pants were unspeakably ragged and dirty—he confessed that he had not had them off for upward of a week—and he was excused from the review. That evening he went to General Taylor's tent on business, entered, and found Lincoln himself there, chatting with Taylor. Abashed, he tried to withdraw; no man in pants like his had any business lingering in the presence of the President of the United States. But Lincoln told him not to leave and asked

Taylor to introduce him. Taylor did so, explaining about the regrettable pants worn out in the country's hard service. Lincoln shook hands, rested his left hand on the boy's shoulder, and said: "My son, I think your country can afford to get you a new pair of breeches."[7]

Lincoln hadn't come all the way down from Washington just to review troops, of course, nor did he spend much time chatting with brigade commanders. He was there primarily to see McClellan and to find out for himself, if possible, just what could be done next with the Army of the Potomac. The war was approaching an unexpected crisis, and much more had been lost than a few square miles of swampland along the Chickahominy. What was fast disappearing was the last chance for a relatively short war; going with it, or soon to go, was the high hope and confidence with which the country had faced the summer's fighting. Unless the war could be won quickly it would become a new kind of war, creating its own objectives, exacting a fearful price; no longer an affair of esprit de corps and hero worship and the élan of highhearted volunteer fighters, but a long, brutal, grinding, and totally unpredictable struggle to which all the agony and heartbreak of the Seven Days' fighting would be only a prelude.

The sky had been so bright that spring, and final victory had not appeared to be far away. In the West, Kentucky and most of Tennessee were safe and New Orleans was taken, and it looked as if the whole length of the Mississippi would soon be open. In the East, amphibious expeditions had seized much of the Confederacy's coast line, and McClellan's army had seemed ready to drive straight through to Richmond. Secretary Stanton had been so encouraged in April that he had blithely closed all of the recruiting offices, which was a black item against him in McClellan's book. Now the brightness was gone and dark clouds were climbing up the sky. The armies in the West were stalled—no actual repulse anywhere, but no victories, either. Every detail of the Virginia campaign had gone awry, and men were thankful because the Army of the Potomac had not actually been destroyed. John Pope had been brought on from the West to make an army out of the scattered commands north of the Rappahannock—McDowell's, Sigel's, and Banks's—but McClellan's army still represented most of the muscle, and it was the big question mark. What could it do now? Or, considering that it was McClellan's army, would *would* it do? Lincoln had to find out.

When the bad news first came in from in front of Richmond, Lincoln had been consoling. In his first message to McClellan he told him: "Maintain your ground if you can, but save the army at all events, even if you fall back to Fort Monroe. We still have strength enough in the country, and will bring it out." Next day he wired McClellan: "If you think you are not strong enough to take Richmond just now, I do not ask you to just now," and promised reinforcements; a new levy of three hundred thousand volunteers was to be raised at once. On the following day he wired that he was satisfied that "yourself, officers and men have done the best you could" and conveyed "ten thousand thanks for it." A day later he repeated his acknowledgment of "the heroism and skill of yourself, officers and men" and assured McClellan: "If you can hold your present position we shall hive the enemy yet." In a letter Lincoln went into detail about reinforcements, again urged the general to hold on and make his army safe, and added in a postscript: "If at any time you feel able to take the offensive, you are not restrained from doing so." Confidently McClellan replied: "Alarm yourself as little as possible about me, and don't lose confidence in this army."

So far, so good; President and general seemed to understand one another. Now the President was on the ground to talk things over.

Yet how could they talk, those two men, even with incalculable matters depending on their coming to agreement? We know both of them by now; we have had two generations to study them and find out what they really meant. But they could never see each other clearly. Too many shadows lay between them. On each man was a pressure; in each man was an ignorance which kept him from understanding just what the other man's pressure was—ignorance of politics, for the one, and of military affairs, for the other. Behind each man, subtly influencing him, were the suspicions his colleagues held, including on each side the dim half belief that perhaps the other man did not really wish a speedy end to the war. (Among the "war Democrats," who had no use for anti-slavery agitation, was the feeling that the Republicans did not want the war to end until it could be made into an instrument to crush slavery. Among the Republicans was the conviction that men like McClellan wanted the war to drag out into an indecisive peace-without-victory which would leave slavery intact. These two feelings were in the backgrounds of the President and the general who were to confer with each other.)

McClellan had bluntly accused the administration of infamous conduct. He had not been rebuked for it. He had had nothing from Washington since then but kind words. How could he interpret that, except as clear proof that there *was* infamous conduct in Washington and that the authors of it—the men who gave him his orders—felt so guilty that they dared not resent his angry words? He had invited them to cashier him and they had not done it; instead, Stanton had sent a note assuring him that "you have never had from me anything but the most confiding integrity," followed by another asserting: "No man had ever a truer friend than I have been to you and shall continue to be. You are seldom absent from my thoughts, and I am ready to make any sacrifice to aid you."

And Lincoln? Among his trusted cabinet members was Gideon Welles, the Secretary of the Navy, who has been described as an irascible Santa Claus with his stern face and his bushy white whiskers, and who was eminently levelheaded, taking no part in the frantic factional efforts to tell Lincoln how to run the war. Welles had visited McClellan on the peninsula shortly after Yorktown fell and had had a long and oddly revealing talk with him. McClellan had confided his great desire to capture Charleston, South Carolina, a city which he would like "to demolish and annihilate." (The general must have been really worked up that day. It is impossible to imagine him demolishing and annihilating any city: for better or for worse, he completely lacked the Sherman touch.) In his diary—that marvelous depository for acid comments—Welles went on with the tale:

"He detested, he said, both South Carolina and Massachusetts, and should rejoice to see both states extinguished. Both were and always had been ultra and mischievous, and he could not tell which he hated most. These were the remarks of the general-in-chief at the head of our armies then in the field, and when as large a proportion of his troops were from Massachusetts as from any state in the Union, while as large a proportion of those who were opposed, who were fighting the Union, were from South Carolina as from any state. He was leading the men of Massachusetts against the men of South Carolina, yet he, the general, detests them alike."[8]

It is easy enough at this day to see McClellan's outburst as a variant of "a plague on both your houses," directed at the fire-eaters of North and South alike, and it is hard to get very disturbed about it. But there was a war on then, and a detached attitude was hard to come by, and, as Welles said, that *was* an odd way for a Northern general to talk. A Northern newspaper correspondent, summing up the Seven Days' Battles, had written that "Massachusetts mourns more dead soldiers, comparatively, than any state's quota in the Army of the Potomac." It is fair to assume that Welles had told Lincoln about McClellan's words. Would not those words inevitably get in between the two men as they talked about the future course of the war?

If those words wouldn't, there were others that would. Phil Kearny had been free in his comments. His insistence that he could march his own division into Richmond, after Lee struck his first blow north of the Chickahominy, and his angry denunciation of McClellan for ordering a retreat were by no means army secrets. Brigadier General Hiram G. Berry, who commanded one of Kearny's brigades, had been present when Kearny sounded off, and Berry, who came from Maine, was in steady confidential correspondence with Vice-President Hannibal Hamlin. Even earlier, Kearny had been writing to a friend in the North that "McClellan is a dirty, sneaking traitor," and was suggesting that back of McClellan's strategy "there is either positive treason or at least McClellan or the few with him are devising a game of politics rather than war." At this distance it is fairly easy to recognize Kearny as a tolerably familiar type in the long history of the American Army—the ardent, hard-fighting, distinguished soldier who just has to blow off at the mouth every now and then. But Lincoln was conferring with McClellan in 1862, and all he could be expected to see was that the most slashing fighter in the army was doubting the loyalty of his commanding general.

And Lincoln was in the mood to heed the words of a hard fighter. At bottom his whole problem was summed up in the fact that the North had the power to win the war but lacked the slugging, driving generals who would use that power. He could form his own judgments of men, and he was not persuaded by all the whispers about McClellan's loyalty; what did bother him about McClellan, from first to last, was McClellan's reluctance to crowd the enemy into a corner and punch until somebody dropped. Perhaps the most revealing remark Lincoln ever made about his relationship with McClellan was one concerning an entirely different general. Earlier that spring Grant fought the battle of Shiloh—fought it inexpertly, suffering a shameful surprise, losing many men who need not have been lost. There was a great clamor against him, he was denounced as an incompetent and a drunkard, and tremendous political pressure was put on Lincoln to remove him. A. K. McClure, the Pennsylvania politician who was intimate with Lincoln, was convinced that Lincoln, as a matter of practical politics, "could not sustain himself if he attempted to sustain Grant," and late one night he went to the White House to argue the point. He told Lincoln "with all the earnestness I could command" that he simply must get rid of Grant. Then, as McClure described it: "Lincoln remained silent for what seemed a very long time. He then gathered himself up in his chair and said in a tone of earnestness that I shall never forget: '*I can't spare this man; he fights.*'" Lincoln had warned McClellan that there were political pressures which even the President could not resist; but to uphold a fighting general he was ready to resist any pressure whatever.[9]

However all of that may be, Lincoln and McClellan had their conference. And McClellan there made his crowning mistake. Having failed to understand that political considerations could modify the best plans of the best military men in a democracy at war, he suddenly switched from military planning to political planning—with disastrous results.

Here he was, barely a week after the battle of Malvern Hill, with the whole future of the war depending on the speed and energy with which the army could be repaired and thrown into a new campaign, with all of the involved problems growing out of that fact resting chiefly on himself for solution, with his own career, the fate of the army, and the safety of the country itself depending on what might come out of his talks with the President: and to the President he gave, not a plan for renewing the fighting, but a long letter telling him how he should shape the high policy of the war.

It was his desire, McClellan wrote, to expound his views regarding the rebellion, even though those views "do not strictly relate to the situation of this army or strictly come within the scope of my official duties." But the policy he was arguing for must be adopted by the

President and put promptly into effect "or our cause will be lost." It was a policy, he said, both "constitutional and conservative," which would "receive the support of almost all truly loyal men" and which, it might be hoped, would even "commend itself to the favor of the Almighty."

Specifically: "neither confiscation of property, political executions of persons, territorial organization of states or forcible abolition of slavery should be contemplated for a moment." In the fighting, Federal armies should protect private property and unarmed persons, and there should be no "offensive demeanor by the military toward citizens"; there should be no military arrests, except in areas where actual fighting was going on, and where military government was set up it should be confined to preserving order and protecting political rights. Military power should never be used to interfere "with the relations of servitude"; if contraband slaves were pressed into service, the rights of their owners to compensation should be recognized. Unless some such policy as this were adopted, the effort to get new recruits for the army would fail; and if the government should adopt "radical views" on the slavery issue, the existing armies would disintegrate.

To put through such a policy, McClellan added, the President would need a sympathetic general-in-chief for the armies. He did not ask that place for himself but would willingly serve "in such position as you may assign me."

Now it is probably true that at least a part of this letter was aimed at the egregious General Pope, who had celebrated the assumption of his new command by issuing ferocious orders regarding the treatment of Rebel civilians within his lines—orders so unduly restrictive that the government quietly let them become a dead letter. To that extent McClellan was on sound ground. But there can be no doubt whatever that the final effect of the letter was to convince Lincoln that McClellan was not the general he could use to win the war.

For two reasons.

To begin with, Lincoln was reluctantly concluding that the war could not be won on the first simple flush of enthusiasm for saving the Union. That would remain the one dominant motive, to be sure: he was presently to write his famous letter to Horace Greeley declaring that he would save the Union in any way he could, whether by freeing no slaves, by freeing just a few, or by freeing all. It was a motive to which he had remained true despite tremendous pressure from his own party. He had disciplined General Frémont, first presidential candidate of the Republican party, for issuing a premature proclamation of emancipation. He had rebuked former Secretary of War Cameron when that slippery individual, deep in trouble because of slovenly administration of his office, tried to wrap the anti-slavery cloak about his bent shoulders. He had disavowed the act of General David Hunter, another hero of the abolitionists, who tried to proclaim abolition along the Southern seacoast that spring. Painfully and patiently he had tried to bring forth some solution for the terrible slavery problem aside from outright, forcible emancipation. He had persuaded a reluctant Congress to adopt a joint resolution for compensated emancipation; there had been something fairly pathetic in his appeal to the people of the slave states to support such a settlement—"I do not argue; I beseech you to make the arguments for yourselves. You cannot, if you would, be blind to the signs of the times."

But the sands were running out. By the end of the first week of July 1862, the President had just about made up his mind that some sort of emancipation program was essential as a war measure. (It was less than a week after this talk with McClellan that he first told Secretary Seward and Secretary Welles that he had come to this conclusion.) In a sense, Lincoln had gone down to Harrison's Landing with a draft of the Emancipation Proclamation in his pocket. Yet here was the general of his most important army saying that the one thing which he, the President, had decided must be done to win the war could not and must not be done; telling him, in so many words, that if the slavery issue were raised the army would not fight—McClellan's army, made in his own image, bound to him by battle-tested ties of devotion.

And in the second place, McClellan's letter forced Lincoln to ask just who was running the country, anyway—the civil administration or a general? Obviously, if he accepted McClellan's advice, the general was running it. At that early date Lincoln was bumping into the ominous fact that when democracy makes all-out war the way is always open for military persons to take control on the plea that the military problem can't be solved unless all related political problems are adjusted, Procrustes-fashion, to fit. There had been plenty of talk for a year and more about the need for a dictator, whether in shoulder straps or frock coat. Some of it had been pumped into McClellan's own ears by none other than his present bitter enemy, Mr. Stanton. McClellan was by no means the only general who had been beguiled by such talk, nor was Stanton the only beguiler, and Lincoln knew it. Indeed, Lincoln's administration had not been a month old before Secretary Seward had given the President a letter, blandly offering to take over the job of running the government himself; did this letter of McClellan's, closing with the courteous disclaimer of any personal ambition, remind the President of that earlier letter of Seward's? The parallel is striking.

Whatever Lincoln might have thought as he read the general's remarkable letter, he gave nothing away. He thanked McClellan politely for it, put it in his pocket, and went back to Washington. Three days later he plucked General Halleck out of the lines along the Mississippi, brought him to Washington, and made him general-in-chief of the nation's armies.

And McClellan wrote to his wife that he had given the President the letter and that "if he acts upon it the country will be saved." He sent her a copy, asking her to preserve it as a document important to the record—a document proving, McClellan felt, "that I was true to my country, that I understood the state of affairs long ago, and that had my advice been followed we should not have been in our present difficulties."

Which is as it may be. It is doubtful if McClellan ever realized exactly what effect his letter had, or why such an effect might have been expected. He was acting, those days, with an incredible innocence. Understanding politics not at all, he put himself inextricably into politics; having given Lincoln a letter which was enough to destroy his own position, he now had to make certain that his enemies in Washington would be able to put the worst possible interpretation on it. He entertained in his camp Fernando Wood, recently mayor of New York, and one of the leaders in what was just beginning to be called the Copperhead movement.

Wood was a character any administration man might well look upon with suspicion. When the Southern states began to secede at the end of 1860 and the beginning of 1861, Wood had proposed that New York City itself secede and become some sort of free city on the coast, friendly to the new Confederacy, bringing from Lincoln the dry comment that the time hardly seemed ripe for the front door to detach itself and set up housekeeping by itself. Wood was by now the complete exemplar of those Northern Democrats who let their old sympathy for the South, their dislike of anti-slavery agitation, and their basic political opposition to the Republicans carry them over to the very edge of being pro-Confederate rather than pro-Union. Like many another Northern general—U. S. Grant, for a random example—McClellan was a Democrat and always had been; but he could not see now that under all the circumstances it was not quite politic for him to confer with Fernando Wood while his army recuperated from defeat within gunshot of Lee's outposts.

He talked politics with Wood, who felt and said that McClellan would be a good presidential candidate. He seems to have prepared for Wood a letter outlining his political views; a letter apparently embodying much the same points as were expressed in his letter to Lincoln, but dangerously susceptible to misinterpretation when given by the commanding general to a reckless conniver like Wood. McClellan showed the letter to one of his closest friends, General William F. Smith—"Baldy" Smith to the army, a good soldier and a stoutly loyal citizen. Smith, according to the surviving reports, read it and found the remnants of his hair standing on end; handed it back with the startled remark that "it looks like treason" and would be the ruin of McClellan and all who were close to him. On Smith's urging, McClellan destroyed the letter. His enemies in Washington, of course, never saw the letter and never knew just what had passed between Wood and McClellan; but they knew that Wood had visited McClellan, they knew that talk of McClellan as the next President was beginning to circulate, and they did know Wood.

After Wood left, Halleck came down for a conference. McClellan was stiffly polite; he considered Halleck an inferior person, in which he was quite correct, and he wrote to his wife that his self-respect would permit him to remain in command of the army "only so long as the welfare of the Army of the Potomac demands—no longer." That tie with the army had become by now the only thing that counted: "I owe a great duty to this noble set of men, and that is the only feeling that retains me. . . . I owe no gratitude to any but my own soldiers here; none to the government or to the country." The conversation with Halleck was inconclusive. McClellan was left with the feeling that his army would be reinforced and would be ordered to resume its advance on Richmond, and Halleck also seems to have promised that McClellan would ultimately be put in command of Pope's army as well as his own. This McClellan took with a grain of salt. He wrote home that as far as he could see the authorities "intend and hope that my army may melt away under the hot sun."

Then the blow fell. At the end of July, Halleck telegraphed that reports from Pope indicated a lessening of Rebel strength around Richmond and suggested a reconnoissance in force by McClellan. Hooker's division, accordingly, was sent forward to the old battle-field of Malvern Hill, and McClellan prayed that the Rebels would incautiously attack—then, with a counterattack, he might create an opening for a real advance on Richmond. But the Rebel attack did not develop, a sputtering of small-arms fire along the picket lines died away in the thickets, and Hooker was withdrawn, furious, like Kearny earlier, swearing that a determined push would have taken the Confederate capital. McClellan himself was hopeful and wired Halleck that if he were properly reinforced he believed he could march his army to Richmond in five days; but Halleck replied that there were no reinforcements to send and bluntly told him that it had been decided to withdraw the entire army from the James to the upper Potomac—McClellan must get busy, send his sick north at once, and put his army on the transports as fast as he could.

McClellan argued, and Halleck, an expert at conducting disputation by telegraph, argued back, and the old business of Pinkerton's overestimate of Confederate strength arose once more to cripple the army. If Lee, said Halleck, actually had two hundred thousand men, as McClellan was insisting, then it was potentially disastrous to leave Lee posted between the armies of Pope and McClellan: with that strength he could easily hold off one army and crush the other. In the face of such numbers the only possible course was to reunite the armies in front of Washington and make the best fight possible. This was unanswerable, and the withdrawal began—as promptly as possible, McClellan felt; slowly and with unpardonable delay, Stanton and Halleck believed.

It was almost a question, by now, whether McClellan was fighting the Confederates or the authorities at Washington. He still saw himself as the man who would finally save the country, but he believed that he would have to do it over the objections of the government, as he was fully convinced that the men in Washington were determined to get rid of him at any cost. "Their game," he wrote to his wife, "is to force me to resign; mine will be to force them to place me on leave of absence, so that when they begin to reap the whirlwind that they have sown I may still be in a position to do something to save my country." Reflectively, and as if there might be doubts about the matter, he added: "With all their faults, I *do* love my countrymen, and if I *can* save them I will yet do so."

So the retreat began, down the peninsula to the wharves around Fortress Monroe. Along the way McClellan found time to be the fond husband thinking of the wife and baby girl at home—he did hope the child wouldn't make too much progress in the way of learning to walk and to talk before he could get home to see her. He sent his wife a pressed flower, picked in an old cemetery at Jamestown, and he tried to imagine what things were like centuries earlier when John Smith first came up this river. He mused about the stateliness and comfort with which the colonial planters managed to surround their lives: "It would delight me beyond measure to have you here to see the scenery and some of the fine old residences which stud its banks."

And the army marched along the narrow roads, leaving much behind it: youthful innocence, many comrades, and the bright hope that the war might yet be won before it settled down into hatred and blind destruction and the deaths of half a million boys.

On the march the men found that less care was being exercised now to prevent the destruction of Rebel property. One division came to a fine old plantation whose owner, somewhat rashly, had defiantly posted a sign forbidding the burial of any dead Yankees on the grounds. The men surged in over the lawn, set fire to the house, and resumed the march, a black pillar of smoke rising behind them in the windless air.

FOUR

An Army on the March

1. Indian Summer

To the people of the North it seemed that September was bringing the outriders of doom up across the Potomac. Lee's army, so unbelievably thin and ragged in actual appearance, so greatly magnified and transfigured by rumor and by fear, came splashing through the shallows of the fording places like a legendary host, and the sound of its bands playing "Maryland, My Maryland" was like the first far-off notes of the last trumpet. The rebellion had not been put down, after all; it was here, over the border, ready with fire and sword to conquer and lay waste. The great war to save the Union, entered into with so many waving flags, so many cries and cheers for departing trainloads of young men in bright new uniforms, might be coming to sudden catastrophe before the autumn leaves had turned. Here was something government could not handle, after all. The war was coming to the people.

All across the North the people reacted, as if the country itself were beleaguered. When the news came that Pope's army had been crushed and driven, Boston bestirred itself. At the urging of Governor Andrew churches were made ready to receive wounded men, and freight-car loads of bandages and medical supplies were hastily prepared and sent to Washington. Martial law was declared in the Ohio River cities of Cincinnati and Covington—for in the West Rebel armies under Braxton Bragg and Kirby Smith had slipped the leash and were driving north in pace with Lee. A self-organized "national war committee" met in New York, proposed that Pathfinder Frémont be reinstated in army command, urged the enlistment of a special corps of fifty thousand men for his special use, appointed a delegation to meet next day at Providence with such governors of the New England states as could be on hand, and then dropped out of sight and was heard of no more. In Pennsylvania, Governor Curtin called for the formation of volunteer militia companies. At least fifty thousand men would be needed, he said, "for immediate service to repel the now imminent invasion by the enemies of the country." The mayor of Philadelphia called on "all able-bodied men" to assemble at election-district precinct houses to be organized for service, and places of business throughout the state were ordered closed at 3 P.M. daily so that the new units might drill

Governor Morton of Indiana told counties bordering the Ohio River to form military companies as speedily as might be. In the Susquehanna Valley people prepared to evacuate their towns, if need be; in Lancaster the citizens formed a committee of public safety and a home-guard company, and advised sister cities and boroughs to do likewise and "to arrest every man who uttered a traitorous sentiment against the government." Several hundred women met in Boston's Park Street Church and resolved that women throughout the country should form "circles of prayer" to pray for "the outpouring of the Holy Spirit on the entire nation." Cincinnati reported that "over 1,000 squirrel hunters from the neighboring counties" had come in to offer their services. From the Army of the Potomac, Major General John F. Reynolds was detached and sent to Harrisburg, to give professional direction to Pennsylvania's home-guard levies.[1]

The Army of the Potomac was pulling itself together in Washington, getting its second wind for a sprint after Lee. The people of the North might arouse themselves with any number of public meetings, emergency volunteer companies, massed squirrel hunters, and committees of public safety on guard against treason: Lee was not going to wait for that frothy, fluid outpouring to harden into tangible military strength. If he was to be stopped, it was the army that would have to stop him, and the army knew it perfectly well.

Even before the army had fully reassembled in the Washington lines, the men in the ranks could see that there had been a great change. The Popes and the McDowells were gone, and the organization was running smoothly once more; scattered brigades were pulled together without fuss, the frantic running around and feverish activity at army headquarters had given way to quiet competence, regular rations were being issued again, new uniforms and equipment were being passed out, and in general it began to look as if there was a man at the top who knew what he was doing. Once again the lounging stragglers were swept up off the streets. Stray detachments of men, posted at odd spots in and around the capital, not knowing why they were posted there and strongly suspecting that no one else knew either, were called in and given regular assignments. There is record of one cavalry command that had been camped in a suburban field for weeks, "waiting for orders," completely forgotten by the authorities; it was found and put to work after someone thought to make a check on the rations issued by the commissary department. In Alexandria a huge camp suddenly came into existence for returning convalescents, wandering soldiers who had lost their papers, detailed men whose regiments had moved off without them, paroled prisoners awaiting exchange, and the like, and there were arrangements for getting these men back where they belonged with a minimum of fuss and delay.

Squadrons of regular cavalry patrolled the streets; they straightened out the endless traffic jams caused by the great wagon trains and put a stop to the ceaseless, useless galloping of couriers, mounted orderlies, and other overenthusiastic horsemen The encircling lines of forts, which had never been quite finished, were put into final shape and were strongly garrisoned as new troops came in from the North. Watching it all, seemingly fascinated and heartened at the way order was swiftly replacing disorder, was President Lincoln; almost daily he would saunter into the offices which had been set up for the defenses of Washington, to inquire gently, "Well, how does it look today?" He remarked that now, for a change, he was not bothered all day and could sleep all night if he chose.

While all of this was going on the army began to move north and west out of Washington, in pursuit of Lee. It was the same army that had gone up the river just a year earlier to picket the fords and season itself in the open country, the same that had embarked from the river wharves that spring with banners flying and hearts high; but it knew a great deal more than it had known then, and many things had happened since the halcyon autumn when the war seemed more than half for fun. Gallic Colonel Regis de Trobriand, leading the Frenchmen of his 55th New York past their old camp at Tennallytown, mused sadly on the changes:

"What a contrast between the departure and the return! We had started out in the spring gay, smart, well provided with everything. The drums beat, the bugles sounded, the flag with its folds of immaculate silk glistened in the sunshine. And we were returning before the autumn, sad, weary, covered with mud, with uniforms in rags. Now the drummers carried their cracked drums on their backs, the buglers were bent over and silent; the flag, riddled by the balls, torn by shrapnel, discolored by the rain, hung sadly upon the staff without cover.

"Where were the red pantaloons? Where were the Zouave jackets? And, above all, those who had worn them, and whom we looked in vain along the ranks to find, what had become of them? Killed at Williamsburg, killed at Fair Oaks, killed at Glendale, killed at Malvern Hill; wounded or sick in the hospitals; prisoners at Richmond; deserters, we knew not where. And, to make the story short, scarce 300 revisited Tennallytown and Fort Gaines on their way to fight in upper Maryland."[2]

But if the colonel fell into a *neiges d'antan* melancholy when he looked back on the past, the army as a whole marched out of Washington in the highest of spirits. It had its old commander back, and it devoutly believed that he would make right all that had gone wrong. It had the pride of men who had fought hard and well, and it was sure that it would win the war the next time it went into battle. Getting into Maryland, too, was like coming home. No longer did the Westerners and the New Englanders feel that this slave state was foreign soil. The farms and the countryside might not be like Massachusetts and Indiana, but they were even less like the flat, dank, wooded country of the Virginia peninsula, and they had not been scorched by the usage of war.

Best of all, the people themselves were friendly. In western Maryland, at least, public sentiment had settled on the side of the Union by the fall of 1862, and the inhabitants welcomed the army joyfully.

Young Captain Noyes, on Doubleday's staff, remarked that girls with buckets of cold spring water waited at almost every gate to give tired soldiers a drink. "If my hat was off once, it was off thirty times," he wrote, adding ecstatically: "Fine marching weather; a land flowing with milk and honey; a general tone of Union sentiment among the people, who, being little cursed by slavery [Captain Noyes was the staunchest of abolitionists], had not lost their loyalty; scenery, not grand but picturesque, all contributed to make the march delightful."[3]

Nearly all of the soldiers who made that march and left a record of their thoughts made the same sort of comment. A diarist in the 22nd Massachusetts felt that the combination of beautiful country and friendly people did wonders for the army; around the campfires, he said, there was universal agreement that they would beat Lee decisively next time they met him. In the 27th Indiana it was agreed that getting back into Maryland made all the difference; the men felt better, and it wasn't because of McClellan—this regiment had never served under him before and had no ingrained hero worship to respond to. General Abram Duryée's brigade—97th, 104th, and 105th New York, plus 107th Pennsylvania—straggled badly coming out of Washington; too many men had loitered, as one writer confessed, to enjoy "the comforts of civilization," and the first day's march was hard. But the stragglers all caught up after a while, and the brigade stepped out gaily; in the town of Frederick, the brigade historian recalled, "hundreds of Union banners floated from the roofs and windows, and in many a threshold stood the ladies and children of the family, offering food and water to the passing troops, or with tiny flags waving a welcome to their deliverers." The 3rd Wisconsin found it hardly needed its army rations in Frederick, "so sumptuous was the fare of cakes, pies, fruits, milk, dainty biscuit and loaves" which the citizens were passing out. A regimental diarist added fondly: "Of all the memories of the war, none are more pleasant than those of our sojourn in the goodly city of Frederick."

Men in the Black Hat Brigade noted that children stood in almost every doorway, offering pies, cakes, drinking water, and the like, and flags were hanging from almost every window. A soldier in the 9th New York found the streets "filled with women dressed in their best, walking bareheaded, singing, and testifying in every way the general joy." Captain Noyes spoke of the passage through Frederick as "one

continuous waving of flags, fluttering of handkerchiefs, tossing of
bouquets," and said the soldiers grew hoarse cheering in response.
A veteran of the 7th Maine extended his grateful benediction to all of
Maryland; the regiment found camp sites "conveniently situated as to
chickens and corn and honey and apple butter, and like the Israelites
of old, we looked upon the land and it was good." Remembering
the hostile people on the peninsula, he added: "The girls no longer
made faces at us from the windows, and the people were down at
their front gates with cold water, at least, if they had nothing better.
It seemed like Paradise, this Maryland, and many were the blessed
damosels we saw therein." As French's division passed through one
town a private looked at the flags, the smiling girls, and the general
air of wholehearted welcome and called out joyously: "Colonel! We're
in God's country again!"[4]

All in all, it was as if a clean wind from the blue mountains had
blown through this army, sweeping away weariness and doubt and
restoring the spirit with which the men had first started out; restoring,
for the last time in this war—perhaps for the last time anywhere—
that strange, magical light which rested once upon the landscape
of a young and totally unsophisticated country, whose perfect embodiment the army was. In a way, this army was fighting against
reality, just as was Lee's army. The dream which possessed the land
before 1861 was passing away in blood and fire. One age was ending
and another was being born, with agony of dissolution and agony of
birth terribly mingled; and in the Army of the Potomac—in its background, its coming together, its memories of the American life which
it imagined it was fighting to preserve—there was the final expression
of an era which is still part of our heritage but which is no longer a
part of any living memories.

And there was for the soldiers, just then, a brief pause in the war,
a quiet, unexpected breathing space between battles, a little Indian
summer of the Army of the Potomac. The country was tense and
anxious, and in Washington the President and Cabinet and general-in-
chief lived through almost unbearable suspense, and beyond the
mountains Lee was somewhere out of sight, his ominous designs
cloaked by silence. But the Union Army itself was, for the moment,
almost peaceful. It moved ahead very slowly, while far in front the
mounted outriders cantered with smoking carbines up against Lee's

shifting patrols, groping to touch the hard solidity of his massed infantry. By night the army rested in green fields that were like the fields of home; by day, if it moved at all, it moved in leisurely style, cheered by the greetings from farmhouse and village. The men were old soldiers by now, able to live entirely in the present moment. As they moved northwest along the old National Road, the white tops of the wagon trains bobbing in the slow columns like the covered wagons of some unimaginable new folk migration, it was as if they passed in unhurried review, fixing in one suspended moment of time the image of the country that had borne them.

There was in the army a regiment called the Bucktails: 13th Pennsylvania Reserves, actually, owning a nickname because a private, in training-camp days, had ornamented his hat with a snippet of fur cut from the carcass of a deer hanging in front of a town meat market, and all the other men in the regiment had seen it and had gone and done likewise. The Bucktails had been enlisted in the spring of 1861 in the mountain country of northern Pennsylvania, where leading citizen Thomas Kane had put up placards in all the towns and hamlets stating that he was authorized to accept for service "any man who will bring in with him to my headquarters a Rifle which he knows how to use," and urging: "Come forward, Americans, who are not degenerate from the spirit of '76!" The men came swarming in to the recruiting places and formed scattered companies; and when it was time to assemble at Harrisburg three of the companies bought lumber and built rafts, with a platform on one raft so that the colonel's horse could ride, too, and rafted it down the West Branch of the Susquehanna, camping out nights along the banks and pausing to sing "The Star-Spangled Banner" jubilantly after they had shot the rapids above Rattlesnake Falls. Another company, the "Raftsman Guards," coming from farther west, likewise went by raft, down the Allegheny to Pittsburgh, and took the cars thence to Harrisburg.

The men had thought they were enlisting for three months, under the first call for troops, but when they got to the capital they found the state's three months' quota was filled, so they signed up for three years instead. Company K, lumbermen from Clearfield County, who were recruited at a mountain inn called "Good Intent and People's Line," was a bachelor company; started out with 123 men, found that only 100 could be accepted, and sent home all the married men. When the regiment was finally assembled for mustering in, good Colonel Kane resigned, stating that he lacked military experience—he used to carry an umbrella for sunshade while drilling the troops—and asking the men to elect Charles Biddle, a Mexican War veteran, in his place. The men did so, but insisted on making Kane lieutenant colonel, and when Biddle resigned a few months later to enter Congress, Kane got the regiment after all. He became an excellent soldier, later winning command of a brigade.

The regiment marched overland from Harrisburg into Maryland in the summer of 1861, and as it drew near to Maryland the men were tense: crossing the Mason and Dixon line would mean stepping into slave territory, into the war itself. So they halted, while a lieutenant seized the colors, ran across the state line, and boldly planted the flag on Maryland soil, whereat the regiment fired a salute, ragged but noisy. They were officially designated a rifle regiment—hangover from the day when a soldier who had and could use a rifle was very much a specialist—and they were equipped with breech-loading single-shot Sharp's rifles.[5]

Then there was the 27th Indiana, which came from what was already beginning to be called Copperhead country—the region west and south of Indianapolis, where Lincoln Republicans were not popular and there were strong ties linking the countryfolk with the Southland. The atrocity stories that were spread after the first battle of Bull Run seem to have had a part in pulling these boys into the army; wild tales of Rebels bayoneting prisoners and mutilating corpses "were as a fire in the bones," the regimental historian recalled. The 27th came into the army without any physical examinations whatever; the mustering officer, an overworked major of regulars, simply looked each company over, man by man, before accepting them, and many physical defects were carefully concealed. Men with gray beards shaved clean in order to look younger, or dyed their hair; hollow-chested men stuffed clothing inside their shirts; recruits with crooked arms held them tightly against their sides so the defect would not be noticed; others who lacked fingers held their fists clenched. Underage boys would write "18" on a slip of paper and put it inside a shoe; then, when asked if they weren't pretty young, they could truthfully say, "I'm over 18." Many of the boys came from homes where there was no sympathy with the Union cause, and regimental officers helped them with these dodges to get by the mustering officer before angry parents could come and haul them back home. Sometimes a company was advised to muster in at twilight, when physical defects were less likely to be noticed.

It was a boast of the 27th that it had the tallest man in the army, Captain David Buskirk, who stood six feet eleven inches in his socks. They tried to give him a solid company of six-footers; couldn't quite make it, but did give him eighty of them. The whole regiment averaged large in size, for all the potential 4-Fs who had slipped in; when the regimental quartermaster drew shoes he had to go around the other regiments, swapping fives and sixes for nines and tens. His favorite regiments for this purpose were the 9th New York and the 29th Pennsylvania, regiments of city chaps who were somewhat undersized. For all that it was from a rural area, the 27th boasted that it was a jack-of-all-trades group. It had bakers, who manned regimental ovens; printers, who could set type and run captured printing presses—they had actually done it while the regiment served under Banks in the valley; engineers, firemen, and brakemen, if they had to operate any railroad trains. The regiment used to wish that it might, in the freakish chance of war, sometime capture a steamboat: it had plenty of steamboat hands, plus a pilot licensed for all Western rivers. As the army marched up into Maryland the 27th's brigade got two new regiments, 13th New Jersey and 107th New York, which came in full strength. The Indiana boys, their own ranks much depleted by hard service, gaped at them. "We had not realized before how large a regiment really was." They noticed, too, that the faces and hands of the new soldiers were white, that their uniforms looked uncreased and new, and that they still had an inexpert way of bundling up and carrying their equipment.[6]

New York City had contributed the famous Irish Brigade—63rd, 69th, and 88th New York, Irish to a man, carrying regimental flags of pure emerald green embroidered in gold with an Irish harp, a shamrock, and a sunburst. Brigadier General Thomas F. Meagher led these soldiers. Famous as an Irish patriot who had had a part in the unsuccessful uprising of 1848 and had been sent to Australia on an English prison ship, he had escaped and come to America and in 1861 saw the Union cause as the cause of freedom. He had raised this brigade with the backing of Archbishop Hughes of New York, and the regimental flags had been presented at a fine ceremony in front of the archbishop's residence on Madison Avenue. Deep-chested, muscular, gay, witty, sporting a trim mustache and imperial, and entirely looking the part of the dashing Irish soldier, Meagher had made the brigade a valiant fighting force. It was in Bull Sumner's corps, and they said that on the peninsula, whenever he had to go into action, Sumner first inquired: "Where are my green flags?" To the brigade had recently been added the 29th Massachusetts, which was Irish enough to keep the average up and fit in all right. As a general rule the brigade did not like New England troops, considering them scheming Yankee bargain drivers and narrow anti-Romanists to boot.[7]

The 40th New York was called the "Mozart Regiment," not because the men were devoted to music, but because the regiment had been organized with the special blessing of Mayor Wood of New York City, whose personal faction in the New York Democratic party was known as the Mozart Hall group, in opposition to Tammany. Six of the Mozart's ten companies came from outside the state, four from Massachusetts and two from Pennsylvania. These companies were filled with men who had simply insisted on getting into the war: independent companies, organized in 1861 after their states' quotas had been filled, which had refused to disband and had gone shopping around looking for some regiment that would take them. Mayor Wood had been having much trouble recruiting the 40th New York, his reputation as a devout patriot not being of the best, so by special dispensation the out-of-state companies were taken in. The regiment stayed up all night when it got word that it was to leave for Washington and the front; played tag and leapfrog and fired blank cartridges from the two brass cannon which were at that time part of the regiment's regular equipment. When they started out they needed ten wagons to carry the regimental baggage; now, in the fall of 1862, they carried their baggage on their backs.[8]

The 1st Minnesota bragged that it was really the first volunteer regiment to be offered for Federal service in the war. Governor Alexander Ramsey of Minnesota happened to be in Washington when Fort Sumter fell, and he hot-footed it over to the War Department early next morning to offer his men for service, thus making Minnesota the first state to respond to Lincoln's call for troops. The regiment had been built around a St. Paul militia company known as the "Pioneer Guards." Mustered in at picturesque Fort Snelling, it found to its disgust that it was to be assigned to duty on frontier posts watching the Sioux Indians, and didn't get away from Minnesota until mid-June. Lacking uniforms, the state had clothed the men in black felt hats, black pants, and lumberjacks' shirts of checkered red; the boys didn't get regular uniforms until after the first battle of Bull Run. Like the Mozart Regiment, the men stayed up all night to celebrate when orders finally came to start east. They left Fort Snelling by steamboat (no railroad in Minnesota at that time) and took a train east from a port down-river; paraded through Chicago, the mayor riding beside the colonel, and were hailed by the Chicago *Tribune* as "unquestionably the finest body of troops that has yet appeared on our streets."[9]

The country was proud of those early regiments, and it knew how to show it. Traveling cross-country, en route to Washington, was for most of them a long succession of cheering crowds, brass bands, spread-eagle speeches, and banquets. The 3rd Wisconsin, which started east in July 1861, recorded that it was cheered on every farm along the track in southern Michigan, was visited at Adrian by a committee with buckets of iced lemonade, was given a grand banquet at Toledo, and was met at Erie by a committee of women bringing baskets of food. At Buffalo there was a parade through the city and a speech of welcome by the mayor, after which there was a banquet at the railroad depot. Next morning "the ladies of Elmira gave us a sumptuous breakfast"; at Williamsport the ladies gave them dinner and also stuffed their haversacks with cakes and cold meats. It was this regiment, incidentally, which treasured one memory of the battle of Winchester, where Stonewall Jackson routed Banks's corps. The rout having taken place, the men had lost formation and were legging it for the rear, and General Banks rode among them to rally them, calling out earnestly: "Men, don't you love your country?" To which a realist in the 3rd Wisconsin yelled back: "Yes—and I'm trying to get back to it as fast as I can."[10]

If they took the enthusiasm and cheers as part of the natural order of things, the men in those early regiments were also suspicious, fancying that treason might be found almost anywhere. Riding the cars from New York to Baltimore, the 12th Massachusetts felt that the train's slow progress could only be due to secessionist leanings on the part of the engineer—who, presumably, wanted the war to end before the regiment got to the front; so at a convenient stop they put the engineer off the train, while a private in Company G who had been an engineer before the war went to the cab and ran the train the rest of the way. The 3rd Michigan had a somewhat similar experience, riding the train down from Harrisburg to Baltimore. The men were told (they were never quite clear about who told them) that the engineer, a Rebel at heart, meant to wreck the train, so they put an armed guard in the cab, notifying the engineer that he would be shot at once if there was any funny business. They had an engineer in their own ranks and could handle the train themselves if they had to.[11]

Like nearly all the other Northern regiments in 1861, this 3rd Michigan was nervous when it came time to march through Baltimore—Baltimore, strongly secessionist in sympathy, where the 6th Massachusetts had been mobbed during the first weeks of the war. The 3rd Michigan marched through town with loaded muskets, its band playing "Dixie"—not yet fully identified as a Rebel tune: many Union bands played it in those early days—and the colonel sternly warned the mayor that "if a man in my regiment is hurt the streets of Baltimore will run with blood." The progress through Baltimore of the 6th Wisconsin was somewhat ignominious. No arms had yet been issued, and the regiment tramped across the city escorted by a detachment of two hundred cops, while city roughs stood on the street corners and hooted. The Frenchmen in the 55th New York met jeers but no violence in Baltimore; the colonel wrote that the men "recompensed themselves by mocking airs and gestures more expressive than polite."

But if going through Baltimore in 1861 was a trying experience for nervous recruits, the army to a man enjoyed going through Philadelphia. At the start of the war a citizens' committee there had organized what was called "The Philadelphia Union Refreshment Saloon" and saw to it that every regiment that went by got proper treatment—airy, roomy washrooms with plenty of soap, hot water and towels, a lobby where the men could rest and write letters, a big dining hall with an abundance of good food. Furthermore, this wasn't just part of the enthusiasm of the first few months of the war; the Philadelphians kept it up right through to Appomattox, and even opened a second "refreshment saloon" when the first became overcrowded. A member of the 37th Massachusetts recorded that his regiment visited Philadelphia six times during the war and got the same friendly treatment each time. A veteran of the 10th Massachusetts Battery, looking back fondly long afterward, wrote: "When supper ended we began our march across the city with such a handshaking with young and old of both sexes, and such a Godspeed from all the population, as came from no other city or town through which we passed, and this was continued until our arrival at the Baltimore depot. Could the wives and sweethearts left behind have seen the affectionate leave-takings at this place it might have aroused other than patriotic emotions in their breasts."[12]

This was a deeply sentimental army, and it sang a great deal; not stirring patriotic songs, full of rally-round-the-flag heroism—they were for stay-at-home civilians—but slow, sad tunes that could express the loneliness and homesickness of boys who had been uprooted and sent out to face hardship and danger and death. Their favorite was a song called "When This Cruel War Is Over," by Charles Carroll Sawyer: a song which might well have been, momentarily, the most popular song ever written in America. It sold more than a million copies during the war, which would be equivalent to a sale of seven or eight million today—and that was before the era of canned music and artful song pluggers, before the day when there was a piano or other musical instrument, plus some sort of musical training, in every home. The song went like this:

> *Dearest love, do you remember,*
>   *When we last did meet,*
> *How you told me that you loved me,*
>   *Kneeling at my feet?*
> *Oh, how proud you stood before me*
>   *In your suit of blue,*
> *When you vowed to me and country*
>   *Ever to be true.*

And the chorus:

> *Weeping, sad and lonely,*
>   *Hopes and fears how vain!*
> *Yet praying, when this cruel war is over,*
>   *Praying that we meet again.*

Men would sing that song and cry. More than any other possession of the army, it expressed the deep inner feeling of the boys who had gone to war so blithely in an age when no one would speak the truth about the reality of war: war is tragedy, it is better to live than to die, young men who go down to dusty death in battle have been horribly tricked. The higher brass didn't admire the song at all; some fathead in shoulder straps at one time actually issued an order forbidding the singing of it in the Army of the Potomac, on the ground that it encouraged desertion—being quite unable to see that it really worked the other way by giving the boys a chance to express their war-weariness simply by opening their mouths and singing rather than by dropping their muskets and running away. As might be supposed, the order was totally ineffective and was soon re-scinded.

Next in popularity, probably, was "Tenting Tonight on the Old Camp Ground"; a song more familiar nowadays because it hung on after the war, being adapted to express the emotions of old soldiers at reunions, whereas "Weeping, Sad and Lonely" wasn't, exactly. There was, of course, not a trace in either song of the jingle and stir of what is commonly thought of as patriotic music. "Tenting To-night" frankly states the soldier's dejection:

> We're tenting tonight on the old camp ground,
>   Give us a song to cheer
> Our weary hearts, a song of home,
>   And friends we love so dear.

The chorus complains:

> Many are the hearts that are weary tonight,
>   Wishing for the war to cease;
> Many are the hearts that are looking for the right,
>   To see the dawn of peace.

And the conclusion, very soft and long-drawn-out:

> Dying tonight . . . dying tonight,
> Dying on the old . . . camp . . . ground.

They were sentimentalists, all right, the boys who sang those songs around their campfires, with the regimental bands lifting the slow melodies up to the dark sky like drifting plumes of wood smoke from the embers; but they weren't milk-and-water sentimentalists. If they chose to make a song about "dying tonight," they were the men who had to go out and do the dying, and they knew it. (In the thrice-valiant 2nd Wisconsin the figures showed that by the end of the war nearly nine out of ten men in combat assignments had been shot. If non-combatants like company cooks, officers' servants, ambulance details, and so on, are included, the proportion is closer to nine out of twelve.)

They liked "Lorena," too, although that was perhaps more popular in the Southern armies—"Lorena" with its sugary, paper-lace-valentine romantics:

> *The years creep slowly by, Lorena,*
> *The snow is on the grass again:*
> *The sun's low down the sky, Lorena,*
> *The frost gleams where the flowers have been.*

North and South, the armies sang Stephen Foster—"My Old Kentucky Home," "Old Folks at Home," "Old Black Joe," and "Nellie Gray," especially the latter. Ranking close to "Tenting Tonight" was "The Vacant Chair"—

> *We shall meet, but we shall miss him;*
> *There will be one vacant chair—*

and they liked old favorites such as "Drink to Me Only with Thine Eyes" and "Auld Lang Syne" and—deeply, tearfully—"Home, Sweet Home." It is recorded that during the long winter after the battle of Fredericksburg, when the two rival armies were camped on opposite sides of the Rappahannock, with the boys on the opposing picket posts daily swapping coffee for tobacco and comparing notes on their generals, their rations, and other matters, and with each camp in full sight and hearing of the other, one evening massed Union bands came down to the riverbank to play all of those songs, plus the more rousing tunes like "John Brown's Body," "The Battle Cry of Freedom," and "Tramp, Tramp, Tramp the Boys are Marching." Northerners and Southerners, the soldiers sang those songs or sat and listened to them, massed in their thousands on the hillsides, while the darkness came down to fill the river valley and the light of the campfires glinted off the black water. Finally the Southerners called across, "Now play some of ours," so without pause the Yankee bands swung into "Dixie" and "The Bonnie Blue Flag" and "Maryland, My Maryland." And then at last the massed bands played "Home, Sweet Home," and 150,000 fighting men tried to sing it and choked up and just sat there, silent, staring off into the darkness; and at last the music died away and the bandsmen put up their instruments and both armies went to bed. A few weeks later they were tearing each other apart in the lonely thickets around Chancellorsville.[13]

Singing on the march was not very common except among recruits. After the first half-hour an army march settled down to a dull question of endurance; there was mud to contend with, or if there was no mud there were choking clouds of dust, and nobody had any breath or enthusiasm to waste on songs. On special occasions, though, the troops might fall into step and strike up a song; one of the German regiments (all especially noted for their singing) came tramping into Frederick with flags uncased, singing the John Brown song lustily. It was noted, too, that when troops were marched through Charles Town, where old Brown had been tried and hanged, they had a way of singing that song. Once in a while, when the day was cool and the road was good, a regiment might sing a bit on the march out of sheer good spirits; but when it did the song was apt to be a homemade ditty, neither sentimental nor patriotic, like the little song of the Zouave regiments:

> Oh we belong to the Zoo-Zoo-Zoos—
> Don't you think we oughter?
> We're going down to Washing-town
> To fight for Abraham's daughter.

When the soldiers used music to complain about their lot, it was not so much the fighting they were protesting against—although, being very human, they would have been glad to be shut of it. Boredom, dirt, disease, bad food, and the general air of doing everything the hard way which is inseparable from army life (it began, no doubt, in Julius Caesar's legions) seemed to cause most of the grousing. A veteran of the 2nd Massachusetts found military martinets the soldier's chief cross. He wrote that his colonel once put a company commander under arrest for talking to a sergeant (during a halt while the army was on the march) without requiring the sergeant to stand at attention—a touch which sounds quite modern, somehow. A man in the 37th Massachusetts thought the worst thing about army life was the long delay, with everyone standing in ranks under full pack, which occurred on every march. In the 21st New York a private wrote that the shoddy uniform was the worst trial; it absorbed the rain and held it next to the skin, keeping the soldier wetter and colder than if he were naked. To the historian of the 3rd Wisconsin, by far the worst feature of the entire war was the camp diarrhea, which hit almost everyone sooner or later and which in many cases became chronic, weakening men and causing them to lose weight, often resulting in death or in a medical discharge. A soldier in the 17th Michigan found war's worst trial "the terrible, nauseating stench that envelopes a military camp." To a young officer in the 57th New York the worst thing was the old army officer from the regular service; such men, he said, "suffered from red-tape-ism, slowness, desire for a comfortable berth, and above and beyond all, jealousy." By contrast, among the enlisted men the regular officers often seemed to be better liked than the volunteers; a private in the 128th New York noted that the one officer in his regiment who tried to look out for the enlisted men was the lieutenant colonel, the regiment's lone regular. The historian of the 4th Rhode Island was bitter about the food given sick and wounded men in hospital; the mainstay, he said, was "shadow soup." He gave the recipe: put a large kettle of water on to boil, then hang a chicken so that its shadow falls in the water, and boil the shadow for half an hour; add salt and pepper and serve.

These were the particularized complaints. But the whole was greater than the sum of its parts. War itself was the real evil, and the charge was never fully formulated. Those soldiers lacked the easy articulateness of the modern youth, and they could never quite say what it was that they hated so much—and so, being unable to say it, they took it out by singing the sad, mournful little songs that come down the years so inexpressibly moving.

Chaplains the army had in plenty—one for each regiment—to give the boys spiritual consolation. Yet as one reads the memoirs and diaries there is a distinct impression that as a group, and with honorable exceptions, the chaplains somehow did not quite measure up. There were too many misfits; in that free-and-easy age, too many unqualified men, perhaps, had taken holy orders. A Massachusetts regiment had a first lieutenant who was a minister in private life; he pulled wires to get himself made regimental chaplain, failed, and wound up by absconding with ninety dollars in company funds. A diarist in another Eastern regiment mentioned a chaplain who was court-martialed for stealing a horse, and added that as a general thing the chaplains were not too highly thought of. For a time the 48th New York enjoyed a special odor of sanctity because so many of its officers had been ministers. It fell from grace, however, when it was put to work opening a channel for gunboats through some tidal swamp during the expedition to Port Royal and the Savannah delta. The work was extremely hard and the weather was very hot and steamy, and all hands became excessively profane, ex-ministers and all. A brigadier, watching them at work one day, asked the lieutenant colonel if he really was a preacher. The officer replied apologetically: "Well, no, General, I can't say I'm a regularly ordained minister. I'm just one of those —— —— local preachers."[14]

With the shepherds backsliding in that way, the 48th as a flock quickly got a reputation for unbridled wickedness. Famous throughout the army was the story told about the 48th in connection with this same coastal expedition. An attack by a new ironclad Rebel gunboat was anticipated, and elaborate plans were made to entrap the monster with submarine obstructions that would cause it to run aground on a mud bank. But then the question arose: how to board the vessel, once it was trapped? It was sheathed in iron and its ports would be closed flush with its sloping sides, and it would be impossible to get into it and subdue the crew. The colonel of the 48th (according to the legend) had the answer. Parading his regiment, he said: "Now, men, you've been in this cursed swamp for two weeks, up to your ears in mud—no fun, no glory and blessed poor pay. Here's a chance. Let every man who has had experience as a cracksman or a safe-blower step to the front." To the last man, the regiment rolled forward four paces and came expectantly to attention.[15]

Which calls to mind the evil repute of yet another New York regiment, the 6th, which had a large enrollment of Bowery toughs— one officer spoke of it as "the very flower of the Dead Rabbits, the crème de la crème of Bowery society." Army rumor had it that before a man could enlist in this regiment he had to show that he had done time in a prison: a libel, beyond question, but the army liked to believe it. And it was alleged that when this regiment was about to take off for the South the colonel harangued the men; thinking to inspire them, he drew out his gold watch and held it up for all to see. They were going, he said, to the Deep South, where every plantation owner, living luxuriously among his slaves, was waiting to be despoiled of a watch quite as good as this one. If they were brave soldiers each might get one for himself. Five minutes later, looking to see what time it was, he found that his watch was gone. (Writing long afterward, the regiment's historian complained bitterly about the "vicious nonsense" which was circulated about the regiment. He blamed the regiment's colonel, who liked the stories, having "that essentially American cynic humor which often finds amusement in wild exaggeration.")

Those New York regiments seemed to breed odd stories. A devout chaplain, it was said, went to the colonel of a Manhattan regiment which had no chaplain and asked permission to hold services. The colonel was dubious; his men were a godless lot, he said, and he doubted that the chaplain would accomplish much. But the chaplain, who believed in saving sinners where he found them, was insistent. He had just held services, he said, in the neighboring Brooklyn regiment, and—but that was enough. Between the Brooklyn and Manhattan regiments there was a great rivalry, and the colonel instantly ordered the regiment paraded for divine worship, announcing that if a man smiled, coughed, or even moved he would be thrown in the guardhouse. The chaplain held his services, and at the end asked if any men would come up and make profession of faith; thirteen men had done so, he said, in the Brooklyn regiment. The colonel sprang to his feet.

"Adjutant!" he bellowed. "Detail twenty men and have them baptized at once. This regiment is not going to let that damned Brooklyn regiment beat it at anything!"[16]

For a few days there in Maryland the army came about as close to contentment as an army on active service ever gets. The future did not exist, and the past would somehow be made up for; there was only the present, with easy marches, friendly country, clear weather, and good roads. A veteran in George H. Gordon's brigade has left a picture of a noonday halt: each man building a tiny campfire, putting his own personal, makeshift kettle (an empty fruit can with a bit of haywire for a bail) on to boil water from his canteen, shaking in coffee from a little cloth bag carried in the haversack. "At the same time a bit of bacon or pork was broiling on a stick, and in a few minutes the warm meal was cooked and dispatched. Then, washing his knife by stabbing it in the ground, and eating up his plate, which was a hardtack biscuit, the contented soldier lit his laurel-root pipe, took a few puffs, lay down with his knapsack for a pillow, and dozed until the sharp command, 'Fall in!' put an end to his nap."[17]

2. Crackers and Bullets

The best thing about being in Maryland, the soldiers agreed, was that the people had plenty of fresh provisions to sell and were quite willing to sell them. The army was in funds; most of the men had put in four months on the peninsula, a war-ravaged country where the people had no food to spare and in any case scorned to deal with Yankees, and there had been little chance to spend anything. It had been but little different along the Rappahannock, although in the larger towns a man could usually make a deal; the 14th New York was alleged to have passed some three thousand dollars in counterfeit Confederate notes—obtained heaven knows how —among the luckless shopkeepers of Fredericksburg. But now, with money in his pocket and things to spend it on, the soldier enjoyed a few days of better eating than the regulations called for.

The Civil War soldier would have stared in amazement if he could have looked ahead eighty years to see the War Department, in World War II, thoughtfully retaining female experts on cookery to devise tasty menus for the troops and setting up elaborate schools to train cooks and bakers. No such frills were dreamed of in his day; the theory then seems to have been that if the raw materials of dinner were provided in quantity the army would make out all right. In a sense, the government might have been right. The army did survive, although, looking back at the provisioning and cooking arrangements, one sometimes wonders why it didn't die, to the last man, of acute indigestion. For while the government provided plenty of food of a sort, the business of getting it cooked and served was left entirely up to the soldiers.

One regimental historian—whose experience was quite typical—recalled that when his outfit was first assembled in camp the authorities simply issued quantities of flour, pork, beans, rice, sugar, coffee, molasses, and bread, made kettles and skillets available, and then suggested that the men had better form messes of from six to ten members and get busy on the cooking. The men did as instructed, and in each mess the men took their turns acting as cooks. (The phrase, "acting as," seems expressive, somehow.) A few of the fancy-pants Eastern militia regiments which turned out in response to the first call for ninety-day service had no trouble; they hired their own civilian cooks and got along fine as long as they stayed close to town in established camps where ranges, bake ovens, and civilian markets were handy. But these were the regiments where private soldiers wore tailor-made uniforms (bought at the individual's expense, as carefully fitted and frequently as gaudy as a Coldstream Guard colonel's) and they were never characteristic, nor did they last very long.

Neither, for that matter, did the extreme sketchiness of the informal regimental messes. Sooner or later the institution of the regular company cook was established: two to a company, detailed to the job by order and excused from drill and combat duty. Naturally, their quality varied greatly. Here and there a regiment was lucky enough to find that it actually had some professional cooks in the ranks, although that didn't happen often; nobody, from first to last, was ever enlisted as a cook. Mostly, the company cooks learned their trade on the job, and the soldiers had to eat what they prepared while they were learning. A soldier in the 19th Massachusetts, considering the matter with an indignation which a quarter century of peace had not diminished, summed it up in words which most soldiers would have endorsed: "A company cook is a peculiar being: he generally knows less about cooking than any man in the company. Not being able to learn the drill, and too dirty to appear on inspection, he is sent to the cook house to get him out of the ranks."[1] A notable exception to all of this was, as might be expected, the 55th New York, full of transplanted Frenchmen. They knew something about cooking, and their officers' mess, at least, was famous. President Lincoln dined with them once while they were in camp on the edge of Washington, and told the officers afterward that if their men could fight as well as they could cook the regiment would do very well indeed. They had given him, he added, the best meal he had had in Washington.

A good deal depended on the higher officers. If they insisted that their men be well fed, the men usually fared pretty well. Phil Kearny used to have a habit of sticking his head into the company mess kitchens just before mealtime to sample the food. If the cooking was bad or if the shack was dirty, the company cooks—plus the company and regimental officers—were sure to have a bad time of it before the general left.

In many cases that strange Civil War figure, the contraband, came to the rescue. Now and then, among the escaped slaves who attached themselves to the army as the campaigns in Virginia progressed, were house servants who could cook, and when a detachment got hold of one it never let him go. One company in the 21st Massachusetts acquired somewhere along the Rappahannock a contraband named (apparently by themselves) Jeff Davis. He was a first-rate cook, and he served also as a sort of unofficial commissary agent and general factotum for the entire company. They picked up a mule for him from some secessionist farmer's stock, and he loaded the beast with his kitchen equipment and supplies. Every pay day he would pass the hat and each man would chip in a quarter or half a dollar which Jeff Davis used as a mess fund, so that the company often enjoyed extras like fresh eggs, butter, and garden truck, most of them lawfully bought and paid for. This priceless contraband served with the regiment to the end of the war and went north with the men after Appomattox; he settled near Worcester, married, raised a family, and, wrote the regiment's historian, lived happily ever after —one case where emancipation worked out nicely.

But even after the kitchen arrangements were formalized there were many, many occasions when cooking was strictly a matter of each man for himself. On any march where speed was essential, or where there were frequent brushes with the enemy, regiments would be separated from their wagon trains for days at a time. Then the men were given "marching rations"—three days' supply of hardtack, coffee, and salt pork per man, plus sugar and salt, all carried in the haversack—and, as far as the army authorities were concerned, that was what the men lived on until the wagons joined them again. As a result, the experienced soldier always carried kitchen equipment with him: a little tin pail or empty can for a kettle, and a tin plate or half a canteen with an improvised wooden handle for frying pan. With these, and a few splinters to make a fire, he could get by, although what the results must have done to his stomach is enough to make a dietitian wince.

The hardtack was the great staple. It was a solid cracker, some three inches square and nearly half an inch thick: solid, hard, nourishing, and—by surviving testimony—good enough to eat when it was fresh, which wasn't always the case. Nine or ten of these slabs constituted a day's ration, and a soldier who wanted more could generally get them, since many of the men couldn't eat that many and would give some away. For breakfast and supper, when on the march, the soldier was apt to crumble the hardtack in his coffee and eat it with a spoon. Now and then a whole hardtack was soaked in water, drained, and fried in pork fat, when it went under the name of "skillygalee" and was, said a veteran, "certainly indigestible enough to satisfy the cravings of the most ambitious dyspeptic." At times the hardtack was toasted on the end of a stick; if it charred, as it generally did, it was believed good for weak bowels. Boxes of hardtack, piled high, often stood in all weathers on open platforms at railway supply depots. If the hardtack got moldy it was usually thrown away as inedible, but if it just got weevily it was issued anyway. Heating it at the fire would drive the weevils out; more impatient soldiers simply ate it in the dark and tried not to think about it.

The issue of salt pork was frequently eaten raw, on hardtack, when the men were on the march, since it was hard to cook without regular kettles and tasted about as good one way as the other, anyhow. Occasionally the salt pork was rancid when the men got it.

When salt beef was issued instead of salt pork the men objected loudly—except, it was noticed, the men who had been deep-sea sailors before the war; no army salt beef could phase men who had eaten it out of the harness cask after six months at sea. The beef was so deeply impregnated with salt that it had to be soaked overnight in running water to be edible, and for that reason it was seldom issued as part of the marching ration. When cooked, it generally stank to high heaven, for it was often very aged. Now and then, when an especially bad hunk of it was served out, the men would organize a mock funeral, parading through camp with the offending beef on a bier and burying it—where the colonel could see, if possible—with fancy ceremonies. Bacon was enjoyed, but on the march the men preferred salt pork: carried in the haversack in hot weather, bacon had a way of giving off liquid grease, staining a man's clothing and quickly becoming unfit to eat.

Herds of cattle usually were driven along with the army, to be butchered nightly to provide fresh meat; the beef thus obtained, one veteran recalled, was "not particularly juicy." The company cooks (naturally) were always accused of keeping the best portions for themselves, and one officer remembered, with a noticeable shudder of distaste, the "odious beef served quivering from an animal heated by the long day's march and killed as soon as the day's march was ended." It was nice, now and then, to get a piece of fresh beef from which steaks could be cut. The company cooks would hand the steaks out raw, and each man would broil his own on a stick.

The coffee ration was what kept the army going. The government bought good coffee and issued it in the whole bean to prevent unscrupulous dealers from adulterating it, and the men ground it for themselves by pounding the beans on a rock with a stone or musket butt. The veteran learned to carry a little canvas bag in which he mixed his ground coffee and his sugar ration, spooning them out together when he made his coffee. The ration was ample to make three or four pints of strong black coffee daily, and on the march any halt of more than five minutes was sure to see men making little fires and boiling coffee. Stragglers would often fall out, build a fire, boil coffee, drink it, and then plod on to overtake their regiments at nightfall. Cavalry and artillery referred to infantry, somewhat contemptuously, as "the coffee boilers."

The favorite ration of all was the army bean. It was no go, of course, on the march, but in settled camps it was one food the men never tired of. Even the most inexpert cook knew how to dig a pit, build a wood fire, rake out the coals, lower a covered kettle full of salt pork and soaked beans, heap the coals back on and around it, cover the whole with earth, and leave it to cook overnight. The mess kettle, incidentally, was simply a heavy sheet-iron cylinder, flat-bottomed, some fifteen inches tall by a foot wide, with a heavy iron cover. When potatoes were at hand they were invariably boiled in such a kettle, and beef was often added to make a kind of stew. A real cook could make such a stew quite tasty by adding vegetables (if he had any), doing an intelligent job of seasoning, and thickening the broth with flour.[2]

As a general thing, even though the coffee was good and the baked beans were palatable, the food the Civil War soldier lived on ranged from mediocre to downright awful. Looking at the combination of unbalanced rations, incompetent cooks, and crackers fried in pork fat, one wonders how the men kept their health. The answer, of course, is that many of them didn't. There were many reasons for the terrible prevalence of sickness in that army—the incomplete state of even the best medical knowledge of the day is certainly one of them: no one then knew how typhoid fever was transmitted, for instance, and typhoid killed tens of thousands of soldiers—but faulty diet must have been one of the most important. (One private who lived through it all left it as his opinion that the great amount of sickness was due to "insufficient supplies and brutal, needless exposure of the men by officers of high rank.")

Surprisingly enough, the health of the soldiers was better when they were actively campaigning than when they stayed in camp. The constant exercise and fresh air seem to have counterbalanced the destructive effects of salt pork and hardtack; or perhaps, bad as that diet was, it nevertheless was better than the stuff the company cooks turned out when they had unlimited supplies to draw on. At any rate, the regiments which suffered the heaviest combat losses were almost invariably the ones with the lowest losses from disease. From first to last, some 220,000 Union soldiers died of disease during the war, and a good fifth of them came from regiments which never got into combat at all. Half of the deaths from disease were caused by intestinal ailments, mainly typhoid, diarrhea, and dysentery. Half of the remainder came from pneumonia—"inflammation of the lungs," as it was called then—and from tuberculosis.

This prevalence of sickness meant that in every regiment there was a slow, steady process of attrition, which began the moment the men got into training camp and never ended. And it almost seems as if the authorities went out of their way to make sure that this attrition would take place. By modern standards the arrangements for keeping a regiment's strength up were appallingly bad. Very little was done to keep physical misfits out of the army in the first place, and there were practically no provisions for replacing such men when the hardships of army life remorselessly weeded them out. The 27th Indiana was by no means unique in getting into Federal service without physical examinations. The same thing happened in many other cases. A member of the 5th Massachusetts wrote that physical examinations for his regiment were informal and were not given by a physician—"zeal and patriotism were recognized as potent factors, and their outward manifestations were given full credence." The recruiting, of course, was not uniformly that carefree, but the physical examinations were never really rigid; the men were expected to be "sound of wind and limb," but that was about all.

Yet if the entrance standards were excessively lax, the standards by which a man could be given a medical discharge—a "surgeon's certificate of disability," in the army jargon of the 1860s—were fairly high. The regimental surgeons were for the most part able and conscientious men, and when they found that a man was unfit for active service they said so, and he was paid off. In the spring of 1861 the 2nd New York discharged 118 men for disability. Most of the men promptly re-enlisted in other regiments, the war spirit running high at the time.

Thus, in actual practice, the rigors of life in camp in the 1860s did what the original entrance examination is expected to do now—eliminate the men who, for one reason or another, just weren't rugged enough to stand the gaff. The result was that no regiment in the army, at any time after the first few weeks of its existence, was ever anywhere near its full paper strength. On paper a regiment was supposed to consist of approximately a thousand men. Actually, very few regiments got to the battlefield with anything like that number.

The 20th Massachusetts was mustered in, full strength, on July 2, 1861, getting its first medical exams, incidentally, after the mustering in. By mid-August, when it left Massachusetts, it was down to 500 men. Recruits and returned convalescents later brought in 250 more, but that was high-water mark: from then on its strength went steadily downward. Within a year of its enlistment the 128th New York was down to 350 men, although it had had few battle casualties. The 125th Ohio, which enlisted in the summer of 1862, numbered 751 men when it left Ohio for the South. Six weeks later it was down to 572. A typical entry in the regimental history, made at a time when the regiment was not in action, shows seven deaths and eight medical discharges for one month. The 12th Connecticut took a thousand men from home and had 600 "present for duty" when it lined up to go into its first fight.

Yet with all these losses there were few replacements. Throughout the war men were recruited by the states, not by the Federal government. The governors liked to form new regiments—each one offered a chance for patronage, with a colonel's commission to be awarded to some distinguished, well-heeled citizen who had exerted himself to round up recruits. (There is a record of one New York merchant who spent $20,000 to raise a cavalry regiment. He became its colonel but was never seen in camp, finding the avenues and hotel bars of Washington much pleasanter. The regiment finally went off to fight without him, while he, having good political connections, became a brigadier and wound up in command of some empty barracks safely inside the Union lines.) The states simply had no arrangements whatever for recruiting replacement troops, since it was politically more profitable to form new regiments. Each regiment had to do its own recruiting when and if it could. Now and then an officer, sometimes a whole company, would be sent home on furlough to drum up men, but this was seldom very effective. Only Wisconsin, of all the states, officially recruited replacements for regiments already in the field, which was one of the reasons why every general liked to have a few Wisconsin regiments around if he could manage it.

The result of all this, naturally, was that the war was fought with what would now be considered skeleton regiments. A colonel who could take 500 men into action considered himself very lucky indeed. By the fall of 1862, when the army was drifting up through Maryland after Lee, a regiment which mustered as many as 350 men was fully up to the average, and many regiments were far under that strength. Technically, a brigade was supposed to consist of four regiments; later in the war we find brigades with six, eight, or even ten, jumbled together in a desperate effort to give the organization the man power a brigade ought to have.

Battle attrition, of course, was deadly. Hardly anybody realized it at the time, but the Civil War soldier was going into action just when technical improvements in the design of weapons had created a great increase in fire power and had given the defense a heavy advantage over the attack. The weapons those men used do look very crude nowadays, but by comparison with earlier weapons—the weapons on which all tactical theories and training of the day were based—they were very modern indeed. It is not much of an exaggeration to say that the armies of 1861 were up against exactly the same thing that the armies of 1914 were up against—the fact that defensive fire power had made obsolete all of the established methods for getting an offensive action under way. As in 1914, the enlisted man paid with his life for the high command's education on this matter.

The basic, all-important weapon, of course, was the infantry musket, and the standard of the war was the rifled Springfield. This was a muzzle-loader, with an involved procedure for loading. Drill on the target range began with the command, "Load in nine times: load!" (The "nine times" meant that nine separate and distinct operations were involved in loading a piece; recruits were trained to do it "by the numbers.") The cartridge was a paper cylinder encasing a soft-lead bullet and a charge of powder. The soldier bit off one end of the paper, poured the powder down the barrel, rammed the bullet down with his ramrod, cocked the heavy hammer with his thumb, and had a percussion cap on the nipple to ignite the charge when he pulled the trigger. For most rifles, these caps came in long rolls which were inserted in a spring-and-cogwheel device in the breech, exactly like the rolls for a child's cap pistol today.

This weapon has long since been a museum piece, but the big point about it then was that it was rifled and had a bullet which took the rifling properly. The bullet was the Minié, named for the French captain who had invented it—the bullets were "minnies" to all soldiers—a conical slug of lead slightly more than half an inch in diameter and about an inch long, with a hollow base which expanded when the rifle was fired and prevented leakage of the powder gases. It would kill at half a mile or more, although it was not very accurate at anything like that distance. Its effective range was from 200 to 250 yards—"effective range" meaning the distance at which a defensive line of battle could count on hitting often enough to break up an attack by relatively equal numbers. A good man could get off two shots a minute.

Compared with a modern Garand, the rifle was laughable; but compared with the smoothbore which had been the standard weapon in all previous wars, it was terrific. Early in the Civil War, before the government got the rifled muskets into mass production, many regiments were equipped with the old smoothbores, which fired a round ball or, sometimes, a cartridge containing one round ball and three buckshot: the "buck and ball" of army legend. Regiments which had to use such muskets were disgusted with them. Extreme range was about 250 yards, and accuracy was almost nil at any range. As one of the backwoodsmen from Wisconsin remarked, it took a fairly steady hand to hit a barn door at fifty paces. At very close range, of course, they were quite effective, especially when firing "buck and ball," which gave a scatter-gun effect. These primitive smoothbores were discarded as fast as new weapons were produced, and by the fall of 1862 few regiments on either side carried them.

Yet it was these ineffective old smoothbores on which all established combat tactics and theories were based. That is why the virtues of the bayonet figured so largely in the talk of professional soldiers of that era. Up until then the foot soldier was actually a spear carrier in disguise, the bayonet was the decisive weapon, and an infantry charge was just the old Macedonian phalanx in modern dress—a compact mass of men projecting steel points ahead of them, striving to get to close quarters where they could either impale their opponents or force them to run away. All offensive infantry tactics were designed to enable a commander to throw that compact, steel-tipped mass against an enemy line of battle.

But with the rifled musket it just didn't work that way any more. The compact mass could be torn to shreds before it got in close. The advancing line came under killing fire four or five times as far off as used to be the case. As one student of Civil War casualties remarked: "There was a limit of punishment beyond which endurance would not go, and the old Springfield rifle was capable of inflicting it."[3] Like the machine gun in 1914, here was a weapon which upset all the old theories. The natural result was that actual hand-to-hand work with the bayonet was a great rarity in the Civil War, for all the fine talk of grand bayonet charges to be found in the generals' memoirs. The bayonet was still carried and it was still a threat, but very few men ever used it. Of some 245,000 wounds treated by surgeons in Union hospitals, fewer than a thousand had been made by bayonets. One reason, of course, may be that when a man did get bayoneted he usually died on the spot; nevertheless, the figure is significant.

The Confederate General John B. Gordon, who got into about as much truly desperate fighting as any man on either side, wrote after the war: "I may say that very few bayonets of any kind were actually used in battle, as far as my observation extended. The one line or the other usually gave way under the galling fire of small arms, grape and canister, before the bayonet could be brought into requisition. The bristling points and the glitter of the bayonets were fearful to look upon, as they were levelled in front of a charging line: but they were rarely reddened with blood."[4] In several private soldiers' memoirs one finds the remark that the bayonet was really most useful as a candlestick: its point could be jabbed into the ground easily and its socket was just the right size to hold a candle.

The rifled musket not only had a greater range and accuracy than anything soldiers had ever used before; it made an uncommonly nasty wound—actually, a good deal worse, in most cases, than the one inflicted by today's rifle, and infinitely worse than that of the round ball fired by the old smoothbore. Its muzzle velocity was high enough to give the bullet considerable shocking power, and the bullet itself was relatively huge; furthermore, it usually mushroomed when it hit bone or cartilage, with dreadful effect. The ghastly number of amputations performed at all field hospitals—veterans repeatedly told of vast, hideous piles of severed arms and legs lying by the hospital tents in battle—did not take place because the surgeons were unskillful, or because they knew less than modern surgeons know about the way to treat gunshot wounds. They took place because when one of those soft-lead rifle bullets hit a bone it usually splintered the bone so horribly that no medical magic could save the limb.

As one army surgeon wrote long afterward, when comparative experience with the effect of modern rifles was available: "The shattering, splintering or splitting of a long bone by the impact of the Minié or Enfield ball were, in many instances, both remarkable and frightful, and early experience taught surgeons that amputation was the only means of saving life." The same surgeon added that a wound in the abdomen inflicted by one of these rifles was almost invariably fatal; the Minié bullet tore the intestines as the old smoothbore ball seldom did.[5] The one advantage that the Civil War soldier enjoyed over today's soldier, in respect to bullet wounds, was that at a moderately long range the old Springfield lacked penetrating power. There were repeated instances of soldiers being knocked down by bullets which failed to break the skin because they were stopped by some unimportant obstruction in the pocket—a deck of cards, a bundle of letters, or a pocket Testament. (How many solemn homilies were delivered, in succeeding years, by devout churchmen on that one subject: the pocket Testament that saved a life!)

All of this meant that the soldier who got hit was likely to be hurt pretty badly. The official casualty figures don't quite tell the story. They show, usually, that from six to eight men were wounded for each man killed outright, which is apt to make a modern reader (to whom a muzzle-loader is more or less a joke, anyway) assume that the weapon was ineffective. What the casualty figures don't show is that a substantial number of the wounded died in hospital; usually, according to one authority, about two thirds as many as were killed instantly. Altogether, about half of the men wounded in any engagement were lost to the army for good: mortally wounded, or permanently disabled. In addition, a fair number of the men reported "missing" were dead—men who fell in dense underbrush or isolated ravines, or men who crawled off into thickets after they were hit and were missed by the ambulance parties and the burial details.

For example, a battle is fought and an army reports a hundred men killed and nine hundred wounded. Of the nine hundred, between sixty and seventy will die, while nearly four hundred will be too badly crippled ever to return to duty. The army, therefore, has not merely suffered a temporary loss of nine hundred men; it has lost, permanently, rather more than five hundred men. The casualty figures for every Civil War battle, ghastly as they are even on the surface, need to be adjusted upward if they are to tell the true story.

If the power of the infantry rifle had been stepped up, so had the power of the artillery. The rifled gun was just coming in, like the rifled musket, and most generals did not quite understand what could be done with it. Standard fieldpiece when the war began was the twelve-pounder brass smoothbore; the famous "Napoleon" one reads so much about in the Civil War stories. When McClellan's chief of artillery set things up for the peninsular campaign he specified that two thirds of the army's guns should be Napoleons. This proportion was greatly reduced later, but the brass smoothbore remained popular right to the end. The gun fired a round ball some four and one half inches in diameter, had an extreme range of about one mile, but was woefully inaccurate at anything over half that distance; was liked chiefly for close-range work, when it fired case shot—thin-walled shell filled with a bursting charge and a hatful of lead slugs—or, by preference, canister. The canister cartridge was a sheet-metal cylinder with a charge of powder in an attached container at one end and a thin wooden plug at the other, and it was filled with two or three hundred round bullets. Firing this, the Napoleon was really a sawed-off shotgun of enormous size, and at close ranges—say up to 250 yards —the effect was murderous beyond belief. The only trouble was that the range of the infantryman's rifle had increased so; troops could often pick off the gunners before they got within canister range, unless the battery could be rushed into action after a charge got under way. In addition, the Napoleon was heavy and hard to move across broken country.

The new rifles were much better for everything except the infighting. They had twice the Napoleon's range, and for that day were exceedingly accurate. The commonest types were the three-inch iron rifle and the ten- and twenty-pounder Parrotts. These were fairly light and easy to handle, and all were muzzle-loaders. Breech-loading cannon did not appear on Civil War battlefields, except for a few English guns the Confederates imported, which fired queer-looking projectiles that were twisted to fit the spiraled hexagonal tubes and raised a horrifying screech as they sped through the air. The muzzle-loaders could be served with fair rapidity, and generals who knew how to use them could often break up an attack before it got well started because of their great range and power. (General Henry J. Hunt, in charge of Union artillery at Gettysburg, insisted to the end of his days that Pickett's historic charge would never have reached the Union line if Hunt had been allowed to do what he proposed—keep the Federal guns out of action during most of the preliminary bombardment in order to save their ammunition and their gunners, and plaster the Rebel infantry with everything he had from the moment it lined up for the charge. He was probably entirely correct.)

The artillerist's big problem throughout the war was with his fuses. They weren't too precise, and the gunner was never quite sure just where a shell would burst or, for that matter, whether it would burst at all. Federals had a big advantage over Confederates in artillery. They had more rifled guns, which meant they could often outrange the Rebel gunners, hitting without being hit; even more important, their fuses and powder were of better quality, so that the Northern gunner had a much better chance of seeing his shells strike and explode where he wanted them to.

What all of this meant—rifled muskets for the infantry, rifled cannon for the artillery—was that the defense had a huge advantage. Field tactics were still built around the idea of sending massed troops smack into and over the enemy line, and all military thinking ran in that direction. But a battle line whose flanks were anchored and which had any kind of protection in front was, in fact, just about invulnerable to that kind of attack. At Gaines's Mill, Fitz-John Porter, with one army corps (plus very moderate reinforcements late in the day), stood off most of Lee's army for six hours and came close to holding his ground for keeps. At Malvern Hill, where the artillery had a clear field, the Rebel assaults just didn't have a chance. Likewise, at Second Bull Run, Jackson's men behind their railway embankment were in shape to hold their ground for the rest of the summer. The fight Gibbon's and Doubleday's men had with Jackson's corps there earlier, with both battle lines standing elbow to elbow and blazing away, might have been in the grand tradition of the earlier wars, but for the 1860s it was utterly useless; murderous enough to satisfy the most bloodthirsty, but almost as out of date as it would be today.

The armies had begun to adjust themselves to the new state of af-

fairs. The skirmish line—which originally had been merely a thin
cordon of scouts going ahead to make sure the enemy didn't have
any unpleasant surprises concealed in advance of his main line—
was being built up, bit by bit, into an attacking line. An assault on
a hostile position was ceasing to imply a steady, unbroken advance
by men whose one aim was to reach a hand-to-hand encounter; the
old lithographs of Civil War battles, drawn by men who weren't
present, have left a false impression. The most spirited "assault" on
a hostile position was apt to be delivered by troops who were completely motionless, hiding behind any obstruction the ground afforded,
moving forward—when they did move forward—by short rushes, advancing small parties here and there under a cover of protective fire,
seeking to build up within effective range a firing line heavy enough
to beat down the opposing fire and persuade the enemy that it was
time for him to go. A battle line which was getting the worst of it
often gave way almost imperceptibly, the men firing and then stepping
back a couple of paces while they reloaded, the attackers moving
forward in the same manner. While this happened the line that was
being beaten would leak men to the rear, as individual soldiers here
and there decided they had had enough and turned to run.

Small inequalities in the ground—an outcropping of rock, a sunken
road, an old fence whose rails could be pulled loose and piled along
the ground to provide protection—were apt to become of decisive
importance. The great defect of the Civil War musket was that only
a contortionist could load it when he was lying down; if he fought
in a prone position, as he very often did, he needed some sort of
protection so that he could load his piece safely. The soldiers early
noticed that a surprisingly high percentage of crippling wounds oc-
cured in the right hand and arm, exposed when a man rammed a new
charge down his muzzle-loader. When regular entrenchments were
dug, so that men were fully protected while they loaded and fired,
direct assault became practically impossible—as Grant finally realized
at Cold Harbor.

It was because a frontal attack was so easily repulsed that the
flanking movement was so important. In front, a brigade might have
the direct fire power of fifteen hundred rifles; caught end-on, at either
extremity of its line, it had a fire power of exactly two, and so was
utterly helpless unless it could shift its position fast. Where a whole

army could be flanked, the way incautious Pope let Longstreet flank him at Bull Run, the inevitable result was complete defeat; in any battle line, a gap between regiments or brigades was a sure invitation to disaster. Impregnable as his position was at Fredericksburg, Jackson had a few bad moments when Meade found an open place between two brigades; if Meade could have been supported, old Stonewall might have had serious trouble. Pickett's great complaint after Gettysburg was that he had to make his assault with no protection for his flanks: the Federals curled around the ends of his line and tore the heart out of him.

To get from marching formation into fighting formation, the soldier had to learn, and become letter-perfect in, a long series of intricate maneuvers, as formalized as a ballet dance. If he had to march any distance at all he did it in column—column of twos, of fours, of platoons, of companies, or what not. To fight, the column had to be spread out into a long line two ranks deep, and the complexities of infantry drill in those days, designed to bring this about, were something today's soldier is happily spared. Furthermore, those complexities weren't just parade-ground maneuvers; they had to be learned if the men were to be able to fight. There were a dozen different ways for shaking a marching column out into line, and the men and their officers had to know all of them—had to know them well enough so that the maneuvers could be performed under fire, for if an organization formed its battle line too soon it was all but impossible to get it forward into action. The wild rout at the first battle of Bull Run is perfectly comprehensible: most of the soldiers just did not know how to perform those maneuvers. Once they got into line, they fought well; the trouble was that neither officers nor men had ever had any experience at swinging a marching brigade into a formation from which it could fight, or vice versa, and they got hopelessly snarled up when they tried it. One participant recalled that a Massachusetts regiment was ordered to open fire while it was still formed in column of companies. Naturally, men in the leading ranks were killed and wounded by the fire of their own inexpert comrades in the rear. The wonder is that either army, in that first battle, was able to do any fighting at all.[6]

Unless troops were expected to capture a remote position and stay there overnight, in which case they would want food and blankets, the usual routine was to leave knapsacks and other surplus equipment in bivouac before moving up to fight. That order was always complied with gladly; no soldier ever enjoyed carrying his knapsack, but the one the Civil War soldier carried seems to have been especially irksome—it was poorly designed, so that its straps cut the shoulders and strained the back even more than its weight and bulk made necessary. Unless the regimental or brigade commander was a stickler for doing everything regular-army style, seasoned troops soon discarded the knapsack altogether and substituted the blanket roll. This was formed by spreading out the half of a pup tent which each soldier carried, laying the opened blanket on top of it, arranging such spare clothing as the soldier might have on top of that, and then rolling the whole business up as tightly as possible, tying it with straps from the discarded knapsack, looping the two ends together to form what the soldier called a horse collar, and then slipping it over one shoulder. The army was mildly amused when the spanking-new 118th Pennsylvania joined up on the way through Maryland. This regiment, known as the "Corn Exchange regiment" (it had been raised and equipped by elderly patriots of the Philadelphia Corn Exchange), carried oversized knapsacks, well filled with spare pants, boots, coats, and other oddments. When it came into camp the veterans urged the men to throw all that truck away and switch to blanket rolls, but the Pennsylvanians refused—they wanted to do things right, and the regulations said knapsacks and extra clothing, and they'd stick with 'em. A man in the 22nd Massachusetts, chuckling at them, noted: "I don't suppose there was a spare shirt in my company," and added that his mates traveled so light one man would carry a towel and another man a cake of soap—no sense in each man loading himself down with both.

Other new regiments besides this one from Pennsylvania came in while the army was in Maryland. They came in gaily enough, looking enormous by contrast with the war-thinned veteran regiments, and their uniforms and equipment were new and unstained. The veterans were glad to see them, and remarked that all that newness would get worn off soon enough. One officer, watching them march into camp, wrote: "Some were singing the John Brown song, and others found occasion for merriment in commenting upon the picturesque appearance of our weathered and sunburnt soldiers. They all seemed cheer-

ful, and as their long columns and full ranks marched by, their
polished arms glistening in the sun, one could scarcely repress a sigh
at the thought that, with a certainty, hundreds of these men would
fall in the battle which all knew was now closely impending."[7]

3. Generals on Trial

Back in Washington there was General Halleck, and the general
was worried. Worrying, he called for incompatibles, demanding in
one breath a dashing pursuit and an extreme of caution. Lee must be
overtaken, brought to battle, and crushed, no matter what; but the
army must remember that its primary function was defensive. If it
did not hurry, Lee might get away; if it went too fast, Washington
might be exposed. McClellan should keep his left firmly anchored
on the Potomac as he advanced, lest Lee slide past him to the south
and dash into the capital. On the other hand, it was dangerous to
stick too close to the river: Lee might angle off in the other direction,
making (so to speak) a sweep around right end, seizing Baltimore
and coming down on the capital from the north. All of these points
glowed and sparkled by turns, like shifting specks before the eyes of a
troubled strategist. Halleck's telegrams to McClellan at this time,
although they were numerous, were nagging rather than helpful.

In the beginning McClellan had asked that the garrison at Harper's
Ferry, some twelve thousand good men, be ordered back to join the
main army. He argued that the place itself was of no great importance, that it could quickly be reoccupied once Lee had been driven
south, and that it was wholly indefensible and could not be held in
any case if Lee wanted to make a snatch at it. Halleck pooh-poohed
at him: the twelve thousand men were safe enough, nothing to worry
about there. Later, when Lee had his army squarely interposed between Harper's Ferry and the Army of the Potomac, Halleck notified
McClellan that the garrison was his to command as soon as he could
go pick it up. It couldn't get out unaided, so it would just have to
hold on until McClellan could go and relieve it, which he had better
do at his early convenience. And so on.

Old Brains was in the top command and he was not being particularly impressive. He was strictly a headquarters operator. General

Pope (whom one could nearly feel sorry for, if he weren't Pope) had called on him, almost prayerfully, to come and take command in the field around the time of the second Bull Run fight, but Halleck felt insecure anywhere except at the Washington end of the telegraph line. He refused to budge then and he was not budging now, and he surveyed the war from his office in the War Department, at 17th Street and the avenue, and looked portentous as the papers piled higher and higher on his desk. As he studied these papers—or, for that matter, when he indulged in thought of any kind—he had a way of rubbing his elbows, slowly and methodically: a mannerism which drove Secretary of the Navy Welles almost frantic.

Welles had a number of dealings with him, there being divers matters on which army-navy co-operation was essential, and he came away from all of them feeling rather baffled. When he put a problem up to Halleck, he wrote, "he rubbed his elbow first, as if that was the seat of thought, and then his eyes," and then made noncommittal remarks; and Welles recorded in his diary the impression that Halleck "has a scholarly intellect and, I suppose, some military acquirements, but his mind is heavy and irresolute." Unvarnished old Andrew Foote, the diligent flag officer who commanded the navy's gunboats in the Mississippi early in the war, when Halleck commanded out there for the army, told Welles bluntly that Halleck was a military imbecile who might just possibly make a good clerk. And James Harrison Wilson, then a young officer of topographical engineers, later to become one of the Union's best major generals and an advocate of making war modern-style with magazine rifles, wrote long afterward of the impression he received when he called on Halleck in his office at the War Department:

"He had already received the sobriquet of 'Old Brains,' but when I beheld his bulging eyes, his flabby cheeks, his slack-twisted figure, and his slow and deliberate movements, and noted his sluggish speech, lacking in point and magnetism, I experienced a distinct feeling of disappointment which from that day never grew less. I could not reconcile myself to the idea that an officer of such negative appearance could ever be a great leader of men. . . . Long before the war ended he came to be recognized by close observers, and especially by the Secretary of War, as a negligible quantity."[1]

The record of Halleck's dispatches during the days just before and after Pope's disaster makes curious reading. At a time when the big problem on which the fate of the Union might depend was to get Pope's and McClellan's armies united before Lee could force a battle, Halleck was sounding partly like a dollar-a-year man worried because the newspapers were impertinently printing confidential memoranda, and partly like a tired bureaucrat fussily absorbed by trifles. He wired Pope to clean all the newspaper reporters out of his army and to let no telegrams go out except those signed by himself—there had been too many news leaks recently. Pope protested; Halleck replied that "your staff is decidedly leaky" and complained that the very order calling for a news black-out had been printed in the papers as soon as it was issued. Virtuously Halleck added that "there has been much laxity about all official business in this army."

Office details engrossed him. Three days before the great collision at Bull Run, Pope protested that he was not being kept up to date about the movements of McClellan's forces. Halleck wired back petulantly: "Just think of the immense amount of telegraphing I have to do and then say whether I can be expected to give you any details as to the movements of others, even when I know them." After the fighting began, when Pope implored Halleck to come out and take charge of things himself, Halleck wired tersely: "It is impossible for me to leave Washington." When the commander of the defenses of Washington complained that he could not man the fortifications owing to lack of artillerymen, Halleck replied: "If you are deficient in anything for the defense of the forts, make your requisitions on the proper office. . . . I have no time for these details and don't come to me until you exhaust other resources."

To anyone who has ever worked in Washington, Halleck is quickly recognizable for what he actually was: a typical old-line government-service hack, to whom the tidy operation of an office is an end in itself, infinitely more important than anything the office can conceivably *do*. If the papers progress smoothly from "incoming" to "outgoing," all is well, even though the Republic fall, and it is much less important to prevent the fall than to make certain that no wreckage lands on one's own desk. The Republic is strong and it has amazing resilience, and it can support people like that ordinarily without much trouble, but it can hardly endure having such a one in command of its armies at the height of a furious war.

In the midst of all the Bull Run confusion Secretary Stanton sent in a demand for the full record regarding McClellan's withdrawal from the peninsula: when was he ordered to leave, when did he leave, was the whole operation handled with such slackness as to endanger the country? Recognizing this as Stanton's search for ammunition to destroy McClellan, but bearing in mind also that McClellan might yet ride out the storm and be the hero of the nation, Halleck sent a facing-both-ways reply. He gave all the dates, stated that the withdrawal was not made with the speed the national safety required, but added that once McClellan did begin to move he moved fast and that McClellan at the time reported the delay as unavoidable. No matter who won, Halleck was safe. His reply could be read as condemnation or as vindication, as circumstances might require.

And so one more attempt by the President to solve the problem of army high command was flickering out in windy futility. Lincoln had demoted McClellan because, with McClellan in the number-one spot, nothing much ever seemed to happen. There had been no way to convey to the young general the terrible urgency of the moment, the need to bring the war to a close before it blew up into a raging flame that might consume more than it saved. For a time the President himself, aided by the Secretary of War, had been running things, which had brought nothing but disaster. Military affairs could not be handled by amateurs, even though the President, with a persistence both ludicrous and pathetic, drew military textbooks from the archives and boned up on strategy in his spare time. So Halleck, the genius recommended by General Scott, had been called in, and for a space Lincoln thought he had what he finally got when he called in Grant; but now Halleck was proving that Lincoln had just made another mistake.

Which was tragic, from any viewpoint. Almost anything—including a change in the American form of government—might happen if the command problem were not solved. McClellan's implied proposal for veto power by a soldier over political decisions by the civil authorities had been pigeonholed neatly enough, but some equally astounding suggestions were coming in from other quarters. Chase and Stanton were leading a drive for government by Cabinet: choice of the top generals, and with it control of the war, should be lodged with a junta of cabinet ministers. This drive was failing, partly because Lincoln would have none of it and partly because of the good sense and Yankee stubbornness of Gideon Welles, who flatly refused to be a party to it. Dimly allied with it was a move by Republican leaders to give executive control to Congress: Congress should pick the generals, pass on strategy, and set all war policies, and the Committee on the Conduct of the War—busily spreading fear and distrust and working with clumsy ruthlessness and undying energy—would be its instrument. Nobody who doubted the need for ending slavery overnight would be allowed to have any hand in army affairs—although private soldiers who were not abolitionists would still, presumably, be allowed to die in battle, if perchance they were hit by Southern bullets.

This pressure by the leaders of his own party was something Lincoln could by no means ignore. He had taken his political life in his hands by reinstating McClellan in command of the Army of the Potomac, and the party leaders were sounding off about it. Senator Zachariah Chandler of Michigan, almost incoherent with fury, underlining words with sputtering pen point, was writing that recent disasters to the army had been caused by "treason, rank treason, call it by what name you will," and could see no hope save in "a demand of the loyal governors backed by a threat" to bring about an immediate change in policy; the President was "unstable as water" and was letting himself be "bullied by those traitor Generals" who would yet create a military dictatorship.[2]

To the Republican leaders, everything was simple. The Army of the Potomac was not aggressively used and was shamefully pushed around by muscular Rebels. The reason, as they saw it, could only be that it was led by men whose hearts were not in the cause; by case-hardened Democrats; by men who sympathized with slavery and who therefore did not really want the rebellion suppressed; by men disloyal, in plain English. The remedy was, of course, obvious: entrust the army only to generals whose abolitionist convictions were strong beyond all question and there would be no more of this pampering and cosseting of treason.

This led them into manifest absurdities. They considered John Charles Frémont ideal material for high command: he was sound on the slavery question, and that was enough. The mere fact that he was totally devoid of military ability was beside the point. They also felt that the ineffable Ben Butler would make a good army commander; he was fully as incompetent as Frémont in the military field, but he was "loyal" on the only issue which mattered—even now he was rubbing slaveholders' noses in it, in New Orleans. Franz Sigel, the transplanted German revolutionary, and David Hunter, who had rashly proclaimed emancipation along the Georgia coast, would be equally acceptable. No one ever accused those men of being especially qualified soldiers, but no one ever accused them of sympathy with slavery, either, and that was all that counted. Lincoln flared up once when burly Ben Wade was insisting on the removal of McClellan; if he removed him, asked the President irritably, with whom should he replace him? "Anybody!" cried Wade. Lincoln shook his head; "anybody" might do for Wade, he said, but he must have *somebody*.

Yet these men had a point. One could almost say that they were right for the wrong reasons—or partly right, at any rate, for reasons that were mostly wrong. There *was* a crippling deficiency in the army command, from the brigades and divisions on up, and it was the kind of deficiency from which the Confederate Army of Northern Virginia did not suffer: a lack of the hard, grim, remorseless, driving spirit that must be on tap if wars are to be won.

Stonewall Jackson in the Shenandoah Valley offers an example: driving his men in pursuit of Banks with remorseless fury, sending them on far past the point of physical exhaustion, continuing to pursue even though most of his army had fallen out from sheer inability to take another step, keeping it up long after a more sober general would have realized that pursuit was impossible—but winning, in the end, because he forced Banks to fight at Winchester before Banks could rally his men and get set for the blow, which meant that Banks got licked disastrously.

Jackson was an undefiled genius, to be sure, and it is hardly fair to expect all corps and division commanders to measure up to his standard. But there was a touch of the same sort of thing in the other Confederate commanders. General A. P. Hill was too heedless and impetuous by far, rushing into the attack without proper caution—but, in the end, providing the killing punch, against the odds, that helped to knock McClellan's right wing back behind the Chickahominy. Longstreet was sullen and balky, ignoring Lee's expressed wish, waiting for his foe to make one more ill-advised maneuver. Yet finally, when the opening appeared, he came down on the enemy's exposed flank like an avalanche, every man in action, no reserves held back for use in case something went wrong; and he turned the second battle of Bull Run into a rout. The Confederacy's other General Hill, D. H. Hill, was a carping dyspeptic who observed that Lee's tactics at Malvern Hill were all wrong and that it was hopeless to assault the massed Yankee guns; but when finally ordered he went in with such a cold fury that he almost turned certain defeat into dazzling victory. The least common denominator of those men was that they fought all-out. If they hit at all they hit with everything there was. They had an exultant acceptance for the chances of war. They fought as if they enjoyed it, and they probably did. The Army of the Potomac just was not getting that kind of leadership. Kearny had had it, but he was dead. Most of the other generals seemed uninspired.

What the radicals really meant when they complained that the Federal generals were too easy with their opponents was that the generals kept missing their chances for lack of that extra ounce of deep combativeness. They were quite wrong in believing that this would be remedied by promoting stanch abolitionists, but they were quite right in insisting that more forceful leaders were needed; and they anticipated Clemenceau in believing that war was far too important to be left to the generals, anyway. The North had not yet found the men who had the flaming spirit of war. McClellan's army was not handled the way Lee's army was: neither as a whole nor in its divisions and brigades. The key perhaps lies in the fact that any attempt to show how a Northern general at this period failed to measure up usually makes its point by showing, for contrast, what his opposite number on the Confederate side was doing.

Canny old Secretary Welles in the Navy Department really had the answer. He was ceaselessly shuffling naval officers, looking for that hard-fighting, driving quality without which all other assets are vain. Over and over in his diary one finds him speaking of some distinguished officer who didn't quite measure up: "He has wordy pretensions, some capacity, but no hard courage . . . scholarly pretensions, some literary acquirements, but not of much vigor of mind. . . . Is an intelligent but not an energetic, driving, fighting officer, such as is wanted for rough work." He summed up the army's problem neatly enough: "Some of our best-educated officers have no faculty to govern, control and direct an army in offensive warfare. We have many talented and capable engineers, good officers in some respects, but without audacity, desire for fierce encounter, and in that respect almost utterly deficient as commanders."

A considerable part of the radicals' suspicion was directed at West Point. Had not that school been under Southern control for a generation or more? Had not some of its most distinguished graduates gone South when the war began? Did it not seem to produce, for the North, bookish and doctrinaire generals who made war by rote and neglected to hit the enemy when he should be hit? And was not war itself, for that matter, really quite a simple matter if a man had his heart in the right place? To the radicals, lack of professional training for army command was a positive asset, not a deficiency. A man whose heart was in the war was infinitely better than a professional who did not care.

Since most of the really successful generals in that war, Northern and Southern alike, finally turned out to be West Pointers, this attitude seems almost willfully obtuse today; yet here again the politicians had a point. The government's experience with the older regular-army officers in the early part of the war had not been too happy. Very few of the regulars had shown enthusiasm for the Northern cause. Many limited themselves to a strict performance of the letter of their duty, were utterly lacking in zeal, openly predicted defeat, and admittedly served the North only because the honor of a soldier required it. The stuffiness that had grown up in a small officer corps limited to routine duties in the long years of peace had not gone unnoticed. Jacob Cox of Ohio, a civilian who rose to become a better than average major general, has recorded that one general to whom he reported early in the war admonished him severely on the importance of obeying orders literally but not going one step beyond: "If you had been in the army as long as I have, you would be content to do the things that are ordered without hunting up others." Cox was quite as caustic as anyone in criticizing the incompetent officers who came in from civilian life, for political reasons, under the volunteer system, but he remarked: "It seems to me an entirely fair conclusion that with us in 1861, as with the first French republic, the infusion of the patriotic enthusiasm of a volunteer organization was a necessity, and that this fully made up for the lack of instruction at the start."[3]

And if the volunteer system elevated many a nincompoop to high command, it also brought up some good men with solid talents for war: more of them than one is likely to realize, reading the blanket denunciations of political generals. The North got men like John Logan and Frank Blair, for instance—untutored civilians who became such good soldiers that each was able to command an army corps under as grim a fighting man as William T. Sherman. Blair and Logan were political generals pure and simple, one the brother of a cabinet minister, the other a prominent Democrat whom it was important to placate, but they were first-rate soldiers as well. It may be that Sherman, with his rough informality and his utterly unregimented mind, had more of a knack for developing fighting men than anyone in the East had; it may be noted that in the Army of the Potomac O. O. Howard never showed a sign of anything but diligent mediocrity, but that when he was transferred west and went under Sherman he presently became an army commander. On his march to the sea Sherman had more ex-civilians than West Pointers among his generals, and they were men of his own choosing. Sherman's favorite corps commander was believed to be Joseph A. Mowrer, who never saw West Point.

In the East, too, some of the volunteer officers were measuring up. One of the best men in the Army of the Potomac was the amazingly warlike Manhattan lawyer, Colonel Francis Barlow, now commanding the 61st New York but ultimately to be an inspired, savagely fighting division commander. Barlow had the quality the Republicans were looking for, if they only knew it—the indefinable something which can best be summed up as a positive taste for fighting. Instead of wearing a regulation officer's sword he carried the heaviest cavalry saber he could find; said that when he whacked a laggard or a straggler with the flat of it he wanted to hit with something that would hurt. He had an obsession about preventing straggling, and he let it gnaw at him until he found the answer, which wasn't until after he came to division command. Then, when on the march, he used to detail a company to form a skirmish line, with fixed bayonets, at the rear of the division column, with orders to sweep up and drive

forward all stragglers. It wasn't a pleasant assignment. Most of the
men in the skirmish line had to scramble over ditches and fences and
fallen logs and work their way through brambles and underbrush
while the rest of the army was tramping the smooth highway, and
they got all the dust the division kicked up. The natural result was
that after an hour of it they were mad enough to bayonet their
own parents, and a straggler who fell into their hands was due to get
very rough treatment. As a consequence: no stragglers from Barlow's
division.

Barlow was no stickler for the niceties of military dress. He wore
his single-breasted uniform coat unbuttoned, and under it he wore a
checked flannel shirt, lumberjack-style. He looked, one of Meade's
staff officers wrote, "like a highly independent mounted newsboy,"
and a Brady photograph shows him as a slouchy, rangy, limber young
man, black felt hat crumpled in one hand, heavy boots on his feet,
clean-shaven, rather handsome, with quiet, deadly-cold eyes. After he
got his division he took it where the fighting was. Somebody totted
up figures after the war and found that in all the Federal armies
there were nineteen regiments which had done so much hard fighting
that each had lost at least sixteen officers killed in action; five of the
nineteen belonged to Barlow's division. He had entered the army as a
private in the spring of 1861; became a colonel a year later, and when
the Maryland campaign began was commanding what might be called
half a brigade—his own regiment, plus the 64th New York, which was
attached to it.

There weren't many Barlows. But the army did contain the kind of
generals the radicals were really looking for, and they were beginning
to make their presence felt. One of them was General Israel B. Richardson, who—for all that he was a West Pointer—carried informality
of dress and behavior to a point that made Barlow look like a fency-
thet Briton in the Horse Guards. Richardson might have been model-
ing himself subconsciously after old Zachary Taylor, or maybe he
just didn't care; at any rate, he went around camp with a battered
straw hat on his head and his hands in his pockets, looking like a seedy
old farmer—uniform coat discarded half the time, so that no insignia
of rank were visible. A dapper young shavetail galloped up to his
division headquarters one time with a dispatch; saw Richardson, took
him for an orderly, and tossed him his bridle reins as he dismounted

with a curt "Here—hold my horse." A few moments later the shavetail was admitted to the headquarters tent, to find the supposed
orderly sitting behind a camp desk, eying him with grim amusement
and asking, "And what do you want, sir?" Another time some privates
of the 57th New York were washing in a little brook. A man whom
they took to be a wagon driver came up and asked if he could borrow
some soap. One soldier told him to go to hell and find his own soap,
but some of the others were more generous; and the shabby wagon
driver, after a wash, sat on the bank and told them stories about the
Mexican War—pleasant enough old coot, the boys thought, in whose
remarks there was a little old-timer lecture about how soldiers should
always share things with their comrades. A day or so later it happened that three of these privates were detailed to take some contrabands to division headquarters. In front of the tent they found this
same old-timer, and they asked him if he could tell them where to
find General Richardson. "Well," he said, "I guess I can tell you.
Sometimes they call *me* General Richardson—and other times they
call me Greasy Dick."[4]

He was not pure eccentricity, however, and all that slouchiness
was strictly confined to camp. In the field he was a first-rate fighter
who had commanded a brigade to the eminent satisfaction of Phil
Kearny and was now pleasing Bull Sumner, in whose corps he was.
His men liked him immensely; called him "Fighting Dick" and
bragged that he was the plainest general in the army. One private
wrote that "he has good common sense, a rare commodity apparently." The men recorded that when they went into battle he would
tell them to come on—"I won't ask you to go anywhere I won't go myself." It was his division, incidentally, which contained the irrepressible Barlow. Like so many of the successful generals in that war,
Richardson had resigned from the army in the 1850s; was a Detroit
businessman when war came, raised the 2nd Michigan Regiment, and
won his general's stars shortly thereafter.

There were others. Among them there was a rising cavalry officer,
Brigadier General John Buford, who had made first-rate use of Pope's
cavalry until Pope's incessant, jumpy countermarching wore out
horses and men alike. Buford was another of the plain-as-an-old-
shoe soldiers; wore corduroys tucked into cowhide boots, always had
a big pipe and tobacco pouch bulging his blouse pockets, and was

beginning to show an ability to persuade the clumsy horsemen of the
Federal cavalry that they might yet face Jeb Stuart's troopers on even
terms. He had that streak of grimness the radicals were unconsciously
looking for. He once hanged a guerrilla, in a neighborhood seething
with secessionist sympathy, and left the body dangling from the limb
of a tree under a big sign: "This man to hang three days; he who
cuts him down before shall hang the remaining time." Also worth a
passing glance was the 5th New Hampshire's Colonel Cross: a tall,
lean, rangy man with reddish whiskers and a balding pate who had
fought in the Mexican War and, later, had held a commission in the
Mexican Army; a man of rough and jocose energy who had made his
regiment one of the best combat units in the army and was obviously
in line for promotion.

And there were better-known men, like Meade, with his flaming
temper, his sardonic smile, and his constant attention to detail—woe
to the regimental officer in his command who frittered away strength
by the unnecessary assignment of men to non-combat jobs; like Hancock, who swore at his officers but always remembered their names
and made them feel somehow that they were intimate with him, and
who had a fine fury in the hour of action; like solid John Sedgwick,
always cool and unruffled, who commanded a division under Sumner,
was known as "Uncle John" to his men, and would one day command
the army's most famous corps. They were there if one looked for
them, the kind of men who could use this army as it was meant to be
used.

But the trouble was that the radicals had the wrong touchstone.
Neither West Point nor civilian life had failed: from both sources the
driving, slashing, fighting type of general was coming up, and in the
end the war would be grim enough to satisfy Ben Wade and his
whole committee. But the men who were going to make it grim—to
drive for the enemy relentlessly, grinding up his strength in pitiless
combat and forcing victory no matter who got hurt—were not going
to be the kind of men whose political beliefs would please the Con-
duct-of-the-War inquisitors. Take the list of Union officers who were
in the key positions when the war was finally won—Grant, Sherman,
Sheridan, Thomas, Meade: not an abolitionist in the lot, not a man
who began the war with any particular animus against slavery.

And it was not just by accident that these men were so long in being called to the top spots. The radical bloc, demanding the kind of warfare which only such men could provide, was actually making it harder for the administration to find these men and use them: for it was providing an ideological qualification for purely professional jobs, and instead of inquiring about men's competence it was asking about their loyalty. The Army of Northern Virginia was able to find its best men quickly and it was able to use them once it found them; with all his problems, Jefferson Davis did not have to fight his war and run his country in the midst of a witch hunt. If the dominant leaders in the Confederate Congress—the men who had created and shaped the war party in the South—had worked night and day to keep the army out of the hands of General Lee, on the ground that Lee had not supported secession before Fort Sumter was fired on and hence must be a disloyal person, the story of the war in the Virginia theater would have been considerably different.

One thing must be said for the radicals. They believed their own gospel, down to the last inspired word. And during the weeks after Pope's inglorious defeat they suffered an agonizing extreme of suspense and gloom. They had had their way and nothing had worked out right. Pope was a hard-war man and he was also thoroughly "loyal" by their standards; but he was used up now, no pressure of politics could save him, and he was under orders to go back into obscurity in the Northwest, far from the Rebel generals whose minds he could not read. He was complaining enough about it, those days, bombarding Halleck with angry letters, reminding Halleck that he was under certain obligations to him, making veiled, ugly threats of political reprisal. There was some secret between the two men, and Pope was trying to let Halleck know that he would not be above telling it, if he had to, to re-establish himself. Whatever hold he might have thought he held over the general-in-chief, he at last let it go loose. But before departing he created one last, festering sore to plague the army. He filed formal charges against several generals, including chiefly Fitz-John Porter, alleging disobedience of orders at Bull Run and angrily claiming that a conspiracy of generals had foully done the North out of an overwhelming victory. With McClellan back in command, Porter had protection, and the charges were held in abeyance; if McClellan should ever leave the army,

Porter would be at the mercy of every force in Washington that was hunting for a scapegoat.

The record of that first fortnight in September makes fantastic reading, showing, as it does, enough ill will and all-round distrust afloat in Washington to lose any war. The Union cause had reached low-water mark for the war, and the infection in its central nervous system had all but induced complete paralysis. Lee was invading Maryland with an army so exhausted, ragged, and ill-equipped that by any ordinary standard it ought to have gone back to some rest camp for a couple of months' refit. But Lee knew what he was fighting against just then, and if his daring in beginning an invasion with a worn-out army can be explained only by the assumption that he held his opponents in supreme contempt, there were ample grounds to justify such a feeling.

The Federal mainspring had run down. That will-o'-the-wisp of the Confederacy, foreign intervention, was on the verge of coming true. The Prime Minister of Great Britain, having compared notes with the Foreign Secretary, was getting ready to propose to the British Cabinet that England take the lead in inducing a concert of powers to step in and bring the Civil War to an end—which, of course, could only mean independence for the Confederacy. The Foreign Minister, agreeing, added that if such a concert of powers could not be arranged, England ought to go ahead on its own hook, granting full recognition to the South. The two men were waiting now to see how the invasion of Maryland turned out before taking final action.

At home the belief in victory had faded. As fine a soldier as General John Sedgwick had given up hope and had accepted the idea of two separate nations, North and South. On September 4 he was writing to his sister: "I am in despair of our seeing a termination of the war until some great change is made. On our part it has been a war of politicians; on theirs [the Confederacy's] it has been one conducted by a despot and carried out by able generals. I look upon a division as certain; the only question is where the line is to run. No one would have dared to think of this a few weeks since, but it is in the mouths of many now."[5]

In the White House, Lincoln had finally come to see that the war could not be carried on any longer as a simple fight to re-establish the Union. There had to be a broader base: the fight had to be pinned to a *cause,* something that would change the entire emotional climate, both at home and abroad, turning the deep vitality of the radical group into an asset rather than a liability, making foreign intervention impossible no matter what military setback might take place on the hills of Maryland or Pennsylvania. There was but one step possible: the war had to become a war for human freedom, a war to end slavery. Otherwise it was lost. So he had in his desk the draft of the Emancipation Proclamation—that amazing document which is at once the weakest and the strongest of all America's state papers.

But as things stood just then he could not issue it. Seward had warned him: Put that out now, when we have been defeated and our armies are in retreat, and it will look like a shriek of despair—not an attempt by us to help the black race, but an appeal to the black race to help us. We must have a victory first.

And Seward was right. The paper lay folded in a pigeonhole. The war could not be won without it, but it could not be issued until a victory had been won. And the rival armies now were drifting up through Maryland, eying each other like two boxers circling in the ring, jabbing tentatively with cavalry, looking for the opening.

It was all up to the army, then. Leadership had failed and chances had been missed, and the climax was here; the bewildered, homesick boys with muskets on their shoulders would finally have to say which way American history henceforth would go. They knew none of these things. They were quite "unindoctrinated," for none of the oratory and the lofty war talk had prepared them for this. All they knew was that there was going to be a big fight pretty soon, and most of the time they tried not to think about it. They had the general they wanted, and they seemed to be back among their own kind of folks, and maybe this time it would work out all right.

FIVE

Opportunity Knocks
Three Times

1. At Daybreak in the Morning

The 27th Indiana never forgot that day at Frederick. The day didn't especially stand out at the time, except for the welcome the townspeople gave, with the fruit and the ice water and the pretty girls waving flags; but afterward the soldiers built it up and made many stories about it, and almost everybody claimed to have been in on it, or to have seen it, or at least to have known about it. It was a Big Thing, as army talk had it, and it all began right in the middle of this Hoosier regiment.

The army got to Frederick on the twelfth of September, the mounted patrols going into town from the east just as the last of Wade Hampton's cavalry went out of it to the west, with a fine rackety-spat of flying hoofs on the turnpike and stray shots from carbines nipping through the orchards and the front-yard flower gardens. The 27th Indiana was pushed through in a long skirmish line next morning, and when it got to an empty field a courier rode up from the rear with orders from corps headquarters: stack arms in the field, put pickets out, and stand by for a while. The men broke ranks, and most of them sauntered about to find bits of wood to boil coffee.

It was a nice morning, and it wasn't too warm, and the men took it easy. The field had been a Rebel camping ground a few days before, and the boys didn't especially like that. It was never too pleasant to occupy a spot where the enemy had just camped, as departing armies weren't too tidy about picking up the litter they had made, and the ground was apt to be messy. Still, this was a big field, and the rest was good, and the men drank their coffee and lit their pipes and talked about nothing much; and two lounging non-coms suddenly became very important men. Corporal Barton W. Mitchell of Company E lay at full length chinning with his pal, First Sergeant John McKnight Bloss. A few feet away, half hidden in the tall, trampled grass, was a long, bulky-looking envelope. The two men stared at it idly for a while, lazily wondering who dropped it there and what might be in it, until at last Mitchell's curiosity got the better of him and he rolled over, stretched out one arm, and picked it up. It was unsealed, and it contained a long paper, covered with writing, wrapped around three cigars.

Three cigars were a find, any day. They appeared to be fresh, and the two soldiers began to feel in their pockets for matches. As they did so, Mitchell's curiosity—which, by one of the stupendous oddities of war, was that day the Republic's greatest asset—gave him another dig, and he uncrinkled the paper that had been folded around the cigars and took a lazy look at it. As he looked he forgot about the matches and nudged the sergeant: hey, would you take a look at this?

The paper was headed "Headquarters, Army of Northern Virginia," and was dated September 9. It was labeled "Special Orders No. 191," and it was studded with names like General Jackson, General Longstreet, General McLaws, and so on—names known to every enlisted man in the Union Army. It was signed "R. H. Chilton, Assist. Adj.-Gen.," and at the bottom was the name of the addressee: "Maj. Gen. D. H. Hill, Commanding Division."

Whatever this might amount to, it seemed altogether too hot for any two enlisted men to hang onto, so the soldiers got to their feet and hurried off to show it to Captain Kopp, skipper of Company E. The captain took one look and sent them to regimental headquarters, where they handed it to Colonel Silas Colgrove, who was having a chat just then with Brigadier General Nathan Kimball, brigade commander from Sumner's corps. These two read it and exchanged glances; Kimball went away and Colgrove got on his horse and went galloping off to his division commander, Brigadier General A. S. Williams. Williams took his turn reading it and beckoned to his assistant adjutant general, Colonel Pittman, who stuck the paper in his pocket, yelled for his horse, and set out for army headquarters as fast as the beast could carry him. And so the paper got to McClellan, while Bloss and Mitchell went back to the field and stretched out on the grass again.

It is irritating, in a mild sort of way, that none of the accounts of this affair mention what finally happened to the cigars. Bloss wrote later that he and Mitchell simply forgot about them; Colonel Colgrove had the impression that the boys had rewrapped the cigars in the paper and put them back in the envelope before they gave it to him. There the trail dies out. Did anybody ever smoke them, in the end—those cigars that were so important in the history of the war?[1]

Fate had not been too kind to McClellan up to now. After that first dazzling, too-lucky stroke that had lifted him from the western Virginia mountains to the top command at Washington he had had nothing but bad fortune. But as he studied the paper the Hoosier corporal had picked up he could see that the opportunity of a lifetime had come to him. For what he had in front of him was nothing less than Lee's official orders, telling where every last division of the Confederate Army was and what it was up to—the plans of Confederate GHQ in complete detail. It was just too good to be true, and McClellan was cautious: could the paper possibly be genuine? His staff examined it. One officer, it developed, had known Colonel Chilton, Lee's assistant adjutant general, quite intimately in the old army and was familiar with his handwriting. He studied the paper and gave his verdict: genuine, beyond a doubt—that was unquestionably written in Chilton's hand.

With that verdict the fog of war which always limits the vision of an army commander suddenly dissolved and everything became clear. McClellan knew as much about Lee's plans as if he had personally attended Lee's last staff conference. The game was being handed to him on a silver platter.

The town of Frederick, where McClellan then was, is some forty miles northwest of Washington. The National Road, as it was called in those days, comes up from Washington, passes through Frederick, and continues west and north until it reaches Hagerstown, about twenty-five miles farther on, where it swings west to reach Wheeling and the Ohio country. From Hagerstown, good roads drop southward to the Potomac and the Shenandoah Valley; other roads lead north into Pennsylvania. Just about halfway between Frederick and Hagerstown the National Road climbs over the long, wooded height of South Mountain—not an isolated peak, as one usually pictures a mountain, but a great, slowly curving ridge that begins on the Potomac nearly opposite Harper's Ferry and runs far up into Pennsylvania, where it passes a few miles west of Gettysburg. Just now it lay on McClellan's western horizon like an ominous thundercloud fifty miles long, full of veiled lightnings: for behind that blue curtain lay the striking power of the Confederacy, embodied in the dusty gray divisions of the Army of Northern Virginia, securely hidden from inquisitive Federal eyes.

Innumerable rumors had been coming in, but they were next to useless. Peaceful civilians who saw a scouting detachment were apt to magnify it into an army corps when they reported it, and the nervous alarms they sent back were sure to be garbled in transmission. The news McClellan had been getting from beyond the mountain proved nothing except that there were a lot of Rebels over there somewhere and that the Union folk in the area were almighty worried. He had his cavalry forward trying to locate the enemy, but every road they took led them straight up against Jeb Stuart's patrols. Rebel cavalry had the gaps in the mountain well covered, and it would take more than Yankee cavalry to open those gaps. A forward lunge by the army itself would of course send Stuart's cavalry flying, but in the absence of any knowledge about Lee's position and intentions it seemed to McClellan that it would be dangerous to make such a lunge. The blow might take the army into the wrong place and enable Lee to go rampaging off unopposed, doing fatal damage among the rich and nearly defenseless cities of the North. Up to this moment Lee had all the advantage.

Now, in a twinkling, this advantage had passed from Lee to McClellan. Lee's Special Orders No. 191, which had been issued just four days ago, told precisely what the Confederate Army was doing and where it was situated. Right now it was in the act of gobbling up that isolated garrison at Harper's Ferry. Stonewall Jackson and his command had been detached from the army and sent back into Virginia, roundabout, to come up on Harper's Ferry from the south. The division of General A. P. Hill was with him. General John G. Walker, commanding another Rebel division, had also gone below the Potomac to approach the town from the east—he was to make for Loudoun Heights, a little mountain that rises on the eastern bank of the Shenandoah, where it joins the Potomac, and overlooks the little town where John Brown once raised the flag of slave revolt. Two more Confederate divisions under General Lafayette McLaws were descending on Harper's Ferry from the north and were to occupy the lofty ridge of Maryland Heights, on the north side of the Potomac, whence they could look right down the throats of the Union garrison. The rest of the Confederate Army—Longstreet's command, plus the division of D. H. Hill, together with the reserve artillery and the supply trains—was to wait at Boonsboro, a little town on the National Road just beyond South Mountain. When Harper's Ferry had been duly captured everybody was to head north and join up with Lee and Longstreet, either at Boonsboro or at Hagerstown, a dozen miles up the road.

There it was, all spelled out, and McClellan had it right on his desk. He was the beneficiary of the greatest security leak in American military history—the only one that ever finally affected the outcome of a great war.

Harper's Ferry, of course, was doomed. It was in the bottom of a soup bowl, and once the Rebels got up on the rim, there would be no stopping them. The place had always been indefensible, and Halleck's refusal to order the garrison out when there was time looked sillier than ever now. But quite unintentionally Halleck had baited a trap, and Lee was stepping right into it. His pause to capture this outpost (he banked heavily on McClellan's extreme caution) was giving McClellan the most dazzling opportunity any Northern general was to have throughout the whole length of the war.

For Lee's army was at this moment completely scattered, and McClellan, his own army united, was closer to the scattered pieces than those pieces were to each other. Lee was entirely at his mercy. There was nothing to keep the Army of the Potomac from breaking through the mountain wall and stamping out those separated segments of Lee's army one at a time. The Army of Northern Virginia could be destroyed, which would win the war overnight, and it could be done by a man whom the radicals in Washington were proclaiming a disloyalist who did not want to win!

There was just one catch in it. McClellan would have to move fast. Those orders would be out of date before long. They were four days old already, and the Rebel army could do a power of marching in four days, as sundry Northern generals had found out. The door was wide open, but it was likely to swing shut quickly. If McClellan was to take advantage of his opportunity he had no time to spare. Every minute might count.

And yet, actually, the situation was even better than McClellan supposed. Having given him this break, the fates were providing him with a little extra bulge to allow for contingencies. Lee's logistics were a trifle off, and the snatch at Harper's Ferry was taking longer than expected. Special Orders No. 191 did not give the time schedule, but Lee had anticipated that the job would be finished by now. The various elements had begun their march on September 10; by the twelfth, it had been believed, Jackson would be taking possession of Bolivar Heights, the long ridge that dominates Harper's Ferry from the south, Walker would be in position across the Shenandoah, and McLaws would be on top of Maryland Heights. On September 13, therefore, according to Lee's plan, the garrison would be held by the throat and would have to surrender, prisoners and captured supplies could be started south, and the victors could be on their way north again.

But nobody had moved as fast as that. Only now, while McClellan was reading the order, was the head of Jackson's column coming within sight of the Federal troops on Bolivar Heights, and it would take another day for Jackson to get fully into position. Only now was McLaws fighting his way up the steep ridge to take possession of the peak north of the Potomac; only now was Walker getting his men in place on the crest of Loudoun Heights. McClellan was getting from one to two full days more than he had any reason to hope for. In addition, the rest of Lee's army was no longer concentrated at Boonsboro, close to the gap through which the National Road crossed

South Mountain. Since writing the order Lee had heard a rumor (later proved false) that Federal troops were coming down from Pennsylvania in some strength, and he and Longstreet had moved up to Hagerstown to head them off. Nobody but D. H. Hill was anywhere near the all-important gateway, and Hill's division was so worn by hard fighting and straggling that it numbered barely more than five thousand muskets. Lee's army was even more scattered than the order showed, in other words, and it would take it longer to get reassembled. When the fates finally gave McClellan this break they went out of their way to make it a good one.

General John Gibbon happened to visit army headquarters early that afternoon. His Black Hat Brigade was getting thin and he wanted to have it strengthened if he could. He and McClellan were on friendly terms, having known each other back in the old army days, and he was admitted to McClellan's tent without delay. When he got in he could see that a good deal seemed to be happening. McClellan asked him to sit tight for a minute and went on dictating orders, receiving reports, sending staff officers hurrying off here and there, everybody energetic and active. Finally there came a lull. McClellan turned to him, taking a folded paper out of his pocket and displaying it jubilantly, his eyes sparkling.

"Here is a paper with which, if I cannot whip Bobbie Lee, I will be willing to go home," McClellan said. "I will not show you the document now, but"—he turned down one fold to show the writing—"here is the signature, and it gives the movement of every division of Lee's army. Tomorrow we will pitch into his center, and if you people will only do two good, hard days' marching I will put Lee in a position he will find it hard to get out of."

Gibbon, of course, was delighted; also, this gave him his opening, and he took it without delay as a good soldier should. He had a brigade, he said, that would do all the marching and fighting the general could ask for—four crack Western regiments that were as good as any in the army, if not a little bit better. But they had been worn down by hard service and the brigade was a little skimpy; when new troops came in could the general assign a good Western regiment to Gibbon's brigade? McClellan listened attentively. He always liked to hear his troops praised, and he glowed as Gibbon talked. When Gibbon finished McClellan promised that he would have the first

Western regiment that came to camp. Gibbon left, feeling highly encouraged, and McClellan returned to the task of getting the ponderous army in motion.[2]

Basically his problem was fairly simple—to get across South Mountain while Lee's army was still in pieces, to overwhelm the separate fragments, and, if possible, to rescue the Harper's Ferry garrison so that those twelve thousand soldiers could be added to the Army of the Potomac.

Of the many roads that crossed South Mountain in various places there were only two that mattered now: the National Road, leading through Turner's Gap to Boonsboro and thence to Hagerstown, and a road that forked off in a more southerly direction west of Frederick, crossed the mountain at Crampton's Gap, six miles south of Turner's Gap, and came out on the far side just five miles north and east of Harper's Ferry. A quick drive through Turner's Gap would bring the army down on what looked like Lee's main body—Longstreet's and D. H. Hill's commands. A simultaneous smash through Crampton's Gap would crush the two divisions led by McLaws, would open the door so that the men at Harper's Ferry could come out, and would leave Jackson and the others completely isolated on the south side of the Potomac. When all of that had been done, Jackson and A. P. Hill and Walker could be hunted down at leisure and there would be nobody of any consequence left in the entire state of Virginia to oppose an irresistible descent on the Confederate capital.

As McClellan faced the mountain range he would be striking at Turner's Gap with his right hand and at Crampton's Gap with his left. Conveniently placed to act as his left hand were some eighteen thousand good men under General William B. Franklin, a solid, highly respected soldier who commanded the VI Corps and who had with him his own two divisions and a third one temporarily attached. They would be a force ample to open the gap, crush Lafayette McLaws, and rescue the Harper's Ferry people. Franklin was ordered to get going—to do a lot of banging away with his artillery, even if he didn't have anything to shoot at, so that the commander at the Ferry would hear and know that help was on the way. Meanwhile the rest of the army, some seventy thousand men, would be the right hand and would go straight through Turner's Gap.

While all of this was going on, McClellan reflected, it would be helpful if somebody could come down on Lee from the north. Governor Curtin was frantically assembling Pennsylvania state troops, and General Reynolds had been detached from the army to help him; and while they probably had nothing that could stand up to Lee's veterans in an open fight, Lee might be bothered and delayed a good deal if a sufficient swarm of these home guards and militia could come edging in on him. So McClellan, having inspected the map, sent off a wire to "the commander of U.S. forces at Chambersburg" to concentrate all available troops and obstruct Lee's march until the Army of the Potomac could come up and make a real fight out of it. He didn't know who was commanding at Chambersburg, but it seemed likely that somebody was there, and the card looked like a good, inexpensive one to play.

As it turned out, this had no effect on the campaign, but it did give a bad forty-eight hours to that eminent Pennsylvania editor-politician, Alexander K. McClure. McClure had been in Washington when Lee marched north, and when Governor Curtin began building up the home guards it seemed wise to have a few of the state's leading citizens on hand to help, so McClure had been hastily given a major's commission and sent north to lend a hand. When McClellan's wire came in, McClure, uncomfortable but game in his new role as army officer, and accompanied by no troops whatever, was posted at Chambersburg. He gulped when he got the wire; combed the town and managed to round up about twenty home-guard cavalry, which were all the "U.S. forces" within reach. With these McClure began patrolling the roads valiantly, preparing to ward off the Army of Northern Virginia if by chance it came his way. Tough old Thad Stevens happened to be in Governor Curtin's office at Harrisburg when the wire came through. The thought of the unmilitary McClure and his twenty men standing between Pennsylvania and invasion tickled the grim abolitionist, and he chuckled. "Well, McClure will do something. If he can't do better he'll instruct the toll-gate keeper not to permit Lee's army to pass through." Then, reflectively: "But as to McClellan, God only knows what he'll do."[3]

McClellan rode through Frederick to make sure that the advance guard of the army was put in motion properly. A little outside of town he overtook the head of General Jesse Reno's IX Corps, which had the advance. Reno's leading division, two brigades of Ohio troops, under General Cox, was moving along, and McClellan stopped to talk a moment with Cox, who had been one of his assistants back in the springtime of the war, when McClellan was out in Columbus trying to get Ohio's first troops housed, uniformed, and drilled. Cox's men had done practically all of their fighting in western Virginia, having come east just within the last month, and they were happy to be with the Army of the Potomac. They had heard that it was far ahead of all other Union armies in drill, discipline, and marching ability, and its record seemed to make their own service in the mountains look commonplace, and they were anxious to make a good impression. There was a subtle difference between them and the rest of the army. They were more informal in bearing and discipline, and it was noticed that they marched with a longer, freer stride; the Army of the Potomac had been rigorously drilled to the regulation pace of twenty-eight inches, while the Westerners had been allowed to set their own gait. Incidentally, the Ohioans were already remarking that the men in these crack Eastern regiments straggled much more than did the mountain brigades. . . . McClellan gave Cox some last-minute instructions and went back to headquarters.

Pretty soon Reno himself came along. He was feeling good just now; had gone south on the Roanoke Island expedition as a brigadier under Burnside, had done well, and now held a corps command, and things seemed to be opening up for him in fine style. While the army was in Frederick, Reno had heard the Barbara Frietchie story, which seems to have been circulating freely among the Federals long before Whittier made a propaganda poem out of it, and he had gone around to the old lady's house to see her. As nearly as can be learned, at this distance, Barbara Frietchie had indeed waved a flag from her window, but she had waved it in welcome to the Union troops, not in defiance to Jackson's "Rebel horde." Some other woman in Frederick did wave a United States flag at Jackson, but he never saw it or her, and there was no blast of rifle fire to rip that or any other Union banner. The stories got all mixed up and added to, and old Barbara became the center and heroine of a garbled blend. Anyway, Reno had gone to her house that morning and offered to buy the famous flag. She wouldn't sell it to him—couldn't, very well, since the flag he wanted to buy didn't really exist—but she did give him a flag she had around the house, and the general had ridden off, well content.[4]

By dark Reno had pushed Cox's division across the Catoctin range, a low ridge that runs north and south halfway between Frederick and South Mountain; and the Ohioans went into bivouac near the tiny village of Middletown, while Rebel outposts on South Mountain saw the ridge to the east blossom out with campfires as darkness came down, and sent word back to D. H. Hill in Boonsboro that quite a lot of Yankees seemed to be coming up to Turner's Gap. Yankee cavalry skirmished with Confederate patrols in the valley and on the lower slopes of South Mountain and sent back their own reports: as far as they could find out, there was nothing in front of Turner's Gap except cavalry.

McClellan, meanwhile, was working on the orders for the rest of the army. The most important was the order for Franklin, and McClellan got it off a little after six that evening. Franklin was down at a place called Buckeystown, six miles south of Frederick and about twelve miles due east of the summit at Crampton's Gap, and McClellan gave him the picture in detail, telling him about the finding of Special Orders No. 191 and explaining the positions of Lee's troops. Cox was at Middletown, he said, and would be off first thing next morning, followed by the rest of the army, to get through Turner's Gap and land on Lee at Boonsboro. Franklin was to move "at daybreak in the morning" for Crampton's Gap. Once through the gap, his first duty was "to cut off, destroy or capture McLaws' command" and relieve the Union troops at Harper's Ferry, after which, depending on events, he would either rejoin the main army at Boonsboro or move west to Sharpsburg to cut off Lee's retreat. In order that it might be perfectly clear to him, McClellan added: "My general idea is to cut the enemy in two and beat him in detail."

All fine, so far. But as the courier galloped south with that order the first thin mist of what would soon be a serious cloud was beginning to rise across the gleaming face of McClellan's good fortune. McClellan's order was clear and precise, and it gave Franklin a perfect picture of the situation, but it was defective in just one respect: nowhere in it was there any hint of the extreme urgency of the moment.

For it was no ordinary strategic advantage McClellan was reaching for; he had it within his power to destroy Lee's army and end the war within the next few days, and every minute might count. South Mountain was still a screen, and there was no way to know how far or how fast Lee's troops might be moving, off on the other side. Franklin's troops were rested, they had not fought since the battles on the peninsula back in June, and presumably they were quite capable of a little extra exertion now, with the outcome of the whole war hanging in the balance.

Reflecting on this order, which lays out a job of work and breathes the very spirit of unhurried calm, one is conscious of that queer feeling of exasperation which, even at this distance, McClellan's acts occasionally inspire. With everything in the world at stake, both for the country and for McClellan personally, why couldn't the man have taken fire just once? To have Franklin march "at daybreak in the morning" was good—but to have him march that same evening, driving for that door through the mountains without giving the enemy an extra minute to repair his faulty dispositions, would have been infinitely better. The roads were good and the weather was clear, and a night march was perfectly feasible; making it, Franklin would be able to go through the gap first thing in the morning. In a great many ways the history of the country (to say nothing of McClellan's own place in it) could have been a good deal different if Franklin's eighteen thousand men had been put on the road that night under the stars.

But Franklin didn't move. McClellan didn't tell him to, and Franklin was no man to exceed the letter of his instructions. To be sure, McClellan had closed his letter by saying that he now asked of Franklin "all your intellect and the utmost activity that a general can exercise," which might have given him the hint; but McClellan was a courtly man who used that kind of language as the small change of polite correspondence, and Franklin was one more of those Union generals who were loyal and capable and conscientious but who utterly lacked that priceless little extra spark. He could drive his men just as hard as he himself was driven, but no harder: a first-rate soldier, in the ordinary way, but lacking the power to be first-rate in an extraordinary way.

So McClellan and Franklin and Franklin's eighteen thousand men got (one supposes) a good sleep that night, and any clock that headquarters might have possessed ticked on, unhurried but inexorable. On the morning of September 14 Franklin's corps broke camp and got off to a good early start, precisely as ordered, and set out on the twelve-mile hike to Crampton's Gap, with the cavalry trotting on ahead and stirring up hedge-hopping fights with Stuart's outposts.

Beyond South Mountain, where Crampton's Gap cuts through, there is an open space two or three miles wide bearing the neatly descriptive name of Pleasant Valley; and on the far side of Pleasant Valley is the humpbacked ridge of Elk Mountain, whose southern end is named Maryland Heights and looks down on the town of Harper's Ferry. Lafayette McLaws, a Confederate general who was almost exactly like the Union's General Franklin—solid, capable, unimaginative— had been dutifully industrious. He had chased the last Yankees off Maryland Heights, and he was putting in the morning getting his artillery up on top so that he could bombard the Yankee garrison in Harper's Ferry. It wasn't easy, the sides of Elk Mountain being very steep and the roads being sketchy, and in the end he had to put two hundred men on each gun and wrestle the ponderous weapons up by sheer muscle. Stuart warned him sometime during the morning that the Federals were coming up to Crampton's Gap, in his rear, and McLaws eventually sent a few regiments back to hold the pass. They didn't get there until midday had gone, and until then the little road over the mountain was guarded by nothing but Stuart's cavalry; but they arrived well ahead of Franklin and they found a good position at the eastern base of the ridge, behind a long stone fence. There they lined up, with dismounted cavalry on either flank.

Those Southerners were good men, but there were not nearly enough of them to keep the Federals out of the pass, and Franklin did not have to put half of his men into action. He planted a row of guns on the left, sent the 27th New York and the 96th Pennsylvania ahead as a heavy skirmish line, and backed them up with the 5th Maine and the 16th New York. The Rebels were well protected behind their stone wall, and there was a brisk fight for a while. McLaws was warned that a real push was on, and some more Southern regiments came up to extend the line, but Franklin sent a brigade of New Jersey troops in on a charge, and the Confederates were driven away from the stone wall and went scrambling back up the mountainside, firing as they went. For a couple of hours after that it was an

Indian fight, the Rebels too few to make a stand but giving ground slowly, Rebels and Yankees shooting at each other from behind trees, the Northerners coming on doggedly.

A private from a Vermont regiment, scrambling up the mountainside, slipped and fell, and went sliding off downhill to land, all in a heap, in a little hollow among the rocks, face to face with a Confederate private who somehow hadn't retreated when the others had. The two soldiers glared at each other for a moment, gripping their rifles; then they agreed that it would be foolish for them to carry on a personal, two-man extension of the war there in the hollow. They would wait where they were, suspending hostilities while everybody else fought, and at the end of the day they would see how the battle had gone. If the Federals got licked and retreated, then the Vermonter was a prisoner, but if the Confederates retreated, then the Reb was a prisoner. So they laid their rifles down and shared tobacco, leaning back among the rocks, and waited for the two armies to settle their fate for them.

Their comrades were having hot work for a while there on the wooded slopes. Firing down from above, the Confederates were shooting just a little high—not high enough to miss, the Northern boys complained afterward, but just high enough to inflict a dreadful number of head wounds, nearly all of which were fatal. Mindful of his orders, Franklin kept banging away with his artillery and made a prodigious racket, and down in Harper's Ferry the Union garrison—which knew perfectly well by this time that it was thoroughly trapped—heard the noise and began to feel hopeful again.

Late in the afternoon the last Confederate resistance dissolved, and the Federal assault waves cleared the crest of the ridge and halted, while the main body of Franklin's troops went marching through the gap and swarmed down into Pleasant Valley. McLaws awoke at last to the realization that he was in desperate trouble as the broken remnants of his rear guard came streaming back down the valley, and he and Stuart took fresh troops and hastened up to repair the dike, while the long shadow of Elk Mountain filled the valley with evening dusk and began to creep up the side of South Mountain to the east. A Confederate brigadier came pelting up to them, crying that all was lost, but McLaws and Stuart didn't think so. They formed a line of battle across the valley and got ready to

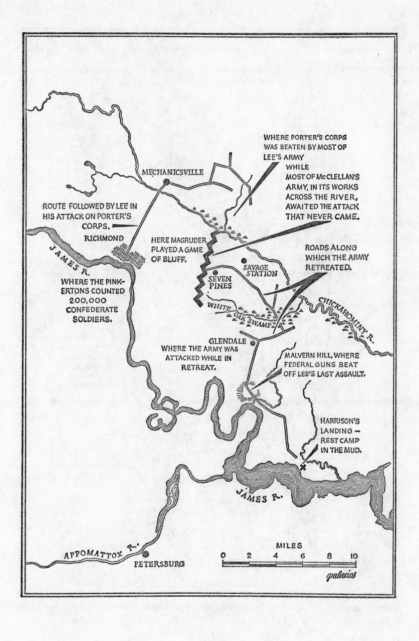

WHERE PORTER'S CORPS
WAS BEATEN BY MOST OF
LEE'S ARMY
WHILE
MOST OF McCLELLAN'S
ARMY, IN ITS WORKS
ACROSS THE RIVER,
AWAITED THE ATTACK
THAT NEVER CAME.

MECHANICSVILLE

ROUTE FOLLOWED BY LEE IN
HIS ATTACK ON PORTER'S
CORPS.

RICHMOND

HERE MAGRUDER
PLAYED A GAME
OF BLUFF.

ROADS ALONG
WHICH THE ARMY
RETREATED.

JAMES R.

SAVAGE
STATION

SEVEN
PINES

CHICKAHOMINY R.

WHERE THE PINK-
ERTONS COUNTED
200,000
CONFEDERATE
SOLDIERS.

WHITE OAK SWAMP

GLENDALE
WHERE THE ARMY WAS
ATTACKED WHILE IN
RETREAT.

MALVERN HILL, WHERE
FEDERAL GUNS BEAT
OFF LEE'S LAST ASSAULT.

HARRISON'S
LANDING —
REST CAMP
IN THE MUD.

JAMES R.

APPOMATTOX R.

PETERSBURG

MILES

0   2   4   6   8   10

palacios

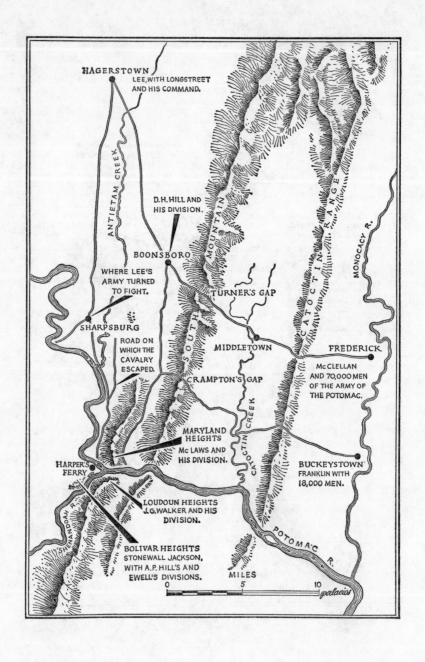

HAGERSTOWN
LEE, WITH LONGSTREET
AND HIS COMMAND.

ANTIETAM CREEK

D.H.HILL AND
HIS DIVISION.

BOONSBORO

WHERE LEE'S
ARMY TURNED
TO FIGHT.

TURNER'S GAP

SOUTH MOUNTAIN

CATOCTIN RANGE

MONOCACY R.

SHARPSBURG

ROAD ON
WHICH THE
CAVALRY
ESCAPED.

MIDDLETOWN

FREDERICK

CRAMPTON'S GAP

McCLELLAN
AND 70,000 MEN
OF THE ARMY OF
THE POTOMAC.

CATOCTIN CREEK

MARYLAND
HEIGHTS
McLAWS AND
HIS DIVISION.

BUCKEYSTOWN
FRANKLIN WITH
18,000 MEN.

HARPER'S
FERRY

LOUDOUN HEIGHTS
J.G.WALKER AND HIS
DIVISION.

SHENANDOAH R.

BOLIVAR HEIGHTS
STONEWALL JACKSON,
WITH A.P. HILL'S AND
EWELL'S DIVISIONS.

POTOMAC R.

MILES
0   5   10

palacios

make the best fight they could, while the fugitives were rallied and formed up to help the fresh troops.

Franklin rode through the gap, surveyed the line of Rebel soldiers a mile or more to the south, and considered that this was no time to be hasty. He had carried out the letter of his instructions, which is to say that he had forced his way through the gap. It still remained to "cut off, destroy or capture McLaws' command," but it seemed to Franklin that he was outnumbered and that the Rebel line was too strong to break, what with darkness coming on and his own troops winded. Also, additional Confederate forces might well be coming down on him from Turner's Gap, for all he knew, and if he was fighting McLaws when they came he would be taken in the rear. So, in the end, he did nothing, deferring his next move to the morrow.

On top of the mountain that night the Federals who had carried the crest slept on the field of battle, gleaning it carefully for discarded valuables. The 4th New Jersey, which had been carrying the old smoothbore muskets, claimed to have re-equipped itself completely with rifled Springfields dropped by wounded or fugitive Rebels. The slopes were covered with the wounded men of both armies, and late at night the soldiers went clambering over the rocks, bringing casualties to the field hospital. They picked up their own wounded first and then brought in Confederates, until at midnight the exhausted surgeons, their linen coveralls streaked and smeared with blood, told them not to bring in any more because no more could be handled that night. So the 16th New York laid out a little camping place on the mountaintop, built fires, and made the wounded Southerners as comfortable as they could, with food and water at hand. They had taken a number of unwounded prisoners, and they detailed two of these to keep the fires going and look after the wounded men, and then they made their own bivouac. In the morning they found that the unwounded men had fled and half a dozen of the wounded had died during the night, and they carried the rest off to the hospital. Then they went down into Pleasant Valley and joined the main body.

Now it happened that night that there was one officer, in all the Union Army, who didn't believe in waiting until tomorrow. He was only a cavalry colonel, and he was inside Harper's Ferry, completely surrounded by Rebels, and there wasn't a great deal he could do about it, but what little he could do he proposed doing. Oddly enough, he was a Mississippian by birth—one of two Mississippians in the regular army, it was said, who had stuck with the Union when the war came. He was Colonel Benjamin F. Davis, called Grimes Davis at West Point and in the old army, and he was roosting in Harper's Ferry as commander of the 8th New York Cavalry. On the night of September 14 he knew as well as anybody else that the place would have to be surrendered next morning: the Confederates finally had all the heights lined with artillery, and the town couldn't be held an hour once those guns opened up, which they would unquestionably do as soon as it was light. What made Davis unique that night was that he didn't intend to fold his hands and wait for the inevitable.

Like its colonel, his regiment was feeling frustrated. The 8th New York had been raised in the country around Rochester in the summer of 1861, and the government had been slow about the matter of providing horses: for a solid year the 8th had worn sabers and talked cavalry lingo but had gone about on foot, not having a horse to its name. The regiment had footed it up and down the Shenandoah Valley with Banks in the spring of 1862, sharing in the humiliations which befell that officer's command and feeling them more keenly because of its utter inability to ride as cavalry should. Finally, about the time Pope was getting licked at Bull Run, the 8th New York got its horses, and it had ridden brightly up the Potomac just in time to get penned up here at Harper's Ferry, where there was nothing whatever for cavalry to do and, currently, no prospect of anything better than a ride off to Libby Prison in Richmond. So when Colonel Davis finished a stormy conference that evening with the post commander and then came outside and whistled up his cavalry, the boys were ready for action—any kind of action, just so it got them out of that hole in the mountains to some place where they could ride.

What Davis proposed was that, since the post was going to be captured, anybody who could get out ahead of time should do so. He had finally won permission to take the cavalry and try it, the cavalry on hand consisting of his own 8th New York, the 12th Illinois, and a mixed handful from the 1st Maryland and 7th Rhode Island. A Unionist who lived in the region and knew all the mountain roads was going to act as his guide; in addition, Davis had one of his own scouts who had just slipped in through the Confederate screen and had a pretty good idea where all the Rebel commands were posted.

As soon as the town got dark, then, Davis lined up his troopers, some thirteen hundred in all. The regimental sutler, knowing that he couldn't get his goods out and that he would inevitably be looted of all he owned next day by needy Rebels, passed down the ranks, giving away tobacco: an act of generosity that almost floored the soldiers, sutlers being men who never gave anything away.

Davis took his post at the head of the column, with his guide and his scout and a picked patrol of twenty-five troopers. The 12th Illinois and the Marylanders and Rhode Islanders came next, and the 8th New York was formed at the rear. In single file, moving at a walk, the little band crossed the Potomac on a pontoon bridge and headed off to the northwest on a narrow, winding road through the mountains —an obscure little road that ran right under the overhanging cliffs of Maryland Heights, the one road out that McLaws had failed to block. (It was the same road, if anybody had stopped to think about it, down which John Brown had moved, with death in his eyes and a monstrous vision of flame and bloodshed in his heart, when he made his descent on the Harper's Ferry enginehouse in 1859.)

The boys had quite a night for themselves. As soon as the head of the column got across the river it moved at a trot, so that the line kept getting longer and longer; Colonel Davis was ten miles up in Maryland by the time the last man left the bridge. The road took them within a few rods of McLaws's camp, but the jingling and the clattering seem to have escaped the notice of McLaws's pickets, and the cavalry got away clean. (Jeb Stuart had warned McLaws earlier to guard that lonely little road, but McLaws had other things on his mind and had paid no attention.) It was pitch-dark there under the trees, and except when they were going uphill—which was a good part of the time—the men rode at a trot. One trooper recalls that "the only way we could tell how far we were from our file leaders was by the horses' shoes striking fire against the stones in the road."

Two miles from the river Davis's advance patrol surprised and scattered a Confederate picket post. Two miles farther the Rebels had erected a road block of fence rails and overturned wagons, the routed pickets having broadcast a warning. Davis anticipated this, however, and led his command cross-lots by some winding woods path his guide knew about, and they left the road block behind. As they got out of the tangled mountain region they moved through cornfields and pastures as much as by road. Altogether it was a tough, grinding ride, and some of the horses gave out. When that happened, the dismounted men were taken up by their comrades; Davis was determined not to leave a man behind.

They swung out to by-pass the town of Sharpsburg, under the starlight, driving off a squad of Confederate cavalry that was patrolling the roads there. A few miles north of town they hit the Hagerstown turnpike and went clattering north in fine style. Then, up ahead in the dark, Davis heard the rumble of wagons. He spurred on past a fork in the road and ran into a big Rebel wagon train, escorted by a small detachment of cavalry, bound for Sharpsburg. It was too dark for anybody to see the color of his uniform, and Davis had a fine Mississippi accent, so he simply posed as a Confederate officer and notified the driver of the leading wagon that he was to turn sharply to the right when he got to the fork in the road; and he told the commander of the Rebel cavalry escort to wait by the roadside and fall in at the rear of the train. Then he galloped back to his own command, formed the 8th New York alongside the fork to take care of the wagons, and got the rest of the men lined up to handle the Confederate troopers.

All unsuspecting, the sleepy wagon drivers took the right-hand fork, starting off on a road that led to Pennsylvania, while the 8th New York, riding single file, fell in beside the train. As the last wagon made the turn and the Rebel cavalry escort came up, Davis sent his Illinois troopers in on the charge with drawn sabers, and the surprised Rebels were broken up and sent scattering down the country roads in the dark. When it began to grow light the wagoners came to a little, noticed the blue uniforms, and asked the troopers what outfit they belonged to. Proudly the soldiers answered: 8th New York Cavalry. The teamsters pulled up in a hurry, swearing and fuming, and some of them jumped down to unhitch their horses, but the New Yorkers drew revolvers and persuaded them to climb back in their seats, and the train went jolting along, drivers very glum, cavalry bubbling over with delight.

At about nine in the morning the whole cavalcade got to Greencastle, Pennsylvania, where Davis called a halt and examined his capture. There he found that he had seized nothing less than General Longstreet's reserve ammunition train—forty-odd wagons, each drawn by six mules, with some two hundred prisoners. He turned the train and prisoners over to the authorities and led his tired command into a field to get a little sleep. News of the capture got through the town, so that by the time the boys had their horses unsaddled and watered and picketed the townsfolk were coming out on foot and in buggies, carrying all sorts of things to eat—fresh bread, hams, baskets of eggs, and so on. The cavalry ate a tremendous breakfast and felt like heroes and stretched out for a good sleep in the shade, and one of their number wrote: "The boys thought that soldiering wasn't so bad, after all."[5]

It was a bright little exploit, all in all, and looking back on it, in its setting, one feels a twinge of regret that Grimes Davis was only a colonel. A little touch of his spirit, just then, in army headquarters or in the various corps headquarters, would have made the story of the rest of the war very different indeed. For by the time he got to Green-castle with his captured train, the garrison at Harper's Ferry had surrendered; and Franklin, with eighteen thousand men, was sitting by the roadside five miles from the scene of the surrender, reflecting on the perils of his situation and warily doing nothing at all. And Lafayette McLaws was in close touch with Stonewall Jackson and A. P. Hill and was no longer in any danger whatever.

2. Destroy the Rebel Army

From his perch on top of South Mountain, Confederate General Daniel Harvey Hill could look down and see the war coming up to meet him like a tremendous pageant, unspeakably grand. Five miles to the east lay the Catoctin ridge, with three roads coming over to the approach to Turner's Gap. Down each of these roads rolled an endless blue column, pouring down the slope and into the open valley as if the weight of unlimited numbers lay behind it, growing longer and longer and spraying out at last, at the foot of South Mountain, into long fighting lines, rank upon rank, starred with battle flags. The general looked, and reflected that the old Hebrew poet who used the phrase, "terrible as an army with banners," must have looked down from a mountain on just such a scene as this. Hill was one of the least timid men in the army, but he confessed afterward that he never in his life felt so lonely as he had that day: all of the soldiers in the world seemed to be marching up against him, and he had only five thousand men to stop them, some of which were still back at Boonsboro.

Over on the Union side there were men who saw the picturesque quality too. It was not very often, even in that day of close-order fighting, that an entire army was massed in the open where everybody could see it. This was one of the times when it happened, and it was enough to take the breath away to look at it. A private in the 9th New York, his regiment pausing for a breather on the Catoctin slope, wrote that it was a "beautiful, impressive picture—each column a monstrous, crawling, blue-black snake, miles long, quilled with the silver slant of muskets at a 'shoulder,' its sluggish tail writhing slowly up over the distant eastern ridge, its bruised head weltering in the roar and smoke upon the crest above." General Abner Doubleday, turning in his saddle to inspect his brigade, cried involuntarily: "What a magnificent view." And McClellan himself, one of the first to come over the ridge, reined up near the village of Middletown to watch his men marching past. As the men came up to him they took fire—the great open amphitheater of war, their own proud strength all on display, and the hero whom they trusted to the death sitting his horse, proud and martial-looking, the one man who could make war seem grand to men who had been in many battles: they broke into wild cheers, yelling until they were too hoarse to yell any more. A Massachusetts veteran described the scene:

"It seemed as if an intermission had been declared in order that a reception might be tendered to the general-in-chief. A great crowd continually surrounded him, and the most extravagant demonstrations were indulged in. Hundreds even hugged the horse's legs and caressed his head and mane. While the troops were thus surging by, the general continually pointed with his finger to the gap in the mountain through which our path lay. It was like a great scene in a play, with the roar of the guns for an accompaniment."[1]

It had taken time to build up this impressive scene, however. McClellan mounted amid the troops, pointing dramatically to the rising slope where the battle smoke was drifting up through the mountain laurel, is the center of an unforgettable picture, but the picture had been some hours taking shape. There had been nothing dramatic about the first two thirds of this day—which, since the stage was all set for drama, simply means that the army had been very leisurely about coming up for the assault. Indeed, during the entire morning a few regiments of cavalry plus General Cox's division of Ohio infantry had had the place pretty much to themselves, except for the Rebels on South Mountain.

Even so, this day—the fourteenth of September, the same day Franklin's men were coming up to Crampton's Gap, off to the south —began bravely enough. Union cavalry went across the valley at dawn, and as the foot soldiers became visible behind them the Confederate cavalry trotted back and went up the winding mountain roads. The sun had not been up very long before Cox started his men after them. The Ohio soldiers left the National Road a mile or two before it began to climb the irregular valley which constitutes Turner's Gap, and followed a country road which goes through another depression a mile or more to the south; two brigades of Western infantry, six regiments in all, perhaps a total of three thousand men. There was a brief delay after the troops took the side road. Cox and General Pleasonton, who had the cavalry, trotted on half a mile along the main highway to arrange a couple of batteries on a little knoll—a dozen twenty-pounder rifled Parrotts, long-ranged guns for those days. The guns began to shell the top of the mountain, and Confederate gunners on top answered them, while the infantry stacked arms and waited in a little field. As they waited a sergeant on horseback, with a big bundle back of the saddle, came rocketing up to the 11th Ohio—mail from home, just arrived. The boys clustered round, and while the guns searched the wood with shell to prepare the way for them they sat on the ground and read their letters—each letter, no doubt, expressing the pathetic hope that the man who received it would survive whatever lay ahead of him, would "take care of himself" and, in the fullness of time, would get back home safe and sound.

Just about the time the letters were finished the orders came, and the men took up their rifles, formed a line of battle, and started up the mountainside. The slope was not too steep, but in most places it was abominably tangled with laurel and other scrubby growth, and the going was tough. At times the men found themselves struggling ahead single file, and regimental formations were badly mixed. As they got near the summit the growth became less dense and the ground was more nearly level, and they came out at last in a more open region of small farm clearings and pastures and found Rebels behind a stone fence. Long volleys of musketry rolled back and forth along the mountain ridge, while a Rebel battery near the gap to the north threw case shot into the Ohioans' ranks. D. H. Hill had sent in one of his best men, Brigadier General Samuel Garland, Jr., to hold this place, with a brigade of North Carolina troops and a few squadrons of dismounted cavalry. Garland stayed up where the fire was hottest, to encourage his men—they were outnumbered and they knew it, and they were a little nervous—and presently a Yankee bullet found him and killed him, and one of the Carolina regiments gave way. The 30th Ohio got through the wall and hung on, and in a couple of places there the Carolina and Ohio boys slugged one another with musket butts and jabbed with bayonets. Cox decided that if he could get some men up on a little rise of ground to the left all of the Rebels would have to go away, so he sent the 11th Ohio off to tend to it.

Accompanied by its regimental dog, Curly—a frisky pooch who enjoyed going out on the skirmish lines—the 11th went forward cautiously, the exact Confederate position along the knoll not being known, and pretty soon the 11th found itself in a nasty pocket, with Confederates shooting at them from three directions, so they got back out in a hurry.[2] Then the 23rd Ohio came up to help, and the two regiments went storming up the hill, firing as they went. The lieutenant colonel of the 23rd, a promising chap named Rutherford B. Hayes, was shot down, wounded; William McKinley, sergeant in the same regiment, was unhurt. The regiments kept on going, struggling through dense thickets that seemed to be alive and humming with bullets, and the Carolina brigade gave way at last and drew off down the western slope of the mountain, most of the men out of action for the rest of the day. This part of the mountaintop now belonged to the Army of the Potomac.

Actually, the whole mountaintop did, had the Army of the Potomac just been on hand to take possession. Of the five brigades in his command, Hill had had only two on South Mountain when the day began: one posted in the center at Turner's Gap, where the National Road came through, and the other one off here a mile to the south, where Cox and his Ohioans made their attack. The other three were hot-footing it up from Boonsboro, but they wouldn't be on hand for quite a while, and until they got there Hill had nothing left but the thin brigade on the National Road, some artillery, a few game remnants of the North Carolina brigade, and such dismounted cavalry as Stuart had been able to leave with him. It was at this time, when he reflected that he was standing there with something like a thousand muskets to stave off the greater part of McClellan's army, that General Hill experienced that great feeling of loneliness.

But the wind is tempered sometimes to the shorn lamb, and so it was here. Thus far the Army of the Potomac was represented only by the division of General Cox—some three thousand men when the battle began. These men did their best, and Cox had the right idea: he turned their faces toward the north, once the Carolinians had been driven off, and prepared to advance along the crest to Turner's Gap. The ground was broken and uneven, and it took time to get the men formed up. The Confederates had a number of guns at the gap, with a good line on the little clearings where the Ohioans were. Somehow they got the guns far enough forward to fire canister, the charges ripping up the sod, as Cox wrote later, "with a noise like the cutting of a melon rind." Cox sent back to his corps commander, Reno, for help, and Reno sent more men forward. By the time they got there and found their way up the difficult slopes it was a couple of hours past noon, and by this time some of Hill's other brigades were coming up. Hill had made a good showing, meanwhile, with the men he did have, and although the heads of McClellan's long columns were coming over the Catoctin ridge, Hill had not yet had to fight anything very much worse than equal numbers. He was in an extremely bad spot, but he had already been given eight hours' leeway.

As more of Reno's men came up the mountain, with Reno himself spurring up after them, Cox made ready to renew the attack. General Orlando Willcox got his division into line somewhere off to the right of Cox's Ohioans, and pretty soon the men went struggling forward. In Willcox's outfit there were two untried regiments going in side by side—the 17th Michigan and the 45th Pennsylvania. The Michigan boys were so painfully new that they could hardly get from marching column into fighting formation. They had been mustered in only a month ago, had been rushed down to Washington in feverish haste when Stanton got panicky over Pope's defeat, and barely a week before this day on the mountaintop one member of the regiment had written sadly that they did not know even "the rudiments of military maneuvering," adding that "there is not a company officer who can put his men through company drill without making one or more ludicrous blunders." For some reason this regiment was made up largely of men nearing middle age—except for Company E, which had been enlisted from students at the State Normal School at Ypsilanti—and they were desperately self-conscious and anxious to do the right thing in this first engagement. They had their best clothes on—dress coats buttoned neatly up to the throat, high-crowned black hats, each with a feather stuck jauntily in the band. One veteran remembered that they even had their dress-parade white gloves carefully folded and stuffed in their pockets; looking back with a rueful smile, he wrote that it was "a wonder we did not put them on, so little know we of the etiquette of war." Anyway, here they were, clumsily forming line of battle in the underbrush, the sweating officers irritably horsing the men into place by hand. They went stumbling forward, their dress uniforms getting sadly torn by thorns and broken branches; and D. H. Hill's veteran artillerists were getting the exact range of the ground they would have to traverse.[3]

The Pennsylvanians who went in with them were not nearly so new, but they were equally ignorant of what battle was like. They had been in service nearly a year and had been sent down to South Carolina on the Port Royal expedition. That had been mere "Sunday soldiering," one of their number wrote afterward; they had occasionally seen isolated Rebels on other islands several miles distant, but their only fighting had been against gnats and mosquitoes, and they had lived high, eating oranges and sweet potatoes, green corn and watermelon, with fresh fish out of the ocean. Now they were in line beside the Michigan boys, forcing their way through a wood where their major, to his shame, found his horse suddenly turned balky, so that he had to dismount and proceed on foot, leaving the faithless beast behind. The regiments came out at last behind a rail fence all grown up with long grass and briars, with a pasture beyond and another of those ominous stone walls eighty yards off on the far side. As usual, the stone wall was held by Rebels, who squatted on their heels, rested their rifles atop the wall, and blazed away with deadly aim.[4]

The Pennsylvania and Michigan men knelt behind their own fence and fired back, discovering immediately that an open rail fence is not nearly as good protection as a solid stone wall. Somewhere beyond the Confederate firing line there were Rebel batteries, which opened with shell and solid shot, sending the fence rails flying. The greenhorns looked around nervously, saw General Willcox calmly sitting his horse right up by the fence, took heart, and kept peppering away at what they could see of the enemy across the field. Reno got some more troops up, and at last the outnumbered Confederates backed away, firing as they went, and disappeared in the forest. Reno sent fresher troops on after them while the two new regiments caught their breath and took stock of the situation. The Michigan men found that they had lost thirty men killed and about a hundred wounded—fairly heavy losses, considering that they took some five hundred men into action (they had been a thousand strong a month earlier, but nearly half the regiment was sick and had been left behind). The Pennsylvania regiment had had almost exactly equal losses. They had had their baptism of fire, and the Michigan men proudly recorded that the veterans who saw them in action told it around that they "fought like tigers." Also, they noticed that there were a good many dead Rebels behind that stone wall.

It was getting late in the afternoon by now, and General Reno—who was up on the mountaintop taking personal charge of the fighting—began to believe that the Confederates had retreated. Riding up to the front, he took as good a look as he could at the checkerboard pattern of clearings, woods, and laurel patches. There was nobody in sight on this side of Turner's Gap, as far as he could make out, and he got ready to march straight north along the crest to cinch matters.

Beside him was the 51st Pennsylvania, which had been fighting hard. He directed it into an open field and told the colonel to have the men stack arms and to let them boil coffee if they wanted to: it would be a few minutes before he had his marching column formed. He turned his horse, to ride back along the line—and just then a body of Confederates, darkly concealed in the woodland ahead, let fly with an unexpected volley that splintered the Pennsylvanians' stacked muskets, broke up the coffee-fire groups, and knocked General Reno out of his saddle, dead. The 51st hurried to grab its muskets and got into a horrible cross fire. There was still another of those green regiments,

the 35th Massachusetts, lined up behind the 51st, and the 35th began
wildly returning the Rebel fire without waiting to let the Pennsylvania
boys get out of the way. There was an infernal mix-up for a while in
that tree-fringed clearing, with a prodigious racket of small-arms fire,
reeking smoke clouds hanging in the air, bullets zipping by from all
directions, men getting hit, and a great shouting and cursing going up;
but it finally got straightened out, and the Federals drove in hard
on the Confederates in the wood and scattered them.⁵

It was now close to four in the afternoon, and all of the fighting so
far had been done here south of the National Road by Reno's men.
The Confederates were in the immediate, visible presence of seventy
thousand Yankee soldiers, but they had not had to fight more than a
tenth of that number. In a sense, McClellan's finding of Special Orders No. 191 was working to his disadvantage this afternoon. According to that document, Boonsboro—which was only a couple of miles
or so beyond the summit of the mountain—was held by both Longstreet and Hill, and as a result McClellan, still clinging to the old, old
idea of Lee's overpowering numbers, believed that South Mountain
was occupied by at least thirty thousand men. Therefore, he played
his cards cautiously, refusing to make a direct stab at the gap until
he had plenty of men in line.⁶

Joe Hooker had been elevated to the command of the I Corps—
McDowell had been relieved, a man unlucky beyond all other generals, taking his demotion in manful silence, without recrimination—
and Hooker brought the I Corps down from the Catoctin ridge.
McClellan had him spread it out for an advance up South Mountain
to the north of the slopes where Reno's men had been fighting so long.
Hooker had three divisions in his corps—Meade's, Ricketts's, and
Hatch's—and he sent Meade's, Ricketts's, and most of Hatch's around
on a big swing a mile or more to the right of the National Road, to
go swarming up the heights that overlook Turner's Gap from the
north. It took a long time to move an entire army corps into position
in those wooded hollows, and it was getting along toward evening
before they were ready to advance. Hooker kept Gibbon's brigade
back, and he had it form right on the highway, with orders to start
for the top as soon as the lines on the right began to move.

Gibbon had his Black Hat boys all keyed up, which was a good
thing, since they had the toughest assignment of the lot. Turner's Gap

is a long, curving valley in the mountain, the road following the narrow floor as it climbs to the summit; the soldiers who went up here would have no chance for any fancy maneuvering but would have to go straight ahead in the teeth of whatever direct fire the Confederates might arrange for them. Since Hill was now being reinforced by Longstreet—whom Lee had started back from Hagerstown in a hurry, first thing that morning, when he learned that McClellan was moving—this frontal fire was apt to be heavy. But Gibbon had told his boys, before they left Frederick, how McClellan wanted two days of good marching and how he had assured the general that this brigade could outmarch and outfight anything in the army, and the men were on their toes. McClellan himself was not far behind, on top of a little hill from which he could see the highway all the way to the summit; whatever they did would be done right under his eye.

Gibbon got his boys astride the road, 7th Wisconsin on one side and 19th Indiana on the other, formed "by the right of companies" —which meant that each regiment was made up of ten parallel columns, each column representing one company marching two men abreast. They couldn't fight in that formation, but they could get over rough ground easily and could be brought up into line of battle without delay. The 2nd and 6th Wisconsin fell in behind. The brigade was thin, with hardly more than eleven hundred men altogether, the four regiments averaging a little under three hundred men apiece. Two twelve-pounder smoothbores from reliable old Battery B were moved up into the roadway, and the command set out.

They came under rifle fire before long, and when they reached the Rebel skirmish line the two guns were wheeled around to blast the Rebels with canister. The skirmishers withdrew, and Gibbon swung his men into line of battle, bringing the two rear regiments up abreast of the two in front—pridefully noting that the men did it as smoothly as if they were on the parade ground, while McClellan watched through his field glasses from the hilltop far below. Confederate artillery was posted at the summit and it had the range: it put a shell into the middle of the 2nd Wisconsin just as those ten company columns were wheeling into regimental front, dropping a dozen men with that one burst. The two guns of Battery B did what they could to quiet the Rebel guns, and the battle line went scrambling up the mountainside.

Up near the summit they found the Rebel line—a formidable affair behind another of those stone walls, with the enemy tucked snugly away where he could shoot downhill. The Rebels were in high spirits, and when the Westerners came within handy range they yelled taunts in the dusk: "Oh, you damn Yanks! We gave you hell again at Bull Run!" Some of the Wisconsin boys called back: "Watch out, Johnny, this isn't McDowell after you now—this is McClellan!" Then both sides gave up the catcalling and began using their rifles, and the fight became hot and heavy, with the Black Hat Brigade unable to advance an inch, and with Gibbon wondering, presently, whether they could even stay where they were. Ammunition ran low, and details were formed to collect cartridges from the dead and wounded. The sun went down and it was pitch-dark, and back on his little hilltop Mc-Clellan could follow the fight by watching the pin points of stabbing flame from the muzzles of the muskets. Along toward nine o'clock the fighting died out from sheer exhaustion, and the Black Hat Brigade prepared to spend the night on the firing line. Since it started uphill it had lost some 280 men, about a quarter of its total number.[7]

Off to the north Hooker's corps had been making progress, although the progress had been slow. Meade had his division of Pennsylvanians in front, and they went clambering up a high, steep-sided spur of the mountain ridge on top of which Confederate Robert Rodes had his fine brigade of Alabama troops. The Alabamians were badly outnumbered, but they had all the advantage of position and were rated as shock troops, under a general who was one of the best brigadiers in the Confederate Army, and before night came down they gave the Pennsylvanians a bad time of it. Coming up through the wood, the Bucktails caught it from a slim Confederate skirmish line hidden behind trees. The Rebels here were expert marksmen, and woods fighting was their specialty. They went dodging back from tree to tree, reloading under cover and drawing a good bead before they fired. But the Bucktails came from mountain country and were pretty good riflemen themselves. They got the wood clear at last, and then Meade's men had nothing but open fields in front of them and the Rebels had to give ground.

There was a delay along toward twilight, when Meade thought he was about to be outflanked, but Hooker sent more troops in and the supposed danger evaporated. The Rebels just did not have enough men on the mountain to make a serious counterattack, and once McClellan got his available strength into action, there could be only one outcome to the battle. By the time it was dark the Pennsylvanians had got to the top and Rodes's brigade took some very rough treatment, with a couple of hundred men shot down and an equal number captured. The firing flickered out in the darkness finally all along the crest, and the exhausted Federals prepared for a cheerless bivouac on the mountaintop. During the night there was a good deal of firing by nervous pickets, and some of the Union commanders feared a counterattack, but actually the field had been won: Union troops were on the heights, where they had full command of the pass, and the Rebels were grateful for the dark and a chance to get away.

The Black Hat Brigade had a little tale to tell around the campfires. Late in the evening the brigade found that it had some prisoners to send back to army headquarters. A corporal and squad were detailed, and the corporal led the way back to a country house which McClellan had taken over. He was misdirected, somehow, when he went inside, and when he opened what he thought was the door of the provost marshal's office he unexpectedly found himself facing McClellan. McClellan, busy with some papers, looked up, frowning at the intrusion, and said somewhat curtly: "What do you want?"

The corporal gulped and explained: he had some prisoners to turn in and he had opened the wrong door by mistake. Softening a bit McClellan asked the boy for his name and regiment. When he was told his eyes brightened.

"Oh, you belong to Gibbon's brigade. You had some heavy fighting up there tonight."

"Yes, sir," said the boy. "But I think we gave them as good as they sent."

"Indeed you did. You made a splendid fight."

The corporal hesitated. Then, greatly daring, he said:

"Well, General, that's the way we boys calculate to fight under a general like you."

McClellan got up, came around the table, and gripped the corporal by the hand.

"If I can get that kind of feeling amongst the men of this army," said McClellan, "I can whip Lee without any trouble at all."

So the corporal went back to his regiment, and the Black Hat

Brigade had a story which went through the whole army: General McClellan had shaken hands with an enlisted man and complimented him on his brigade's fighting qualities.[8]

At dawn there was a heavy mist on the mountaintop, as if the battle smoke of the previous day's fighting had lingered under the leaves. The commands there cautiously sent out patrols, which presently brought back word: no Rebels in sight. Pleasonton's cavalry came up the National Road and went down the western slope into Boonsboro as the mist evaporated, driving out Fitz Lee's Confederate troopers and provoking a series of running fights across the fields and down the country roads. A double handful of Rebel stragglers were combed out of the town, and McClellan ordered Sumner to push his corps through and take up the pursuit. Sumner put Richardson in front, and the 5th New Hampshire had the advance, sweeping along the road past dead cavalry horses, occasional wrecked caissons, and various other signs of a hasty retreat. The New Hampshire boys legged it so fast that they later remembered with pride that other commands had dubbed them "Richardson's cavalry." In French's division, which followed Richardson's, was the brand-new 130th Pennsylvania, whose untried soldiers gaped, wide-eyed, as they saw their first live Rebels—a band of prisoners being escorted to the rear. In this band was a dapper young Confederate officer, trim in a new gray uniform; one of the Pennsylvania rookies called out to him: "Are there any more Rebels left?" The officer replied grimly that they would see lots of Rebels very shortly—a prophecy, said the 130th's historian, which was amply fulfilled.[9]

Back on the mountaintop the brigades that had done the fighting the day before pulled themselves together, took stock of their losses —altogether, eighteen hundred Union soldiers had fallen—and sent out parties to bury the dead and pick up discarded equipment. Young Captain Noyes grew thoughtful as he watched one party laying dead Confederates in a trench, and noted in his diary: "How all feeling of enmity disappears in presence of these white faces, these eyes gazing upward so fixedly in the gray of the morning hour." And a soldier of the 9th New York, viewing a similar scene, remarked that "there was no 'secession' in those rigid forms, nor in those fixed eyes staring blankly at the sky." Less melancholy, a private in the 51st Pennsylvania recorded that he and his buddies looted the haversacks of dead

Rebels and found them full of good food—better rations, he remarked, than the Union men were carrying. On the way down the mountain the 12th Massachusetts saw Joe Hooker, well pleased with the work of his new corps, "in the saddle taking his brandy and water, looking as clean and trim as though he had just made his morning toilet at Willard's."[10]

Piece by piece the army reassembled and took to the road, following Sumner. Without ceremony the XII Corps, which had been under the luckless Nathaniel P. Banks, found that it had a new commander —a white-haired, wintry-faced old regular named Joseph K. F. Mansfield, who had been graduated from West Point away back in 1822, before most of the soldiers in this corps had been born, and who showed up this morning in a fine new blue uniform, an improvised staff trotting at his heels. He took hold strong, while his corps was in the act of getting on the road, and one of the soldiers noted with approval that while he appeared to be "a calm and dignified old gentleman" he quickly showed that he "was the personification of vigor, dash and enthusiasm." Another recorded that he rode "with a proud, martial air and was full of military ardor."[11] Several new regiments, fresh from training camps at home, came plowing up through Frederick and joined the army—or tried to, anyway. There was a great traffic jam on the road between Frederick and Boonsboro, with ambulances and details of prisoners going back against the tide and with long wagon trains clogging the road as they tried to slip in between the marching divisions, and the recruits had to stand by in the cornfields to wait their turn.

The army was feeling good. It was enjoying an experience which, from one end of the war to the other, the Army of the Potomac did not have very often—chasing a Confederate army which was in full retreat, after a battle which had been a clear-cut Union victory—and it was like a tonic. The men had been told a day or so earlier that they were going to relieve Harper's Ferry and had not yet been informed that that place had already surrendered; and as the long miles passed underfoot the men in the ranks made good-natured gibes about it, asking one another: "Who in hell is this Harper, and where's his ferry?" Early in the afternoon the 5th New Hampshire passed through a little hamlet and came out on a chain of low heights overlooking a pleasant, winding little creek, with rising ground beyond and the steeples and housetops of a town showing over the hills. They were halted there, since the Confederates had guns posted on the opposite hills and seemed disposed to contest any further advance, and the rest of the army slowly came up and poured off into fields and farmyards on either side of the road. Pretty soon McClellan and his staff cantered up amid a long wave of cheers, and the general rode to a hilltop and spent a long time examining the lovely, rolling countryside with his field glasses, while a Confederate battery tossed so many shells at him that he sent his staff back into a hollow for protection.

The little town that he could just see beyond the hills was the town of Sharpsburg. The stream that wound through the open valley was Antietam Creek, gleaming brown in the afternoon sun and looking like a promising place to fish in the cool of a summer evening. A couple of miles away, in front and to the general's right, there was a little white church with a wood behind it: a church of the Dunker sect, whose members believed church steeples a vanity and held that war was sinful. Flags and guns and moving men were to be seen on the slopes between the church and the town. Lee and his army had stopped retreating and had turned to fight.

The sporadic cannonading died away and the afternoon became peaceful again. McClellan was in no mood to hurry things. Most of his army was still spraddled back over a long stretch of road, and it would take a good many hours to assemble all of it. Franklin was some miles away, near Crampton's Gap, and it might not be wise to call him in until it was certain that the Rebels who had seized Harper's Ferry were up to no more mischief in that area. So McClellan established headquarters on the lawn of a pleasant house on a hill overlooking the valley. That morning he had sent his wife a hasty telegram, saying that the army had "gained a glorious victory"; this he had followed with a note saying that he was pursuing the enemy "with the greatest rapidity, and expect to gain great results." The air had been full of jubilant talk that morning, and McClellan had written: "If I can believe one-tenth of what is reported, God has seldom given an army a greater victory than this." He had also reported the victory to the President, incautiously telling him that "General Lee admits they are badly whipped"—a statement which caused Secretary Welles to wonder tartly to whom Lee made this statement that it should be so promptly brought to McClellan's ears. In another message home McClellan proudly asserted that the victory had "no doubt delivered Pennsylvania and Maryland."

No doubt. And yet the sky was slowly but steadily darkening. The finding of Lee's lost order had put the game in McClellan's hands; forty-eight hours had passed since then, and two chances had been missed. The Harper's Ferry garrison had not been relieved, and the separate pieces of Lee's army had not been destroyed before they could unite. Two states might well have been "delivered," but the war had not been won—and it was final, shattering victory which McClellan had originally been thinking about. D. H. Hill had had some terribly lonely hours on top of South Mountain, but not until late afternoon had he been compelled to meet more of an attack than his slim numbers could handle, and it was dark before the Federals had brought up men enough to seize the crest by sheer force. The fight had been a Union victory beyond question, and yet, as Hill himself remarked, "if it was fought to save Lee's trains and artillery, and to reunite his scattered forces, it was a Confederate success." And it was precisely that kind of success which McClellan could not afford to let the Confederates win just then.

If this point was obvious to the Confederate soldier, it was also dimly visible to Lincoln back in Washington, watching and waiting in almost unbearable suspense as the war came to its greatest moment of climax. Receiving McClellan's triumphant announcement that the mountain passes had been forced, Lincoln sent him this reply:

"God bless you and all with you. Destroy the Rebel army if possible."

3. Tenting Tonight

The country around Sharpsburg is surpassingly lovely, with low hills rolling lazily down to the Potomac on the west, and little patches of trees breaking up the green-and-brown pattern of the farmers' fields. The river comes down unhurried, going to the south in wide loops and then swinging to the east; and just before it turns again to go south the copper-colored Antietam comes down and joins it—another unhurried stream that makes little loops and bends of its own as it follows a north-and-south line to enter the river. Between the creek and the river is the town of Sharpsburg, lying on the western slope of a gentle ridge that slants off, east and west, to the two streams.

This ridge is not sharply defined; just a stretch of higher ground, tapering off to the south in the blunt angle where the creek meets the river, and merging imperceptibly with the hills of the Maryland countryside a mile or two north of town. It is full of minor heights and hollows, with easy spurs and valleys running east toward the creek, dotted here and there with little open groves. The main road from Sharpsburg to Hagerstown runs north from the town along the broad crest of this ridge. The other principal road goes east from the town, gets over the height, and goes down a long slope to cross Antietam Creek on an arched stone bridge, after which it runs off northeast to Boonsboro. Half a dozen miles to the east the blue mass of South Mountain lies upon the land.

All of this is good farming country, with a look of quiet and uneventful prosperity. There are many cornfields and pastures, orchards and gardens surround the farmhouses, and there are huge barns. Little country roads zigzag in between the fields, worn down by many generations of use until, in some places, they are below the level of the ground they cross. They are bordered by fences—mostly barbed wire, nowadays; weathered rail, two generations ago. Here and there the ground is broken by an outcropping of rock.

Now this country town, together with the streams and the principal roads, had names before the armies came together there, because men have to have names for such places in the daily routine of living. But most of the landscape lay nameless, except for purely local, informal titles like Piper's cornfield, or Poffenberger's wood, and it serenely and happily lacked history and tradition. Nothing had ever happened there except the quiet, undramatic, unrecorded round of births and deaths, christenings and weddings, cornhuskings and barn-raisings, the plowing of the ground in the spring and the harvesting of fat crops in the fall. Life moved like the great tide of the Potomac a mile or so to the west—slowly, steadily, without making a fuss, patiently molding the land to its own liking.

As one comes up the hill on the road from Boonsboro, after crossing the creek and just before entering the town, there is the National Cemetery, green and well kept, white headstones marking the places

where many dead men lie in orderly military formations, with pleasant trees casting broken shadows on the lawn. It is a large cemetery,
and it was not there at all on the morning of September 16, 1862;
there was nothing there then but the broad crest and the peaceful
grove, with the spires and roofs of Sharpsburg half hidden beyond.
If a man stood in this grove and looked to the north he could see the
white block of the little Dunker church, a mile away, beside the
Hagerstown pike. And on that September morning in 1862, anyone
who looked at the church would have seen two bits of woodland
lying near it—one west of the Hagerstown road, surrounding the
church on three sides and stretching northward for half a mile or
more, and the other east of the road, separated from it by open
fields several hundred yards wide. Two quieter bits of woodland
could not have been found in North America, and no one outside the
immediate neighborhood had ever heard of them; no one had ever
taken human life in either of them. But ever since then, because of
what was about to take place there, those two wood lots have had a
grim, specialized fame and have been known in innumerable books
and official records as the West Wood and the East Wood—as if, in
all that countryside, there were no other bits of wood that lay just
east and west of a country road. In the same way, there was a forty-
acre cornfield lying on the east side of the road, between the two
plots of trees, which ever since has simply been *the* cornfield, as if
there had never been any other.

The woods have been cut down since then, and where the cornfield used to be there is a macadamized roadway flanked by gleaming, archaic-looking monuments and statues, with little markers here
and there unobtrusively beckoning for attention. But in the fall of
1862 no one was dreaming of statues, and because they had had
good growing weather the corn was in fine shape—more than head-
high, strong, richly green, the tall stalks waving slowly in the last
winds of summer.

And over and above all of this perfection of peace and quiet, on
the sixteenth of September, there was a silent running out of time
and a gathering together of the fates, as issues that reached to the
ends of the earth and the farthest borders of national history drew
in here for decision. The peace and quiet had already been destroyed.
In the grove where it would soon be necessary to lay out a cemetery

(grass waving in the summer breeze beside the tiny faded flags: it's all right now, it's all right) men in trim gray uniforms sat on their horses and looked to the east through field glasses. Many other men, much less neatly dressed in gray and tattered brown and every imaginable shade between, were filling the zigzag country lanes and trampling down the grain in the farmers' fields all along the ridge. Dust hung in the air as long columns of six-horse teams labored up the roads, swung off into the fields at higher places on the ridge, and sent polished guns into battery to the tune of crackling bugle calls. Now and then a set of these guns would shoot out quick jets of bright flame and rolling clouds of soiled smoke, the guns jarring backward with each discharge, scarring the ground beneath their trails and breaking the air with heavy sound.

On the eastern side of the Antietam, a mile away, the scene was much the same, except that here the men wore blue—very dusty, worn, and dirty, much of it—and there were many more of them. They brought guns up to the low heights bordering the east side of the creek: iron rifles, mostly, many of them bearing at the breech the heavy band that marked the long-range Parrott. From time to time they fired at the Confederate guns to the west, battery and section commanders standing a little apart, peering under the smoke to spot the shots. Behind the guns, safely under cover in valleys and hollows, were dense masses of infantry, the men glancing incuriously up at the guns as they moved into their places, each youthful face a tanned, expressionless mask. Now and then the crash of the rival batteries rose to a great tumult that sent long echoes rolling cross-country to the mountains off to the east; then the noise died down and the country seemed quiet, and the unending thump-shuffle of feet and the creaking of wagon wheels could be heard. When the guns were being fired it seemed as if a great battle were being waged, yet this was not really a battle at all; this was merely the preliminary feinting and sparring, most of it due to nothing but the overeagerness of the battery commanders and none of it doing very much harm.

On the right-hand side of the road from Boonsboro, nearly a mile before the road crosses Antietam Creek, there is a little rise of ground running out in a low spur overlooking the valley, and here a man named Pry had built a fine big two-story house of brick, with broad lawns and tidy outbuildings, and a grand view opening off to the west and south. In his yard, on the crest of the western slope, General McClellan had pitched his headquarters tents. Orderlies had driven tall stakes into the ground in front of the tents, and telescopes were strapped to the tops of these stakes, ready for use by any military eye that cared to search the Rebels' side of the Antietam. Camp chairs from the headquarters wagons had been set up, and a few regular armchairs had been brought out from Mr. Pry's house, and the commanding general had taken his post here, surrounded by his staff, their orderlies, the headquarters guard, and all the rest, with the headquarters flag flying from a tall pole in the center. The morning wore away and McClellan studied the long ridge to the west, and the generals came in to report and to receive their orders. What was going to be the battle of the Antietam was beginning to take shape, piece by piece, in the general's mind.

It was hot, that morning, with a blazing sun, and no air was stirring in the protected hollows where the troops took shelter. All through the morning the army kept coming up, the men filing into place to right and left of the Boonsboro road, headquarters officers cantering up and down the dusty road with papers in their hands to see that each unit got to the proper location. Now and then groups of soldiers would leave their places and walk to the top of some hill to see what the prospect might be. They never stayed long because the Confederate gunners were watchful and sprayed shell at any hillock where one of these groups appeared. When that happened the Union batteries would strike at the guns that had fired the shells, and the roar of the cannonade would rise to a brief crescendo, only to die away again as the men took cover. Toward noon the sky became overcast and a little breeze sprang up, and it was a bit cooler. McClellan stayed close to headquarters, conferring with his officers and studying the Rebel position through telescopes. Except for the guns and an occasional glimpse of moving men, there was not a great deal to see. Undulations in the ground kept most of the Confederate Army out of sight.

But the general felt that he was getting a tolerably good idea of its position, and as the day lengthened, his battle plan was formed. As far as McClellan could make out, the Confederate line ran north and south along the ridge, its southern end anchored among the hills south of the Boonsboro road, the other end going into the woods somewhere beyond the white Dunker church. The position was strong, and it was not going to be too easy for the Federals to reach it, because before they could get at it they would have to cross the Antietam, and good crossings seemed to be few. The bridge by which the Boonsboro road crossed the creek offered nothing but a direct frontal assault on the center of the Confederate line, where many batteries were clustered. A mile downstream there was another bridge, built of stone and arched like the first, from which a road followed a little ravine to cross the ridge and get into Sharpsburg from the southeast. This gave an approach to the southern end of the Confederate line, but the ground was bad. Steep hills looked down on the bridge from the Confederate side of the creek, and those hills appeared to be full of armed Rebels, and the guns in front of Sharpsburg commanded both the bridge and the road that led from it up the ravine. Forcing a passage over that bridge and up onto those hills would be just plain murder, unless Lee's attention could first be directed elsewhere.

North of the Boonsboro road the situation was more promising. In front of the Pry house, a mile upstream from the place where the Boonsboro road crossed the stream, there was a third bridge, sheltered in the valley so that the Rebel guns could not reach it, with a winding road that went off through the farmlands to the north and west; and still farther upstream there were a couple of shallow places where men could wade the creek well out of sight of the enemy's artillery.

It looked, therefore, as if the sensible course was to cross the Antietam at these protected upstream crossings, get troops over to the Hagerstown road well north of the Confederate position, and send them sweeping down on top of the ridge, rolling up the Rebel line as they went. At the same time, in spite of the obstacles, it would be well to make a secondary attack at the bridge farthest downstream. That might be costly, but it would keep Lee busy at both ends of his line and prevent him from sending troops from his right, below the town, to support his left, up by the Dunker church. Then, as a final touch: when these two attacks were under way, watch the situation closely, and if all seemed to be going well make a third smash right through the middle—Lee would probably have weakened his center to support his two ends, and this third attack ought to break his line and finish him off.

Thus McClellan figured it out, while the troops waited in the valleys and the guns boomed heavily, fell silent, and broke into action again, and the hot day slowly passed. The whole Union Army was on hand except for Franklin, who was still watching the Rebel detachments over near Harper's Ferry. Franklin must be called in. Presumably he would be able to get his men up to the Antietam sometime next day. McClellan studied the landscape again, talked with corps commanders, and waited, while the sweating gunners brought more and more guns up to the low bluffs that overlook the Antietam from the east. He was going to have everything ready before he opened the fight, and nothing was going to be lost through overhasty action.

Or gained, either. He still had all the advantage, but time was continuing to run out on him, and the bright opportunity that had been handed to him by grace of the Indiana non-coms three days ago was getting dimmer and dimmer. Crampton's Gap: one chance missed. South Mountain: a second chance missed. His luck was still in, a third chance was offering, but there might be such a thing as stretching good luck too far. For it was not by any means the whole of Lee's army that faced him, this sweltering sixteenth of September. The afternoon before, when the weary Confederates planted themselves on the Sharpsburg heights and turned at bay, only the commands of Longstreet and D. H. Hill had been present. This morning Jackson and Walker had brought their men in—very tired and footsore men who had made an exhausting seventeen-mile night march from Harper's Ferry. (Night marches were feasible, after all, if the man who wore general's stars demanded them.) Three full Confederate divisions were still at Harper's Ferry and could not reach Sharpsburg until the next day. Lee had barely twenty-five thousand men on the field, while McClellan pondered his battle plan and weighed his chances and decided not to attack until everything was ready. The higher officers of the Army of Northern Virginia were frankly amazed as they saw Lee serenely awaiting attack with this slender force, while the blue columns were visibly building up overpowering strength on the far side of the creek. General Longstreet, who was a hard man to impress, wrote later that this day-long, ostentatious assem-

bling of Federal legions was "an awe-inspiring spectacle." Yet it remained a spectacle and nothing more, all through the day, while the
slow minutes ticked away.

For McClellan was facing an imaginary army rather than the real
one which was spread so thin on the Sharpsburg ridge: an army that
drew upon fabulous numbers and transcended all of the limitations
which poor transportation and insufficient supplies always imposed
on Confederate commanders. Whether the fault lay with the Pinkerton reports, with McClellan himself, or somewhere else, the incredible fact remains that McClellan was preparing to fight an army that
simply did not exist. He believed Lee to have a hundred thousand
men at his command that day. The Federal army was outnumbered;
that offensive thrust which he must presently make, to drive the invader back below the Potomac, was an enormously risky venture
which could not be undertaken at all except for the great valor of the
troops and the undying love which they had for their commander.

Between this imaginary Rebel army and the flesh-and-blood army
that was awaiting his attack there was an enormous difference. In
his invasion of the North, Lee had taken a gamble even more desperately daring than the one he had taken on the Chickahominy,
when he divided his army and wagered the Confederacy's independence that McClellan would never find out how thin was the screen
that stood between him and Richmond. Lee crossed the Potomac
with an army that was on the verge of complete exhaustion. Shoeless
men who could tramp the dirt roads of Virginia without too much
discomfort just could not march on the hard roads of Maryland; they
had fallen out by the thousands, along with other thousands who felt
that they had enlisted to defend Virginia's soil, not to invade the
North, and who in their unsophisticated way had turned back when
they got to the Potomac, planning to join up again once the army
returned to Virginia where it belonged. Altogether, from ten to
twenty thousand Southerners had left the ranks between Pope's defeat
at Bull Run and the arrival at Sharpsburg. Even when the troops
at Harper's Ferry came up, Lee would have barely forty thousand
men to throw into action.

In a way this was almost an advantage. Every faintheart, every
weakling, every man whose spirit and body were not of the stoutest,
had been winnowed out. The ones who were left were the hard-rock

men who would be a long time dying. But even so, the odds were fantastic. It is hard to find in all of Lee's career any act more completely bold than his calm decision to stand and fight on the Antietam.

When Franklin came up McClellan would have, by his own estimate, eighty-seven thousand men—with abundant reinforcements not far off. His advantage, actually, was not as great as the figures seem to show, because Confederates and Federals reckoned their numbers differently. The Rebels counted only the men who would actually be carrying muskets, and the Federals counted all who were "present for duty"—which meant that they included all the cooks, orderlies, train guards, ambulance details, and others who had non-combat assignments. Such details were particularly wasteful just then; a Northern general who fought at Antietam said that it was necessary to knock fully 20 per cent off the "present for duty" total to get the actual combat strength. But even with that reduction, McClellan had every advantage. Never before and never afterward, until the last gray days between Petersburg and Appomattox, were the two armies to collide with the Rebel strength so greatly reduced. In addition, Lee must fight with his back to the Potomac, so that any blow which really crumpled his line would mean nothing less than absolute disaster. Retreat would be out of the question if the Yankees ever broke through.[1]

But McClellan saw the imaginary situation, not the real one. And he had, by any reckoning, abundant reason for caution. He might have been the man who could win the war in an afternoon; what he could not for a moment forget was that he was also the man who could lose it in an afternoon. Defeat north of the Potomac would mean the end of everything. The army had just been reorganized, and it had many raw troops; from a military point of view it was hardly an army so much as a collection of soldiers, fit to be taken into battle only in a great emergency.

And on top of everything else the old poison of distrust and hatred was still working. McClellan's own position was unstable, not to say downright irregular. He had been restored to command by President Lincoln personally, over the violent objection of the War Department, the Republican majority in Congress, and most of the Cabinet. Nobody had actually ordered him to take the army up here and

fight the Confederates. All that showed on paper was that he had
been put in command of troops "for the defense of Washington," and
if anything went wrong here on the Antietam it was quite likely that
Secretary Stanton would proceed against him for lawlessly exceeding
his authority. McClellan wrote later that he fought the battles of
South Mountain and the Antietam with a noose around his neck—
which is to say that he fought, believing he would be executed for
treason if he were beaten—a consideration hardly designed to make
a bold, dashing fighter out of a man of McClellan's temperament.

So he bided his time: studying, calculating, attending to details.
Noon came and went. Clouds formed in the sky and there was a
little breeze to make the day cooler, and the guns on the hills fell
silent. One of McClellan's staff officers wrote that "nobody seemed
to be in a hurry. . . . Corps and divisions moved as languidly to
the places assigned them as if they were getting ready for a grand
review instead of a decisive battle."[2] McClellan rode from end to
end of his lines, moving a detachment here and there into better
position, endlessly watching the opposing heights. Once he detected
a change in the position of a couple of Rebel batteries and conceived
that Lee was regrouping his forces; that called for further delay,
while additional surveys were made. Ammunition trains were coming
up, and McClellan, always the good administrator, personally super-
vised the arrangements for supplying troops and batteries.

As he perfected his plans he let himself create a mix-up in the
chain of army command—unimportant enough, on the surface, but
due to have far-reaching effects on the way the battle was fought.

Somewhat informally, McClellan had recently grouped his army
into three principal sub-commands, or wings. General Sumner, commander of the II Corps, had been given command over General
Mansfield's XII Corps as well. Franklin had his own VI Corps and
Porter's V Corps; and General Ambrose E. Burnside, who had joined
on the march up from Washington, had the direction of Reno's old
IX Corps and of Hooker's I Corps. In planning his attack, however,
McClellan scrambled this grouping—partly, his staff whispered, at the
urging of Joe Hooker, who considered that he could make a better
fight and win more glory if he were out from under Burnside's control. At any rate, the attack on the extreme right had been entrusted
to Hooker, who was to have Mansfield's corps in immediate sup-

port, with Sumner standing by to lend a hand if necessary. In Franklin's absence Porter was to hold the center and act as army reserve, and when Franklin came up he would be put in wherever he seemed to be needed most. Burnside was on the extreme left, facing the downstream bridge, where he would attack as soon as Hooker's drive was rolling well.

Thus the new wing commands had completely fallen apart, and nobody in particular had general charge of anything. Hooker, theoretically under Burnside, was off on his own at the other end of the line. Mansfield, technically under Sumner, seemed to be temporarily attached to Hooker. Sumner, supposedly commanding a third of the army, had only his own corps and was to help Hooker, although Hooker was not empowered to give him any orders. And Burnside, who was new to the Army of the Potomac, was left to play a lone hand on the hardest front of all, attacking the bridge that crossed the Antietam under the overhanging hills to the south. All of the lines of responsibility had been cut, and if the next day's fighting was going to be co-ordinated in any way, the co-ordination would have to be provided by McClellan himself—and McClellan was a general who, like Lee, much preferred to leave the actual conduct of the fighting to his subordinates once a battle was begun.

The arrangement promised to make Hooker the hero of the next day's fight, and so that general, always eager for distinction, was very happy about it. It didn't sit at all well with Burnside, however, and it unquestionably had a grave effect on the fighting his men were to do.

There was to be a time when the Army of the Potomac would dislike and distrust Burnside intensely—not because he was personally objectionable, but because he presently developed an almost unfailing knack for bringing on defeat whenever he went into action. That time had not yet come, however, and in September 1862 he was immensely popular with the IX Corps, which knew him, and was generally respected by the rest of the army. Neither he nor the corps had been with the army very long, but both the general and the men brought a first-rate record in with them. Judging strictly by past performance, Burnside was a good man with the habit of success.

In 1861 he had been a Rhode Island businessman of some prominence, a West Pointer who had resigned from the army because garrison life in peacetime seemed unbearably dull. He got back in quickly enough when Fort Sumter was fired on, and raised the first of Rhode Island's troops. Late in that first summer of the war he proposed that an amphibious expedition be fitted out to descend on the North Carolina sounds, taking possession of seacoast cities and forts, giving Jefferson Davis a new front to defend, and closing the ports of entry for blockade runners. The suggestion was a good one and the administration accepted it, appointing Burnside to organize and lead the expedition. He got it under way early in January 1862, sailing from Hampton Roads with a heterogeneous fleet of transports and strong navy support.

Everything worked out fine, and the expedition was a brilliant success. Burnside made a good impression even before the fleet sailed. In the job lot of transports that had been collected so hurriedly there were some remarkably unseaworthy old tubs, and the soldiers protested strongly about having to go to sea in them: they had signed up to face Rebel bullets, but they didn't want to be drowned. Burnside promptly ended all grumbling by moving himself and his headquarters staff off the fine new steamer that had been set aside for him and embarking the smallest and most rickety little vessel of the lot—and almost paid for it with his life when the fleet ran into a gale off Cape Hatteras and the little steamer came within an inch of foundering.[3]

He seems to have been a very likable person, this Burnside. McClellan was very fond of him (until after the Antietam had been fought, anyhow) and used to write informal, chatty letters to him beginning "Dear Burn." Lincoln appears always to have retained a good deal of faith in him, even after Burnside had repeatedly demonstrated that it had been a military tragedy to give him a rank higher than colonel. One reason might have been that, with all his deficiencies, Burnside never had any angles of his own to play; he was a simple, honest, loyal soldier, doing his best even if that best was not very good, never scheming or conniving or backbiting. Also, he was modest; in an army many of whose generals were insufferable prima donnas, Burnside never mistook himself for Napoleon. Physically, he was impressive: tall, just a little stout, wearing what was probably the most artistic and awe-inspiring set of whiskers in all that bewhiskered army. He customarily wore a high, bell-crowned felt hat with the brim turned down and a double-breasted, knee-length frock coat, belted at the waist—a costume which, unfortunately, is apt to strike the modern eye as being very much like that of a beefy city cop of the 1880s.

At any rate, McClellan's order of battle for September 17 seems to have touched off all of Burnside's troubles. In a sense it left him all dressed up with no place to go. He was supposed to command two army corps, but one corps had been taken away from him. The one that remained had been commanded by Reno, and Reno had been killed on South Mountain; and Burnside, getting a bit stuffy for once in his career, refused to resume direct command of it because he felt that to do so would be to consent to a demotion. So he told General Cox, the ranking division commander, to assume command of the IX Corps; he, Burnside, would remain a wing commander even though the wing had been cut in half.

The result was that the IX Corps in this battle had two commanders—and no commander at all. McClellan gave his orders to Burnside, and Burnside majestically passed them on to Cox, and neither man was quite responsible for operations. Once the action began, there was likely to be a mix-up of the first magnitude.

On the afternoon of September 16, however, nobody foresaw any of that trouble. Along about four o'clock Hooker's corps pulled itself out of the fields along the Boonsboro road, followed a country lane back of the Pry house, and went splashing through the upper fords of the Antietam, with Hooker in the lead riding a magnificent white horse and looking every inch and quite consciously the gallant general. A soldier in the 6th Wisconsin remembered afterward that the way led through apple orchards and that the boys ducked out of ranks to fill their pockets and haversacks with the ripe fruit. Signal stations had been set up on the hills far ahead, and as they marched the men could see the flags wigwagging furiously. The corps began to climb through the rising farmland on its way to strike the Hagerstown road, and from the ridge to the west the move became visible, and Confederate guns banged away, groping ineffectually for the range.

The line of march led near the East Wood—that parklike open grove that lay half a mile northeast of the Dunker church—and the wood was occupied that afternoon by the Confederate division of

John B. Hood: two brigades of Texas and Mississippi troops who were generally considered the hardest fighters in all of Lee's army, which is about all the compliment any troops need. They had their pickets well out in front, and before long the Yankee skirmishers brushed into them and there was a brisk interchange of small-arms fire. General Meade came riding up, brusque and impatient, to look the situation over. He sent couriers dashing off, and in a few minutes he had his Pennsylvania division deployed in line of battle facing the wood, and the Bucktails went forward in a long skirmish line. The rifle fire became heavy, and the colonel of the Bucktails was killed, and smoke and early twilight filled the fringes of the wood. Both sides rolled guns forward to take a hand in the fight, and as these opened, the guns farther back reached out at long range to make their own contribution, and for an hour or more there was a really vicious little battle there under the trees. Far off to the Federal left, soldiers of the 8th Ohio crept up on a hill to watch in the gathering dusk, and one of them—filled with all of a soldier's enthusiasm for a fight in which he himself does not have to take part—wrote: "Nothing could have been more grand. The red glare of flame along the Rebel line for more than a mile, the bright streams of light along the track of the shell, and the livid clouds of smoke as the shell burst in the air, constituted a spectacle brilliant beyond comparison."[4]

The firing was heavy and sustained enough to make Longstreet believe that a major attack had been made and repulsed. But the Federals didn't want the East Wood just then—Hooker was simply trying to protect the flank of his corps as it marched into position farther north and west—and the firing died out at dusk. Meade drew his division off, and only the rival picket lines were left to snipe at each other, sullenly, in the evening dark. On the Confederate side Hood's division was drawn back out of the wood, and replacement troops were sent up to bivouac where they had fought.

Hooker took his men well to the north before halting for the night. Doubleday's division, in the lead (Hatch had been wounded at South Mountain, and Doubleday had the division now), got to the Hagerstown road and formed up facing directly to the south, with Meade's Pennsylvanians on its left and a little more to the south, and the third division, that of Ricketts, to the left of the Pennsylvanians. Having thus reached what looked like a good jumping-off place for the next day's battle, Hooker established his headquarters in a farmer's yard a little east of the turnpike, and his men spread their blankets where they had halted and turned in for a little sleep.

It wasn't a very good night for sleeping. It began to rain after the sun went down, and there were intermittent spells of what one veteran recalled as "dismal, drizzling rain" all through the night; and out in front the pickets were nervous, opening up now and then with a blaze of firing that occasionally stirred some of the batteries and caused them to join in, although it was too dark for the gunners to hit much of anything. The gunfire rose to such a pitch, once, that an aide roused Hooker and called him out of his tent, fearing that the Rebels might be beginning a night attack. Hooker stood in the farmyard and listened, the raindrops glistening on his florid, handsome face, and looked at the spurts of flame off in the dark, estimating the direction of the fire. Then he shook his head. "The Rebels must be firing into their own men—we haven't any troops off that way," he said. Then he went back to bed.

There was a tension in the atmosphere for the whole army that night. Survivors wrote long afterward that there seemed to be something mysteriously ominous in the very air—stealthy, muffled tramp of marching men who could not be seen but were sensed dimly as moving shadows in the dark; outbursts of rifle fire up and down the invisible picket lines, with flames lighting the sky now and then when gunners in the advanced batteries opened fire; taut and nervous anxiety of those alert sentinels communicating itself through all the bivouacs, where men tried to sleep away the knowledge that the morrow would bring the biggest battle the army had ever had; a ceaseless, restless sense of movement, as if the army stirred blindly in its sleep, with the clop-clop of belated couriers riding down the inky-dark lanes heard at intervals, sounding very lonely and far off. The 16th Connecticut, a new and almost completely untrained regiment, which was lying along the Antietam near the downstream bridge, fell into a panic and sprang wildly to arms once when some clumsy rookie accidentally discharged his musket. Veteran regiments nearby cursed them wearily, cursed the high command for banning all campfires—the Rebels had had all day to spot the Union positions, but the top brass had ruled out fires that night for security reasons— and glumly munched the handfuls of ground coffee they couldn't

boil. In Richardson's division the men were marched to the ammunition wagons in the darkness to draw eighty rounds per man, twice
the usual allotment; they accepted the grim omen in expressionless
silence.

Not far from the Pry house Mansfield's corps had turned in for the
night. The men had been there since the afternoon of the day before,
and they had their pup tents up and were feeling snug; but along
toward midnight Mansfield came riding up from the Pry house to corps
headquarters and the outfit was summoned to move—no drums and
no bugles, just officers going down the regimental streets from tent
to tent, quietly rousing the men and telling them to pack up. The
sleepy soldiers made up their blanket rolls, took their muskets, and
went off in the darkness, crossing the Antietam where Hooker had
crossed in the afternoon, and following the guides he had sent back,
old Mansfield riding at the head. They stumbled along, blind as moles
in the drizzling night, holding their canteens and bayonets as they
went, to keep them from jingling, following the obscure roads while
the sky to the left was periodically lit by the mock lightning of the
fitful cannonade.

They tramped for several miles and finally were halted on somebody's farm to the north and east of where Hooker's men were
posted. General Mansfield spread a blanket for himself on the grass
in a fence corner next to a field where the 10th Maine had turned in.
The Maine boys were wakeful and did a lot of chattering—the march
in the rain had roused them, and the thought of what was coming
in the morning made it hard to go back to sleep—and the old general
got up once and went over to shush them. They recalled that he was
nice about it and not at all like a major general: just told them that
if they had to talk they might as well do it in a whisper so that their
comrades could get a little rest. And at last, long after midnight,
there was quiet and the army slept a little.

How far they had marched, those soldiers—down the lanes and
cross-lots over the cornfields to get into position, and from the distant corners of the country before that; they were marching, really,
out of one era and into another, leaving much behind them, going
ahead to much that they did not know about. For some of them
there were just a few steps left: from the rumpled grass of a bed in a
pasture down to a fence or a thicket where there would be an ap-

pointment with a flying bullet or shell fragment, the miraculous and infinitely complicated trajectory of the man meeting the flat, whining trajectory of the bullet without fail. And while they slept the lazy, rainy breeze drifted through the East Wood and the West Wood and the cornfield, and riffled over the copings of the stone bridge to the south, touching them for the last time before dead men made them famous. The flags were all furled and the bugles stilled, and the hot metal of the guns on the ridges had cooled, and the army was asleep—tenting tonight on the old camp ground, with never a song to cheer because the voices that might sing it were all stilled on this most crowded and most lonely of fields. And whatever it may be that nerves men to die for a flag or a phrase or a man or an inexpressible dream was drowsing with them, ready to wake with the dawn.

SIX

Never Call Retreat

1. Toward the Dunker Church

The morning came in like the beginning of the Last Day, gray and dark and tensely expectant. Mist lay on the ground, heavy as a fog in the hollow places, and the groves and valleys were drenched in immense shadows. For a brief time there was an ominous hush on the rolling fields, where the rival pickets crouched behind bushes and fence corners, peering watchfully forward under damp hatbrims. Little by little things began to be visible. The outlines of trees and farm buildings slowly came into focus against blurred backgrounds; the pickets grew more wary and alert, and when one of them saw movement in the half-light he raised his musket and fired. The two armies, lying so close in the rainy night, had been no more than half asleep; once aroused, they began to fight instinctively, as if knowing that the very moment of waking must lead to the fatal embrace of battle.

The random picket-firing increased as the light grew, and the advanced batteries were drawn into it. On the high ground around the Dunker church Stonewall Jackson had massed his artillery, and the gunners were astir early. As soon as they could see any details on the ridges to the north they sprang to their places and fired, and the men who were still in bivouac could feel the earth beneath them tremble faintly with the jar of the firing. Farther west, half a mile from the

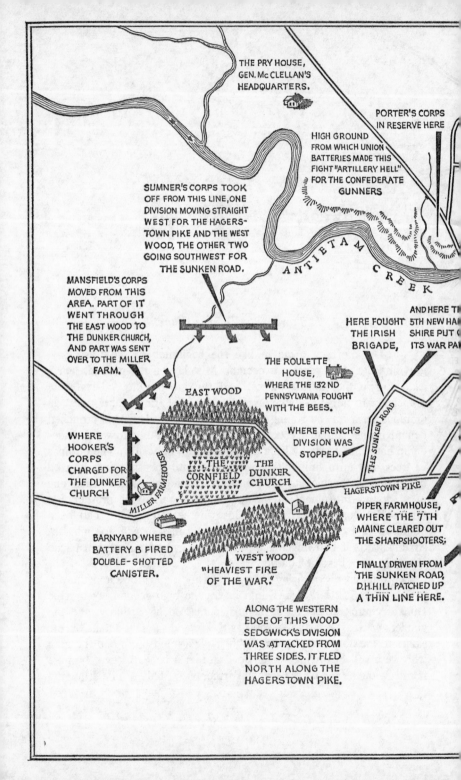

THE PRY HOUSE, GEN. McCLELLAN'S HEADQUARTERS.

PORTER'S CORPS IN RESERVE HERE

HIGH GROUND FROM WHICH UNION BATTERIES MADE THIS FIGHT "ARTILLERY HELL" FOR THE CONFEDERATE GUNNERS

SUMNER'S CORPS TOOK OFF FROM THIS LINE, ONE DIVISION MOVING STRAIGHT WEST FOR THE HAGERS-TOWN PIKE AND THE WEST WOOD, THE OTHER TWO GOING SOUTHWEST FOR THE SUNKEN ROAD.

ANTIETAM CREEK

MANSFIELD'S CORPS MOVED FROM THIS AREA. PART OF IT WENT THROUGH THE EAST WOOD TO THE DUNKER CHURCH, AND PART WAS SENT OVER TO THE MILLER FARM.

HERE FOUGHT THE IRISH BRIGADE,

AND HERE T 5TH NEW HA SHIRE PUT (ITS WAR PA

THE ROULETTE HOUSE, WHERE THE 132 ND PENNSYLVANIA FOUGHT WITH THE BEES.

EAST WOOD

WHERE FRENCH'S DIVISION WAS STOPPED.

THE SUNKEN ROAD

WHERE HOOKER'S CORPS CHARGED FOR THE DUNKER CHURCH

MILLER FARMHOUSE

THE CORNFIELD

THE DUNKER CHURCH

HAGERSTOWN PIKE

PIPER FARMHOUSE, WHERE THE 7TH MAINE CLEARED OUT THE SHARPSHOOTERS;

BARNYARD WHERE BATTERY B FIRED DOUBLE-SHOTTED CANISTER.

WEST WOOD "HEAVIEST FIRE OF THE WAR."

FINALLY DRIVEN FROM THE SUNKEN ROAD, D.H.HILL PATCHED UP A THIN LINE HERE.

ALONG THE WESTERN EDGE OF THIS WOOD SEDGWICK'S DIVISION WAS ATTACKED FROM THREE SIDES. IT FLED NORTH ALONG THE HAGERSTOWN PIKE.

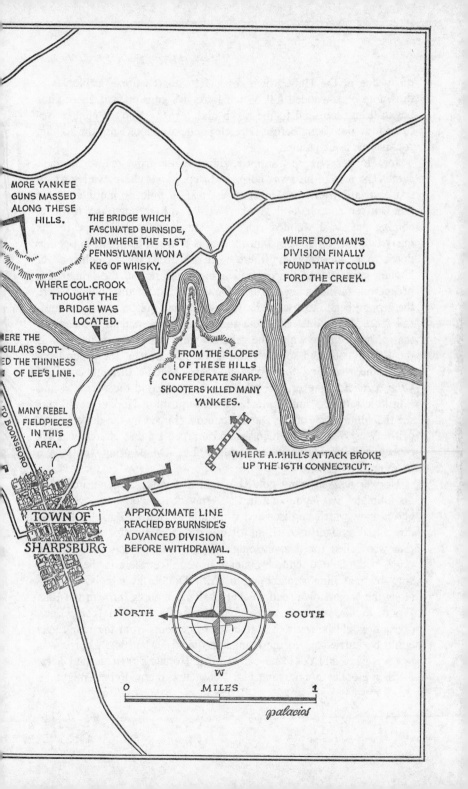

MORE YANKEE GUNS MASSED ALONG THESE HILLS.

THE BRIDGE WHICH FASCINATED BURNSIDE, AND WHERE THE 51ST PENNSYLVANIA WON A KEG OF WHISKY.

WHERE RODMAN'S DIVISION FINALLY FOUND THAT IT COULD FORD THE CREEK.

WHERE COL. CROOK THOUGHT THE BRIDGE WAS LOCATED.

ERE THE GULARS SPOT- ED THE THINNESS F OF LEE'S LINE.

FROM THE SLOPES OF THESE HILLS CONFEDERATE SHARP- SHOOTERS KILLED MANY YANKEES.

MANY REBEL FIELDPIECES IN THIS AREA.

TO BOONSBORO

WHERE A.P. HILL'S ATTACK BROKE UP THE 16TH CONNECTICUT.

TOWN OF SHARPSBURG

APPROXIMATE LINE REACHED BY BURNSIDE'S ADVANCED DIVISION BEFORE WITHDRAWAL.

E

NORTH

SOUTH

W

0   MILES   1

palacios

dusty line of the Hagerstown road, Jeb Stuart's horse artillery was drawn up on a wooded hill. When Jackson's guns opened, these guns began firing, too, and to the north and east the Yankee gunners returned the fire. Long before six o'clock the air shook with the rolling, rocking crash of gunfire.

Joe Hooker was up promptly, riding to the front before the light came. The men of his army corps had slept in a sheltered valley which ran eastward from the Hagerstown road, a mile or more north of the Dunker church, and Hooker went south through the bivouac, coming out on a wooded ridge and studying the landscape in the misty twilight. In front of him there was a broad field, sloping gently down to a hollow where there were an orchard, a patchwork of kitchen gardens and fences, and a big stone house, the home of a prosperous farmer named Miller. On the far side of the hollow, where the ground began to rise again, Mr. Miller had built a stout post-and-rail fence, going due east from the Hagerstown road to the edge of that pleasant grove which the generals were noting on their maps as the East Wood; and south of the fence, filling all of the ground between the road and the wood, was Mr. Miller's thriving cornfield —*the* cornfield, forever, after that morning. Beyond the cornfield and a little less than a mile from his present position Hooker could just see the white block of the Dunker church, framed by the dark growth of the West Wood. The high ground marked by that church was his objective; if it could be seized and held, Lee's whole army would have to retreat.

Hooker was an army politician and a devious man, approaching his ultimate goal—command of the Army of the Potomac—by roundabout ways which he discussed with nobody; but as a fighter he was direct and straightforward, and it was direct, straightforward fighting that was called for this morning. His army corps was camped due north of the Dunker church plateau; it would get there in the obvious way—by marching straight south, with Doubleday's division going along the Hagerstown road, Ricketts's division going through the East Wood, and Meade's Pennsylvanians going in between them. Each division would be massed so that reinforcements from the rear ranks could be hurried up to the front line quickly. Mansfield's corps was not far away and could be called on if Hooker's men needed help. Neither Hooker nor anyone else knew how many Rebels might be waiting in the cornfield and the wood. This was one of the things the advancing battle lines would have to find out for themselves. Meanwhile, it was time to get moving.

It was still early, and the gray light of the dawn was still dim. The army was awake, the men coming reluctantly out of sleep to the sound of the guns, knowing that this fight was going to be worse than anything they had ever been in before. Aroused by the cannon, the men reacted in their different ways. The 1st Minnesota, still safely behind the lines near McClellan's headquarters, noted the mist and the cloudy sky and profanely gave thanks that they would at least be fighting in the shade this day. (They were wrong, as it turned out; in another hour or two the mist would vanish and there would be a scorching sun all day.) Abner Doubleday found the men of his division hard to rouse; they took up their muskets and fell into ranks sluggishly, and they did not even grumble when they were marched off without time to boil coffee. Over in Mansfield's corps there was less of a rush and the men cooked sketchy breakfasts. There were many new regiments in this corps, and the veterans—quietly handing valuables and trinkets to members of the ambulance corps and other non-combat details for safekeeping—noticed with grim amusement that most of the straw-feet were too nervous to eat. In the 27th Indiana men stood up by their campfires to jeer and curse at one desperate soldier whose nerves had given way, out on the picket line, and who was running madly for the rear, oblivious of the taunts and laughter—a man whose legs had simply taken control of him. From one end of the army to the other, bivouacs were littered with discarded decks of cards. Card games were held sinful in that generation, and most men who were about to fight preferred not to have these tangible evidences of evil on their persons when they went out to face death.[1]

The men of Hooker's army corps left their bivouac and in heavy columns made their way through the timber to the ridge which was to be their jumping-off point. Some of the columns could be seen by the distant Confederate gunners, and the shells came over faster—the men had hardly started when one of Stuart's guns put a shell right in the middle of the 6th Wisconsin, knocking out thirteen men and bringing the column to a halt while stretcher-bearers ran in to carry off the wounded. The 90th and 107th Pennsylvania, moving up toward the outer fringe of the East Wood, also came within Stuart's

range and had losses; and men were maimed for life who saw no
more of the battle than a peaceful field and a sandy lane in the wood
in the early light of dawn. As they reached the ridge the leading
elements of the divisional columns sent out skirmish lines, and in the
broad hollow of the Miller farm the sporadic pop-pop of picket firing
became much heavier while the skirmish lines went down the slope—
each man in the line separated from his fellows by half a dozen paces,
holding his musket as if he were a quail hunter with a shotgun, moving
ahead step by step, dropping to one knee to shoot when he found a
target, pausing to reload, and then moving on again, feeling the army's
way into the danger zone.

Rebel skirmishers held the Miller farm in some strength, and there
were many more along the fence by the cornfield. The sound of the
musket fire suddenly rose to a long, echoing crash that ran from the
highway to the East Wood and back again. The Confederate batteries to the south and off to the right stepped up the pace, and the
shells came over faster. Beyond the hollow ground the green cornfield
swayed and moved, although there was no wind. The glint of bayonets
could be seen here and there amid the leafage, and long, tearing
volleys came out of the corn, while wreaths of yellowish-white smoke
drifted up above it as if the whole field were steaming. More men
were hurt, and the Yankee skirmishers halted and took cover.

There was a pause, while the battle lines waited under fire. Then
there was a great rush and a pounding of hoofs as Hooker's corps
artillery dashed up into line—six batteries coming up at a mad gallop,
gun carriages bouncing wildly with spinning wheels, drivers lashing
the six-horse teams, officers riding on ahead and turning to signal
with flashing swords when they reached the chosen firing line. In some
of these batteries orders for field maneuvers were given by bugle, and
the high thin notes could be heard above all the racket, the teams
wheeling in a spatter of rising dust—veteran artillery horses knew
what the bugle calls meant as well as the men did, and would obey
without waiting to be told. In a few minutes three dozen guns were
lined up on the slope, limbers a dozen yards to the rear, teamsters
taking the horses back into the wood, gun crews busy with ramrod
and handspike. The guns began to plaster the cornfield unmercifully,
and the air above the field was filled with clods of dirt and flying

cornstalks and knapsacks and broken muskets as the canister ripped the standing grain.

Far off to the left, beyond the Antietam, McClellan's long-range rifles came into action, hammering hard at the Rebel guns by the Dunker church and reaching out to plow the cornfield with a terrible cross fire of shell and solid shot; and the waiting Federal infantry hugged the ground, half dazed by the tremendous waves of noise. Hooker exaggerated a little, but only a little, when he wrote afterward that "every stalk in the northern and greater part of the field was cut as closely as could have been done with a knife"; and he exaggerated not at all when he wrote that in all the war he never looked upon "a more bloody, dismal battlefield." The Confederates in the northern part of the cornfield went down in rows, scores at a time. Then after a while the great thunder of the guns died down a little and the Yankee infantry went forward.

It all looks very simple and orderly on the map, where the advance of the I Corps is represented by a straight line following neat little arrows, three divisions moving snugly abreast and everyone present presumably knowing at all times just what was going on and what the score was. But in reality there was nothing simple or orderly about any part of it. Instead there was an appalling confusion of shattering sound, an unending chaos of violence and heat and intense combat, with fields and thickets wrapped in shifting layers of blinding smoke so that no man could know and understand any more of what was happening than the part he could see immediately around him. There was no solid connected battle line neatly ranked in clear light; there was a whole series of battle lines swaying haphazardly in an infernal choking fog, with brigades and regiments standing by themselves and fighting their enemies where they found them, attack and counterattack taking place in every conceivable direction and in no recognizable time sequence, Northerners and Southerners wrestling back and forth in the cornfield in one tremendous free-for-all. The black powder used in those days left heavy masses of smoke which stayed on the ground or hung at waist level in long tattered sheets until the wind blew it away, and this smoke deposited a black, greasy film on sweaty skins, so that men who had been fighting hard looked grotesque, as if they had been ineptly made up for a minstrel show.

The fighting surged back and forth from the East Wood to the highway and beyond, and the most any general could do was push new troops in from the rear where they seemed to be needed—or, at times, rally soldiers who were coming disorganized out of action and send them back in again: what was happening up front was beyond anyone's control and depended entirely on the men themselves. And a wild, primitive madness seemed to descend on the men who fought in the cornfield: they went beyond the limits of sanity and endurance at times, Northerners and Southerners alike, until it seems that they tore at each other for the sheer sake of fighting. The men who fought there are all dead now, and it may be that we misinterpret the sketchy accounts which they left of the combat; yet from the diaries and the reports and the histories we get glimpses of what might well have been the most savage and consuming fighting American soldiers ever engaged in.

General Ricketts sent his men in through the East Wood—New York regiments, mostly, with a few from Pennsylvania and Massachusetts—and they fought step by step through the thickets and over the rocky ledges and fallen trees in the misty light of early morning, slowly driving the tenacious Confederates out and swinging around unconsciously until they faced toward the west, so that as they came out of the wood they went into the cornfield, with Stuart's cannon hitting them hard from the western hills. They pulled themselves together on the edge of the cornfield, getting an enfilade fire on a Confederate brigade there and sending it flying; then they advanced again, and as they moved the regiments were separated, each one automatically adjusting its lines to face whatever formation of Rebels might be in front of it. When they got deeper into the field the opposition became heavier, until at last whole brigades were shaken by the deadly, racking volleys—the most terrible fire, one veteran wrote, that they ever had to endure. Rifles were splintered and broken in men's hands, canteens and haversacks were riddled, platoons and companies seemed to dissolve. They closed ranks as well as they could amid the cornstalks, sweating officers gesturing with swords and yelling orders no one could hear in the overpowering racket, and they kept pushing on. They attacked and they were counterattacked; they drove certain Rebels and were themselves driven in turn; at times they exchanged stand-up volleys at incredibly close ranges, wrecking their enemies and seeing their own lines wrecked, while the smoke settled thicker and thicker and they fought in utter blindness.

At last they went back, straggling through the East Wood to reform in the rear—a full third of the division shot down and half of the survivors hopelessly scattered. The 12th Massachusetts—the kidglove boys from Boston who had brought a great song to the war and carried a noble flag of white and blue and gold presented by the ladies of Beacon Hill—took 334 men into action and lost 220 of them, and when it tried to rally behind the wood fewer than three dozen men were still with the colors. Duryée's brigade of four regiments found hardly a hundred men to form a line when it finished its retreat. For the time being, except for a few valiant fragments which hung on at the edge of the wood, the entire division was out of the fight.

Meade's Pennsylvanians had gone into the cornfield at the center of the line, and their story is just about the same: advance and retreat, charge and countercharge, victory and retreat all blended. Once the center brigade broke under a driving Rebel charge and went streaming toward the rear. Meade came thundering up with the battle fury on him, yanked the 8th Reserve Regiment back into line, hurried it off to a vantage point by Mr. Miller's fence. A Georgia regiment, lying unseen in the corn, let fly with a volley from a distance of thirty feet, knocking out half the regiment at one sweep. The Pennsylvania color-bearer went down with a foot shot off, struggled to his knees, jabbing his flagstaff into the ground, and struck wildly at a comrade who tried to take the colors away from him. A charging Georgian shot him dead and was himself killed by a Pennsylvania lieutenant; and there were wild tumult and heavy smoke and crazy shouting all around, with the entire war narrowed to the focus of this single combat between Pennsylvanians and Georgians. Then the Pennsylvanians broke and ran again—to be stopped, incomprehensibly, a few yards in the rear by a boyish private who stood on a little hillock and kept swinging his hat, shouting: "Rally, boys, rally! Die like men, don't run like dogs!"

Strangely, on that desperate field where men were madly heroic and full of abject panic by turns, this lone private stopped the retreat. What was left of the regiment fell in beside him. Fugitives from other regiments in the shattered brigade fell in with them, and Meade—who had gone galloping away to bring up a battery to plug the gap—came back and got the uncertain line straightened out, while canister from the new battery uprooted green cornstalks and tore the bodies of Rebels who crouched low on the powdery ground. Then presently the brigade went forward again.[2]

Over by the turnpike the Black Hat Brigade charged around the Miller farm buildings, driving out the Confederate skirmishers but breaking apart somewhat as the men surged past dwelling and outhouses under heavy fire. There is a glimpse of a young Wisconsin officer standing by a gap in a fence, waving his sword and crying: "Company E! On the right, by file, into line!" Then a bullet hit him in his open mouth and he toppled over dead in mid-shout; and the brigade got by the obstructions and went into the cornfield near the highway. Here it seemed to be every man for himself. There was Rebel infantry west of the road, pouring in a tremendous fire; some of the men formed a new line facing west, lying down behind the turnpike fence to fight back. Gibbon sent a couple of regiments across the road to deal with this flank attack, and a moment later Doubleday sent four New York regiments over there to help; part of his division was going south through the cornfield and part of it was struggling desperately in the fields and woods to the west, and shells and bullets were coming in from all directions at once. Men said afterward that the bullets seemed to be as thick as hail in a great storm. Formations were lost, regiments and brigades were jumbled up together, and as the men advanced they bent their heads as if they were walking into a driving rain. And under all the deafening tumult there was a soft, unceasing clip-snip-clip of bullets shearing off the leaves and stalks of corn. Near the highway some officer was yelling the obvious—"This fire is murderous!"—and then, at last, the sweating mob of soldiers came out by a fence at the southern edge of the cornfield, and as they did so a long line of Confederates arose from the plowed ground in front of them and the high sound of rifle fire rose to a new intensity.

A terrible frenzy of battle descended on the fighting line. Men were possessed by a hysterical excitement, shouting furiously, bursting out in shrill insane laughter, crowding up to the fence to fire at the Rebel line. A survivor of this attack, recalling the merciless fire that greeted the men at the line of the fence, wrote: "Men, I cannot say fell—they were knocked out of ranks by the dozen." Cartridges were torn with nervous haste. Muskets became foul from much firing, so that men

took stones to hammer their ramrods down. Wanting to fire faster
than ever before, they found they could not—a nightmare slowness
was upon them as the black powder caked in hot rifle barrels. Some
soldiers threw their pieces away and took up the rifles of dead men.

All along the fence the men were jostling together, with soldiers in
the rear ranks passing loaded rifles forward to the men in front; battle
flags waved in sweeping, smoke-fringed arcs, color-bearers swinging
the flag staffs frantically, as if the mere fluttering of the colors would
help bring victory. Brigades and regiments were all helter-skelter—
Pennsylvanians and New Yorkers were jammed in with men from
Wisconsin and Massachusetts, everyone was cheering hoarsely, new
elements were coming up from the rear to add to the crush along
the fence, the noise of battle was one great unending roar louder than
anything the men had ever heard before. And at last, as if by common impulse, the whole crowd swarmed forward over the fence and
started up the open field toward the Dunker church—very near now,
its whitewashed walls all splotched and patchy from flying bullets.
The Confederate line, terribly thinned by rifle fire, broke in wild flight.
Some of the Southerners tried to escape over the turnpike fences and
were left spread-eagled on the rails as the Federals shot them; others
fell back into the wood around the church. The Northerners raised a
great new shout and went ahead on the run, with victory in sight.[3]

Then, dramatically, from the wood around the church a new Confederate battle line emerged, trotting forward with the shrill yip-yip-
yip of the Rebel yell—John B. Hood's division, swinging into action
with an irresistible counterattack.

Hood's men had been pulled out of the front lines late the night
before, after their brush with the Pennsylvanians in the East Wood.
They had been on short rations for days, and early this morning the
commissary department finally caught up with them, delivering ample
supplies of bread and meat. The division had been in the act of cooking the first solid meal in a week when word came back that they
were needed up front without a moment's delay—the Yankees had
broken the line and would have the battle won unless somebody did
something about it. So the Texans and Mississippians left their half-
cooked breakfasts, grabbed their rifles, and came storming out into
the open, mad clean through: and here, within easy range, were the

Yankees who were the cause of it all, the Yankees on whom the overmastering anger of hungry men could be vented.

Hood's men drew up and delivered a volley which, said a Federal survivor, "was like a scythe running through our line." It hit the Federals head-on and stopped them. There was a brief pause, and then the Northern soldiers turned and made for the rear on the run, back over the fence and into the raddled cornfield and down the long slope, Hood's men following them with triumphant, jeering shouts, while three brigades from D. H. Hill's command came in from below the East Wood and added their own weight to the pursuit.

Down in the open ground by the Miller house the flight was checked. General Gibbon had brought up old Battery B, and its six brass smoothbores were drawn up in a barnyard west of the road. The Rebels were advancing on both sides of the pike, converging on the barnyard—the Federals west of the road had had to retire when the cornfield was lost—and the guns became a strong point where the beaten soldiers could make a stand again. Some of the fugitives fell in behind the battery, kneeling and firing out between the guns. Gibbon got two of his regiments drawn up farther west, a little ahead of the guns and facing east; General Patrick brought his four New York regiments up amid the crush; and the charging Confederates came out of the corn from the south and east, smashing straight at the battery, firing as they came.

Battery B was pounding away furiously, but Gibbon, looking on with the eye of a gunner, noticed that in the mad excitement the gun crews had let the elevating screws run down so that the guns were pointing up for extreme long range, blasting their charges into the empty air. He shouted and gestured from the saddle, but no one could hear anything in that unearthly din, so he threw himself to the ground, ran to the nearest gun, shouldered the gun crew aside, and spun the little wheel under the breech so that the muzzle slowly sank until it seemed almost to be pointing at the ground. Gibbon stepped aside, the gunner jerked the lanyard, and the gun smashed a section of rail fence, sending the splintered pieces flying in the faces of Hood's men. The other gunners hastily corrected their elevation and fired double-shotted rounds of canister at the range of fifty feet, while the Northern infantry cracked in with volleys of musket fire. In all its history the battery never fired so fast; its haste was so feverish that a veteran regular-army sergeant forgot to step away from his gun when it was discharged, and as it bounded backward in recoil a wheel knocked him down and crushed him.

The front of the Confederate column was blown away, and the survivors withdrew sullenly into what was left of the cornfield. Some of the Federals west of the road raised a yell and went into the cornfield after them, were struck in the flank by unseen Confederates farther south, and came streaming back across the pike again to take shelter among the rocky ledges west of the guns. The Rebels re-formed behind a low ridge, then came on again. A soldier in the 80th New York, helping to defend the battery, called this assault "one of the finest exhibitions of pluck and manhood ever seen on any battlefield." But the heroism served only to swell the casualty lists. There were too many Yankees there and the guns were firing too fast; the charging Rebel line simply melted away under the fire, the men who were not hit ran back into the cornfield again, and for a moment there was something like a breathing spell, while the rival armies lay, as one soldier wrote, "like burnt-out slag" on the battlefield.[4]

Two hours of fighting in one forty-acre field, with the drumming guns never silent for a moment; Northerners and Southerners had fought themselves out, and the fields and woods for miles to the rear were filled with fugitives. A steady leakage had been taking place from each army as all but the stoutest found themselves carried beyond the limit of endurance. The skulkers and the unabashed cowards, who always ran in every battle at the first chance they could get —and there was hardly a regiment, North or South, which did not have a few of them—had drifted away at the first shock. Later others had gone: the men who could stand something but not everything, men who had stood fast in all previous fights but found this one too terrible to be borne; the men who helped wounded comrades to the rear and then either honestly got lost (which was easy to do, in that smoking madness) or found that they could not quite make themselves go back into it. All of these had faded out, leaving the fighting lines dreadfully thin, so that the loss of strength on each side was far greater, just then, than the casualty lists would show. Hooker's corps had lost nearly twenty-five hundred men killed and wounded—a fearful loss, considering that he had sent hardly more than nine thousand into action—but for the moment the story was much worse than that.

The number of uninjured men who left the ranks was probably fully as great as the number of casualties. The proud I Corps of the Army of the Potomac was wrecked.[5]

On the Confederate side the story was about the same. The troops who had held the cornfield and East Wood when the fight began had been splintered and smashed and driven to the rear. Their dazed remnants were painfully trying to regroup themselves far behind the Dunker church, fugitives were trailed out all the way back to the Potomac, and field and wood were held now by the reinforcements, Hood's men and D. H. Hill's. There was still fight left in these men, but they had been ground down unmercifully. At the height of his counterattack Hood had sent back word that unless he could be reinforced he would have to withdraw, but that meanwhile he would go on as far as he could. He had gone to the northern limit of the cornfield, had seen the striking spearhead of his division broken by the Yankee guns and rifles around Miller's barnyard, and he was holding on now in grim expectancy of a new Federal attack. The cornfield itself was a hideous spectacle—broken stalks lying every which way, green leaves spattered with blood, ground all torn and broken, littered everywhere with discarded weapons. Inconceivable numbers of dead and wounded lay in all parts of the field, whole ranks of them at the northern border where Hooker's first blasts of cannon fire had caught them—after the battle Massachusetts soldiers said they had found 146 bodies from one Rebel brigade lying in a neat, soldierly line. Hood wrote afterward that on no other field in the whole war was he so constantly troubled by the fear that his horse would step on some helpless wounded man. The Rebel brigades that were in the field when the fighting began had lost about 50 per cent of their numbers.

But there could be no lull. Hooker had Mansfield's corps at his disposal, and when the Rebels drove his men back through the cornfield he sent for it. Old General Mansfield went galloping up to his troops, his hat in his hand, long white hair and beard streaming in the wind. The men in Gordon's brigade jumped up and ran for their rifles as soon as they saw him coming, falling in without waiting for orders, cheering loudly. Something about the old soldier, with his air of competence and his unexpected mixture of stiff military dignity and youthful fire and vigor, had aroused their enthusiasm during the two days he had been with them. Mansfield reined up in front of them, calling:

"That's right, boys, cheer—we're going to whip them today!" He rode down the line from regiment to regiment, waving his hat and repeating: "Boys, we're going to lick them today!"

They were a mile and more from the battlefield, and the uproar beat upon their ears as they moved forward. The noise seemed to be coming in great, swinging pulsations, as if whole brigades or divisions were firing successive volleys. The booming of the cannon was continuous, so steady that no individual shots could be heard; and before the field could be seen the men could make out great billowing clouds of smoke drifting up in the windless air. As they got nearer they met wounded men going to the rear—chipper enough, most of them, all things considered, calling out that they "had the Johnnies on the run." Gordon's brigade came out on the ridge near the Miller farm, with the northern border of the cornfield in view. Federal regiments were withdrawing across the hollow, stepping backward, loading and firing as they retreated. One pitiful skeleton of a beaten regiment saw the fresh 27th Indiana coming up behind it. Heedless that they were still under fire, the men shouted with joy, threw caps, knapsacks, and canteens in the air, waving jubilant welcome to the reinforcements; and when the Indiana soldiers came abreast of them the retreating soldiers halted, re-formed ranks, and started back into battle again without orders.

Mansfield went in at the head of his first brigade, heading straight for the northern part of the East Wood. The situation was not at all clear to him, and he halted the column briefly while he tried to make out what was in front of him. Hooker came cantering up, crying: "The enemy are breaking through my lines—you must hold this wood!" Then Hooker rode away and Mansfield started putting his leading regiments, 10th Maine and 128th Pennsylvania, into line of battle. The East Wood presented almost as ghastly a sight as the cornfield, by now—dead and living bodies everywhere, little groups of men trying to help wounded comrades to the rear, shattered limbs of trees lying on the ground in a tangle, wreckage of artillery equipment strewn about, with unseen Rebels keeping the air alive with bullets, and streaky sheets of acrid smoke lying in the air. Nobody knew whether there were Union troops in front or not. The ground was uneven, crossed with rocky ledges and ridges. Organized bodies of troops could be seen in the distance now and then, but the light was bad and the skirmishers, shooting at everything that moved, did not know whether they were firing at friends or enemies.

Brigadier General Samuel Crawford made his way through the wood, trying to get his brigade into line: an unusual man, doctor turned soldier, who had taken an unusual route to his general's commission. He had been a regular-army surgeon before the war and was in the Fort Sumter garrison. Back at the beginning of 1861, when Major Anderson moved the garrison from Moultrie to Sumter, all the line officers being busy, the doctor was posted at a loaded columbiad to sink the Confederate guard boat if it tried to interfere. He didn't have to shoot just then, but either that experience or the later bombardment itself apparently inspired him to give up medicine for line command, and when the garrison came north he got a brigadier's star. His brigade had been badly cut to pieces at Cedar Mountain early this summer, when Pope's advance guard had its first meeting with Stonewall Jackson. Since then Crawford had been vainly writing applications to have the brigade withdrawn for reorganization and recruitment, pointing out that his four regiments numbered only 629 men altogether, with so many officers gone that three of the regiments were in command of inexperienced captains. His 28th New York had been consolidated into four companies and was going into action today with sixty-five men. Crawford had got nowhere with his applications, but a couple of days before this battle the high command had given him three brand-new regiments of Pennsylvania recruits, and with this lopsided command—four understrength regiments of veterans and three big, half-trained regiments of rookies—he was now going into action against Hood and D. H. Hill. Understandably, he was nervous about it.

Most of the enemy fire seemed to be coming from the cornfield at the western edge of the wood, so Crawford wheeled his regiments in that direction. The Rebel skirmishers were playing Indian again, dodging back from tree to tree and ledge to ledge and firing from behind the piles of cordwood that some thrifty farmer had stacked here and there; but the Maine regiment, the veteran 46th Pennsylvania, and the tiny 28th New York finally got to the edge of the wood, with two of the greenhorn regiments struggling up on their right, and began to fire at moving figures among the shattered cornstalks. Mansfield rode up, worried; he still didn't know where the enemy was, and Hooker had given him the impression that Meade's Pennsylvanians were still in the field. He made the Maine regiment cease firing—"You are firing into our own men"—then put his horse over the fence and rode on ahead to get a better look. Some soldier called out, "Those are Rebels, General!" Mansfield took a last look, said: "Yes—you're right"—and then a volley came out of the cornfield. Mansfield's horse was hit, and when the old man dismounted to clamber over the fence he himself got a bullet in the stomach.

Some of the rookies from the 125th Pennsylvania picked him up, made a crude litter of muskets, and got him back into the wood, where they laid him down, uncertain what to do next. They had been soldiers for only a month, this was their first battle, and what did one do with a badly wounded major general, anyhow? Three boys from the 10th Maine took over—as veterans, one gathers, they knew a good excuse to get away from the firing line when they saw it—the Pennsylvanians went back to the fence, and the down-Easters tried to lug the general back to the rear. And they found, in the wood, a bewildered contraband who was company cook in one of Hooker's regiments and who, with a clumsy incompetence rare even among company cooks, had chosen this time and place to lose, and then to hunt for, a prized frying pan. The Maine boys seized him that he might make a fourth at carrying the general, who was heavy and helpless. The contraband demurred—he had to find the captain's frying pan, and nothing else mattered—but the soldiers pounded him with their fists, the whine of ricocheting bullets cutting the air all around, shells crashing through the branches overhead, and he gave in at last and poor General Mansfield somehow was got back to a dressing station. There a flurried surgeon pressed a flask of whisky to his mouth, almost strangling him; and, what with the wound and the clumsy handling, the old man presently died. He had had the corps only two days, but he had already made the soldiers like and respect him; it seems likely that he might have made quite a name if he had been spared.[6]

But there was no holding up the fight because a general had been killed. Crawford went down, too, with a bad wound, and a colonel took over the brigade, and the veterans and the rookies got into a tremendous fire fight with some of D. H. Hill's men along the east side of the cornfield. Farther west General Gordon drove his brigade in past the Miller farm buildings and over the pitiful human wreckage that littered the ground in front of Battery B. The Rebels in the corner of the cornfield and along the fence on the northern side were not disposed to go away, and the 3rd Wisconsin took a beating when it got up to the fence; but Gordon worked the 2nd Massachusetts around on the right and got an enfilade on the Texans, and the 27th Indiana came up on the other side, and the Confederate line gave way.

So once more there was a bitter fight in the cornfield, with the Federals coming in from the north and the east; and Hood, as he had foreseen, was compelled to withdraw, with half of his men shot down. As Gordon's lines went in Hooker got a bullet in the foot and rode to the rear, dripping blood, and command of this part of the battle passed temporarily to Mansfield's senior division commander, General Alpheus S. Williams, who rode about the field with the unlighted stub of a cigar gripped in his teeth and who was called "Pop" by his troops—sure sign that they liked him. The retreating Rebels made a desperate fight of it. One of Crawford's men asserted that "on all other fields, from the beginning to the end of our long service, we never had to face their equals," and the 27th Indiana came to a halt in the middle of the smoky field, standing erect in close order and firing as fast as it could handle its muskets, which finally became too hot to be used. One Hoosier, badly wounded, laid down his rifle and went a few yards to the rear, where he sat down, opened his clothing, and examined his wound. After studying it, he mused aloud: "Well, I guess I'm hurt about as bad as I can be. I believe I'll go back and give 'em some more." So he picked up a discarded musket and returned to the firing line.

The regiment shot up all its ammunition, a hundred rounds per man, and sent details around the field to loot the cartridge boxes of the dead and wounded. In this fight the 27th lost a good non-com —Corporal Barton W. Mitchell, who had caused the battle in the first place by finding Lee's lost order; he went down with a wound that kept him out of action for months. His company commander, Captain Kopp, to whom he had first taken the lost order, was killed.

At last the 2nd Massachusetts came in on the right, its colonel jubilantly waving a captured Texas battle flag, and the Confederate defense began to crumble. Crawford's men came out of the East

Wood at last, rookies and veterans all yelling and firing as they came, and the Rebels gave way and went back, running south and west across the turnpike and into the West Wood. Once more the corn-field, for whatever it was worth, belonged to the Union. Gordon's and Crawford's men tried to get across the turnpike and pursue, but nobody had ever yet cleaned up on the Rebel strength to the west of this highway—Mansfield had sent a brigade over there when he first took his corps into action, but the regiments had been put in clumsily and had been driven off—and the Federal advance was halted along the rail fence, and that dusty country highway once more became a lane of death.

Half a mile farther east things were going better. General George Sears Greene, a relative of Revolutionary War hero Nathanael Greene, had the rest of Mansfield's troops—a battle-worn division of some seventeen hundred men—and these had cut through the eastern fringe of the East Wood and had gone driving straight for the Dunker church. Some of the Confederates who had been driven out of the cornfield rallied and hit them in the flank as they got past the timber, some of Hill's men gouged at their other flank, and Lee brought reinforcements over from the right of his line to make a stand in front of the church. The Northerners had a hard time of it for a while, coming under fire from three directions, and when the Confederates came in with a counterattack the outlook was bad; but just in time a Rhode Island battery came galloping up, the infantry broke ranks to let the guns through, and the counterattack was smashed with canister and rifle fire. Then one of Crawford's rookie regiments—125th Penn-sylvania, seven hundred strong, a giant of a regiment for that field—came up, separated from its brigade and slightly lost but anxious to get into the nearest fight; and Greene's division ran on past the guns and got into the West Wood around the Dunker church, forming a solid line on the far side of that battle-scarred building. Here was victory, if someone could just bring up reinforcements.

But the reinforcements didn't show up. This spearhead had got clear through the Confederate line. The high ground around the church, objective of all the morning's fighting, had been seized at last. But Greene had lost a third of his men, more than two hundred of the Pennsylvania straw-feet were down, and the survivors could do no more than hang on where they were, the Rebels keeping them under a steady fire. Completely wrecked, Hooker's army corps was trying to round up its stragglers and reassemble on the hills a mile to the north. The rest of Mansfield's corps was in position around the Miller barnyard and along the western edge of the cornfield, solidly posted but too busy to send any help. Greene's boys had reached the goal, but they couldn't do anything with it now that they had it. The fire that was being played upon their lines was not strong enough to drive them out, but it was too strong to advance against; and off to the southeast they could make out the movement of marching bodies of men, as if heavy Confederate reinforcements were coming up. The right wing of McClellan's army was beaten out, with this one advanced detachment huddling under the trees to mark high tide.

2. The Heaviest Fire of the War

It may be that life is not man's most precious possession, after all. Certainly men can be induced to give it away very freely at times, and the terms hardly seem to make sense unless there is something about the whole business that we don't understand. Lives are spent for very insignificant things which benefit the dead not at all—a few rods of ground in a cornfield, for instance, or temporary ownership of a little hill or a piece of windy pasture; and now and then they are simply wasted outright, with nobody gaining anything at all. And we talk glibly about the accidents of battle and the mistakes of generalship without figuring out just which end of the stick the man who died was holding. As, for instance:

By seven-thirty in the morning a dim sense that something had gone wrong had reached McClellan's headquarters. The signal flags had been wigwagging ever since it was light enough to see them, and at one time McClellan came out of his tent, smiling and saying, "All goes well—Hooker is driving them." But all had not gone well thereafter, and presently white-haired old General Sumner was ordered to take his corps across the creek and get into action. Sumner moved promptly, and before long, from Mr. Pry's yard, McClellan could see the three parallel lines of John Sedgwick's division threading their way up the farther hillsides, heading for the East Wood.

Sumner rode with Sedgwick, letting the two remaining divisions of his corps follow as best they could. He was strictly the Indian fighter of the Western plains this morning, putting himself in the front rank of the column of attack, ready for a straight cut-and-thrust onslaught on the Rebel lines. He knew almost nothing about what had happened so far—had the impression, even, that the right wing of the army had gained a victory and that he was being sent in to make it complete. But when he got to the East Wood the omens under the shattered trees were sinister. The place was packed with wounded men, and there were far too many able-bodied soldiers wandering around trying to help them. (One of Sedgwick's colonels wrote sagely: "When good Samaritans so abound it is a strong indication that the discipline of the troops in front is not good and that the battle is not going so as to encourage the half-hearted.")[1] And when the division came out on the far side of the wood, facing west, the picture looked even worse. Sumner could see smoke and hear gunfire off to the right, where tenacious Rebels and Northerners still disputed possession of the Miller barnyard and adjacent pastures, and some firing seemed to be going on to the south by the Dunker church; but in front, as far as Sumner could see, there was nothing at all except for the ghastly debris that filled the cornfield. From the sketchy evidence he had, Sumner concluded that two whole army corps had ceased to exist: the right wing of the army was gone, except for scattered fragments, and he had this end of the battle all to himself.

The plan of attack which he decided on was very simple. If he was now beyond the Federal flank, then he must be beyond the Rebel flank as well: so he would move straight west, at right angles to the earlier lines of attack, advancing until he was in rear of Lee's left. Then he would wheel to his own left and sweep down the ridge behind Lee's line, crumpling the Army of Northern Virginia into McClellan's net. He had Sedgwick form his division in three lines, a brigade to each line, five thousand men altogether, and he started out across the cornfield full of confidence: if Sedgwick's men got into any trouble they could cut their way out, and besides, two other divisions were following.

Sumner supposed they were following, at any rate. They had been told to do so. But he was the cavalry colonel, riding in the front line as he led his men to the charge, not the corps commander staying back to make sure that everybody understood what he was to do and did it; and his second division was even now going astray, swinging about for an attack on the high ground southeast of the Dunker church, half a mile or more away from Sumner's target. The third division had not even started, staff work having been fouled up. Worst of all, Sedgwick's division was formed for a head-on attack and nothing else. The three brigade lines were so close together that maneuvering would be almost impossible, and if the division should be hit in the flanks there would be great trouble.

The five thousand enlisted men who would have to foot the bill if anything went wrong were not thinking of possible errors in tactics as they moved forward. They were veterans and they were rated with the best troops in the army, but the march so far had been rather unnerving. They had come up through all the backwash of battle, seeing many wounded, hearing many discouraging remarks by demoralized stragglers; they had seen ambulances jolting to the rear from advanced operating stations, carrying men who held the stumps of their amputated limbs erect in a desperate effort to ease the pain of the rough ride. When they formed line at the edge of the wood, even the veteran 19th Massachusetts had been so visibly nervous that its colonel had put the men through the manual of arms for a few minutes to steady their nerves. (This was another of the old fancy-Dan regiments; in the beginning it had elected not merely its officers but its enlisted men as well, just like a club, and when it left Boston in 1861 it had two complete baggage wagons for each company, four for regimental headquarters and four for the commissary—enough, as one member said, for an army corps, by later standards. It had learned much since those days.)

The division went west across the cornfield, the lines wavering as the men stepped carefully to avoid the dead and wounded, and it came under artillery fire. Stuart's horse artillery had moved south to a hill behind the West Wood, firing over the treetops, and the division was so wide and solid that the gunners could not miss—a shot that carried over the first battle line was sure to hit the second or the third. (One veteran wrote disgustedly afterward: "We were as easy to hit as the town of Sharpsburg.")[2] The men could see the shells coming, but they had learned by now that it was useless to duck and dodge, and they went straight ahead, bending their heads a little as if they were walking into a high wind. From the rear they made a handsome sight —long lines carefully aligned, battle flags fluttering, little white smoke clouds breaking out overhead here and there as shells exploded, green wood ahead of them: very nice to look at, so long as you could look from a distance. Far away, near McClellan's headquarters, staff officers swung their telescopes on the moving lines and remarked to one another that this was going to do it—that division could not be stopped.

Out of the cornfield and over the turnpike they went, past narrow fields and into the West Wood, that long belt of trees which ran north and south from below the Dunker church to a spot opposite Mr. Miller's barnyard. The trees gave protection from the shells, and the only Rebels in sight were skirmishers who faded back and disappeared as the division came on. The wood was open enough so that the brigade lines were maintained without much difficulty, and in a few minutes the leading brigade came out on the far side, facing open fields that rose slowly to an irregular ridge several hundred yards off. Stuart's guns were up there, and a few thin lines of infantry, but nothing very solid. The division was halted, with nobody able to see anything much except the men in the leading brigade. Sumner's idea might be right: he was on the flank, and all he had to do now was get his cumbersome battle lines out into the open, chase the last Rebels off that ridge, perform a left wheel, and march down toward Sharpsburg.

But it wasn't going to be that way. The left of Lee's line had been mangled quite as badly as the right of McClellan's, but in the precise nick of time Lee had sent up strong reinforcements—McLaws's division and Walker's, with Jackson's indomitable lieutenant, Jubal Early, bringing in his own brigade and such other stray elements as he could collect. And all of these, totaling more men than Sumner had with him, were now poised to attack just where it would hurt most—from the left.

The blow came with demoralizing suddenness, and for most of the men it was completely invisible, and there was nothing whatever they could do about it. One minute Sumner was sitting his horse amid the leading brigade, watching the firing that was coming from the Rebels on the ridge, sizing up the situation; the next minute there was a great uproar of musketry and screaming men in the wood to

the left, the air was full of bullets, an unexpected host of new Rebels
was going into line on the ridge in front, guns were appearing from
nowhere and going into battery there, and there was complete and
unmerciful hell to pay.

It hit the rear ranks first. One-armed General Howard had four
Pennsylvania regiments in the third brigade—all the men came from
Philadelphia, and the outfit was known as the "Philadelphia Brigade"
—and these men, who had been standing at ease in the wood, abruptly
found themselves under a deadly fire from behind. Regiments broke,
men scrambled for cover, officers shouted frantically; the enemy was
out of sight, dense smoke was seeping in through the trees, the air
was alive with bullets, fugitives were running every which way. Howard—never an inspirational leader, but a solid citizen who was never
scared, either—went riding along the line trying to get the men realigned, which was hard because nobody knew which way the men
ought to be faced in order to fight effectively. Sumner galloped up,
shouted something, and galloped off again. In the unceasing racket
Howard could not hear a word he said; an aide yelled in his ear that
Sumner had been shouting: "My God, Howard! You must get out of
here!"—an idea which by now had seized every man in the brigade.
The 72nd Pennsylvania, at the far left, gave way completely, its
frantic stragglers adding to the confusion. Some detachments were
faced by the rear rank and started off, but that didn't seem to work
—more often than not the men found themselves marching straight
into a consuming fire; and presently the whole brigade simply dissolved and the men ran back out of the wood and into an open field,
a disordered mob rather than a brigade of troops. In the field they
were caught by artillery, the Rebels having wheeled up guns to sweep
the open ground, and the rout of the brigade became complete. In
something less than ten minutes the brigade had lost more than five
hundred men and had hardly been able to fire a shot in reply.

Up front it was a little better, but not much. A savage Rebel charge
came in from the open field, and the 15th Massachusetts took it
head-on, exchanging volleys at a scant fifteen yards. One soldier in
this regiment later wrote that "the loss of life was fearful; we had
never seen anything like it." The 34th New York, which was at the
left end of the front line, tried to move over to help and somehow
got squarely in between two Confederate lines and took a horrible

fire from front and rear at the same time, losing half of its men in a few minutes. General Sedgwick hurried back to his second brigade, trying to get a regiment or two wheeled around for flank protection, but it was simply impossible—there just was no room to maneuver in all that crush even if the Rebel fire had permitted it, which it didn't. Sedgwick got a wound in the arm and an aide urged him to go to the rear. He refused, saying that the wound was a nuisance and nothing more; then another bullet lifted him out of the saddle with a wound that kept him in hospital for five months. (He made a bad patient, it seems. Impatient with hospital routine, he jokingly said that if he ever got hit again he hoped the bullet would finish him off—anything was better than a hospital. Cracks like that are bad luck for soldiers: Uncle John got his wish at Spotsylvania Courthouse in 1864, when a Rebel sharpshooter hit him under the eye and killed him.)

Minutes seemed like hours in the uproar under the smoky trees. The sound of rifle fire rose higher and higher as more Rebel brigades got into action. Over and over, in official reports and in regimental histories, one finds Federals giving the same account of it—the heaviest, deadliest fire they ever saw in the entire war.[3] The rear brigade was gone and the second brigade was going. General Dana, commanding the second brigade, managed to get parts of the 42nd New York and the 7th Michigan swung around to meet the fire from the left, but they couldn't hold on. When Howard's brigade went to pieces the Rebels came in from the rear and the two regiments were overwhelmed, with a few platoons managing to keep some sort of formation as they backed off to the north.

The colonel of the 59th New York rode back and forth with a flag, bawling: "Rally on the colors!" His men grouped themselves around him and tried to return a heavy fire that came out of the wood in front; and in the smoke and the confusion they volleyed into the backs of the 15th Massachusetts, and there was a terrible shouting and cursing amid all the din. Then a Confederate regiment worked its way around and fired into the 59th from the rear, and the New Yorkers lost nearly two thirds of their numbers. Young Captain Oliver Wendell Holmes of the 20th Massachusetts went down with his second wound of the war; and somehow, amazingly, that wandering rookie regiment from General Samuel Crawford's brigade, the

greenhorn 125th Pennsylvania, showed up and fell into line beside
the battered 34th New York, where it fought manfully. (Nobody
ever knew quite how it got there; it had been fighting with Greene's
boys south of the Dunker church, and in some incomprehensible
manner it had got detached and in all the fury of this infighting had
managed to get into the middle of Sedgwick's front line. Those rookies
seemed to have a genius for wandering into fights, and they were
packing a whole year's experience into one desperate morning.)

If the time seemed endless, it was really very short. Just fifteen
minutes after the first shot had been fired, the last of the division
retreated. From first to last, the division had not had a chance; it
was attacked from three sides at once—front, left, and rear—and the
collapse ran from rear rank to front rank. It left more than twenty-
one hundred men dead or wounded in the West Wood, and a good
half of its units had never been able to fire a shot; some of those
that did fought facing by the rear rank. Confederate losses in this
fight had been negligible; the sacrifice of Sedgwick's division had accomplished nothing whatever.

A few regiments got out in good order. The 20th Massachusetts
proudly recorded that it left the West Wood at a walk, in column
of fours, muskets at right shoulder; and the 1st Minnesota, which
had been lucky—it had lost only a fourth of its men—went out beside it, similarly formed. These and a few other unbroken units were
lined up perpendicular to the Hagerstown pike, a few hundred yards
north of the spot where the division had crossed the road on its way
in, and they laid down a strong fire when the triumphant Rebels came
out of the wood to finish the rout. The Rebel lines swept into the
cornfield—one more charge across that cornfield!—where wounded
men cursed wearily and pressed their faces against the dirt, hoping
that pounding feet and bursting shells and low-flying bullets would
not hurt them further as they lay there helpless—and for a few minutes it looked as if this counterattack might destroy the whole right
wing of McClellan's army and end the battle then and there. But
the remnant of Sedgwick's division gave ground stubbornly and at
a price, Gordon's tired brigade from Mansfield's corps came in to
help, a good deal of rifle fire was still coming out of the East Wood,
and an enormous line of fieldpieces was waiting on the slope north
of the cornfield. For the last time that day the cornfield was swept

by murderous fire, and the Confederates slowed down, halted, and went back to the shelter of the West Wood, while the beaten Federals withdrew to the ridge in rear of the guns, leaving a fringe of pickets and skirmishers behind.

And while this area north of the Dunker church was smoldering and fitfully exploding all the rest of the day with long-range rifle and artillery fire, there was no more real fighting here. There had been enough, in all conscience. In a square of ground measuring very little more than one thousand yards on a side—cornfield, barnyard, orchard, East and West Woods, and the fields by the turnpike—nearly twelve thousand men were lying on the ground, dead or wounded. It had not taken long to put them there, either. The fighting began with daylight—around five-thirty or six o'clock. It was now nine-thirty; four hours, at the most, from the time Hooker's batteries began to rake the cornfield to the end of the last Rebel countercharge. They fought with muzzle-loaders in those days, the men who got off two shots a minute were doing well, and it took, as one might say, a real effort to kill a man then. But considering their handicaps, they did pretty well.

When the beaten elements of Sedgwick's division crept north to safety, Sumner rode east to see about the rest of his army corps. The old man had done his best, and after that first desperate "My God, Howard! You must get out of here!" he had been as cool in all that fire as if he had been on parade, riding his horse at a walk amid the broken ranks of panicky soldiers, doing the little that could be done to pull fighting lines together, calming men by his stout refusal to recognize personal danger. But his best had been tragically inadequate: good enough to serve in the moment of disaster, but not good enough to keep the disaster from happening. He had been given an entire army corps, the biggest one in the army, eighteen thousand men in all; and he had left two thirds of it behind when he made his big attack. The one division which went astray and the other which was late in starting—these two, banked up beside Sedgwick's men, might well have broken Lee's flank beyond all hope of repair and the war would have been won by noon. The old man thought about them and went back to see about them after his attack had failed.

(Back by the Pry house sat McClellan, getting the messages of triumph and disaster from the wigwagging signal flags, studying the far-off slopes through his telescope, sending his aides here and there, watching the battle that he had planned, but not laying his own hand upon it: climax of the war taking place before his eyes, climax of his own personal fate, life or death for many thousands of young men depending on this day's battle. McClellan, quiet, composed, thoughtful, almost detached, listening with an inner ear for the still voice of caution and doubt, letting the battle go on without him.)

Yet the thing could still be done, and perhaps Old Winkey was the man to do it. Brigadier General William H. French, who had the second of Sumner's divisions, was red-faced and bluff, with a fantastic habit of bringing both eyes tightly shut spasmodically as he talked—thus "Old Winkey" or "Old Blinky" to his men. (One buck private, in the early days of the war, accosted by French about something or other while the division was on the march, had given way to laughter at all of this blinking. Since French was a hot-tempered man, the private had been hung by the thumbs from the nearest tree and left there to reflect on the sober respect that is due a general, until the following division cut him down.) French took his division across the Antietam in the wake of Sedgwick, under the impression that he was to strike for the Rebel line to the south of the Dunker church. As he brought his men up the hills west of the creek he had on his right hand a pillar of flame—the farmhouse of one Mumma, a solid citizen who had given the land where the Dunker church was built, his dwelling set ablaze that morning by D. H. Hill's outposts, who feared it might become a strong point for Yankee sharpshooters.

The division halted briefly to perfect its alignment, and about the time the last of Sedgwick's fugitives got back to the northern hills French had everything ready and the men started up out of the creek valley. The sun came out and the light was bright; ahead was the Roulette farm, a pleasant cluster of buildings on a broad knoll, surrounded by an orchard, shade trees, and a well-kept lawn. As the line reached this high place the officers back at headquarters got another look at the deceitful pageantry of war: broad, orderly lines of infantry going on in the sunlight, tiny puff balls of smoke appearing around the house as the Rebel skirmishers went into action, battle flags making high lights of gay color, officers posturing on their horses with glinting swords, a battery of artillery riding up fast and unlimbering dramatically; all very fine and bloodless-looking, just like the colored lithographs. Then the battle line divided as the men went by the Roulette house, the Federals combing belated Southern skirmishers out of stables and springhouse at bayonet point. Regimental surgeons, following close behind, moved into the big barn under the brow of a hill and prepared their operating tables, while orderlies spread out straw for wounded men to lie on. They would have plenty of work to do presently.

As the lines closed up beyond the farmhouse, with sharper rifle fire coming down from the crest of a rise in front, some of the men went through a yard where there was a long row of beehives; and just then a round shot from some Southern gun smashed through the length of these hives, and the air, which was already full of bullets, was now abuzz and humming with angry bees. The rookie 132nd Pennsylvania got the worst of it, and for a moment the bees almost broke up the battle. The green soldiers were marching into the rifle fire bravely enough, but the bees were more than they could take and the regiment went all to pieces as the men leaped and ran and slapped and swore. It took the united efforts of General Kimball, the brigade commander, his staff and the regimental officers to get the boys out of the yard and back in ranks again. To the end of their days the soldiers of the 132nd remembered the fight with the bees in the Roulette farmyard.

The Confederates who were defending the line in here belonged to D. H. Hill, and he had them cunningly posted at the crest of a hill, lying down almost invisible, firing steadily. As the Northerners came nearer these Rebels found themselves outnumbered and backed off; and when the advancing Yankee line got to the crest it looked down the reverse slope a hundred yards or more to a sunken road packed full of Rebels who yelled furious defiance. The Northerners' faces were already blackened by powder smoke, and a couple of regiments wore brand-new uniforms of blue darker than ordinary, which looked black in the morning sun, and the Southerners shouted: "Go away, you black devils—go home!" along with much else.

It was a bad layout. An eighth of a mile south of the Dunker church a country lane runs zigzag east and south from the Hagerstown road, going for a quarter of a mile under the lee of a long hill, climbing to a plateau for another quarter mile, and there making a sharp elbow as it turns south. By years of usage and erosion this

lane had been worn down several feet below the surface of the
ground, and it was bordered on both sides by snake-rail fences. On
the northern side the Rebels had taken these rails down and piled
them in a low breastwork, and they were lined up strongly in the
low road behind this obstruction, as securely entrenched as if they
had been digging all night. Lying below the brow of the hill, the
lane could not be reached by Federal artillery. The men who defended it were almost wholly protected; the men who tried to take it
would have to advance in the open, exposed to a crippling fire. It
was as nasty a strong point as the army ever ran up against: the
famous sunken road, known forever after (for sufficient reason)
as Bloody Lane.

The Yankee line halted on top of the hill, dressing its ranks. In
the road below the Rebels held their fire, waiting for them. For a
moment this part of the field was almost silent, and the waiting Confederates could hear the shouted commands of the Northern officers
as the assaulting lines started forward. Down the slope they came,
four ranks deep. A colonel in the sunken road paid his tribute to the
brilliance of the spectacle: "Their gleaming bayonets flashed like
burnished silver in the sunlight. With the precision of step and perfect
alignment of a holiday parade this magnificent array moved to the
charge, every step keeping time to the tap of the deep-sounding
drum."[4]

Down the slope they came, nearer and nearer, the Confederates
crouching low in their trench, officers standing just behind them, the
whole field seeming breathless with suspense. Then, at a shouted
command, the Rebels leveled their muskets and fired, and a long
sheet of flame ran from end to end of the sunken road, a wave of
smoke drifted up the hillside, and the Yankee charge ceased to look
like a holiday parade. The first line of the assaulting wave was almost torn to pieces. The men halted, tried to re-form, and the
Southerners, reloading with desperate haste, stood up and whacked
in another volley. Back up the hill went the Northerners, to pull their
broken lines together and come down again; but the Rebel fire was
too heavy. The lines swayed to a halt halfway down the slope, and
the men sprawled on the ground to return the fire from the sunken
road, both sides volleying away at the closest range, while the terrible
tumult of battle rose to a higher pitch than ever. The leading Federal

brigade finally faded back, and French sent another one in to take its place.

Beyond the sunken lane were more Rebels in a cornfield (not *the* cornfield: this one belonged to a man named Piper), and they fired over the heads of the men in the lane, tearing the Yankee lines. Rebel guns came up on the high ground back by the Hagerstown road, and the great uproar of the battle was deepened and increased as Federal guns beyond the Antietam marked these Rebel batteries for destruction. The Southern gunners were in a hard spot. They were under orders to forget about the Yankee guns and attend to the infantry —this was the last line of defense, and if the Yankees broke through here it would be the end; and whole batteries of long-range rifles beyond the creek concentrated their fire on the Confederate guns, hammering the line from end to end, smashing gun wheels and limber chests, dismembering gunners, sending shells through whole ranks of waiting battery horses. Once a shell found a Confederate caisson and blew it up with a crash that resounded above all the din, while an immense cloud of black smoke shot upward. Never had the Southern batteries taken such a fearful pounding; throughout the rest of the war they remembered this battle as "artillery hell."

It was hell for the infantry too. The strange, frenzied, illogical exaltation of spirit that descended on the fighting men at times in this battle visited the troops who assaulted the sunken road and the troops who defended it. Once a group of Rebels scrambled out of the road and charged straight up the hill in a mad, doomed counter-attack, shook the Yankee line briefly, and then went all to bits in the fire; one Federal who helped to repulse this attack said none of the Confederates got back to the lane. Farther north, some courageous Southern artillery officer rolled two guns out into an open field, and a mass of yelling Rebel infantry came out to beat in the right flank of the Yankee line. Red-faced French, storming and swearing with excitement, pulled the 8th Ohio and 14th Indiana out of line and sent them over to meet the threat, and the Westerners fired until their muskets were hot and foul, their ammunition gone, and half their men down. From somewhere in the rear a section of Yankee guns came clattering up, and the Rebel advance was driven back.

An immense sheet of smoke covered the battlefield, like a low thundercloud that was forever pulsing and glowing with lightning.

The ground underfoot shook and trembled with the everlasting jar
of the guns. The barn by the Roulette house was jammed with
wounded men. Screams, prayers, and curses made it a horrible place,
with hundreds of anguished men packed together on the straw begging the surgeons to attend to them—surgeons bare-armed and fear-
somely streaked and spattered with blood, piles of severed arms and
legs lying by the slippery operating tables, the uproar of the battle
beating in through the thin walls. Stragglers from the fighting line
crept into house and outbuildings and drifted downhill toward the
creek, where the valley gave shelter.

French's division was fought to a standstill, but new troops were
coming up. Franklin arrived on the field with his army corps from
the valley north of Harper's Ferry, and he put a brigade in line on
French's right to prevent any further flanking maneuvers by the
Rebels there. What was left of Greene's division was pulled back
from its lines around the Dunker church, to join this brigade of
Franklin's; and to the south Sumner's third division, Richardson's,
got across the creek at last and prepared to go into action. Richardson rode along the line—strictly business this morning, with the ec-
centricities of camp all shelved—and he shook out the Irish Brigade
with the golden harps on its emerald flags to spearhead the attack.

Between the general and the Irishmen there was a warm friend-
ship, and it all started because of a sly dodge worked by a member
of Richardson's staff. Early in the war, when the Irish Brigade was
first assigned to Richardson's division, this staff member—Captain
Jack Gosson, himself as Irish as Dublin—felt that it would be fine
if the general got a good first impression of the new brigade. So when
Richardson started over to make his first inspection Gosson rode on
ahead of him. He found the three regiments all drawn up, waiting,
and he spurred up and addressed them eloquently about the merits
of their new commander.

"And what do you think of the brave old fellow?" he cried at
last, inspired to a great and beautiful lie. "He has sent to our camp
three barrels of whisky, a barrel for each regiment, to treat the boys
of the brigade; and we ought to give him a thundering cheer when
he comes along."

This made sense to the Irishmen, and when Richardson came up
they threw their caps in the air and gave him one of the most spirited

ovations of the war. Naturally this pleased Richardson very much, he being ignorant of Captain Gosson's stratagem, and ever afterward he was especially devoted to the Irish Brigade. The complete non-appearance of the whisky was not held against him, somehow; probably the boys could recognize an artful Irish trick when they saw it. At any rate, this was Richardson's pet brigade and he was the brigade's pet general, and when he came up they yelled loudly and went swinging up the hill with their green flags snapping.[5]

They came up just in time, for French's men were in serious trouble. One brigade had been broken and the other two had been taking a deadly pounding, and the Rebels had mustered some new men and sent them forward beyond the lane, on the higher ground, to crush the Union left flank. The Irishmen went charging into this flank attack with savage power, the oncoming Confederate line halted to meet them, and on the open field there was a terrible shock of point-blank fire too hot for any troops to endure for long. General Meagher, who led the Irishmen, decided that the only way out of it was straight ahead—his men could charge or they could retreat; the one thing they could not do much longer was stand there and take it. He edged a few squads forward to tear down a fence that rose in their way, and then he stood up in his stirrups, raised his sword high, and shouted over all the battle thunder: "Boys! Raise the colors and follow me!" The green flags went tossing up and onward, the Irishmen cheered again, and the Rebels slowly fell back into the sunken road, where they rallied and poured out a fire which the Irish Brigade remembered afterward the way Sedgwick's men remembered the fire in the West Wood—the heaviest they had to face in all the war. Half of the 63rd New York fell in that first volley, all of the brigade color-bearers went down, and the men who snatched up the fallen flags went down likewise—carrying the colors was a mean job in that war, for hostile fire was always directed at the flags. A bullet killed Meagher's horse in full gallop, and the beast fell heavily, knocking Meagher out so that he had to be carried to the rear. The advance came to a halt a hundred yards from the sunken road, the Irishmen hugged the ground, and the last of their ammunition gave out.

Richardson was close behind, and he sent a fresh brigade through them while the Irish soldiers went to the rear to get more cartridges.

Still under fire, they marched to the rear in columns as orderly as
if they were on the drill field, with no straggling, although the four
regiments in the brigade were down to five hundred men now. Richardson met them as they came out, rode up to Lieutenant Colonel
Kelly of the 88th New York, and cried: "Bravo, 88th—I shall never
forget you!" and the exhausted soldiers gave him three cheers. Then
Richardson rode back to the front, and his fresh troops pushed forward until they were within thirty yards of the sunken lane. All up
and down the half-mile length of that little country lane in front of
French and Richardson the air was ablaze beneath the smoke, and
all the fury of the battle was coming to a new climax.

Everything seemed to happen at once. D. H. Hill found a gap between French and Richardson and sent troops forward, while other
Confederates went prowling around to the south and east, trying still
another flank attack around Richardson's new line. The first counterattack was broken up easily, and Richardson spotted the second
one just in time and sent the 5th New Hampshire off to meet it. This
regiment's Colonel Cross had a scalp wound, and had bound a red
bandanna around his head. He took his men in with the grim warning: "If any man runs I want the file closers to shoot him. If they
don't, I shall myself." The New Hampshire boys set off on a run
through a ragged cornfield, collided with a North Carolina regiment
on a little knoll, and halted for a vicious fire fight amid the tattered
cornstalks. Richardson came up on foot—hatless, bare sword in hand,
his face like a storm cloud. He had just pricked some skulking major
out of a hiding place, and the men heard him shouting: "God damn
the field officers!" He got into the front line, the men surged forward
with him, the North Carolinians gave way, and the flank attack was
beaten off.

There was a pause. The sunken lane and the main Confederate
line lay just ahead, the heated air was full of drifting smoke and
flying bullets, winded men snatched breath in convulsive gulps as they
nerved themselves for a new advance. Colonel Cross, the old Indian
fighter, got in front and turned to face them, face black with smoke,
eyes flaming.

"Put on the war paint!" he yelled. The soldiers grabbed grimy
cartridge papers and smeared their sweaty faces with soot.

"Now give 'em the war whoop!" shouted Cross.

Cheers went up in a wild falsetto chorus. The colonel swung his arm, and the line moved on. To the right the 81st Pennsylvania began to advance at the same moment. Still farther to the right, Colonel Barlow got the 61st and 64th New York regiments up to high ground where they could enfilade part of the sunken lane. For the first time the Southerners there came under a fire that was too hot to take, and they began to back away. Then at last the whole line caved in, the sunken lane was abandoned, and yelling Federals ran down the slope, clambered over the fence rails, and fired at the backs of the retreating enemy.

French's men were too dead-beat to do more than form a new line in the captured roadway, but Richardson's men were fresher, and anyway, Richardson was a driver. He lost little time sorting out the scrambled commands but took them on as they were, into the rolling fields south of the lane, so that they swarmed over the Confederates' second line, broke it, and went plunging down into hollow ground in the angle between the sunken road and the Hagerstown pike.

Once more the battle had come to a moment of supreme crisis, and final victory was within reach. The Confederate General Hill, imperturbable in the midst of disaster, somehow scraped the ultimate bottom of the barrel and got together a handful of men from his beaten command and led them forward in a new countercharge—taking a musket himself, it is said, to lead them in person. Barlow saw it coming and broke it up, and Richardson went off to get some artillery. His infantry got down into the hollow and drove the Confederates out of Mr. Piper's farm buildings, but there the disorganized attack lost its impetus, and by a supreme, despairing effort the Rebels kept them from going any farther. Richardson reappeared with Battery K, 1st U.S., and planted it on a hill south of the sunken road; it silenced a couple of Rebel smoothbores near the Hagerstown road, then came under a heavy fire and began to lose men. Richardson had the battery commander move back, cautioning him to save his guns and men: there would be a big advance just as soon as Richardson could get his division realigned, and the general wanted the battery in shape to accompany it.

The battery withdrew readily enough, as ordered, getting into a more sheltered spot where the Rebel fire wasn't quite so bad; and, apparently from nowhere and by magic, there appeared a well-dressed civilian with a two-horse carriage, who drove up without paying any attention to all the bullets, pulled up his horses, alighted, and began to hand baskets of ham and biscuits to the dumfounded gun crews. This done, he invited the wounded men to get into the carriage so that he could carry them back to a dressing station. As they got in he walked forward to inspect his team, a shell fragment having slightly wounded one of his horses. Satisfying himself that the animal was not badly hurt, he saw that the wounded men were comfortable, waved his hat cheerily to the astounded battery commander, and drove off—an unnamed man of good will who shows up briefly in the official reports and then vanishes as mysteriously as he came.[6]

At this moment Lee's battle line was a frayed thread, held by scraps and leftovers of tattered commands who clung to the ridges by the Hagerstown road and fought like automatons. Batteries had been hammered all to pieces: a mile to the rear, officers and men were working feverishly with wrecked gun carriages and limbers, trying to make patchwork repairs so that at least some could be put back in service. Longstreet, who held top command along this part of the line, had sent his own staff officers in to work the guns of one ravaged battery and was standing nearby holding their horses and helping to correct the ranges. The only infantry in his immediate vicinity was a lone regiment which was completely out of ammunition, waving its flags vigorously to create an illusion of strength. He had called for reinforcements, but there were none to be had, except for a few worn-out skeletons of regiments and some stragglers rounded up and sent back into the fight. The Confederates were still keeping up a brave fire, but there was no weight back of it—no possibility that it might suddenly flare up into a great, obliterating wave of destruction in case of need. Many years later Longstreet confessed that at that moment ten thousand fresh Federals could have come through and taken Lee's army and all it possessed.

The ten thousand fresh Federals were at hand, and to spare. Franklin's army corps was on the field, and Franklin believed that he had brought it there to fight. Richardson's division was still in good shape despite its terrible losses. Franklin was preparing to advance and Richardson was moving guns up, getting his ranks reassembled, making ready to attack beside him; and at this distance it is very hard to see how that attack could ever have been stopped.[7]

The only trouble is that it never was made. Bringing some guns up to a new location, Richardson was hit by a rifle bullet and was carried off the field—only slightly wounded, it seemed, but in a few days an infection set in and the wound killed him. Barlow went down, desperately wounded. McClellan detached Hancock from his own brigade and sent him in to take Richardson's place, so there was still a fighting commander up front; but white-haired old Sumner, senior officer on this part of the field, shaken by the disaster in the West Wood and by the killing he had seen since, countermanded the order for an offensive and forbade Franklin and Hancock to attack. Franklin argued hotly, but Sumner was unyielding; he had seen nothing but catastrophe that day and he firmly believed half of the army had been scattered, and he told Franklin that if his attack should fail the day would be lost beyond saving.

One of McClellan's staff officers rode up, bearing from the commanding general a suggestion that the army attack if possible, and Sumner cried out to him: "Go back, young man, and tell General McClellan I have no command! Tell him my command, Banks' command and Hooker's command are all cut up and demoralized. Tell him General Franklin has the only organized command on this part of the field!"[8]

Back to headquarters went this gloomy message. McClellan reflected on it briefly, considered once more the danger of being overbold—and upheld Sumner. The ten thousand fresh Federals Longstreet was talking about stayed where they were, and Lee's frayed line held.

Late that afternoon there was one final flare-up. The 7th Maine was detached from the front line and sent forward to drive Rebel sharpshooters out of the Piper farm buildings, down where Richardson's drive had reached high-water mark a few hours earlier. The little regiment got to the farmyard, chased the sharpshooters, found itself surrounded in an orchard, cut its way out, and came staggering back to the lines with sixty-eight men around the colors—it had set out with 240. A Vermont brigade which had watched the whole performance stood up in the lines and cheered as the exhausted soldiers came back. The skipper of the Maine regiment remarked afterward that if only that Vermont brigade had been sent forward in support they could have broken the Rebel line even then; up at close quarters he had seen for himself how weak the Confederate defenses really were.

But that was just one more of the might-have-beens. North of the town of Sharpsburg the fighting was over. The Federals drew their line partly in front of and partly behind the sunken road—the road itself was so full of dead men, so horrible with its torn fragments of flesh, its congealing pools of blood in ruts and hollows, that it could no longer be used as a trench.

3. All the Landscape Was Red

In the four years of its existence the Army of the Potomac had to atone for the errors of its generals on many a bitter field. This happened so many times—it was so normal, so much the regular order of things for this unlucky army—that it is hardly possible to take the blunders which marred its various battles and rank them in the order of magnitude of their calamitous stupidity. But if some such ranking could be made, this battle of the Antietam would surely be represented. Here, if anywhere, the soldiers were thrown into action and left to fight their way out. There would have been unqualified disaster if the generals had not been commanding men better than themselves.

The battle was fought in three separate parts. The first part was the fight around the cornfield, and the second was the fight in the West Wood and along the sunken road; and the third part—tardy, disjointed, and almost totally unco-ordinated, as if it had no relation to the rest of the battle—took place along the banks of the creek and on the hills and high ground beyond those banks, to the southeast of the town of Sharpsburg.

McClellan had planned to have the Union attack down here made at the same time as the attacks at the other end of his line, along the Hagerstown road, and if it had happened that way there can be very little doubt that Lee's army would have been crushed by the middle of the day. But somehow McClellan had very little control over this battle, and it did not work out at all as he had planned. The great assault on his left was hopelessly flubbed: a knockout punch, aimed at an enemy almost helpless on the ropes, which somehow turned into a mere shove. The private soldier fought as well here as he fought elsewhere, but he got no help whatever from the top.

When the day began the IX Corps was lying on the east side of Antietam Creek, south of the Boonsboro road, sprawled out among the low hills and sloping meadows which border that part of the stream. The Antietam runs in slow loops here, with steep high hills on its western bank, and these hills were held that morning by Rebel soldiers who opened fire as soon as they could see anything to shoot at; and as the light grew the Confederate batteries on the high ground in front of Sharpsburg joined in, to be answered promptly by the Federal guns east of the creek. So when the great uproar of the engagement north of the Dunker church filled the morning air there was an answering wave of sound from these hills on the left. For a while this was sound and nothing more (quite a number of men died under the shelling and the sharpshooting, to be sure, but their deaths were incidental, contributing nothing to victory or defeat); but somewhere around nine o'clock McClellan sent word to Burnside to attack the Rebel lines in his front immediately—Hooker and Sumner were hard pressed and a blow over here would greatly relieve them.

The two armies lay close together here with nothing between them but the valley of the Antietam. The valley itself is fairly broad, but the creek is insignificant—fifty feet wide, or thereabouts, and so shallow that a man could wade it in most places without wetting his belt buckle. For some unaccountable reason, however, this modest creek was treated that day as if it were quite impassable: a veritable Rhine River, not to be crossed except dry-shod on a bridge.[1] A little country road comes down over the hills on the eastern side, meanders close to the creek through the low meadows for a few hundred yards, and then makes a ninety-degree turn to the left, crossing the stream on a narrow bridge and following a winding ravine up to the high ground near Sharpsburg; and this road and this bridge, fatally, were the only features of this part of the landscape which the high command could think about that morning. When the order came to attack the enemy it was interpreted in terms of the bridge, as if the placid little creek could be passed in no other way. Corps and army command had had more than twenty-four hours to examine the terrain, but it seems to have occurred to no one in all that time to test the depth of this water the way young Lieutenant Custer had tested the Chickahominy

—by going out in it and measuring it personally. There was rumored to be a ford half a mile or more downstream from the bridge, but the search for this ford consisted chiefly in an unavailing hunt for some farmer who knew where it was and could lead the way to it. Meanwhile, orders were to attack; to attack meant to cross the creek; and to cross the creek, in the foggy light that pervaded corps headquarters, meant to cross the bridge—that and nothing else. And the bridge was the worst of all possible places to make an attack: an ideal defensive spot where a few regiments could hold off a whole division.

Orders went bumping down the echelons of command, from corps to division to brigade, and presently Colonel George Crook, who had three regiments of Ohio troops, got the nod. Crook was a good man and made a fine record later in the war—and afterward in the Indian wars out West—but that morning he seems to have been infected by the mental paralysis which beset his superiors. He had his brigade in a little valley an eighth of a mile northeast of the bridge; formed line of battle, went boldly forward over the low hill, and lost his way completely, missing the bridge altogether and coming out on a low plateau in a bend of the creek upstream, with enough Rebel guns trained on him to make the place highly uncomfortable. He got his Ohioans forward to the bank, and they lay down behind fences and underbrush and fired away at some Confederates across the stream, who promptly began to fire back. This brought about the killing of some dozens of boys but contributed nothing whatever to the capture of the bridge. Burnside's first assault was hardly even a fizzle.

Try again: and this time the order went to General Sturgis, he who had sat in Colonel Haupt's office less than a month ago and explained patiently his intense dislike for General Pope. Sturgis had one asset—he at least knew where the bridge was—and he got the 2nd Maryland and the 6th New Hampshire lined up and sent them down the country road and along the riverbank toward the bridge. This was playing into the Rebels' hands. They had the hills on the western side covered with sharpshooters, with a couple of regiments drawn up under good cover in an old quarry overlooking the bridge itself, and they also had a substantial number of fieldpieces trained on the bridge and on the road that led to the bridge. All of these laid down a killing fire, and it was just too much for any troops to stand. The boys from Maryland and New Hampshire tried, but their lines were broken up before they reached the bridge, and presently the survivors went scampering back to the woods for shelter. General Cox got some infantry up to keep the Rebel defenders under rifle fire, and a tremendous bombardment was opened by the Federal artillery; and General Isaac Rodman was ordered to march his division downstream to hunt for that missing ford, which was the last anybody heard of that for some little time. Meanwhile, the morning had gone and the hour was past noon, and the right wing of Lee's army had hardly been annoyed.

About this time McClellan began to realize that although a great deal of noise was being made on Burnside's front nothing very much in the way of an assault was going on. He had already sent several messages urging haste, and now he sent a staff colonel with peremptory orders: get across the stream immediately and open an attack on the high ground. Burnside was sitting his horse beside a battery on a hilltop, surveying the battlefield with impressive calm, and the sharp tone of this latest order jarred him. He told the colonel: "McClellan appears to think I am not trying my best to carry this bridge; you are the third or fourth one who has been to me this morning with similar orders." The colonel agreed that McClellan was getting anxious, and Burnside rode off to see Sturgis about it.

Presently Colonel Edward Ferrero, commanding Sturgis's second brigade, came trotting up to his two pet regiments—51st New York and 51st Pennsylvania, waiting side by side in a protected valley a couple of hundred yards back from the bridge.

"It is General Burnside's especial request that the two 51st's take that bridge," called Ferrero. "Will you do it?"

There was a brief pause while the regiments presumably reflected on the consuming sheet of fire that lay upon the bridge and its approaches and nerved themselves for a desperate deed. Then some corporal in the Pennsylvania regiment sang out:

"Will you give us our whisky, Colonel, if we make it?"

Between the Pennsylvanians and the colonel, whisky was a sore point. Somehow the regiment had earned a reputation as a heavy-drinking crowd: its colonel once remarked that if the regiment were put ashore on some completely uninhabited desert island, the foragers would come back in the evening loaded down with demijohns of the stuff; and for this reason and that Ferrero had recently ordered their whisky ration suspended. (It should be explained that there was no

regular issue of whisky to the troops in the Civil War. Regimental
commanders were authorized to issue it, however, whenever they
thought fit—in bad weather, after a hard march, after a battle, and
so on—and many of them were fairly liberal about it.)

Ferrero—a trim, dapper, black-haired little man, something of a
dandy in his dress—blinked for a moment, then laughed.

"Yes, by God!" he cried.

The regiments cheered, and Ferrero got them lined up side by side,
each regiment in column of twos. They would dash straight downhill for the bridge instead of going along the road parallel to the
Confederate line of fire, and when they got across, one regimental
column would turn to the left and the other to the right. When the
tail of the column was across, both outfits would face to the west,
and they would have a two-regiment battle line ready to charge up
the hill. Cox got the 11th Connecticut down to a stone wall by the
creek to put a covering fire on the defenders, the 11th losing its colonel
and suffering heavily but sticking to it manfully. Upstream a bit,
Crook worked a battery down to the bank to blast the Rebels away
from the western approaches. The fieldpieces on the bluffs stepped
up their fire, throwing shells at every Confederate gun that could bear
on the bridge, and the tumult of battle became a great, unbroken roar.
Battle flags waving at the head of the column, the two regiments
came up over their little hill and ran full-tilt for the bridge, shouting
madly, men falling at every step as muskets and cannon slashed the
column; and there was a wild chaos of smoke, flame, thunderous
noise, and yelling men.

The Rebels across the creek were only twenty-five yards away and
they could make every shot count, but they were under a furious fire
now and it hurt, and there were not really so very many of them
there, anyway, and they began to drift back up the hillsides. The
colonel of the Pennsylvania regiment got to the near end of the bridge
and stood there, one hand on the stone coping, waving his hat in great
circles and yelling words of encouragement. The fighting men surged
past him; his voice gave out, and the men could hear him rasping:
"Come on, boys, I can't holler any more"—and then suddenly the
column was across, fanning out into a line of battle, the handful of
Confederates who remained were running, and the bridge had been
won. The two regiments made their way to the crest of the hill, saw

nothing in front of them but skirmishers—and, far away, Rebel batteries, which were keeping up a heavy fire but which had lost the
range: shells were passing just overhead to explode harmlessly over
the valley, and a man was safe enough if he stayed close to the
ground—and they hugged the crest, waiting for reinforcements and
further orders.[2]

They had been hit hard, those two regiments, and they were
winded, and presently they left a chain of pickets up front, slipped
back down the hillside where there was shelter, lit little fires, and
began to boil coffee. . . . A few days later there was a fancy ceremony in front of the brigade, with Colonel Ferrero getting a brigadier's commission as reward for the valor of the New Yorkers and
Pennsylvanians. Just as he was given the commission—everything very
formal, field all aglitter with high brass, Ferrero sitting his horse in
front of regiments stiff with military reverence—some irrepressible in
the Pennsylvania regiment called out, side-of-mouth fashion: "How
about that whisky?" Ferrero heard it, grinned, and turned his head
long enough to say: "You'll get it"—and next morning, according to
the regimental historian, a keg of the stuff came over from brigade
headquarters and the long dry spell was over. . . .

Meanwhile, the army was losing time. Sturgis got the rest of his
division across and sent the 21st Massachusetts up front—a battle-
wise regiment which had educated its officers under fire and was proud
of it. They had gone into action for the first time some months earlier
at New Bern, North Carolina, where they had had to cross a shallow
stream in a swamp with Rebel bullets whacking in all around them,
men getting hit and everybody pretty tense. One of the officers had
been a noted fiddler back home, much given to playing for country
dances at which, in the custom of the day, he would call out the
movements for the dancers while he fiddled; and at this river crossing
he became greatly excited, so that pretty soon he was skipping about
shouting all sorts of useless orders as fast as he could think of them,
jittery himself and making everybody else the same way. So after a
while one boy piped up: "All promenade!" and then another called
out: "Ladies—grand change!" and the regiment crossed the stream,
shouting with laughter. The officer became quiet and, said a veteran,
"behaved like a little man" for the rest of the war.[3]

Anyway, the 21st was out in front, and after a while the rest of the

division was massed close behind it, and Sturgis got ready to advance
—only to discover that in the wild fusillading of the morning his boys
had used up all of their ammunition. No one, somehow, had thought
to check on their supply and see that they got more before they
crossed. So he sent back word that somebody else would have to
make the attack, adding that his boys were all exhausted, anyhow;
and finally his troops were ordered aside into reserve while a new
division came across the narrow bottleneck of the bridge, and more
minutes slipped by. There was a bad traffic jam there, with marching
men, ammunition wagons, field guns, and caissons all trying to make
the bridge at once. The Confederate gunners up near Sharpsburg
were still shelling the place, and altogether two hours passed before
everything was in order and the advance could begin.

General Willcox was in charge of the new division and he started
his men off astride the little road in the ravine, getting them up to the
higher ground with the 79th New York leading—the old Highlanders
who had mutinied against Tecumseh Sherman back in the army's
gawky adolescence and had made up for it since by hard fighting.
They passed the crest and came out on open ground: fields full of
haystacks, cut up by stone walls, Confederates shooting at them from
under cover, batteries in front and to the left, a scorching fire coming
in. The Highlanders came to a halt, the 17th Michigan moved up
and charged one of the batteries, sending it flying in hasty retreat,
and the fighting line went on and found more Rebels in an orchard
and halted to drive them out with musket fire.

Confederate man power here was fantastically thin, even though
it didn't seem that way to the Federals in the front line. All morning
Lee had pulled men away from this part of the line (Burnside's attack
not developing) to reinforce the defense up by the Dunker church
and the sunken lane, and when the Federals finally got up on the
plateau, about three in the afternoon, there were no more than twenty-
five hundred Rebel infantrymen left to stand them off, with no help in
sight. Confederate batteries and used-up parts of batteries were clattering up from wherever they could be found, and they had to play
the same role here they had played along the Hagerstown road—ignore
the Yankee guns and concentrate on the advancing infantry, getting
hit without being able to hit back: artillery hell all over again, the
Federal gunners having worked out a system of concentrating all

their fire on one Rebel battery at a time, wrecking it and then moving on to the next. Some of Fitz-John Porter's regular infantry and some dismounted cavalry had got across the stream by the Boonsboro bridge and were sending sharpshooters forward to pick off the Rebel gunners—and, all in all, the Army of Northern Virginia, hammered almost into a daze, was staggering on the very edge of final defeat.

But the Federal commanders did not know it. McClellan, back at headquarters, was meditating on the fearful slaughter of the morning and wondering if his right wing could hold its ground. Sumner had already forbidden the assault which Franklin and Richardson had prepared and was thinking only of the reserves which must be kept in hand to repulse a possible Rebel counterattack. (Lee had no reserves whatever just then; every unit which could stand up and hold muskets was in there shooting, and parts of the line were being held by pure bluff.) And Burnside—well, it is impossible to figure out just what Burnside was thinking. He was across the creek at last and he had something like twelve thousand fighting men in his command, with barely a fifth of that number opposing them; but he had one of his four divisions completely out of action, resting and replenishing its ammunition, he had another in reserve behind the front, and a third was floundering around looking for that ford half a mile below the bridge. The upshot was that instead of driving into Sharpsburg with twelve thousand men he was making his big attack with three thousand.

The three thousand were making progress, but it was slow going. The tired Rebels who held this part of the line were few in number, but they kept laying down a heavy fire, and by now there were plenty of Confederate fieldpieces in action to help them despite the counter-battery work from across the stream. These stout Southern gunners were covering the open ground with a nasty cross fire, and the Yankees who were actually up in front doing the fighting were getting no benefit whatever from the fact that the defense in here would be completely swamped if Burnside could just get all of his men into action. The roar of battle grew louder and louder, choking smoke blanketed the hilltops and went rolling through the streets of Sharpsburg, and although the Rebels were giving ground they were being very stubborn about it. A sergeant in an advanced Pennsylvania battery, coming up to his guns after delivering a message to some other outfit, was walking across a field of dry standing timothy which seemed to be alive with wriggling, whistling rifle bullets; and he found himself ludicrously stepping high and walking on tiptoe to keep from treading on these venomous creatures whose trails he could see in the waving grass.

Rod by rod, going in little rushes from fence to fence, the Federal battle line got nearer and nearer to Sharpsburg. They had the high ground now, and the men who were farthest forward could see, down the western slope, the Rebels' behind-the-lines tangle of baggage wagons, stragglers, ambulances, and broken batteries. A stone mill on the edge of town was a strong point briefly, but the 45th Pennsylvania finally drove the Southern sharpshooters out of it. The Pennsylvanians insisted that the miller himself was there in his straw hat and overalls, taking pot shots at them from an upper window, and next day they wanted to find him and hang him but were dissuaded, at last, by the argument that the Rebels were a tattered lot and that the man they thought a civilian was probably a soldier who just didn't have a uniform.

Slowly the Rebel line of defense faded away—brigades up front all cracked, Sharpsburg filled with demoralized stragglers looking for shelter, the last desperate hour of the Confederate Army visibly at hand. On the northern side General Willcox found his men out of ammunition and called a brief halt so that he could dress his lines and get more cartridges; then he would go on, take Sharpsburg, and get squarely across Lee's only line of retreat.

While all of this had been happening General Rodman had been having his troubles downstream. His orders were to find that ford, get his men across, and flank the Rebels who were defending the bridge, and he had started out just as Sturgis got his first orders from Burnside. He had a guide picked up on some farm thereabouts, but the guide couldn't seem to find the ford—one suspects that he had "sesesch" sympathies and was laughing up his sleeve at the misguided Yankees—and the division did a power of more or less haphazard marching around and the whole morning was wasted. Finally, about the time Ferrero was sending in his valiant 51st's to storm the bridge, one of Rodman's brigadiers had the 8th Connecticut deploy two companies as skirmishers and moved them down to the stream to look for the ford. Quickly enough they found it—or at least found that they could wade the creek, which came to the same thing—and with this climactic revelation Rodman got his men over and prepared to join in the final assault on Lee's right.

Rodman's division was not too strong. He had seven regiments in all, and one of these had been detached earlier to support a battery on the east bank; altogether he might have taken close to three thousand men across the little creek. The ground he had to fight on was a bit perplexing. The hills came down to the creek steeply, where he was, all cut up by ravines and gullies and long hollows, with the upper slopes planted in corn. It took a little time to get the two brigades lined up abreast on the western side, with the right wing of the right brigade extended in order to get in touch with Willcox's men upstream. The Rebels were waiting in the various cornfields and they put a stinging rifle fire down on the slopes. Rodman's regiments drifted apart a little while they were forming. When the advance began the left wing somehow didn't get the order; it got off to a late start, and there was a gap between it and the other brigade.

There were three New York regiments in the brigade on the right, and they went plodding up a long hill, with Rebels behind a stone wall at the top and a Rebel battery off at one side plowing the slope with accurate shell fire. All of this fire seemed too much to buck, and the brigade commander had the men lie down halfway up the hill; but the Confederate gunners in here were marksmen and they shaved the ground with solid shot that mashed prostrate men and kicked up great clods of earth. Lying there was worse than charging; one veteran recalled that the Federal line broke out with "the most vehement, terrible swearing I have ever heard"; it became quite unendurable, and at last the men scrambled to their feet and made for their tormentors. Muskets blazed all along the stone wall, the artillerists fired double-shotted charges of canister, and the New Yorkers bent low and ran hard in the loose dirt, struggling for the hilltop. One well-read member of the 9th New York wrote long afterward: "The mental strain was so great that I saw at that moment the singular effect mentioned, I think, in the life of Goethe on a similar occasion—the whole landscape for an instant turned slightly red." And finally they got to the fence and drove the Confederates away, one regiment overran and captured a battery, and the brigade dressed its ranks for a new advance.[4]

The other brigade had gone off at a divergent angle, and the two were now out of touch. Much to his surprise, Rodman was finding Rebel infantry on his left, far south of Sharpsburg, and the brigade swung over to face it. It was hard to make things out very clearly, with the smoke and the irregular hills and the tall corn, and the brigade came to a halt, strung out on a long hillside, plenty of bullets coming in but most of the men unable to see just where they were coming from. The extreme left of Rodman's line—extreme left of the whole army—was held by the 16th Connecticut, most pathetically unlucky of all the Federal units in the battle. This was a brand-new regiment which had been mustered in just three weeks ago. It was nine hundred strong, but it was totally unready for battle: had loaded its muskets for the very first time only the evening before, and today it was maneuvering as a regiment for the first time, and doing it under fire. The boys were willing enough, but they were completely bewildered; they were lying down in a cornfield now, very frightened, trying hard not to show it, well aware that they had no business being on the firing line, discovering that battle was not at all as they had imagined it. The grand and picturesque business of charging a Rebel line, which had sounded so impressive and inspiring back home, had come down to this—hiding in a cornfield and being shot by people who were completely out of sight.

Rodman came up, a quiet, conscientious man with a little pointed beard, worried now because the Rebels were still overreaching his left. He peered off over the corn tops, and from what he could see he gathered that a strong flank attack was about to hit him, and he told the Connecticut colonel to swing his regiment around so that it faced to the south. The colonel barked out the order—"Change front forward on the tenth company!"—and the three-week soldiers got to their feet and tried it. This was one of those maneuvers that made long weeks on the drill ground essential in the Civil War soldier's battle training: company at the left end of the regimental line does a ninety-degree wheel to the left, each succeeding company tramps through a forty-five-degree turn and then marches straight ahead until its left reaches the new line, whereupon it does another forty-five-degree turn and then comes to a halt. Simple enough, in a way, but the sort of thing that called for a lot of practice, which the Connecticut boys had not had. Even on the parade ground they would have had trouble with it; here they were trying it from a bent line, with the corn and smoke making it impossible to see anything, and with a brisk Rebel fire knocking men out at every step. Inevitably they fell into a confused, trampling huddle, with different companies getting in each other's way and everybody tangled up; and while they tried to sort themselves out a tremendous volley swept the field, breaking what formation they had all to pieces.

Then, while the rookies were still trying to get collected, a hostile battle line came shouldering through the cornstalks, firing as it came, and it was too much—the 16th just fell apart and the men turned to run. Rodman was bringing up the 4th Rhode Island to help, and for a moment that made things even worse. The Confederates on this part of the field were wearing blue uniforms (part of the loot from captured Harper's Ferry, the Rebels being necessitous men) and between an advancing blue line in front and another advancing blue line in the rear, the confusion became absolute. The Connecticut boys could not make head or tail out of any of it, and the Rhode Islanders were all mixed up too—saw men in blue running away from other men in blue, held their fire just too long, and became involved in the rout, the oncoming Confederates being the only men on the field who knew just what was going on. Rodman was killed, and the two regiments together went streaking for the rear. A couple of Cox's Ohio regiments were brought over, but the advancing Rebels suddenly seemed to have become very numerous, and their charging line overlapped the reinforcements. Some of the Ohioans were puzzled by those blue uniforms and waited too long before they opened fire, and in the end the whole line gave way and the Federals all the way up to Sharpsburg had to withdraw. At the last possible minute Lee's army had been saved from defeat.[5]

What had saved it was the arrival from Harper's Ferry of A. P. Hill and the leading brigades of his division, which was one of the most famous organizations in the whole Confederate Army. These soldiers came upon the field at precisely the right time and place, after a terrible seventeen-mile forced march from Harper's Ferry, in which exhausted men fell out of ranks by the score and Hill himself urged laggards on with the point of his sword. A more careful and methodical general (any one of the Federal corps commanders, for instance) would have set a slower pace, keeping his men together, mindful of the certainty of excessive straggling on too strenuous a march—and would have arrived, with all his men present or accounted for, a couple of hours too late to do any good. Hill drove his men so cruelly that he left fully half of his division panting along the roadside—but he got up those who were left in time to stave off disaster and keep the war going for two and one half more years.

This A. P. Hill was probably as well known and deeply respected in the Union Army as any general in the Confederacy, just then. He was always a driver and his men were valiant fighters, and the Federals had the impression that whenever they were prodded especially hard the prod was being applied by A. P. Hill. They were so convinced of this that they had evolved a legend to account for it. Back before the war, they said, Hill and McClellan had been rivals for the hand of beautiful Ellen Marcy, daughter of an army officer. She chose McClellan at last, and (so the soldiers believed) Hill carried a great anger against the successful suitor, which accounted for the violence of his attacks. And one morning, when a rattle of firing aroused the army and told it that Hill's men were attacking again, one veteran raised his head and growled disgustedly: "God's sake, Nelly—why didn't you marry him?"[6]

It was late in the afternoon now, and Burnside had been beaten—Burnside and his generals, strictly speaking, rather than Burnside's army corps. The rout of his left had been disastrous, but after all it had involved only about a fourth of the men under his command. Even after Hill's men came in there were still twice as many Federals as Confederates in this part of the field. Willcox's division, waiting on the outskirts of Sharpsburg, was hardly under fire at all now and was about ready to walk in and take possession, and Sturgis's division was still under shelter in the Antietam Valley, resting and refilling its cartridge boxes, the men so far out of the fight that they were wandering about examining the haversacks and knapsacks of dead Rebels. The Ohio division was closer to the front—some of its regiments had gone over to help when Rodman's line collapsed—but as a division it was not in serious action. There were more than enough men present to check Hill's charging ranks, hold the ground around Sharpsburg, and stage a new attack. The trouble was that it did not occur to anyone to try it. The Union commanders just took it for granted that they were beaten, and they were quite right: they had been whipped, even if their men had not been.[7]

So Willcox was told to bring his troops back, a new line was formed on the brow of the hills overlooking the creek, and Burnside sent word to headquarters that he thought he could hold his ground all right, although it would help if he could be strongly reinforced. Altogether he had lost twenty-three hundred men, nearly half of them from Rodman's luckless division—the 16th Connecticut alone had lost more than four hundred, and when it called the roll that evening only three hundred men were present, although a couple of hundred more came wandering in during the night. For the rest, Burnside's worst losses had been incurred in the attacks on the bridge.

McClellan had stayed at the Pry house all day except for one brief excursion to the right to talk with Sumner, after Franklin's attack had been called off. The battle swung and surged back and forth in front of him, and he was like a bemused spectator; he accepted the decisions made by his subordinates but went no farther. Once or twice, it seems, something struck a spark in his mind, and he was on the verge of demanding a new offensive all along the line. But that old, crippling belief in Lee's overwhelming numbers was still working. Every time the fighting reached the stage where one more hard drive would finish matters McClellan thought of the terrible fix he would be in if the Rebels should make a great counterattack and find him without reserves, and so one more hard drive was never ordered.

There is a story—probably garbled, but nevertheless perfectly in character—of McClellan at the end of the afternoon, sitting his horse beside Porter and Sykes near where the Boonsboro road crosses the creek. Up ahead, near Sharpsburg, some of Sykes's regulars had been sharpshooting on the outskirts of the town, their skirmish line a link connecting the troops who had assaulted Bloody Lane with the advanced elements of Burnside's command. An infantry captain in the skirmish line had seen for himself how thin the Rebel defenses in front of him really were, and he sent back word of it, begging that an attack might be made—the attack was bound to win, he said, and it would break Lee's army in half. Sykes liked the idea, it is said, and urged that his division be sent in, followed by the rest of Porter's corps and everybody else who was available. (Here, for the last time, were those ten thousand fresh Federals of Longstreet's.) For a moment McClellan seemed ready to approve. And then Porter said: "Remember, General—I command the last reserve of the last army of the Republic"—and the attack was not made.[8]

It is only fair to point out that Porter, a perfectly reliable witness on other matters, said that no such conversation ever took place, and the story undoubtedly was much embellished in the telling. Nevertheless, it is the tip-off. Lee's army could have been broken then and there, and it was not broken because the men who might have done it had to be saved as the vital last reserve. The Northern fighting men had done their best, but they had not been able to shake their general's belief that his real responsibility was defensive. Whatever might have been the relative merits of the two armies, there is not a shadow of doubt that the Southern commanders that day had an unbeatable moral ascendancy over the commanders of the North.

Another story: In midmorning, young Lieutenant Wilson of McClellan's staff finished a ride through the battered brigades of Hooker's and Mansfield's corps. He had seen the tired men forming new ranks behind the massed artillery which was anchoring McClellan's right, and he reflected that although these boys were deeply dejected—they had given their best and it hadn't been quite good enough —there were still enough of them to go sweeping in over the Rebel flank if proper inspiration were given them. He remembered, too, that next to McClellan Joe Hooker was the most popular general in the army, and while Hooker had been wounded he knew that Hooker's wound was comparatively slight. Lieutenants, of course, do not tell major generals what to do, but sometimes there are ways to work things. At headquarters just then was George Smalley, war correspondent for the New York *Tribune,* who was a good friend of Hooker; and Smalley told Wilson that Hooker, his injured foot bandaged, was lying in a farmhouse a mile or so from the place where his troops were.

"Smalley!" cried Wilson, excited. "Ride rapidly to Hooker and tell him to rally his corps and lead it back to the field, for by doing so he may not only save the day but save the Union also!"

Smalley's horse had been wounded, and he himself was weary and covered with dust from riding about the field, but he was game; he pointed out, however, that Hooker's wound would probably make it impossible for him to mount a horse.

"That makes no difference," said Wilson. "Let him get into an ambulance and drive back to the field. Or, what is still better, put him on a stretcher and with his bugles blowing and his corps flag flying over him let his men carry him back to the fighting line while his staff take the news to the division and brigade commanders."

Smalley took fire. "Hooker will go back—I'll answer for it!" he said, and he galloped away—to return crestfallen half an hour later with the report that Hooker said his wound was too painful to let him make the attempt. Wilson, always a caustic critic of Federal generals, wrote of Hooker: "From that day forth I regarded him as possessing but little real merit."[9]

Just what, if anything, would have been accomplished if this flamboyant project had gone through is, of course, an open question; but the young lieutenant's suggestion does stand out as the one proposal made at any time during the day to make use of the great reserve of enthusiasm and ardor which was possessed by that youthful army. Here were soldiers not yet grown battle-weary and army-cynical: young men still romantic enough to respond to the waving flag and the blaring bugle, foolish enough to try the impossible, and to do it, too, if the right man asked them to. McClellan had that force at his disposal as no other commander of this army ever had it—and he could never quite bring himself to the point of using it. As one of his veterans wrote long after the war: "It always seemed to me that McClellan, though no commander ever had the love of his soldiers more, or tried more to spare their lives, never realized the metal that was in his grand Army of the Potomac. . . . He never appreciated until too late what manner of people he had with him."[10]

And it seems that McClellan's great love for his soldiers actually worked to prevent him from making full use of them. He knew that his men had fought harder that day than they had ever fought before; believed, in fact, that they were completely fought out, that they had done all that any man could ask them to do. He dreaded to see their bloodshed and suffering, and he had been seeing nothing else all day. From one end of the war to the other the Army of the Potomac never lost so many men in one day's fighting as it lost here on the Antietam: not at Gettysburg, not in the Wilderness, not anywhere.

McClellan's capacity for sending his men in to be hurt had simply been exhausted. So they were hurt no more that day—and were to go on fighting until 1865.

And the long day ended at last, and the long battle ended, and both sides were about where they had been at dawn. The sun went down over the western hills, blood-red in the smoky air: an observer at headquarters saw it, just as it was setting, with the gunners of one isolated battery silhouetted black against its enormous disk as they loaded for a final shot, seeming to stand in the sun. As the land grew dark, fires were visible; shells had ignited innumerable hay-stacks on the fields, and these glowed in the twilight. On Burnside's front, boys from the 21st Massachusetts carried their wounded into a farmhouse where an energetic young woman named Clara Barton had set up a dressing station. The sound of the guns died down, and a more dreadful noise rose from the battle lines—the steady, unceas-ing, unanswerable crying and moaning of thousands upon thousands of wounded boys who lay in the open where the stretcher-bearers could not reach them; a crying that continued throughout the night. A survivor of the mangled 16th Connecticut wrote afterward: "Of all gloomy nights, this was the saddest we ever experienced."

4. The Romance of War Was Over

It all happened a long time ago, and that part of the reality which is represented by smoke and flame and bloodshed casts a thin shadow now, its original darkness bleached out by the years. Yet something endures, even if it is no more than the quiet truth that nothing is ever wasted, and the story of what happened along the Antietam is not just the story of young men who passed needlessly through the fire to Moloch. For in the end the young men who passed along that path were triumphant, and the incapacity which cost them so much has ceased to matter.

Their triumph was not the winning of a battle, for this battle seemingly was not won by anybody; to all appearances it was simply a stalemate that wrecked two armies. Yet victory was in it. After it had been fought—because it had been fought—history came to a turning point. Indecisive tactically, the battle shaped all the rest of the war: meant, at the very least, that the war now must be fought to a finish. There could no longer be a hope for a peace without victory. The great issues that created the war were going to be settled, at no matter what terrible cost. This fight was decisive.

Yet at the moment it did not look decisive. It looked like a stand-off, and the morning after the battle the two exhausted armies lay on the field staring blankly over the silent guns, as if they were ap-palled by what they had done to each other. Here and there men on the rival lines made an informal truce so that the wounded could be carried in, but the pickets were alert and scattered shots rang out now and then, warning the ranging stretcher-bearers not to go too far. All day long the soldiers awaited a new outburst of fighting. Heavy reinforcements came into McClellan's lines, and generals went out to study new angles of attack; McClellan listened to them, nodded sagely, and decided to delay the offensive until next day. On the opposite side Lee considered an attack north of the Dunker church, regretfully gave it up when Jackson reported the Federal position there too strong to be carried, and waited for the day to end; and the hot sun came down on fields and copses where lay thousands of unburied bodies. And at last it was night again, and after dark the Federals heard in their front a steady, unbroken sound like the flowing of a great river, hour after hour—the tramping of the brigades of Lee's army moving back to cross the Potomac on the return to Virginia. When morning came the noise had ceased and the Union Army had the field to itself, with none but dead men in front of it.

The cavalry and Fitz-John Porter's infantry were sent on to the river to make sure the last Rebels had gone. They rounded up a few belated stragglers, and they did a good deal of sniping across the water at Lee's rear guard. Porter ran some artillery down to the bank, and that night some of his regiments crossed, captured a few guns, and went forward to see what further damage they could do. The Confederates struck back savagely in the gray of the next morn-ing: A. P. Hill's division again, lashing out at McClellan for the last time. A new Pennsylvania regiment, which, having been armed with condemned muskets, somehow found itself on the front line, discov-ered that its weapons could not be fired, and took a brutal beating before it could get back to the northern shore. There was no more fighting. The Army of Northern Virginia withdrew slowly up the Shenandoah Valley, and the Army of the Potomac stayed where it was, too worn to pursue, and wearily went to work to tidy up the battlefield.

This battlefield was unspeakably awful by now. Swollen corpses darkened by the sun lay everywhere, giving off a frightful stench, and burial parties were put to work. (Any regiment which had got into the bad graces of its brigadier, a veteran wrote later, was sure to be given this assignment.) Great fires were built to consume the innumerable carcasses of dead horses, and nauseating greasy smoke went drifting down-wind and compounded the evil. The men dug long trenches for mass burials of dead Confederates—McClellan said they buried twenty-seven hundred of them, but the count seems to have been too high—and they tried to make individual graves for their own comrades, putting up little wooden markers with names and regimental numbers wherever they could.

Even men who had been in the thickest of the fighting were astounded when they went about the field and saw how terrible the killing had really been. One officer counted more than two hundred dead Southerners in a five-hundred-foot stretch of the Bloody Lane. An Ohio soldier wrote that the lane was "literally filled with dead." Stupefied Pennsylvania rookies gossiped fatuously that the Confederate bodies they were burying had turned black because the Rebels ate gunpowder for breakfast. One Northern soldier, moved by a somewhat ghoulish curiosity, carefully examined a body which hung doubled over a fence in rear of the Bloody Lane and found that it had been hit by fifty-seven bullets. Under the ashes of burned haystacks, in front of Burnside's corps, soldiers found the charred bodies of wounded men who had feebly crawled under the hay for shelter and had been too weak to crawl out when the stacks took fire.

Worst of all, perhaps, was the Hagerstown turnpike between the West Wood and the cornfield, where charge and countercharge had swept back and forth repeatedly, and where the post-and-rail fences on each side of the road were grotesquely festooned with corpses. The colonel of the 6th Wisconsin called this place "indescribably horrible" and said that when he rode through his horse "trembled in every limb with fright and was wet with perspiration." This officer served throughout the war, and when he wrote his reminiscences, in

1890, he said that what he saw along the Hagerstown road that morning was worse than anything he saw later at Spotsylvania's Bloody Angle, at Cold Harbor, or in front of the stone wall at Fredericksburg: "The Antietam turnpike surpassed all in manifest evidence of slaughter." Yet General Gibbon felt that the cornfield itself was even worse; the dead were actually piled on top of each other in places, and it seemed as if whole regiments had gone down in regular ranks. One soldier wrote that it would have been possible to walk from one side of the cornfield to the other without once stepping on the ground. There were two dozen dead horses and scores of human corpses in Mr. Miller's barnyard.[1]

There had been a great deal of killing, in other words. McClellan's official casualty list, which was made up a few days later, showed more than two thousand Federals killed in action and about ten thousand wounded. Rebel casualties were apparently slightly lower, although exact figures are lacking. Altogether, bearing in mind the number of wounded men who were to die, it is probable that five thousand young men lost their lives here; and whatever the correct figure may be, there seems no reason to doubt the accuracy of the contemporary writers who called the Antietam the worst single day of the entire war. Some regiments were down to pathetic remnants. Captain Noyes recorded that he met a company officer the morning after the battle who was carrying a huge piece of salt pork and was wondering what on earth to do with it—it was the day's meat ration for his company, just issued, and he was the company's sole survivor. Noyes added that he checked on this officer's amazing statement and found that it was true. Company G of the 12th Massachusetts had been reduced from 32 men to five; the whole regiment, even after it called in all convalescents and detailed men, numbered only 119 when it was formed for a review two weeks after the battle. The 80th New York had only 86 men to answer roll call the day after the battle, and the 28th New York—which had been a skeleton to begin with—was down to 53. The Irish Brigade had received 120 recruits just before the battle; it reported that 75 of the new men had been shot. Regimental losses of 50 per cent were common; had been suffered, for instance, by three of the four regiments in Sedgwick's front line during the fifteen-minute ambush in the West Wood.

The stragglers were at least coming back to the fold. General

Meade, who was temporarily in command of Hooker's corps, wrote to his wife that the corps' "present for duty" total rose by five thousand in the three days after the battle, explaining that the increase was made up of "the cowards, skulkers, men who leave the ground with the wounded and do not return for days, the stragglers on the march, and all such characters." He added bitterly that this sort of thing was entirely due to the inefficiency of regimental and company officers.[2] Like a good brigadier, Gibbon made a careful check of his own returns and discovered that the Black Hat Brigade's strength had increased by eighty in those three days; and he wrote proudly that *"everyone* of these were men who had returned from detached service and hospitals so that I had *no* stragglers." To add to his pride, he was learning that his brigade now had a new nickname, used by the whole army—the Iron Brigade, a name it carried for the rest of the war. Nobody was quite sure where it came from. The accepted story was that McClellan, watching its progress up the gap at South Mountain, had exclaimed in admiration: "That brigade must be made of iron!" Whatever its origin, the name stuck, and the brigade lived up to it valiantly the next summer at Gettysburg.[3]

The soldiers themselves were slow to realize just what they had achieved. All through the eighteenth of September, when the two armies waited in each other's presence for a renewal of the fighting, the battle had seemed unfinished. The Federals held part of the Rebel position, but only part of it; every offensive had been stopped just short of the goal, and the soldiers who had been driven back from the Dunker church, the Piper farm, and the edge of Sharpsburg knew perfectly well that their enemies had not been routed. It was only after Lee's army went back to Virginia that the Army of the Potomac began to see that it had gained more than it had lost. Meade probably expressed the general feeling when he wrote, three days after the battle, that the retreat of the Confederates proved that "we had hit them much harder than they had us, and that in reality our battle was a victory."[4]

A victory, indisputably, even if a negative one. Lee had invaded the North with high hopes; he had been compelled to fight along the Antietam, and after the fight he had had to go back into Virginia. At enormous cost the Army of the Potomac had won a strategic victory. The invader had been thrown back; or, if not precisely thrown back, he had been fought to a standstill and then had been allowed to *go* back, his late hosts very glad to see the last of him. However qualified this triumph might be, at least the invasion was over. There would be a new campaign now, and it would take place south of the Potomac.

McClellan was looking ahead to it. A week after the battle, when the last of the dead had been buried, he was making his plans: possess Harper's Ferry with a strong force, then reorganize the army thoroughly, get an abundance of new equipment and supplies, make proper replacements for the fallen generals, get those rookie regiments into better shape, and—all of this done—start south afresh. Privately he was jubilant. He had been cautious at first, writing his wife only that "the general result was in our favor"; but as the days passed his very need for inner reassurance made him see it in brighter colors. He wrote about the stacks of captured battle flags that had been brought to him and told his wife gaily: "You should see my soldiers *now!* You never saw anything like their enthusiasm. It surpassed anything you ever imagined." He had no doubt that his enemies in Washington would keep trying to get rid of him, and they might succeed, but that hardly mattered: "I feel now that this last short campaign is a sufficient legacy for our child, so far as honor is concerned." It seems that at last, as he thought it all over, he could see himself measuring up to some private, invisible yardstick. He wrote rather pathetically—for this was the commander of a great army, not a schoolboy mulling over his part in last week's football game—"Those in whose judgment I rely tell me that I fought the battle splendidly and that it was a masterpiece of art."

Masterpiece of art it assuredly was not: rather, a dreary succession of missed opportunities. Not once had the commanding general put out his hand to pull his battle plan together and to undo the mistakes of his subordinates. The battle had been left to fight itself, and the general was a spectator; and in the end it had been a victory by the narrowest of margins—tactically, a victory only in the sense that the army had fought hard and then had not retreated afterward. Meade had said the most that could be said: we hurt them a little more than they hurt us.

Yet it was finally, and irrevocably, *the* decisive battle of the war, affecting the whole course of American history ever since.

For this stalemated battle—this great whirlwind of flame and torn earth and shaking sound, which seemed to consume everything and to create nothing—brought about the Emancipation Proclamation and put the country on a new course from which there could be no turning back. Here at last was the sounding forth of the bugle that would never call retreat.

All summer Lincoln had been waiting for a victory. Here it was, now: an uncertain victory, looking very much like no victory at all, but for all that, and with all of its imperfections, a victory, the all-important victory which he had to have if the war was to be won. One week later he issued the preliminary Emancipation Proclamation, and the war was transformed.

Like the battle itself, the Proclamation at first seemed an achievement of doubtful value. It was just words, promising much but doing nothing. They were not even bold, straightforward words, it seemed. Perversely, they ordained freedom in precisely those places where the Union armies could not make freedom a fact and left slavery untouched elsewhere. They infuriated all sympathizers with secession—Gideon Welles noted glumly that "this step will band the south together"—and they left the abolitionists unsatisfied. They seemed to be neither hot nor cold, a futile attempt to find a middle course in a struggle which had no middle course—and in the end they had more power than a great army with banners.

Their real effect was first seen afar off, in London, where they gave this war in America a new aspect, so that statesmen found to their surprise that it was something with which they could not interfere. In October the Emperor of France formally proposed that England, France, and Russia step in and bring about a six months' armistice—which, in its practical effect, would mean (and was meant to mean) independence for the Confederacy. Britain's Foreign Minister recommended acceptance of the proposal. But the British Cabinet rejected it, for a pro-Confederate in England now was an apologist for slavery, whether he liked it or not. By mid-January, American Minister Adams was writing in his diary: "It is quite clear that the current is now setting very strongly with us among the body of the people," and a little later Jefferson Davis himself recognized that the chance for intervention was dead and withdrew those famous emissaries, Mason and Slidell. By June, when it seemed in Britain most certain that the Confederacy must win—Hooker had been beaten at Chancellorsville, Lee was north of the border again, the Northern cause had never looked worse—public opinion had completely hardened and recognition was impossible.

In substance, then, the Proclamation meant that Europe was not going to decide how the American Civil War came out. It would be fought out at home.

And it would be fought to the bitter end. The chance for compromise was killed.

Until now there had always been the prospect that sooner or later the war might simply end, with neither side victorious. Reunion, continuation of slavery, some adjustment, perhaps, on the thorny issue of states' rights: the whole body of Northern sentiment on which the Copperhead movement was based had exactly that in mind, and there was plenty of feeling along the same line in the South. But the Proclamation made that impossible. The war had been given a deeper meaning and had become something that could not be adjusted. The deep, tangled issues underneath the war—slavery, the permanence of the Union, the dawning concept that a powerful central government might protect the people's freedom rather than endanger it—all of these, now, must be settled, not evaded; and settled by violence, violence having been unleashed.

It might still be argued that they could far better be settled in some other way, but the argument was no longer relevant. The war now was a war to preserve the Union *and* to end slavery—two causes in one, the combination carrying its own consequences. It could not stop until one side or the other was made incapable of fighting any longer; hence, by the standards of that day, it was going to be an all-out war—hard, ruthless, vicious, with Sheridan carrying devastation across the Shenandoah and Sherman swinging a torch across Georgia and Grant pitilessly grinding two armies to powder so that the Confederacy, if it would not die in any other way, might die of sheer exhaustion. (Exhaustion of spirit, of people, of resources, of culture: a bleeding-white from which the country would be generations recovering.) The war must ultimately go that way henceforward. It had come through its period of uncertainty, the period in which it might lead to anything. Now it could lead only to this. It could no longer be fought on simple enthusiasm like a swords-and-roses romance of knightly legend. From now on it would be all grim.

Which meant, finally, that McClellan's part in it was finished. The men who wanted to be rid of him at all costs—who would even have been glad to see him beaten, because that would give grounds for dismissal—could act against him now, not because he had been beaten but precisely because he had won. His victory meant the last thing on earth he would have wished it to mean: sweeping triumph, not merely for the abolitionists whom he hated and considered traitors, but for the implacable spirit of force that was to take control of the nation's destiny. He had let himself be made a political symbol: symbol of the belief in a limited war for limited objectives, a war consciously aimed at something less than destruction of the Southland's way of life, a war that would not bring about profound alteration in the national government. The battle he won meant that the cause he symbolized was not to prevail, and so the symbol itself would have to vanish.

By one of the great ironies of history, this cause and McClellan himself might have been triumphant if the victory along the Antietam had been complete instead of partial. And a complete victory had been within his grasp, over and over again. Run down the might-have-beens for a moment:

He might have had it if there had been more drive and determination in the forty-eight hours immediately after the finding of the lost order. Later, he might have had it by attacking one day earlier at the Antietam. Still later, he might have had it by co-ordinating his blows so that they came together instead of in succession, by using instead of husbanding the ten thousand fresh troops Longstreet was brooding about, by driving Porter's column into Sharpsburg at the close of the action, or by renewing the battle vigorously the next day. Lastly, all else failing, he might have used his own unique magnetism to evoke in his soldiers a sustained enthusiasm to sweep Lee's army off the smoking ridges and drive it into the river. If, just once, he could have transcended his own limitations, he might have won the kind of victory which would have ended the war in the fall of 1862. A peace made then would not have been an abolitionist's peace. It would have been the kind of peace McClellan wanted.

But those are might-have-beens. McClellan did what he did, not what he can be imagined having done. And because his victory was exactly the kind of victory it was—no bigger and no smaller—his own military career had to end. The battle and what it brought with it left him no room to stand.

McClellan himself seems to have had some dim inkling of this when the Proclamation first came out. The day after it was published he told his wife that it was doubtful if he would remain in service much longer—"the President's late proclamation, the continuation of Stanton and Halleck in office, render it almost impossible for me to retain my commission and self-respect at the same time." A fort-night later he told her how a friend had been urging him that "it is my duty to submit to the President's proclamation and quietly con-tinue doing my duty as a soldier"; he was not sure that this advice was sound, but he would at least think it over very fully. What held him in the service seems to have been a deep, mystic feeling that he and the army had become part of each other. To a member of his staff, about this time, he said: "The Army of the Potomac is my army as much as any army ever belonged to the man that created it. We have grown together and fought together. We are wedded and should not be separated."[5]

Lincoln came up early in October to talk to McClellan and to review the troops. The dead men were all underground by now, and the review seems to have been successful, as such things go, although the troops were somewhat subdued: President and general together did not quite draw the spate of cheers and applause that had come on former occasions. One veteran wrote that Lincoln was melancholy: "He rode around every battalion and seemed much worn and dis-tressed and to be looking for those who were gone"—who were, heaven knows, numerous enough to distress a much less sensitive person.[6] McClellan, who was subtle enough in most ways although never subtle enough to understand Lincoln, found the President in good spirits. Their conversation would seem to have had a vaguely unreal quality. McClellan recorded that "I urged him to follow a conservative course, and supposed from the tenor of his conversation that he would do so"—a conservative course, in the jargon of that day, meaning one which would go directly counter to everything said or implied by the Emancipation Proclamation—and this two weeks after the paper had been signed and published.

The melancholy which a soldier thought he saw in the President was genuine enough. Lincoln was at grips with the problem of just whose army it was that he had been reviewing. Every general always says "my army" in ordinary speech. It is no more than easy shorthand for "the army which I am now commanding." Yet when McClellan said it, it seemed to mean more than that. Lincoln dispiritedly told a friend just after this review that it was not the Army of the Potomac he had been looking at—it was "General McClellan's bodyguard." From the record it looked as if that might be the case. The amazing, hysterical transformation that had taken place on the Virginia hillsides after the second battle of Bull Run meant that the men had for this general a devotion which they gave no other man; it might easily mean that he was literally irreplaceable. That devotion had compelled the administration to reinstate McClellan, much against its will; at that point he had been the only man alive who could turn the mob of disorganized soldiers into an army again. That he had done it, with his own peculiar magic, events proved. The men had instantaneously pulled themselves up from the depths of complete demoralization when he came back to them, and they had come up here to Sharpsburg to fight as they had never fought before. He had made this army, he spoke of it as "my army," and the men themselves seemed to feel exactly the same way about it. They were boys who had gone out blithely to fight a picture-book war, victims of a nationwide innocence, filled with a boyish yearning for impossible romance and adventure; nothing was left of that early spirit now except their love for McClellan. He remained as the justification of their early hopes, their last defense against complete disillusionment. Could the war go on if he were taken away? And yet could it be fought, in the only way now remaining, if he stayed?

For a time the wheel remained at dead center, and if Lincoln came to any final conclusion during his visit he kept it to himself. He went back to Washington, and McClellan busied himself with the job of reorganization. He needed much new equipment and he was not getting it fast enough; he argued endlessly with Halleck and the supply people in Washington, refusing to move until he felt the army was fully ready, insisting again that he must be heavily reinforced because Lee still outnumbered him. Lincoln prodded him ineffectually to get him to advance; lost his patience once, and when McClellan reported his cavalry horses worn out asked sarcastically just what his cavalry had been doing lately that would tire anybody's horses. Once Halleck sent peremptory orders, in Lincoln's name, to cross the river. Mc-Clellan ignored them; and while he was continuing to re-equip and reorganize, Jeb Stuart got north of the river with his cavalry and rode gaily clear around the army, getting back unhurt, while Federal detachments ran all over western Maryland looking for him. The bickering became sharper, much of it due to the old two-way mis-understanding—Washington's inability to see the need for proper or-ganization and supply, and McClellan's own inability to realize that the enemy was in worse shape than himself and needed to be crowded a bit. But at last, seven weeks after the battle, the great army slipped down the river, crossed to the Virginia side, and started south.

McClellan seems to have planned this campaign intelligently. He took his army down the eastern side of the Blue Ridge, evidently aiming to box Lee up in such a way that Lee would have to come out and fight at a disadvantage, and there is some reason to believe that he might have had the Rebel army in a bad spot had he been allowed to continue. But his number was up. It was a different war now, and he was due to go out of it, and it was really only a question of time. Lincoln appears to have made up his mind that he would re-move him if he let Lee get east of the Blue Ridge and stand in his path to Richmond; and when Lee got his army—or part of it, at any rate—to Culpeper Courthouse ahead of McClellan, that pulled the trigger. But that was only the immediate excuse. If it had not been that it would have been something else. Whenever the actual decision was made, it had been in the cards for weeks. So . . .

November 7, near midnight; a snowy night, with a cold wind out of the mountains, and everybody huddled under shelter; McClellan in his headquarters tent, writing a letter to his wife. A special train had come down from Washington that afternoon, and a War De-partment functionary had left it and had ridden several miles in a snowstorm, not to see the commanding general, but to call on Gen-eral Burnside. This much McClellan knew, and he had a fair idea what it meant, but he said nothing and stayed in his tent, his staff all asleep. Finally there came a knock on his tent pole, and on his in-vitation two men came in—Burnside, looking very troubled and

embarrassed, and the War Department's General Buckingham, powdered snow lying in the folds of his neat, unweathered uniform. Mc-
Clellan was cordial and seemed unworried; sat them down and
chatted pleasantly about this and that, quite as if a midnight call like
this were an everyday occurrence. Buckingham at last remarked that
maybe the general had better know what they were there for, and
handed over the papers. Letter to McClellan from Halleck—"you
will immediately turn over your command to Maj.-Gen. Burnside
and repair to Trenton, N.J. [McClellan's home], for further orders";
and an order from the adjutant general setting forth that "by direction
of the President of the United States" the command of the army was
passing from McClellan to Burnside.

McClellan read them, seeming quite unruffled—apparently the man
could take it when he had to—and looked up at Burnside with a
little smile. "Well, Burnside, I turn the command over to you." Almost tearfully, painfully conscious that he was not qualified to command the army, Burnside begged him to delay the transfer for at least
a day or two so that Burnside might be brought up to date on troop
movements, intelligence reports, campaign plans, and the like. Mc-
Clellan agreed and the visitors left, and McClellan went back to the
letter he was writing. He gave his wife the news and added: "Alas
for my poor country! I know in my inmost heart she never had a truer
servant."

True servant or false, it was all one now, and his part was finished.
There were a couple of days of earnest activity at headquarters while
Burnside was fitting his own staff into place—something of a scramble for assignments going on, with many jobs open for new men and
with the men who were being displaced trying to find suitable billets,
every officer who had a wire to pull yanking on it for all he was
worth. Burnside conscientiously went to work to study the intricate
web of facts, pending orders, and strategic plans which he was in-
heriting. Evidently they were just too much for him; he hesitated for a
time, and all army movements were halted, while off to the south
Lee's officers wondered briefly why the Yankees had stopped moving
just when they seemed to be maneuvering effectively. Then Burnside
canceled everything and decreed that the army should move east. It
is hard to tell just what he had in mind, the sure professional touch
at GHQ having departed with his arrival, but he seems to have had

some notion of slipping unobserved around the Confederates' right flank—the one maneuver which no Federal general ever succeeded in accomplishing against Robert E. Lee. So the army pulled itself together and made ready to move.

Meanwhile, one little ceremony remained: to say good-by to General McClellan. On November 10, the order of removal having been published, McClellan rode through the camps around Warrenton, and for the last time the fighting men raised their shouts to the wintry sky as the jaunty little man on the great black horse came riding down the lines.

There they were, brigade after brigade, desperately yelling their farewell: the men who had been a loose militia muster until he made them an army, the men who had found pride and strength in being soldiers because it was he who taught them soldiering, the men who, for all their hard knowledge of battle, could still see a shine and a color in war as long as he led them. They had struggled in the Chickahominy swamps and sweltered in the noisome camp at Harrison's Landing, they had gone laughing under the flags at Frederick and had stormed through the smoke to the Dunker church, and he was part of it all; he had lived through those things with them and somehow had given them meaning, so that endurance and hope had been easier because of him. And now he was going away and they would never see him again, and if they were to have endurance and hope they would have to find them for themselves because no one at the top was going to provide them any more.

McClellan passed by the long ranks, and the cheers went up as long as his figure was in sight; and in his wake there rang out yells of "Send him back! Send him back!" Here and there a regiment threw down its arms, swearing angrily, saying it would fight no more. One general was heard (or was reported to have been heard) to call out: "Lead us to Washington, General—we'll follow you!" He came down the Centreville pike at last—that already historic road of battle, the road that had led Pope and McDowell to Bull Run, the road along which the Iron Brigade had found its first experience of combat—and Sumner's corps was lined up on one side of the road, Porter's corps on the other. (Porter himself was doomed now, a sure sacrifice to the vindictive charges filed by Pope; only with McClellan in command could he be protected, and the same officer who brought down the orders relieving McClellan had brought other orders relieving Porter. He was to be court-martialed and cashiered before the winter ended.) These two corps, where affection for McClellan ran higher than anywhere else in the army, stood in long ranks facing the roadway, batteries of field artillery drawn up here and there in the intervals between brigades. They snapped to present arms as the general came up, and then the rigid rows of muskets jerked all askew as the men began to yell, and there was a great cry all along the road.

He passed by and went out of sight, and came finally to the railroad station, where a guard of two thousand men had been drawn up for a final salute. McClellan got on the special train, the guns boomed out—and then the men broke ranks, swarmed about the car, uncoupled it, swore that he should not leave them. McClellan came out on the rear platform and raised his hand, and they all fell silent.

"Stand by General Burnside as you have stood by me, and all will be well," he said. The demonstration stopped. Silently the men recoupled the car, the conductor waved a signal to the engineer, and the train clanked out of the station. A veteran recorded: "When the chief passed out of sight, the romance of war was over for the Army of the Potomac."[7]

Washington seems to have breathed a collective sigh of relief when he went. There had been fears that the army would mutiny—fears that seemed well grounded, if the loose talk that had been flying around army headquarters was listened to. Young Lieutenant Wilson noted that staff officers had been drinking heavily and had been "talking both loudly and disloyally," and there was a good deal of campfire chatter to the effect that the army ought to "change front on Washington," oust the government, and put McClellan in control of civil and military affairs alike. But this was just staff talk, after all, and it reflected the hysteria of individuals rather than the temper of the soldiers. The men who yelled and wept and threw down muskets were expressing grief and anger, but it does not appear to have entered their heads that the order from Washington might actually be disobeyed by one hundred thousand trained men who had weapons in their hands. Washington need not have worried; they just were not that kind of army.

Indeed, there were mixed feelings among the men here and there. In Burnside's IX Corps the change was actually welcomed; those men had not served under McClellan very long, they did not yet realize how Burnside had misused and wasted them on the hills southeast of Sharpsburg, and they felt that their likable corps commander should do very well indeed at the head of the army. In the New England regiments, where abolitionists were numerous, there was very little grumbling. Some soldiers comforted themselves with a tale that McClellan was really being called back to Washington to replace Halleck. And there were a few men who had seen enough of the final thinness of the Rebel lines at the Antietam to feel that McClellan had failed them there: men who recorded that after that battle the army's cheers for the general had not quite had the warmth they had had before.[8]

It was left for a campfire group in the 17th Michigan to provide the characteristic soldier's comment. These men discussed pros and cons that evening. They were profoundly depressed—the regiment had fewer than three hundred men now, and it had left Detroit in August a thousand strong; the boys had learned a lot these last three months. They suspected that the worst would come of this change in generals, and now that they thought about it they concluded that none of their generals really amounted to very much. So, said their historian, they finally agreed that Lincoln ought to retire all of the generals "and select men from the ranks who will serve without pay, lead the army against Lee, strike him hard, and follow him until he fails to come to time." Having expressed this crude front-line wisdom, they grinned ruefully, wagged their heads, and went off through the sleety rain to their pup tents.[9]

And presently the army began to move again; not down the line of the railroad, where McClellan's plan would have taken it, but southeast along the Rappahannock toward Fredericksburg, where Burnside wanted to go. The bugle calls spattered through the camps, wagons were loaded, and regiment after regiment swung into column and marched out into the muddy road. The veteran who put it down on paper was right: the romance was gone from the war now. They had left it behind them, with the lemonade and fried chicken of the ladies' committees at the railway stations, with the brightness of the uniforms that had never known mud or smoke, with the lighthearted inconsequence of those early days when it seemed as if the war might be more than half a lark, when the sky was bright with wonder and the chance of death was only a challenge to set vibrant nerves tingling.

The romance had gone—inevitably, because the war itself was not romantic. The young soldiers were veterans at last. They were not McClellan's army any longer, and they never could be again; they were Lincoln's army now, or the country's, or the army of some inscrutable tide that was flowing down the century to change everything they were used to and break the way for something unimaginable. They had been that army all along, as a matter of fact, and now the war was something that could not be fought on tag ends of youthful hero worship. Now it was going to be ugliness and dirt and pain and death, with the good men getting all the worst of it while the shirkers went straggling off to safety; and the men knew it, and put their feet on the Virginia road to go where it might lead them.

The road ahead was long, and it was to lead them to worse than they had had: to Fredericksburg and Chancellorsville, to Gettysburg and the Wilderness, to the sickening meadows at Cold Harbor and the squalid trenches around Petersburg; to the ultimate misery and bleak wisdom that lie at the end of all the roads of war. They were on their own now, fighting for something they had not been asked about; they had made the victory through which the war had been given its lasting meaning, and now they would have to go on to the end of it, marching doggedly to the dark fields where they would be called on to give the last full measure of a devotion which they themselves could never understand or define.

One after another, flags cased under a gray sky, the regiments moved out of the camp grounds and took to the road for Fredericksburg. The 24th New Jersey kept the cadence a little while after it got on the road, instead of lapsing at once into route step, and struck up a little ditty which it had composed to the tune of the John Brown song:

> *"We'll soon light our fires on the Rappahannock shore;*
> *We'll soon light our fires on the Rappahannock shore;*
> *And tell Father Abraham he needn't call for more—*
> *While we go marching on."*

Down the road they went, and the song died away, and the army trudged off to the east.

Bibliography

The principal source regarding troop movements, battle orders, etc., is of course that voluminous and invaluable set of volumes, *The War of the Rebellion: A Compilation of the Official Records of the Union and Confederate Armies* (Washington: Government Printing Office, 1902). In addition, the following works were consulted:

BOOKS DEALING WITH THE WAR AS A WHOLE, AND WITH ITS POLITICAL AND MILITARY BACKGROUND

Abraham Lincoln: The War Years, by Carl Sandburg. 4 vols. New York, 1939.

Abraham Lincoln and Men of War Times, by Alexander K. McClure. Philadelphia, 1892.

Battles and Leaders of the Civil War. Grant-Lee edition, 4 vols. New York, 1884–87.

Campaigns of the Army of the Potomac, by William Swinton. New York, 1866.

The Diary of Gideon Welles. 3 vols. Boston & New York, 1911.

The Diary of a Public Man, with Prefatory Notes by F. Lauriston Bullard. Rutgers, 1946.

The Hidden Civil War: The Story of the Copperheads, by Wood Gray. New York, 1942.

History of the Civil War, by James Ford Rhodes. 1-vol. edition. New York, 1917.

Lincoln's War Cabinet, by Burton J. Hendrick. Boston, 1946.

The Movement for Peace without Victory during the Civil War, by Elbert J. Benton. Publication No. 99 of the Western Reserve Historical Society, Cleveland, 1918.

Pictorial History of the Civil War, by Benton J. Lossing. 3 vols. Philadelphia, 1886.

Photographic History of the Civil War, edited by Francis Trevelyan Miller. 10 vols. New York, 1911.

The Rebellion Record, edited by Frank Moore. 12 vols. New York, 1862–71.

AUTOBIOGRAPHIES, BIOGRAPHICAL STUDIES, ETC.

Advance and Retreat, by John B. Hood. New Orleans, 1880.

Autobiography of Oliver Otis Howard. 2 vols. New York, 1907.

Correspondence of John Sedgwick, Major General. 2 vols. Privately printed, DeVinne Press, 1902.

Days and Events: 1860–1866, by Colonel Thomas L. Livermore. Boston, 1920.

Four Years with the Army of the Potomac, by Brevet Major General Regis de Trobriand. Translated by George K. Dauchy. Boston, 1889.

From Bull Run to Chancellorsville, by Brevet Major General Newton Martin Curtis. New York, 1906.

General Hancock, by Brevet Brigadier General Francis A. Walker. New York, 1894.

General Philip Kearny, Battle Soldier of Five Wars, by Thomas Kearny. New York, 1937.

Grant and Lee: A Study in Personality and Generalship, by Major General J. F. C. Fuller. New York, 1933.

Jeb Stuart, by John W. Thomason, Jr. New York, 1930.

The Life and Letters of George Gordon Meade, by Colonel George Meade. 2 vols. New York, 1913.

Life and Letters of Wilder Dwight, Lieutenant Colonel, 2nd Massachusetts Infantry. Boston, 1868.

Life of General George Gordon Meade, by Richard Meade Bache. Philadelphia, 1897.

Lee's Lieutenants, by Douglas Southall Freeman. 3 vols. New York, 1942.

Major General Hiram G. Berry, by Edward K. Gould. Portland, Me., 1899.

McClellan's Own Story, by Major General George B. McClellan. New York, 1887.

Meade's Headquarters, 1863–65, by Colonel Theodore Lyman. Boston, 1922.

Military Reminiscences of the Civil War, by Jacob Dolson Cox. 2 vols. New York, 1900.

Personal Recollections of the Civil War, by Brigadier General John Gibbon. New York, 1928.

The Pinkertons: A Detective Dynasty, by Richard Wilmer Rowan. Boston, 1931.

Reminiscences of General Herman Haupt. Milwaukee, 1901.

Reminiscences of the Civil War, by General John B. Gordon. New York, 1905.

R. E. Lee: A Biography, by Douglas Southall Freeman. 4 vols. New York, 1934.

Robert E. Lee, the Soldier, by Major General Sir Frederick Maurice. Boston, 1925.

Selections from the Letters and Diaries of Brevet Brigadier General Willoughby Babcock, by Willoughby Babcock, Jr. New York, 1922.

The Spy of the Rebellion: Being a True History of the Spy System of the United States Army during the Late Rebellion, by Allan Pinkerton. New York, 1883.

Stonewall Jackson, by Colonel G. F. R. Henderson. London & New York, 1936.

Under the Old Flag, by Major General James Harrison Wilson. 2 vols. New York, 1912.

SOLDIERS' REMINISCENCES, REGIMENTAL HISTORIES, ETC.

Awhile with the Blue, by Benjamin Borton. Passaic, N.J., 1898.

The Bivouac and the Battlefield: or, Campaign Sketches in Virginia and Maryland, by Captain George Freeman Noyes. New York, 1863.

A Brief History of the 28th Regiment New York State Volunteers, by C. W. Boyce. Buffalo, 1896.

The Diary of an Enlisted Man, by Lawrence Van Alstyne. New Haven, 1910.

The Diary of a Line Officer, by Captain Augustus C. Brown. New York, 1906.

The Diary of a Young Officer, by Brevet Major Joseph Marshall Favill, 57th New York. Chicago, 1909.

A Duryée Zouave, by Thomas P. Southwick. Privately printed. New York, 1930.

Following the Greek Cross: or, Memories of the 6th Army Corps, by Brevet Brigadier General Thomas W. Hyde. Boston, 1894.

Four Years Campaigning in the Army of the Potomac, by Daniel G. Crotty. Grand Rapids, 1874.

Forty-six Months with the 4th Rhode Island Volunteers, by Corporal George H. Allen. Providence, 1887.

Hardtack and Coffee, by John D. Billings. Boston, 1887.

A History of the "Bucktails," by O. R. Howard Thomson and William H. Rauch. Philadelphia, 1906.

History of Duryée's Brigade, by Franklin B. Hough. Albany, 1864.

A History of the 11th Regiment Ohio Volunteer Infantry, compiled from the Official Records by Horton and Teverbaugh, Members of the Regiment. Dayton, 1866.

A History of the 5th Regiment New Hampshire Volunteers, by William Child. Bristol, N.H., 1893.

History of the 51st Regiment of Pennsylvania Volunteers, by Thomas H. Parker. Philadelphia, 1869.

History of the First Brigade New Jersey Volunteers, by Camille Baquet. Trenton, 1910.

History of the First Regiment Minnesota Volunteer Infantry, by R. I. Holcombe. Stillwater, Minn., 1916.

History of the 40th (Mozart) Regiment, by Fred C. Floyd. Boston, 1909.

History of the 45th Regiment Pennsylvania Veteran Volunteer Infantry, by Allen D. Albert. Williamsport, Pa., 1912.

History of the 100th Regiment of New York State Volunteers, by George H. Stowits. Buffalo, 1870.

History of the Second Army Corps, by Brevet Brigadier General Francis A. Walker. New York, 1886.

History of the 16th Connecticut Volunteers, by B. F. Blakeslee. Hartford, 1875.

History of the 10th Massachusetts Battery, by John D. Billings. Boston, 1881.

History of the 3rd Indiana Cavalry, by W. N. Pickerell. Indianapolis, 1906.

History of the 3rd Regiment of Wisconsin Veteran Volunteer Infantry, by Edwin E. Bryant. Madison, Wis., 1891.

History of the 12th Massachusetts Volunteers, by Lieutenant Colonel Benjamin F. Cook. Boston, 1882.

The History of a Volunteer Regiment, by Gouverneur Morris. New York, 1891.

I Rode with Stonewall, by Henry Kyd Douglas. Chapel Hill, 1940.

The Irish Brigade and Its Campaigns, by Captain D. P. Conyngham. New York, 1867.

Letters of a War Correspondent, by Charles A. Page. Boston, 1899.

A Military History of the 8th Ohio Volunteer Infantry, by Franklin Sawyer. Cleveland, 1881.

Music on the March, by Frank Rauscher. Philadelphia, 1892.

Musket and Sword, by Edwin C. Bennett. Boston, 1900.

Notes of a Staff Officer of Our First New Jersey Brigade on the Seven Days Battle on the Peninsula, 1862, by E. Burd Grubb. Moorestown, N.J., 1910.

Opdyke Tigers: 125th Ohio Volunteer Infantry, by Charles T. Clark. Columbus, 1895.

Personal Recollections of the Civil War, by James Madison Stone. Boston, 1918.

Recollections of a Boy Member of Co. I, 14th Maine Volunteers, by Ira B. Gardner. Lewiston, Me., 1902.

Recollections of the Civil War, by Mason Whiting Tyler. New York, 1912.

Recollections of a Private, by Warren Lee Goss. New York, 1890.

Reminiscences of the Civil War, by Theodore M. Nagle. Erie, Pa., 1903.

Reminiscences of the 19th Massachusetts Regiment, by Captain John G. B. Adams. Boston, 1899.

The Road to Richmond: Civil War Memoirs of Major Abner R. Small, edited by Harold Adams Small. Berkeley, Calif., 1939.

Service with the 6th Wisconsin Volunteers, by Brevet Brigadier General Rufus R. Dawes. Marietta, O., 1890.

The Seventh Regiment: A Record, by Major George L. Wood. New York, 1865.

A Sketch of the 8th New York Cavalry, by Henry Norton. Norwich, N.Y., 1888.

A Soldier's Diary: The Story of a Volunteer, by David Lane. Privately printed, 1905.

The Story of the 15th Regiment Massachusetts Volunteer Infantry in the Civil War, by Andrew E. Ford. Clinton, Mass., 1898.

Three Years in the Army of the Potomac, by Henry N. Blake. Boston, 1865.

The 20th Regiment of Massachusetts Volunteer Infantry, by Lieutenant Colonel George A. Bruce. Boston, 1906.

The 27th Indiana Volunteer Infantry in the War of the Rebellion, by a Member of Company C. Indianapolis, 1899.

The "Ulster Guard" and the War of the Rebellion, by Theodore B. Gates. New York, 1879.

Under Five Commanders, by Jacob H. Cole. Paterson, N.J., 1907.

"War Music and War Psychology in the Civil War," by James Stone. *Journal of Abnormal and Social Psychology,* Vol. 36, No. 4, October 1941.

War Years with Jeb Stuart, by Lieutenant Colonel W. W. Blackford. New York, 1945.

BOOKS RELATING TO SPECIFIC BATTLES AND
CAMPAIGNS, MILITARY TACTICS AND WEAPONS, ETC.

The Antietam and Fredericksburg, by Brevet Brigadier General Francis Winthrop Palfrey. New York, 1882.

The Army of Northern Virginia in 1862, by Lieutenant Colonel William Allan. Boston, 1892.

The Army under Pope, by John C. Ropes. New York, 1881.

Atlas of the Battlefield of Antietam. Prepared by the Antietam Battlefield Board. Published by the War Department, 1904.

Camp and Outpost Duty for Infantry, by Brigadier General Daniel Butterfield. New York, 1862.

The Campaign in Maryland and Virginia, by Lieutenant E. W. Sheppard of the 10th Battalion, Manchester Regiment. New York & London, 1911.

Campaigns in Virginia. Vols. I and XIV, *Papers of the Military Historical Society of Massachusetts,* edited by Theodore Dwight. Boston, 1895.

General John Sedgwick: An Address, by Adjutant General Martin T. McMahon, VI Army Corps, before the Vermont Officers Reunion Society at Montpelier, Vt., Nov. 11, 1880.

The Generalship of Ulysses S. Grant, by Colonel J. F. C. Fuller. New York, 1929.

A History of the United States Navy, by Edgar Stanton Maclay. 3 vols. New York, 1898.

History of the Campaign of the Army of Virginia, by Brevet Brigadier General George H. Gordon. Boston, 1880.

In Memoriam: George Sears Greene. Published by authority of the State of New York under supervision of the New York Monuments Commission, 1909.

Indiana at Antietam. Report of the Indiana Antietam Monument Commission. Indianapolis, 1912.

Joseph K. F. Mansfield: A Narrative of Events Connected with His Mortal Wounding, by John Mead Gould. Portland, Me., 1895.

The Long Arm of Lee, by Jennings C. Wise. 2 vols. Lynchburg, Va., 1915.

Manual of Instruction for the Volunteers and Militia of the United States, by Major William Gilham. Philadelphia, 1861.

New York at Antietam. Published by the New York Monuments Commission. Albany, 1923.

Papers of the Kansas Commandery, Military Order of the Loyal Legion of the United States. 1894.

Papers Read before the Missouri Commandery, Military Order of the Loyal Legion of the United States. St. Louis, 1887.

The Peninsula: McClellan's Campaigns of 1862, by Major General Alex S. Webb. New York, 1885.

Pennsylvania at Antietam. Report of the Antietam Battlefield Memorial Commission of Pennsylvania. Harrisburg, 1906.

Record of Dedicatory Ceremonies held on the Battlefield of Manassas, or Second Bull Run . . . under Auspices of the Veterans Association of the 5th Regiment New York Volunteer Infantry.

Regimental Losses in the American Civil War, by Lieutenant Colonel William F. Fox. Albany, 1889.

Report of Major General George B. McClellan, from July 26, 1861, to Nov. 7, 1862. Washington: Government Printing Office, 1864.

Rifle and Light Infantry Tactics, by Brevet Lieutenant Colonel William J. Hardee. Philadelphia, 1855.

The Second Admiral: A Life of David Dixon Porter, by Richard S. West. New York, 1937.

The War of Secession, 1861–62, by Major G. W. Redway. London & New York, 1910.

Notes

The general bibliography lists all of the works which were consulted in the preparation of this text. No attempt has been made to cite the authority for every statement of fact. It has seemed advisable, however, to list the sources for direct quotations and to give at least a general indication of the works which have been principally drawn on for each chapter. This material is as follows:

CHAPTER ONE

1. There Was Talk of Treason
A full account of the railroad man's meeting with McClellan, his dealings with Hooker, Sturgis, and Stanton, and the problems which were visited on him in connection with the second battle of Bull Run is to be found in General Herman Haupt's *Reminiscences*. Use has also been made of material in the *Official Records*, Series I, Volume XII, Part 3, and of McClellan's autobiography. In his *Military Reminiscences*, General Jacob Cox shows what the second defeat at Bull Run looked like from the fortified lines near Alexandria. Good sketches of Hancock appear in the works cited under Footnote 3.
Specific references are:
1. *Reminiscences of General Herman Haupt.*
2. Ibid.
3. *History of the Second Army Corps*, by Brevet Brigadier General Francis A. Walker. See also the same author's *General Hancock; Following the Greek Cross*, by Brevet Brigadier General Thomas W. Hyde; *Meade's Headquarters*, by Colonel Theodore Lyman, and Brevet Major Joseph M. Favill's *Diary of a Young Officer.*
4. Haupt's *Reminiscences.*
5. *Military Reminiscences of the Civil War*, by Jacob D. Cox.

2. We Were Never Again Eager
The innocent, romantic spirit in which young men went off to war in 1861

(and which they shed quite as rapidly as need be) is reflected in any number of the accounts written by participants. Sometimes the account expresses the writer's individual point of view, as in the case of *The Bivouac and the Battlefield,* by Captain George Freeman Noyes, who wrote his book while the war was still going on—and who, being a staff officer, seems to have retained his innocence a trifle longer than most. Sometimes it is revealed in the accounts of the things green officers and men did as they struggled to turn themselves into soldiers. Two appealing pictures of the formation of the famous Black Hat Brigade are available—one in the memoirs of its first commander, General John Gibbon, and one in the regimental history of one of its components, the 6th Wisconsin Infantry.

Specific references are:

1. *Three Years in the Army of the Potomac,* by Henry N. Blake; *Following the Greek Cross,* and *The Diary of an Enlisted Man,* by Lawrence Van Alstyne.

2. *The Bivouac and the Battlefield.*

3. *Personal Recollections of the Civil War,* by Brigadier General John Gibbon. (A book well worth reading; a likable and admirable soldier unconsciously reveals himself in it.)

4. For the foregoing incidents, see *Service with the 6th Wisconsin Volunteers,* by Brevet Brigadier General Rufus R. Dawes.

5. *War Years with Jeb Stuart,* by Lieutenant Colonel W. W. Blackford.

This amazing fight which introduced the Black Hat Brigade to actual combat is of course described briefly in all standard accounts of the second battle of Bull Run. Most of the details in the text are from General Gibbon and General Dawes.

3. You Must Never Be Frightened

Federal reports of the second battle of Bull Run are to be found in the *Official Records,* Series I, Volume XII, Part 2. Running accounts of the battle from the Federal viewpoint are contained in General George H. Gordon's *History of the Campaign of the Army of Virginia* and in *The Army under Pope,* by John C. Ropes. For the Confederate side, see Douglas Southall Freeman's exhaustive accounts in his *R. E. Lee* and *Lee's Lieutenants,* and Colonel G. F. R. Henderson's *Stonewall Jackson.* General Pope's curious special pleading about the battle is in Volume II, Part 2, of *Battles and Leaders of the Civil War.*

Specific references are:

1. *The Bivouac and the Battlefield.*

2. *Under the Old Flag,* by Major General James Harrison Wilson.

3. A good study of that extremely fascinating character, Kearny, is contained in *General Philip Kearny: Battle Soldier of Five Wars,* by Thomas Kearny, from which the quotations in this paragraph are taken.

4. *Four Years Campaigning in the Army of the Potomac,* by Daniel G. Crotty.

5. *Service with the 6th Wisconsin Volunteers.*

6. Ibid.

7. *A Duryée Zouave,* by Thomas P. Southwick.

8. *History of the 12th Massachusetts Volunteers,* by Lieutenant Colonel Benjamin F. Cook.

9. *Personal Recollections of the Civil War,* by General Gibbon.

10. *General Philip Kearny.*

4. Man on a Black Horse

There are innumerable accounts of the disorder and despair attending the retreat from the field of Second Bull Run. One of the most detailed is in General Regis de Trobriand's fascinating *Four Years with the Army of the Potomac*. See also Charles A. Page's *Letters of a War Correspondent*, General Oliver Otis Howard's autobiography, the second volume of *Battles and Leaders*, and any number of regimental histories. The soldiers' odd distrust of General McDowell also crops out in many of the regimental histories.

Specific references are:

1. "Personal Experience under Gen. McClellan," by Brigadier General Henry Seymour Hall, from *Papers of the Kansas Commandery, Military Order of the Loyal Legion of the United States*.

2. For the preceding quotations, see *Three Years in the Army of the Potomac*, by Henry N. Blake; *History of the 3rd Regiment of Wisconsin Veteran Volunteer Infantry*, by Edwin E. Bryant; *History of the 12th Massachusetts Volunteers*, and *Service with the 6th Wisconsin Volunteers*. There is a good discussion of the soldiers' antagonism toward McDowell and Pope in General Cox's *Military Reminiscences*.

3. This quotation, and the ones in the immediately preceding paragraphs, are from General de Trobriand's book mentioned above.

4. *Autobiography of Oliver Otis Howard*.

5. *Military Reminiscences* of General Cox.

6. *Personal Recollections* of General Gibbon.

7. Articles by Captain William H. Powell and George Kimball in *Battles and Leaders*, Vol. II, Part 2.

8. *Following the Greek Cross*.

CHAPTER TWO

1. A Great Work in My Hands

No bit of Civil War literature is much more interesting than *McClellan's Own Story*—that oddly organized autobiography which tells so much more about its author than the author can possibly have dreamed. The quotations from McClellan in this chapter are taken from that work, and it has hardly seemed necessary to clutter up the text with footnotes identifying each quotation.

Specific references are:

1. For a good account of McClellan's Ohio experience, see General Cox in Vol. I, Part 1, of *Battles and Leaders*.

2. Ibid.

3. *Under the Old Flag*.

4. *Selections from the Letters and Diaries of Brevet Brigadier General Willoughby Babcock*.

5. *Three Years in the Army of the Potomac*.

6. *Reminiscences of the 19th Massachusetts Regiment*, by Captain John G. B. Adams.

7. *Military Reminiscences* of General Cox.

2. Aye, Deem Us Proud

Since it was an unimportant engagement in a military sense, Ball's Bluff gets little space in most histories of the war. There is a good account in Volume II,

Part 2, of *Battles and Leaders,* and the histories of the 15th and 20th Massachusetts regiments give interesting details. Colonel Baker is described in Volume I of Carl Sandburg's *Abraham Lincoln: The War Years.*

Specific references are:

1. *The Story of the 15th Regiment Massachusetts Volunteer Infantry in the Civil War,* by Andrew E. Ford.

2. *Personal Recollections of the Civil War,* by James Madison Stone.

3. *Four Years with the Army of the Potomac.*

4. *History of the First Regiment Minnesota Volunteer Infantry,* by R. I. Holcombe.

5. *The 20th Regiment of Massachusetts Volunteer Infantry,* by Lieutenant Colonel George A. Bruce.

6. *The Story of the 15th Regiment Massachusetts Volunteer Infantry.*

7. For a summary of this strange case, see "Ball's Bluff and the Arrest of General Stone," by Richard B. Irwin, in *Battles and Leaders,* Volume II, Part 1.

3. I Do Not Intend to Be Sacrificed

It is one of the oddities of Civil War history that General McClellan's handling of his purely military problems cannot be understood unless the purely political problems of President, Cabinet, and Congress are understood also. Along with the military histories, it is necessary to consult such books as Sandburg's *Abraham Lincoln,* whose rambling, discursive, all-inclusive account of the currents that swirled about Lincoln makes clear so much that McClellan never understood at all. *Lincoln's War Cabinet,* by Burton J. Hendrick, sheds a good oblique light on the situation, while books by such contemporaries as Gideon Welles and Alexander K. McClure are invaluable. Again, the McClellan quotations in this chapter are from *McClellan's Own Story.*

Specific references are:

1. *The Diary of a Public Man,* with Prefatory Notes by F. Lauriston Bullard.

2. Scott's letters are found in *Battles and Leaders,* Volume II, Part 1.

3. See Volume II of *A History of the United States Navy,* by Edgar Stanton Maclay, and *The Second Admiral: A Life of David Dixon Porter,* by Richard S. West.

4. Nothing in Douglas Southall Freeman's monumental biography of Lee is much more significant than its picture of Lee's great tact and depth of understanding in his handling of a political problem which was, potentially, quite as explosive as the one which confronted McClellan. It was a problem which was altogether too much for as able a soldier as General Joseph E. Johnston.

5. *Following the Greek Cross.*

CHAPTER THREE

1. But You Must Act

The argument over the rights and wrongs of the administration's interference with McClellan's peninsular campaign will not end, probably, until the Civil War itself drops out of discussion. Where certainty is impossible, about the most that can be done is to try to see *why* the administration did the things McClellan complained of so bitterly. A very good detailed analysis of the way in which McClellan laid himself open to the charge of failing to protect Washington adequately is found in *Campaigns in Virginia,* Volume I, *Papers of the*

Military Historical Society of Massachusetts. The growth of the misunderstanding is traced in two nearly contemporaneous works—William Swinton's *Campaigns of the Army of the Potomac,* and Benton J. Lossing's *Pictorial History of the Civil War.* See also *The Peninsula: McClellan's Campaigns of 1862,* by Major General Alexander S. Webb.

Specific references are:

1. *The Rebellion Record,* edited by Frank Moore.

2. For an interesting examination of this point, see Alexander K. McClure, *Abraham Lincoln and Men of War Times,* pp. 221–22.

3. Two good discussions of this savage little fight and its far-reaching effects are in Freeman's *Lee's Lieutenants,* Vol. I, and Henderson's *Stonewall Jackson.*

4. *Following the Greek Cross.*

2. The Voice of Caution

The reader who cares to see a complete account of McClellan's espionage and intelligence system in operation can do no better than read *The Spy of the Rebellion: Being a True History of the Spy System of the United States Army during the Late Rebellion,* by Allan Pinkerton. A good analysis of the troubles his faulty reports got McClellan into is to be found in General Cox's *Military Reminiscences.* Pinkerton's reports appear in the *Official Records,* Series I, Vol. XI, Part 1, pp. 268–70.

Specific references are:

1. *General Philip Kearny.*

2. *A Duryée Zouave.*

3. *History of the First Brigade New Jersey Volunteers,* by Camille Baquet.

4. *Following the Greek Cross.*

5. *The Diary of a Young Officer.*

6. *Autobiography of Oliver Otis Howard.*

7. For Meade, see *Letters of a War Correspondent* and *Meade's Headquarters.*

8. *Under the Old Flag.*

9. De Trobriand: *Four Years with the Army of the Potomac.*

10. For McClellan's remarks to the soldiers, see *The Rebellion Record.*

3. Tomorrow Never Comes

An odd and frequently overlooked fact about the fighting on the peninsula is that in no single battle was anything like the whole strength of the Army of the Potomac put into action. The climactic struggle of Gaines's Mill was, for most of the soldiers, simply off-stage noises. In many ways McClellan himself was not much better off than the man in the ranks. A study of his letters and telegrams in *McClellan's Own Story*—from which, in this as in previous chapters, quotations have been drawn liberally—unmistakably depicts a man who never quite knew what was going on.

Specific references are:

1. Howard's autobiography.

2. For a good view of Cross—an uncommonly talented regimental commander, and an interesting person—see *Days and Events,* by Colonel Thomas L. Livermore, and *A History of the 5th Regiment New Hampshire Volunteers,* by William Child.

3. *The Diary of a Young Officer.*

4. Moore's *Rebellion Record,* Vol. V.

5. *Recollections of a Private,* by Warren Lee Goss.

6. *General Philip Kearny.* See also *Major General Hiram G. Berry,* by Edward K. Gould, for an extended description of this incident by Major H. L. Thayer.

7. *Battles and Leaders,* Vol. II, Part 1, p. 375.

8. Ibid., Part 2, p. 431.

9. *Recollections of a Private.*

10. *Battles and Leaders,* Vol. II, Part 2, p. 432.

4. Pillar of Smoke

One of the things McClellan seems never to have understood, in his dealings with the Lincoln administration, was the weight which the Copperhead movement in the North threw into the scales against him. There is a wealth of literature on this move for a negotiated peace. Two studies which were found especially helpful are *The Hidden Civil War,* by Wood Gray, and *The Movement for Peace without Victory during the Civil War,* by Elbert J. Benton.

Specific references are:

1. *Pictorial History of the Civil War,* Vol. II.

2. See *A Military History of the 8th Ohio Volunteer Infantry,* by Franklin Sawyer, and *Recollections of a Private...*

3. *Under Five Commanders,* by Jacob H. Cole.

4. *A History of the 5th Regiment New Hampshire Volunteers.*

5. *General Philip Kearny.*

6. *Four Years Campaigning in the Army of the Potomac.*

7. *Notes of a Staff Officer of Our First New Jersey Brigade,* by E. Burd Grubb.

8. *Diary of Gideon Welles,* Vol. I, p. 107.

9. *Abraham Lincoln and Men of War Times.*

CHAPTER FOUR

1. Indian Summer

The innumerable regimental histories now gathering dust on the shelves of libraries and secondhand bookshops are a rich mine of material on the kind of men who enlisted in 1861, the spirit with which they came forward, and the strangely innocent way in which the process of turning them into soldiers was undertaken. In many ways, most of these histories are very dull—poorly written, uncritical, full of an inexpert rehash of military history culled from standard texts. But despite these faults they provide the flavor of the young army as nothing else could do, giving the homely and often almost incredible little touches which make those far-off soldiers suddenly come alive. They have been a principal reliance in the preparation of this book and were used extensively in the preparation of this chapter.

Specific references are:

1. For a newspaper roundup of these rather effervescent activities, see Vol. V of *Rebellion Record.*

2. *Four Years with the Army of the Potomac.*

3. *The Bivouac and the Battlefield.*

4. References to the friendly reception in Maryland have been taken from

Musket and Sword, by Edwin C. Bennett; *Following the Greek Cross; The 27th Indiana Volunteer Infantry in the War of the Rebellion,* by a Member of Company C; *History of the 3rd Regiment of Wisconsin Veteran Volunteer Infantry; History of Duryée's Brigade,* by Franklin B. Hough; *Service with the 6th Wisconsin Volunteers,* and *Battles and Leaders,* Vol. II, Part 2, p. 556.

5. For the story of this regiment, see the delightfully artless little book, *A History of the "Bucktails,"* by O. R. Howard Thomson and William H. Rauch. Incidentally, while the name "Bucktails" belonged to this regiment alone, the rest of the army often applied it indiscriminately to the entire division of Pennsylvania Reserves.

6. Another charmingly unsophisticated history is *The 27th Indiana Volunteer Infantry in the War of the Rebellion.*

7. *The Irish Brigade and Its Campaigns,* by Captain D. P. Conyngham.

8. For a good side light on the way in which a regiment was sometimes recruited, see *History of the 40th (Mozart) Regiment,* by Fred C. Floyd.

9. *History of the First Regiment Minnesota Volunteer Infantry.*

10. *History of the 3rd Regiment of Wisconsin Veteran Volunteer Infantry.*

11. For these incidents, see *History of the 12th Massachusetts Volunteers* and *Four Years Campaigning in the Army of the Potomac.*

12. *History of the 10th Massachusetts Battery,* by John D. Billings. See also *Recollections of the Civil War,* by Mason Whiting Tyler.

13. For a fine study of the Civil War soldier and his songs, see "War Music and War Psychology in the Civil War," by James Stone, in the *Journal of Abnormal and Social Psychology,* October 1941.

14. *Under the Old Flag.*

15. *Battles and Leaders,* Vol. II, Part 1, p. 6.

16. *Recollections of a Private.*

17. *History of the 3rd Regiment of Wisconsin Veteran Volunteer Infantry.*

2. Crackers and Bullets

The fact that the Civil War soldier was compelled to solve, under fire and without much help, a set of quite modern-looking tactical problems raised by the improvement in his weapons is a point that deserves more emphasis than it usually gets in Civil War histories. Two interesting discussions of this matter, written by professional British soldiers shortly before World War I, are *The Campaign in Maryland and Virginia,* by Lieutenant E. W. Sheppard, and *The War of Secession,* by Major G. W. Redway. See also *The Generalship of Ulysses S. Grant,* by Colonel J. F. C. Fuller.

Specific references are:

1. *Reminiscences of the 19th Massachusetts Regiment.*

2. For a good review of Civil War rations, cookery, and camp life in general, see John D. Billings's entertaining *Hardtack and Coffee.* Good details are also to be found in *The Diary of an Enlisted Man.*

3. *Regimental Losses in the American Civil War,* by Lieutenant Colonel William F. Fox.

4. *Reminiscences of the Civil War,* by General John B. Gordon.

5. From "Field and Temporary Hospitals," by Deering J. Roberts, M.D., in Vol. VII, *Photographic History of the Civil War.*

6. The reader who is interested can study these tactical details in such standard Civil War texts as *Rifle and Light Infantry Tactics,* by Brevet Lieutenant Colonel William J. Hardee; *Manual of Instruction for the Volunteers and Mili-*

tia of the United States, by Major William Gilham, and *Camp and Outpost Duty for Infantry,* by Brigadier General Daniel Butterfield.

7. *History of Duryée's Brigade.*

3. Generals on Trial

A considerable volume of correspondence between Halleck and Pope, covering the period of the second Bull Run campaign and ending with Pope's exile to the Indian wars on the Western frontier, is available in the *Official Records,* Series I, Vol. XII, Part 3; and while nothing of very great importance is contained in it, it is worth reading for the picture it gives of the queer deficiencies of the army's high command. Studying it, one senses that the army's chief command problem just then was at the very top, embodied in the person of the general-in-chief. If McClellan was overcautious, Halleck was just a plain fussbudget; and if the need of the day was for someone to infuse drive and energy into army commanders, Halleck's own dispatches make it clear that he was the last man for the job. Gideon Welles seems to have been almost alone in his realization that it was the iron-hard spirit of war that was needed, and Vol. I of his *Diary* has been drawn on for quotations. For a consideration of the danger of foreign intervention in the fall of 1862, see James Ford Rhodes's *History of the Civil War.*

Specific references are:

1. *Under the Old Flag.*
2. Quoted in *The Hidden Civil War.*
3. *Military Reminiscences* of General Cox.
4. *Under Five Commanders.*
5. *Correspondence of John Sedgwick, Major General.*

CHAPTER FIVE

1. At Daybreak in the Morning

Extensive use has been made in this work of Major General James H. Wilson's spirited memoirs, *Under the Old Flag.* Wilson was a young engineer lieutenant who served on McClellan's staff for a time and who later became a very distinguished cavalry leader. As a young aide he appears to have been brash and cocky, with a knack for confusing his own functions with those of the major general commanding—altogether, it would seem, an uncomfortable young man to have around headquarters. Opinionated as his book is, however, it casts a most revealing light on the shortcomings of the high command at this period. The staff of the commanding general of the Army of the Potomac was no place for an ardent young perfectionist—not until Grant came along, which is another story.

Specific references are:

1. For details about the finding of the lost order, see "Antietam and the Lost Dispatch," by John McKnight Bloss, in *Papers of the Kansas Commandery, Military Order of the Loyal Legion of the United States.* Brigadier General Silas Colgrove tells the story in *Battles and Leaders,* Vol. II, Part 2.

2. Gibbon's *Personal Recollections.*

3. *Abraham Lincoln and Men of War Times.*

4. For Reno and Barbara Frietchie, see *Personal Recollections of the Civil War,* by James Madison Stone.

5. An enthusiastic account of this surprising little exploit occurs in a quaint pamphlet, *A Sketch of the 8th New York Cavalry,* by Henry Norton.

2. Destroy the Rebel Army

Regimental histories usually give a very faulty picture of a battle as a whole, since each author is responsible only for what he himself saw and relies on other authority—camp gossip, as often as not—for events which took place out of his sight. But when they are used to supplement the more formal reports and narratives, these histories are invaluable. They bring life and color; with their help these battles of the long ago cease to be bloodless set pieces out of military textbooks and become as real and as moving as something out of today's newspaper.

Specific references are:

1. For these quotations, see *Battles and Leaders,* Vol. II, Part 2, pp. 551 and 558.

2. Details from *A History of the 11th Regiment Ohio Volunteer Infantry.*

3. See *A Soldier's Diary: The Story of a Volunteer,* by David Lane.

4. *History of the 45th Regiment Pennsylvania Veteran Volunteer Infantry,* by Allen D. Albert.

5. See the sprightly *History of the 51st Regiment of Pennsylvania Volunteers,* by Thomas H. Parker.

6. Writing some years after the war, General Hill made this argument himself, but indignant Southerners—who were inclined to blame him for losing Special Orders No. 191 in the first place—howled him down. It does seem, however, as if he almost had a point.

7. For the experiences of the Black Hat Brigade, see Gibbon's *Personal Recollections* and Dawes's *Service with the 6th Wisconsin Volunteers.*

8. Gibbon's *Personal Recollections.*

9. See *History of the 5th Regiment New Hampshire Volunteers* and *Pennsylvania at Antietam.*

10. *Battles and Leaders,* Vol. II, Part 2, p. 558; *The Bivouac and the Battlefield; History of the 51st Regiment of Pennsylvania Volunteers,* and *History of the 12th Massachusetts Volunteers.*

11. *History of the 3rd Regiment of Wisconsin Veteran Volunteer Infantry* and *Joseph K. F. Mansfield: A Narrative of Events Connected with His Mortal Wounding,* by John Mead Gould.

3. Tenting Tonight

The literature on Antietam is, of course, extensive, but most of it pays little attention to the wasted day of September 16, when McClellan was flexing his army's muscles. The various articles in *Battles and Leaders,* Vol. II, Part 2, are helpful, particularly the one by General Cox. Palfrey's *The Antietam and Fredericksburg* is excellent and draws attention to the strange mix-up which occurred in connection with the command of the three "wings" of the army. Henderson's *Stonewall Jackson* makes clear the opportunity which McClellan lost by his inactivity on this day. It should go without saying, probably, that anyone who writes about the Army of the Potomac will get an invaluable indirect light on that army from Douglas Southall Freeman's books about its great opponents— *R. E. Lee* and *Lee's Lieutenants.*

Specific references are:

1. For an analysis of the discrepancy between the numbers on McClellan's

rosters and the numbers that could actually be put on the firing line, see Francis Winthrop Palfrey's *The Antietam and Fredericksburg.*

2. *Under the Old Flag.*

3. For Burnside's account of this, see his article in *Battles and Leaders,* Vol. I, Part 2, pp. 660–63. One would give a good deal for a stenographic report of his staff's remarks about the transfer.

4. *A Military History of the 8th Ohio Volunteer Infantry.*

CHAPTER SIX

1. Toward the Dunker Church

Considering the fact that Antietam was a head-on, slam-bang fight with no involved tactical maneuvering, it is a battle whose details are uncommonly hard to trace. Principal reliance, of course, is placed on the innumerable reports in the *Official Records,* Series I, Vol. XIX, Part 2; but one is hampered by the fact that each commander, from corps down to regiment, seems to have assumed that his own outfit had the hardest assignment and gave and received the deadliest blows. In addition, there are great discrepancies from report to report in the descriptions of the ground, statements of numbers involved, and accounts of time sequences. And if the reports of the Federal commanders are hard to reconcile, it is even harder to dovetail them with the Confederate reports; one sometimes has the feeling that the Federals and Confederates are describing two different battles.

Palfrey's *The Antietam and Fredericksburg* is perhaps the best account of the battle. General Cox wrote of it extensively, both in *Battles and Leaders* and in his own *Military Reminiscences.* An excellent narrative is contained in Lieutenant Colonel William Allan's *The Army of Northern Virginia in 1862,* and the descriptions in Freeman and Colonel Henderson are extremely detailed and vivid.

Specific references are:

1. For details, see *History of the First Regiment Minnesota Volunteer Infantry; The 27th Indiana Volunteer Infantry in the War of the Rebellion; Life and Letters of Wilder Dwight, Lieutenant Colonel, 2nd Massachusetts Infantry,* and *Service with the 6th Wisconsin Volunteers.*

2. "How Does One Feel under Fire?" by Captain Frank Holsinger, in the *Kansas Loyal Legion Papers.*

3. There is a good picture of this fighting in *Service with the 6th Wisconsin Volunteers.*

4. General Gibbon described the fighting of Battery B in his *Personal Recollections.* See also *The "Ulster Guard" and the War of the Rebellion,* by Theodore B. Gates, and Theodore M. Nagle's *Reminiscences of the Civil War.*

5. This may be a good place to indicate the vast difference between the numbers listed as "present for duty" and the numbers actually engaged. On the books, Hooker had 14,856 men in his I Corps, and it is usually assumed that he sent approximately that number into the fight. Actually, it is very hard to see how he could have had more than 9,000 men in action. He had three divisions —those of Meade, Ricketts, and Doubleday. In the official reports Meade stated that his division went into action "under 3,000 strong," and Ricketts said that he took 3,158 men into the fight. Doubleday did not give the strength of his division, but it seems quite certain that it was no stronger on the firing line that

morning than the other two. It contained four brigades. One—Hoffman's—was detached as flank guard and did not get into the fighting at all. Of the other three, at least two were far under strength. Gibbon's four regiments were probably under 1,000 strong, all told: he says he had fewer than 1,200 men at South Mountain, where he had 280 casualties. Phelps's brigade, according to the report of its commander, took only 425 men into action at Antietam. The remaining brigade, Patrick's, consisted of four New York regiments which had seen much service, and 1,500 would be a liberal estimate of the brigade's strength.

6. For Mansfield in action, see *Joseph K. F. Mansfield: A Narrative of Events Connected with His Mortal Wounding; A Brief History of the 28th Regiment New York State Volunteers,* by C. W. Boyce; *Pennsylvania at Antietam; The 27th Indiana Volunteer Infantry in the War of the Rebellion,* and *History of the 3rd Regiment of Wisconsin Veteran Volunteer Infantry.*

2. The Heaviest Fire of the War

A detailed description of the way in which Sumner put his corps into action, with especial reference to the unwieldy formation adopted for Sedgwick's division, is contained in Walker's *History of the Second Army Corps.* The same points are also considered at some length in Palfrey's *The Antietam and Fredericksburg.* Sumner did not survive the war and so is not represented in the polemics which cluster around all Civil War battles; his own ideas about the action, however, are presented in an article by his son, Major General Samuel S. Sumner, in Vol. XIV of the *Papers of the Military Historical Society of Massachusetts.*

Specific references are:

1. *The Antietam and Fredericksburg.*

2. *History of the First Regiment Minnesota Volunteer Infantry,* by R. I. Holcombe. This author remarked that his entire brigade had been drilled to fight in close order, in the obsolete elbow-to-elbow manner. The Confederates, he added, never made that mistake: "a hundred of them would string out for more than a quarter of a mile, or cover an acre." It may actually be true that the Confederate private's refusal to concern himself overmuch about the niceties of drill was a positive asset on the battlefield.

3. Two of Sedgwick's three brigade commanders, Generals Gorman and Dana, in their official reports characterized the Confederate fire here as the deadliest they ever saw. One of the most striking things about this whole battle, indeed, is the frequency with which Federal survivors described the Southern fire as the worst in their experience. That testimony comes from men who fought in the cornfield and along Bloody Lane, as well as from the men in Sedgwick's division.

4. *Reminiscences of the Civil War,* by General John B. Gordon. The good general's memory may have betrayed him in regard to the use of the drum during this charge.

5. For a gay account of this incident, see *The Irish Brigade and Its Campaigns.* In his *Days and Events,* Colonel Livermore records that General Sumner once exploded at Gosson: "Mr. Gosson, if you were not such an incorrigible rascal I would cashier you." A graduate of Dublin University, Gosson had seen service in a European hussar regiment.

6. This amazing anecdote appears, not (as one would suppose) in some imaginative regimental history, but in the official report of Captain William M.

Graham of Battery K, 1st U.S. Artillery. It can be found in the *Official Records,* Series I, Vol. XIX, Part 2, pp. 343–44.

7. Another misconception of the number of Federals engaged at Antietam arises from the common assumption that Franklin's corps was thrown into offensive action. Actually, only one of Franklin's brigades saw any serious fighting—a total of five men were killed in all the rest of the army corps—and most of the loss of the one brigade which did fight was incurred by one regiment, the 7th Maine.

8. *Under the Old Flag.*

3. All the Landscape Was Red

One of the things which helped to make the Antietam a badly fought battle appears to have been a misunderstanding as to the nature of the attack which Burnside's IX Corps was supposed to make. Burnside and Cox evidently understood that the attack was simply to be a diversion, to relieve the pressure on the right of the Federal battle line, while McClellan seems to have wanted an attack that would more or less go hand in hand with Hooker's. An argument on this point—which, happily, we need not go into here—became quite heated, during and after the war, and led to coolness between the once firm friends, McClellan and Burnside. Anyone who is interested may study the pros and cons in *McClellan's Own Story* and in Cox's account of Antietam in Vol. II of *Battles and Leaders.*

Specific references are:

1. Major Henry Kyd Douglas of Stonewall Jackson's staff lived in the immediate vicinity of Sharpsburg and had an intimate personal acquaintance with Antietam Creek. In his book, *I Rode with Stonewall,* he is extremely sarcastic about Burnside's difficulty in crossing the stream. ("Go and look at it," he writes, "and tell me if you don't think Burnside and his corps might have executed a hop, skip and jump and landed on the other side."

2. For the story of the whisky, the attack on the bridge, and Ferrero's subsequent promotion, see the engaging *History of the 51st Regiment of Pennsylvania Volunteers.*

3. *Personal Recollections of the Civil War,* by Stone.

4. *Battles and Leaders,* Vol. II, Part 2, pp. 661–62.

5. For a rather pathetic picture of the plight of the rookie soldiers, see *History of the 16th Connecticut Volunteers,* by B. F. Blakeslee. Additional interesting details are to be found in *Forty-six Months with the 4th Rhode Island Volunteers,* by Corporal George H. Allen, and in the official reports of Colonel Edward Harland, commanding Rodman's second brigade, and Colonel Joseph Curtis of the 4th Rhode Island.

6. Interestingly enough, in a letter to his wife from in front of Richmond, just after the battle of Seven Pines, McClellan told of receiving a flag-of-truce message from a Confederate commander in his front, and said: "Well, whom do you think the letter came from? From no one else than A. P. Hill, major-general commanding the Light Division."

7. An examination of that grim barometer of military pressures, the list of killed and wounded, shows what happened in Burnside's corps. Rodman's division was almost torn to pieces by Hill's counterattack, and Sturgis's division lost heavily during the assaults on the bridge, but the divisions of Cox and Willcox had losses which—by the standards of that terrible day—were comparatively

light. It is to be noted that no two of these four divisions were at any time under heavy fire simultaneously.

8. *Battles and Leaders*, Vol. II, Part 2, p. 656.

9. *Under the Old Flag.*

10. *Following the Greek Cross.*

4. The Romance of War Was Over

Military critics are still discussing Lincoln's removal of McClellan, and the majority seems to feel that the removal was a profound mistake. Considered strictly from a military point of view, this is possibly correct. The basic problem with McClellan, however, was always more political than military, and to understand and appraise Lincoln's action it is necessary to study the political history of the times rather than the reports of military action. After September 1862 the dominant fact was the Emancipation Proclamation. Nothing in the *Official Records* sheds any real light on the change in commanders. Actually, the explanation is in McClellan's letters, if you read them carefully, and the thing to study now is the fascinating self-portrait which is so unconsciously and revealingly painted in *McClellan's Own Story*. The McClellan quotations in this chapter are, with one exception, drawn from that book. The verse at the end of the chapter is from *Awhile with the Blue*, by Benjamin Borton.

Specific references are:

1. Gibbon's *Personal Recollections; Service with the 6th Wisconsin Volunteers.*

2. *The Life and Letters of George Gordon Meade.*

3. Gibbon's *Personal Recollections.*

4. *The Life and Letters of George Gordon Meade.*

5. *Under the Old Flag.*

6. *Musket and Sword.*

7. *History of the Second Army Corps.* Be it noted that this talk about the romance of war comes from an officer, and a general at that. The private soldier who had fought at Antietam had no more illusions about war's romance than the veteran of Okinawa.

8. See *History of the 3rd Indiana Cavalry*, by W. N. Pickerell, and *Forty-six Months with the 4th Rhode Island Volunteers.* The theory that McClellan was to replace Halleck is recorded in *A Duryée Zouave.*

9. *A Soldier's Diary.*

Index